Jean Tinguely

Prestel

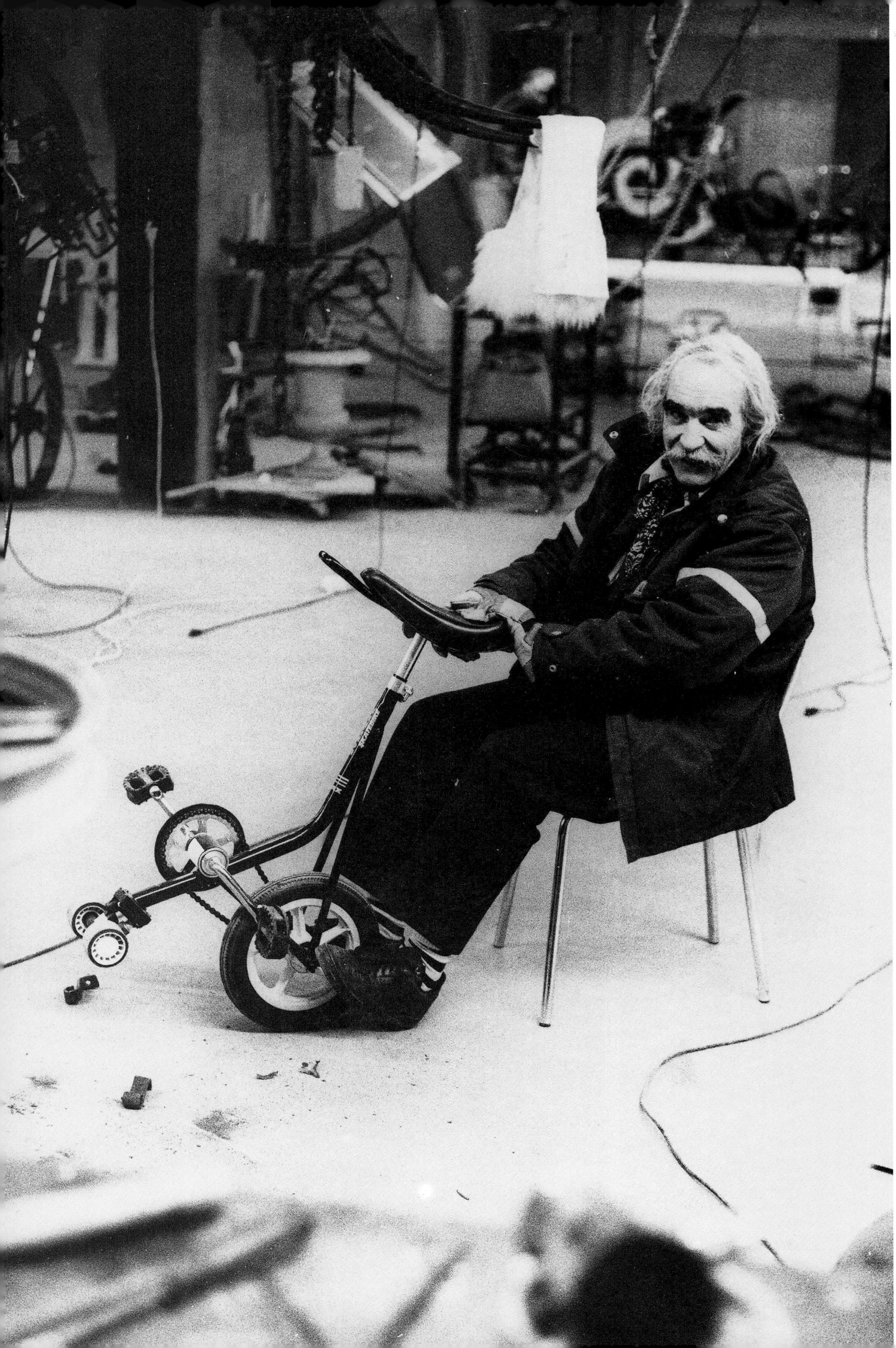

Heidi E. Violand-Hobi

Jean Tinguely

Life and Work

Received from Hans & Dunja Zollinger
of Zurich — December 27, 1996

Jim Richmond

Prestel

Munich · New York

This publication was partly funded by
PRO HELVETIA, Swiss Cultural Foundation

Cover: *Requiem for a Dead Leaf*, 1967
(detail; see fig. 40)
Frontispiece: Jean Tinguely in La Verrerie,
1991 (photo: Leonardo Bezzola)

Photograph credits on p. 179

Prestel books are available worldwide.
Please contact your nearest bookseller or
write to either of the following addresses
for information concerning your local
distributor:
Prestel-Verlag
16 West 22nd Street, New York,
NY 10010, USA;
Tel. (212) 627-8199;
Fax (212) 627-9866
Mandlstrasse 26, D-80802 Munich,
Germany; Tel. (89) 3 81 70 90;
Fax (89) 38 17 09 35

Copy-edited by Andrea P. A. Belloli

Typeset by O.K. Satz, Unterschleissheim
Offset lithography by ReproLine, Munich
Printed by Pera Druck Matthias GmbH,
Gräfelfing
Bound by Auer, Donauwörth

Printed in Germany

ISBN 3-7913-1430-0 (English edition)
ISBN 3-7913-1473-4 (German edition)

Contents

Acknowledgements

This book grew out of my doctoral thesis on Jean Tinguely. I am deeply grateful to my adviser, the late Gert Schiff, for his constructive guidance and an immensely enriching friendship. I also want to acknowledge the continuous encouragement of the faculty of the Institute of Fine Arts, New York University.

My research was enormously facilitated by the pioneering monograph on the artist's work by Pontus Hulten, to whom I remain deeply indebted. I have also learned much from the perceptions of Calvin Tomkins and Margrit Hahnloser.

Furthermore, I owe inspiring insights to the international coterie of Tinguely's friends. I am particularly grateful to Lukas Burckhardt, Lucius and Anne-Marie Burckhardt, Heinrich Koechlin, Gustav Kyburz, Werner Muster, Vera and Jakob Oeri, Rolf Ramstein, Josy Schaub and René Theler, who live in Basel and who were able to highlight many aspects of Tinguely's personality and work as they relate to that city. Monique Barbier-Müller, Walter A. Bechtler, Werner Düggelin, Virginia Dwan, Elsie and Theo Hotz, Paul Jolles, César Keiser, Billy Klüver, Dominique de Menil, Monique and Roger Nellens and Annalena Wibom were all extraordinarily kind in sharing with me memories of specific events and of their friendships with Tinguely.

I am indebted to Johannes Cladders, Michelle Facos, Olle Granath, Knud W. Jensen, Kaspar König, Ulf Linde, Guido Magnaguagno, Rainer Michael Mason, Franz Meyer, Ad Petersen and Pierre Restany for valuable information freely disclosed. Thanks also to artists Claude and François Lalanne, Ursi and Bernhard Luginbühl, Gerald and Muriel Minkoff, Milena Palakarkina, Julia Ris, Daniel Spoerri, Per Olof Ultvedt and Rico Weber and to photographer Leonardo Bezzola for lively discussions and for recollecting their rapport with Tinguely. In addition, I am most grateful to Tinguely's assistant, Joseph Imhof, for his manifold help extended with good humour.

Above all I am indebted to Jean Tinguely, this ingenious creator of an oeuvre unique in the history of art. The book would not be the same without his brilliant and generously given input. His encouragement was delivered by mail—unmistakable yellow envelopes containing wondrously collaged letters with the magic of fireworks.

Special thanks to Niki de Saint Phalle. Listening to her recollections and spending time with her in her house in Soisy remain most cherished memories. Her immense and essential contributions to the persona and work of Tinguely and those of his first wife, Eva Aeppli, still need to be told.

Most importantly, I want to thank Pro Helvetia, Swiss Council for the Arts. The publication of this book was made possible thanks to their generous grant and additional funds received from the Swiss Center Foundation.

Finally, I am deeply grateful to Hans-Joachim Mattke for his critical intellect and spiritual depth and for the enrichment of shared experiences. To him, to my friend Irene Mantel and to my daughter Nicole I lovingly dedicate this book.

Tinguely at the opening of his exhibition at the Palazzo Grassi, Venice, 1987

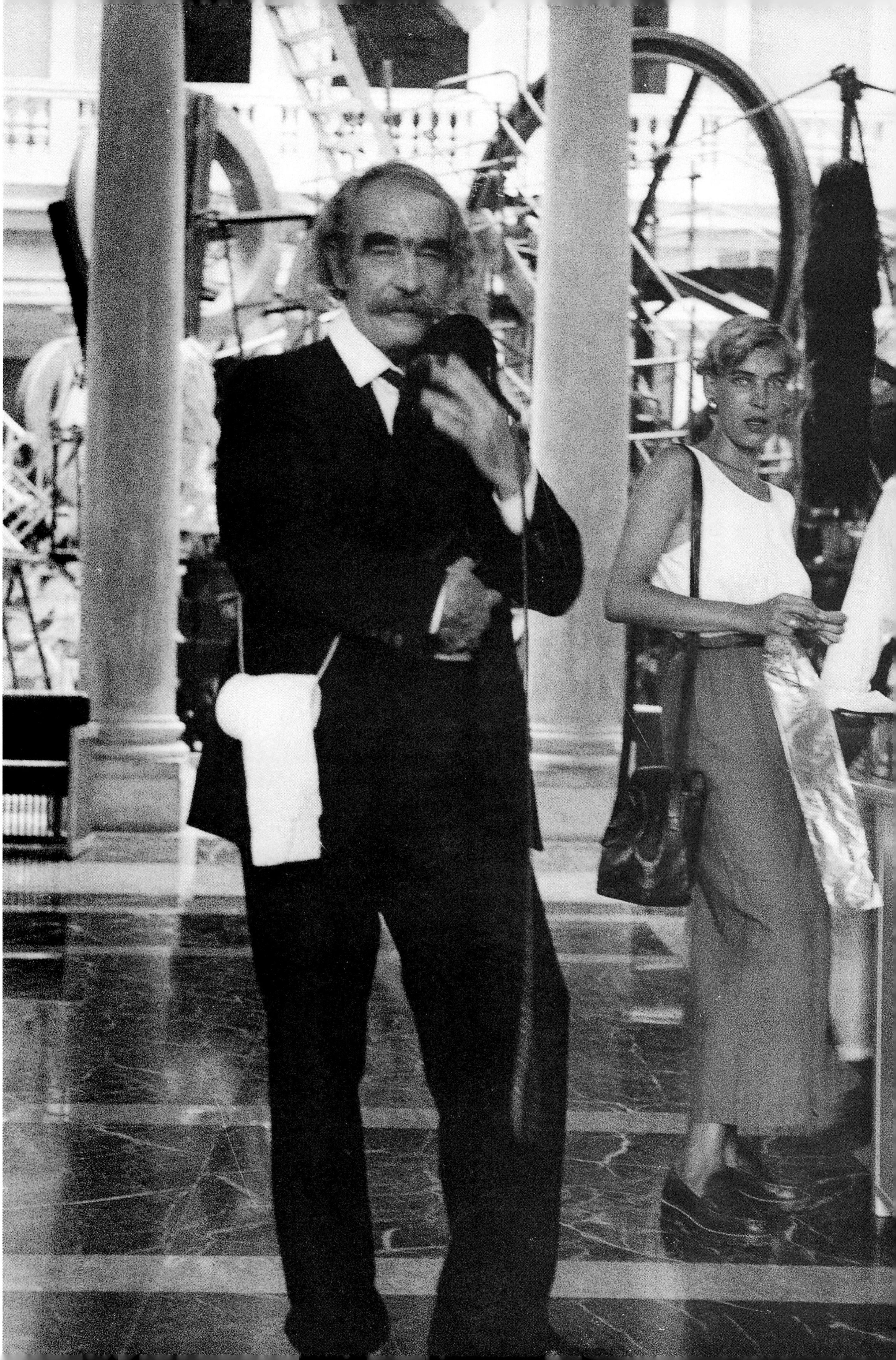

'Luckily, there is no good and no evil'

Introduction

I first met Jean Tinguely at an opening at the gallery of his assistant, Joseph Imhof, in Solothurn, Switzerland, in 1986. As soon as Tinguely arrived, everybody gathered around as he explained why he was late. I was confronted with a charismatic person whose voice and gestures turned a banal incident into a tension-ridden tale: 'It should not happen, but it happened: my Mercedes broke down on the way, and I took a taxi, and I left my fancy English raincoat in the cab, a thing that cost six hundred francs.' When he talked, Tinguely's face was animated; intensifying the effect of ceaseless motion, his long handlebar moustache seemed to bob in time with his words. I began to understand why he had been compared to movie stars and variously called 'the Swiss Marlon Brando' or 'the James Bond of sculpture today'.

Tinguely was a great showman who cast himself most often in the role of the clown. The audience could be the public at openings, his friends or the occupants of neighbouring tables at restaurants. He projected the image of the artist/fool when he appeared for important film interviews attired in party hats. He also involved those close to him in farce and buffoonery. At the elegant opening of his exhibition at the Palazzo Grassi in Venice in 1987, his companion appeared wrapped stylishly by the artist in a piece of fabric of his own design and crowned with a funny cap, likewise improvised by Tinguely. When his young dachshund, not yet house-trained, relieved herself on the polished floor of the museum, Tinguely promptly equipped himself with a roll of toilet paper which he hung round his shoulder from a string in readiness for the next mishap, willingly posing for photographers (illus. p. 7). His antics were improvised according to circumstances, not laboured.

Tinguely addressed large audiences or the eye of the camera with great ease, helped by an unusual facility with verbalisation, a quick mind and genuinely expressive body language. This man of medium height moved with the sinuous, decisive grace and pent-up power of a feline. He underlined the rapid staccato of his voice, now soft-edged, now steely, with correspondingly eloquent movements of face and body.

The artist I met at Solothurn had lost weight, and his recent illness had evidently chiselled his facial features more deeply. However, Tinguely retained his charm. He looked out from under his bushy eyebrows like an eagle. As he sized up the crowd, it seemed that nothing could escape him, not the slightest move, gesture or hesitation. Tinguely's wife, Niki de Saint Phalle, later told me that he was quick to make up his mind about people and that he was rarely proven wrong.

The artist seemed to be driven by a vibrant inner energy. He was a pressure cooker of intensity, his energies constantly seeking an outlet. His hands spoke; they would ball up in fists, caress his moustache and slice the air as he threw himself into a discussion. He could be as outrageous as a *Monty Python* character, bellow in anger or be all charm and sweetness. One could say that to be in his company was like taking a shot of gin. He communicated his vitality effectively, and people responded to him very strongly and positively. They were protective of their friendships with him and fearful of committing faux pas, as he was reputed to possess a tenacious memory for slights. Even at his most congenial, Tinguely was never completely relaxed.

Tinguely almost always wore a blue mechanic's outfit completed by a navy blue polka-dottet mousseline-desoie foulard around his neck. The workman's overalls and foulard were practical, of course, for the artist at work, but the rough costume took on a different meaning away from the workplace. Tinguely told de Saint Phalle that he'd had enormous success with women when dressed like this.[1] He was not uneasy with conventional fashion—his tailor was the finest in town. Regardless of his clothing, he maintained the bearing, the gestures, the look of a grand seigneur. Tinguely's unconventional dress was part of his persona, part of the myth of the artist as the handyman of the absurd, the hero whose spiritual kin were Sisyphus and Don Juan.

Tinguely was an unapologetic, uninhibited philanderer, prankishly sexy, frolicsome and cunning, unfailing

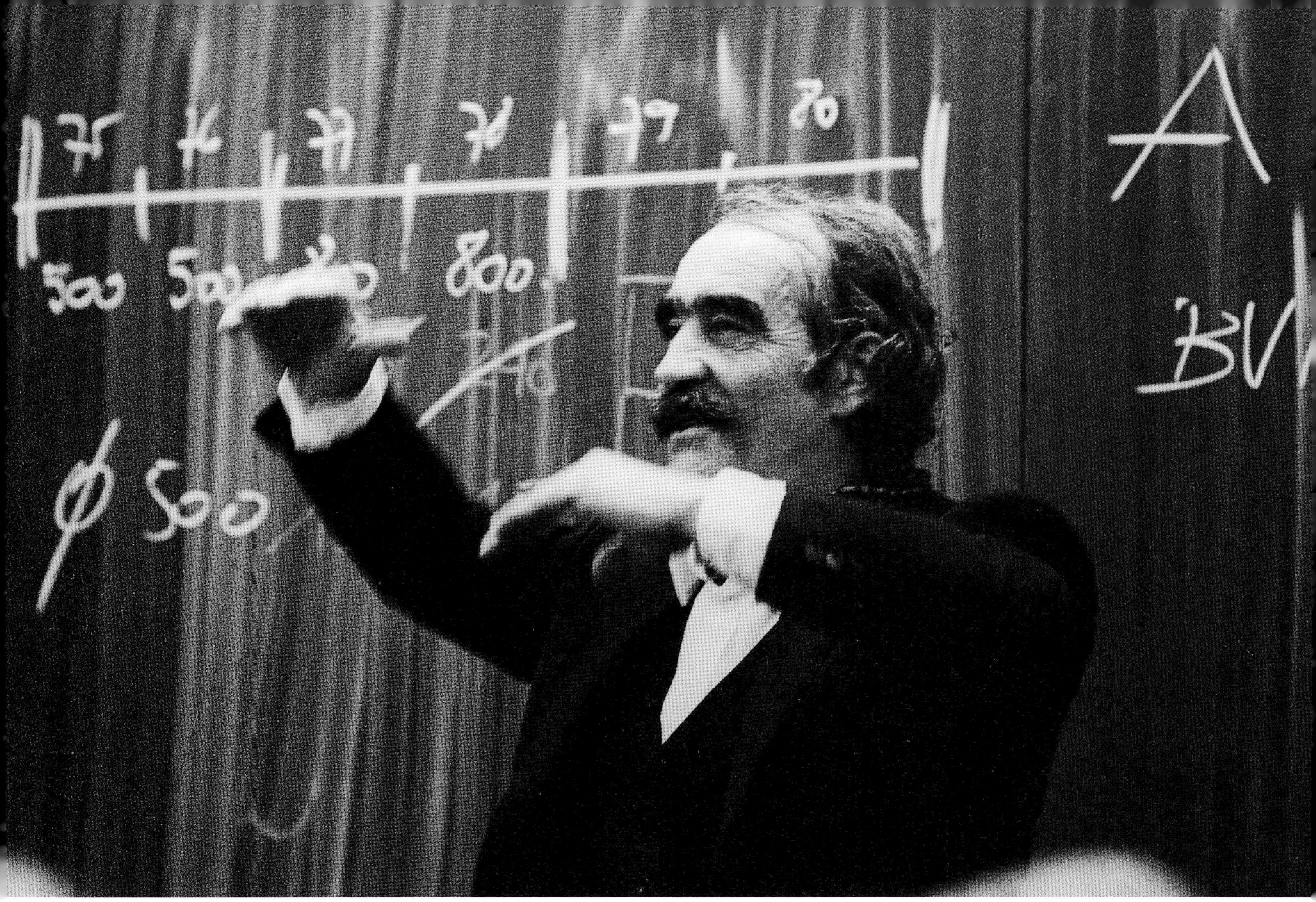

in spotting anyone's Achilles' heel. He had a particularly entangled sentimental life that seemed to correspond to an inner need to replicate the condition of his youth, the kind of tense, charged atmosphere that had driven him to a creative life. He was paradoxically puritanical in being honest about his lack of virtue.

He was, above all, a lover of life in all its manifestations, somewhat like Tomas, the hero of Milan Kundera's novel *The Unbearable Lightness of Being*, a womaniser who believed in the 'lightness' that comes with the recognition that one will go through life only once. Tinguely was a kind of exile whose 'lightness' partook of the floating, suspended exile's state. He was the lonely, isolated, exceptional person in a conventional society, valuing everything and everybody who shared his 'lightness' and who was as strong as he was in accepting the freedom that came with it. He acquired compensatory weight and strength from earthbound things and people, from living near nature in ancient ruins and old farmhouses, from participating in recurring rituals such as the carnival or witnessing rites still practised in the mountainous regions of Switzerland.

Tinguely said: 'I do not know happiness for myself.' He thus was in agreement with many who believe that humans cannot be happy: happiness is the longing for repetition and not part of life's agenda as he understood it.

Tinguely at the University of Berne, 1980

To attempt to hold fast an instant is doubtful.
To bind an emotion is unthinkable.
To petrify love is impossible.
It is beautiful to be transitory.
How lovely it is not to have to live forever.
Luckily, there is no good and no evil.[2]

'Sink or swim'

Formative Years

Some of the anecdotes that make up legends tend to perpetuate themselves and infiltrate an artist's biography. One such recurrent story presents the artist as a child prodigy. As a prerequisite to fame, biographers feel the need to detect in the young child traces of inborn skills and precocious abilities that signal future talent.[1] This is true of Jean Tinguely. An anecdote he told about himself around the age of 12 went as follows:

I began to make something pretty original: I spent weekends, Saturday and Sunday, one after another, beside a stream, rigging up lovely little wooden wheels ... Art never entered my head ... I used a stream in a wood, but I must point out that was a pine wood, a kind of cathedral, and with a cathedral's acoustics ... the sound was magnified fantastically. I built up to a dozen of these little wheels. They all turned at different speeds, and the speeds sometimes changed with the flow of the water. Every wheel had one cog . . . This one cog made the wheel rotate irregularly—as follows: it turned, struck a small hammer, which in turn struck small tin-cans of various kinds, some rusty, some not, and with different resonances. These sounds with their different rhythms were placed at intervals of between five and six metres, and sometimes the sound of the concerts carried for a distance of a hundred metres through the woods. Then I speculated whether somebody walking alone in the woods would be aware of the concert before hearing the sounds of the woods themselves. Sometimes the setup went on functioning for several weeks. Of course it was bound to fall apart in the end, but some of the wheels went on running for months.[2]

This story is retold in every major essay on the artist's work that includes biographical details. In it one can detect many elements of Tinguely's future work: movement and the element of chance, the importance of variegated sounds and speeds, attention to the immediate environment, the element of water as part of the work and a concern with the viewer's response. Furthermore, the wheels were an ephemeral construction, built with junk materials. Thus, the young Tinguely's artistic potential was documented and confirmed as the story revealed premonitory signs of his future accomplishments.

Jean Tinguely was born at 5:00 a. m. on 22 May 1925, in the canton hospital at Fribourg, Switzerland, the first and only child of Charles and Jeanne Tinguely-Ruffieux. Two years later, the family moved to Basel, where Tinguely's father, a warehouse superintendent with Nestlé, had been transferred. They lived in Gundeldingen, then a proletarian sector of Basel, and worshipped at the nearby Catholic Church of the Holy Spirit.

Tinguely's parents never learned to speak German well. Jeannot, as the boy was called by everyone, grew up speaking French at home and learned the Swiss German dialect of Basel with his playmates and High German in school: 'German was difficult for me,

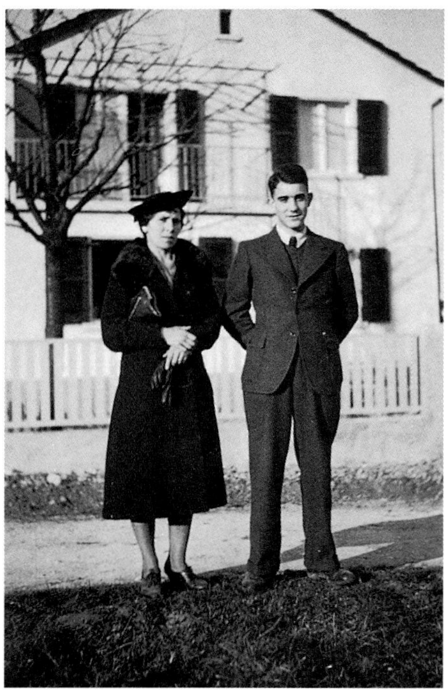

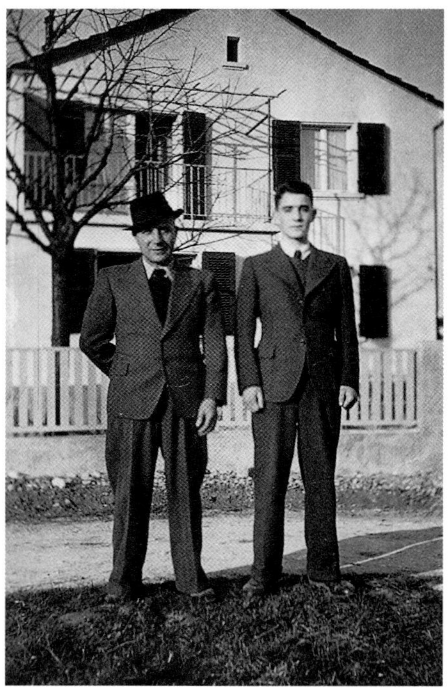

Jean with his parents, Jeanne and Charles Tinguely-Ruffieux, Basel

and I did not get any support from my parents, who were unable to help out with schoolwork. I was a bad pupil, which didn't worry me at all.'[3] The artist recalled skipping classes regularly and spending many hours avidly devouring biographies of such personalities as Alexander the Great, the Caesars, Napoleon and Lord Byron. As a Swiss Frenchman and Catholic in a predominantly Protestant, German-speaking environment, he developed a marked sense of belonging to a minority that took pride in being different and felt in no way inferior.

The Tinguely household was dominated by the authoritarian, choleric Charles, who terrorised mother and child alike. The artist's earliest childhood memories were of traumatic conflicts with paternal authority:

My first memory is also the first nightmare which I remember. . . . I was maybe four or five years old. One night, my father came home very late, drunk reeking of white wine. He was in a violent temper. He erupted into my room, woke me up and asked me if I had said my prayers and for whom I had prayed. My answer, that I had prayed for the Child Jesus, infuriated my disappointed father, who had expected me to pray for him or for Mother. He grabbed my bed with me in it and turned it upside down, to the desperate, horrified cries of my mother, who was afraid he had killed me. I did not have any physical injuries, but I learned what it meant to be afraid . . . This fear is there, and I have to surmount it every time I begin a new work.[4]

Jeannot adored his pretty mother all the more and later reflected upon how profoundly he had lived out the childhood anxieties that Freud termed the Oedipus complex. He added:

My father was unjust, but on the other hand he was very tactful and didn't ask questions. I think my mother didn't observe her marital fidelity vows too closely, and maybe my father thought I was not really his son since I was so odd, even though I do have his physiognomy.

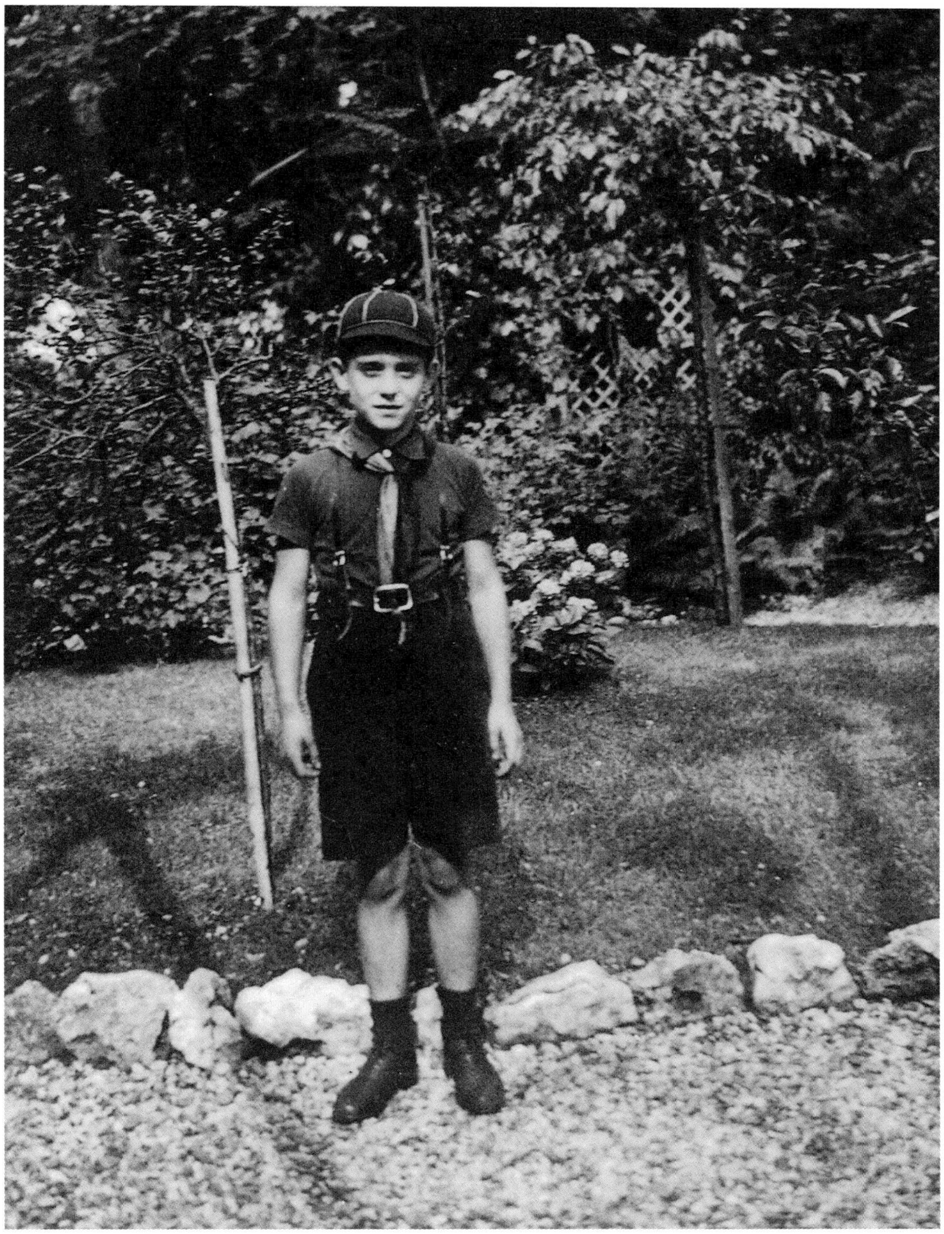

Jean in the Catholic Scouts

During the Second World War, Tinguely was confronted with another kind of fear:

It was on the 17th of December, 1940, at 2:00 or 3:00 o'clock in the morning. Bombs were being dropped during the night, and one bomb by mistake fell on Basel and hit our house. I had heard a similar dry whizzing in the movies, and it was exactly like that, only this time it was for real. One woman lost her life. I was under the impression the Germans were attacking, and I was scared.

Gustav Kyburz, former Director of the Gewerbemuseum, Basel, ran into Tinguely the next day and recalls his striking description of this wartime accident as 'that splinter of the bomb which had entered his body here and left it here—without trace'.[5] The episode had obviously shaken the youth. Typical of the artist's later storytelling, his account was not strictly factual, but combined facts with descriptions of their psychological impact.

Religion was a decisive influence upon the young Tinguely. The Church became crucial as his second family, where he met a formidable role model in the figure of an unusual priest:

Religion was something with which I had been indoctrinated ... For me, religion was a form of shock from which I still have not recovered. I grew up in Gundeldingen, in the Church of the Holy Spirit, and I say that as if it were a family headed by a famous and deeply respected priest, Father Mäder. Father Mäder had a conception of Catholicism which was very puritanical and combative... He ... considered the Protestants as heathens... He supervised all the Catholic youth organisations into which one gets enrolled, such as the Catholic Scouts, where one could find such phenomena as Gustav Kyburz.[6]

Kyburz was Tinguely's group leader in the Catholic Scouts (illus. p. 11). He describes the artist as a sprightly, very lively youth with a vivid fantasy life. Kyburz believes that the Scouts imbued Tinguely's life with meaning and remembers him as doing things others would not dare to do, sweeping everyone along with his enthusiasm. Kyburz also recalls fetching Tinguely from Bellinzona, where the then 14-year-old was being held in police custody. Having been caught on a freight train going to Italy, he had explained that he was en route to Albania to help the freedom fighters against the fascist invader. Kyburz believes that Tinguely submitted to the strictness of the Church out of respect for the towering figure of Father Mäder, his genuineness and absolute sincerity, but also because the Church provided discipline with a purpose, not just senseless formality.[7]

At the end of nine obligatory years of school, Tinguely applied for and passed the qualifying examinations given by the Globus department store and began his apprenticeship as a decorator on 2 May 1941. However, conflicts over discipline led to his dismissal on 25 August 1943. Deliberately rebellious, he liked to wait to clock in just a few minutes late. He finished his apprenticeship with Joos Hutter, an independent interior decorator and artist.[8] During this period, Tinguely attended classes irregularly at the local Allgemeine Gewerbeschule. The curriculum included the usual drawing classes, in which he excelled:

I was packed with talent, but talent is nothing, and one would be better off without it. It's a handicap to have talent and facility. Hence, Theo Eble, himself trained by a Bauhaus pupil, forced me to re-learn how to draw. With the left hand one cannot bluff. It's more honest.[9]

Tinguely added:

It was through others that I learned many things, beginning with Julia Ris, who also made it difficult for me in her innovative and precocious course entitled 'material studies.' She taught in the spirit of the Bauhaus and made me discover modern art from the beginning of the century, with the Cubists, the Futurists, the Constructivists, the Rayonnists, Schlemmer and the Bauhaus, de Stijl, Mondrian, the Dadaists, Arp, Schwitters, Duchamp, etc.

The English-born, Berlin-trained Ris (facing page) not only transmitted to her students her sound art-historical knowledge but also challenged their imaginations with her weekly assignments. She encouraged originality, forbade plagiarism and fostered in them the ability to think and talk critically about their own work, to develop a discerning eye and to trust their own judgement. This is how she remembered Jean Tinguely:

He was a rather square-built, short young man of who wasn't particularly handsome but rather the darkly pondering type, with his heavy black eyebrows meeting above his nose, and, under them, his dark eyes blinking critically. Very quickly, Tinguely's many-sided, outstanding talents became apparent; strikingly intelligent and quick at repartee, he was a brilliant, sensitive draftsman, whose 'material compositions' were full of an unlimited phantasy and astonishing precision, whose remarks were to the point, critical and often bitingly ironic. He was well read in a variety of fields and was open to all artistic, political and intellectual and otherwise interesting questions in which his exceedingly powerful intellectual vitality was already at this young age obvious. Sentimentality was not his thing. He was very much in demand by all the young ladies, and the effeminate youths, too, and was the cause of many nervous breakdowns and tragi-comic scenes of jealousy, which seemed at most to amuse him. Once, when I told him to his face that he treated matters of feeling much too lightly, he bellowed with laughter and said, 'That's the way I am, I can't help it'. Moral considerations were not his forte and he continued cold-bloodedly to practice his tricks with naive men and women, who adored him.[10]

It was during his apprenticeship that Tinguely met Theo Wagner, a decorator at Globus and a homosexual. Tinguely was fascinated by Wagner's way of life, by the man's refinement and sensibility, about which he explained:

My world had been all grey, *and I had just recently discovered that there is such as thing as* rose*—and Theo introduced me to*

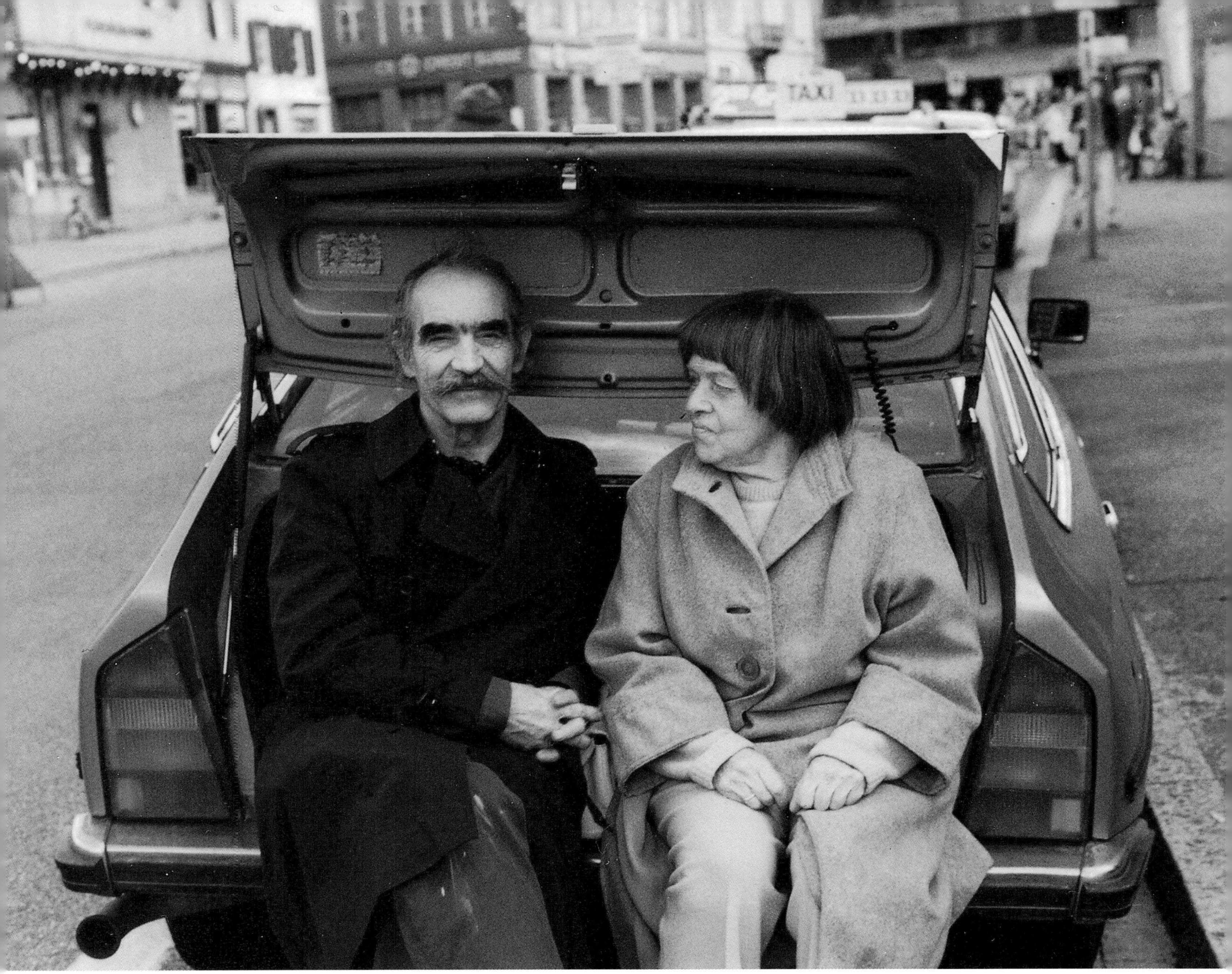

Tinguely with Julia Ris in front of the Gewerbeschule, Basel, 1986

the exotic world of vieux rose. *I was without prejudice against homosexuals and divorced women. The department store employed also many divorced women. They wanted to save me from homosexuality. But I was not at all homosexual.*

He added that once he had discovered sexuality, it immediately lost any problematic aspect it might have had due to his ultra-Catholic upbringing. He responded to the sensuality of men and women alike. A friend of Tinguely's is still bemused by the remarkable scenes that occurred at the time of their military service, when the soldiers would observe Tinguely being fetched by his lover at the barracks. He recalls that the servicemen were both baffled by and envious of Tinguely's flaunted freedom.[11] Tinguely identified totally with his own manhood, driven by a powerful libido, his machismo was masterfully clad in charm and part and parcel of his charisma. He sought a specific type of woman to share his life with, one who, not unlike his mother, was frightened and traumatised, but who had a strong personality: 'I am attracted by women who have problems. Myself, I exteriorise problems through my works. Eva Aeppli, my first wife [illus. p. 15], was always on the brink of suicide. This fascinated me and forced me to be positive, to counterbalance her pessimism.' Having met Aeppli at the Allgemeine Gewerbeschule, they were married in 1951.

Tinguely explained that during and after the Second World War, he stopped nearly all activity except for occasional baby-sitting and dog-walking and began to read avidly: 'I read Stirner, Marx, Bachofen, Hegel, Kropotkin, Bakunin, Proudhon and others; I pondered certain questions and discussed them with friends who were political refugees and others who were students of Karl Jaspers. They were bizarre; they were well versed in Greek philosophy.' Tinguely came into contact with a circle of young anarchists and with Heiner Koechlin, who was finishing his doctoral thesis on the Paris Commune. The ensuing intense interchange of ideas shaped the artist's philosophical and political attitude.

When Koechlin and Tinguely met, the artist sympathised with Communist ideals and had, as he put it, 'switched from the religion of Catholicism to that of Communism'. Tinguely recalled the event that decisively changed his attitude towards Catholicism:

Good Friday in 1939 was a dramatic experience which awakened me to the political world. On that day, the fascist troops of Mussolini attacked Albania. The fact that this attack was launched on that sacred day by the Navy, which had been blessed three months before by the Pope in Ostia, was a terrible shock for all of us puritanical, Protestant-influenced Catholics in the German-speaking regions of the North. This was one of the most crucial rupture-points in my life.

For a short time, Koechlin shared his flat with Tinguely. He still recalls the artist's saying that if he had known Jesus personally, he could have imagined becoming His disciple. For Koechlin, this seemed an amazing statement coming from someone as nihilistic as Tinguely was at the time. Koechlin felt simultaneously attracted to and repulsed by Tinguely:

He was then an anarchist ... He was ruthless toward persons around him. He was a relentless fighter, and ruthlessness was probably a necessity for him. In his way of life, he went completely his own way, without looking left or right, without concessions to bourgeois morality and expectations, and that impressed me. He never used the municipal garbage-disposal service in the soon-to-be demolished house where he lived with Eva Aeppli and others. They simply accumulated all garbage in one room, until one day it took fire. Things like this illustrate his attitude: he did what suited him best at the moment. He was actually never actively involved with politics; he was always more an artist. But everything radical impressed him favourably.[12]

In Tinguely's opinion, the book that influenced him most profoundly was *Der Einzige und sein Eigentum* (The Ego and His Own) by the German anarchist philosopher Max Stirner (a pseudonym for Johann Kaspar Schmidt). Originally published in Leipzig in 1844, the book postulated complete individualism at a time when European thought had discarded traditional philosophical, religious and political dogmas and was adopting new '-isms' such as socialism, liberalism, communism or materialism. Stirner was one of the great libertarian thinkers whose writings belong to the individualist end of anarchist theory, but stand outside the historical anarchist movement of the nineteenth century. He believed that a person is free only if (s)he renounces all dogmas and becomes a unique individual.[13]

Stirner's doctrine is a plea for the integration of the personality as it was developed later by such psychologists as Carl Jung and Erich Fromm. The latter explained in his study on love that '[a]ttitudes toward others and toward ourselves ... are basically conjunctive':[14] from this point of view, Tinguely's selfishness as described by Koechlin can be understood as springing from his very lack of fondness for himself.

In search for Tinguely's view of love, one can find a good number of works in his oeuvre that include erotic imagery. They can be divided into two groups. Those in the first group contain elements that evoke masturbatory friction (see fig. 1). These images of onanistic love seem on one hand absurd, and on the other hand defiant. Works in the second group portray love as penetration (see fig. 2). Here, the ambiguity lies between good-humoured teasing and ruthless aggression. Actually, Tinguely's images of love and his images of obsessive struggle are interchangeable. Both share the relentless repetition of forward and backward motion, a sense of provocation and of being on the offensive. For Tinguely, as for the hero Don Juan as described by Albert Camus,[15] love was an occasion for life, with each new encounter a renewal of total engagement with existence. Tinguely's profound identification with Camus's absurd man can explain why images of love and war coalesce so often in his work.

In Stirner's vigorous emphasis on will and instinct rather than reason and in his relentless exposition of freedom, Tinguely—and artists before him such as Marcel Duchamp—discovered a philosophy they could make their own.[16] Stirner warned that freedom was not possible while one longed for something beyond this life. Most importantly, Stirner's concern was not for revolution, but for individual

Jean and Eva Aeppli with Ursi Luginbühl, Moosseedorf, 1960

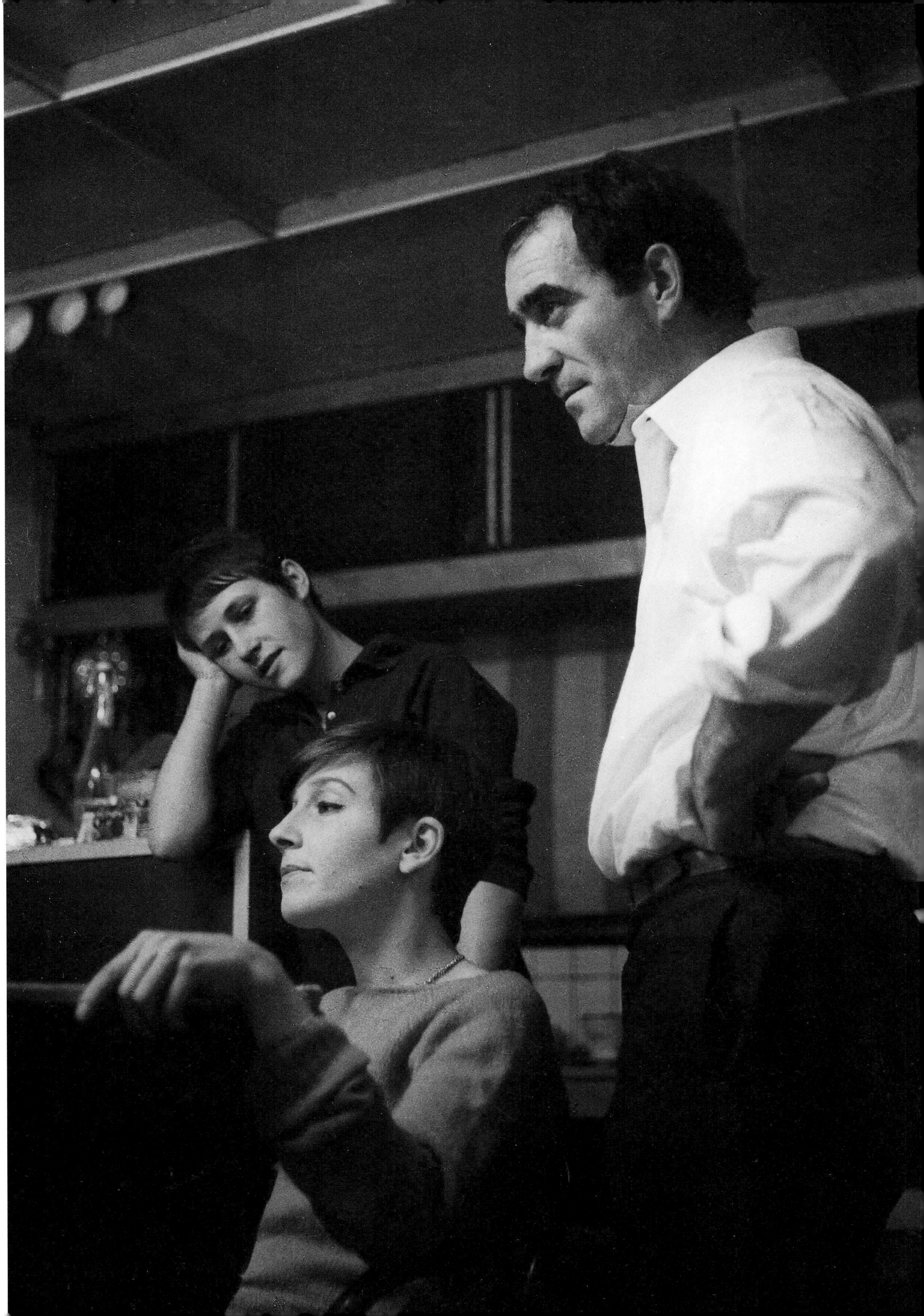

revolt—the liberation of the self. Furthermore, Stirner advocated the enjoyment of life 'like the candle,which one uses in burning it up . . . Enjoyment of life is using life up'.[17]

Anarchism also interested Tinguely. He spoke up for anarchist ideals, such as the necessity to abolish centralised power structures:

With Dada I . . . have in common a certain mistrust toward power. We don't like authority, we don't like power. To me art is a form of manifest revolt, total and complete. It's a political attitude which doesn't need to found a political party. It's not a matter of taking power; when you are against it, you can't take it. We're against all forms of force which aggregate and crystallize an authority that oppresses people. Obviously this is not a characteristic of my art alone—it's much more general, a basic political attitude. It's a clear intention, more necessary today than ever, to oppose all forms of force emanating from a managing, centralising political power.[18]

The Swiss federalistic state was built on the idea of mutuality. To a certain degree, it still embodies the ideals of anarchism, which combines individual freedom with collective responsibility in a system of direct democracy, something which Tinguely advocated:

I love federalistic communities of people. I am a total patriot of the region. I'm against nationalism and for a new old Europe with about 72 counties and then united, with five cultures: supra-federal as well as local art. Thus art would be integrated—namely locally and would not be 'international,' made to float around as wood on a river by the media, but would be anchored within each corresponding body of the people.[19]

Thus, Tinguely viewed political regionalism as beneficial to an integration of art within local culture. He felt that art springs from the same lifegiving force

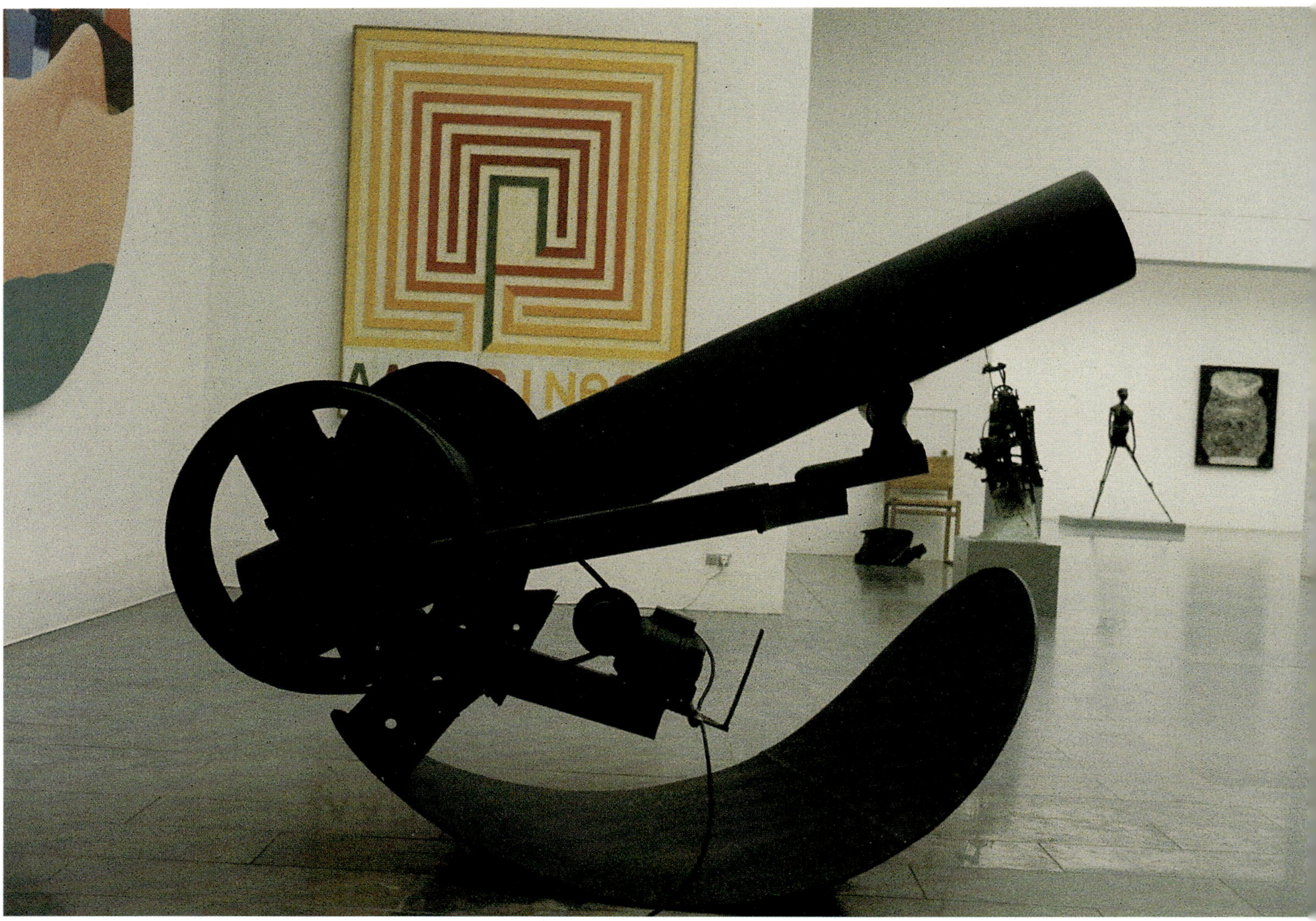

1 *Bascule VII*, 1969

that shapes people. In his own case, it was through the integration of, and identification with, local traditions, such as the Basel Carnival that Tinguely established a connection with the wellsprings of the universal. The debacle of the Second World War intensified the alienation between artists and society. Like his Dadaist predecessors, Tinguely turned to an art of revolt, exposing, mocking and criticising.

During the post-war years, Tinguely enjoyed a bohemian life-style, supporting himself as a free-lance decorator (see figs. 3-7). In 1947/48, this is how Rolf Ramstein, the owner of an optical store, encountered Jean Tinguely:

We were modernising our store and were making the window space fairly narrow and elongated, a novelty in those days. One day, a young man came in, presented himself and asked me if he could create the inaugural window for us. He said that this modern conception of a shop window was attractive and challenging and that he would like to work in this kind of space. When I asked him how much he would charge, he replied: 'This is not really relevant. I can quote you something outrageous or something acceptable—let me simply do my work and we will see about the financial question later.' I liked the young man; he was different from all the others, and I agreed to have him do the window. He used simple wire, which he shaped into abstract forms and painted white against a black background—in those days something completely new. Passers-by would actually stop and look at the display. Many years later he would confess to me that he had taken the wire for this window from a city park enclosure. From then on, he would create many more window decorations for us, and they always would attract a great deal of attention, especially those which included movement. Even after he left Basel to live in Paris, he would from time to time arrange a window for us.[20]

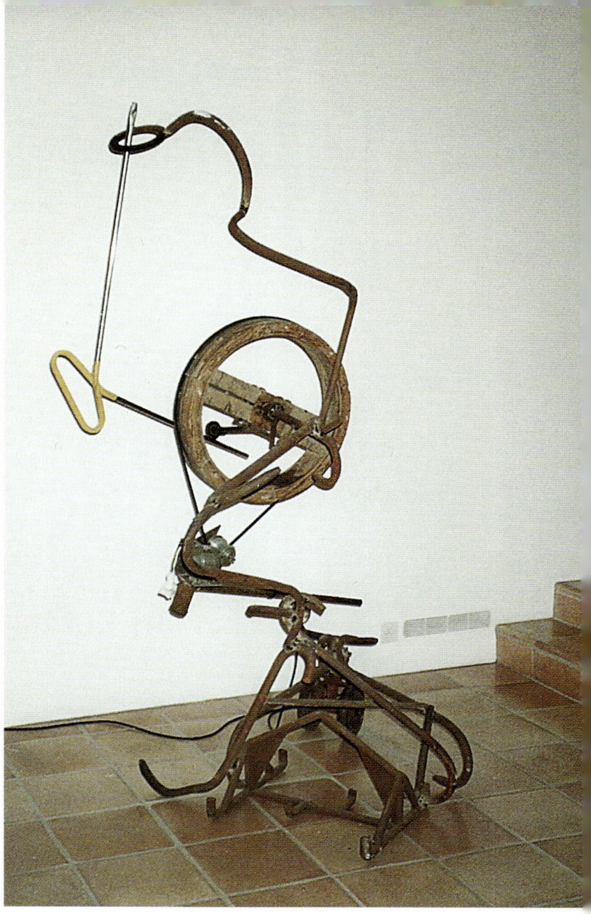

2 *Hegel*, 1988

Tinguely's talent earned him commissions to decorate fair pavilions abroad, in Paris in 1948 for the Association des Femmes Communistes and in 1950 for the Swiss pavilion at the Fiera Campionaria in Milan. The kinetic window decorations allowed him to experiment with movement, a direction which Julia Ris had also suggested to him.

The artist described his other experiments with motion to Richard Calvocoressi, who reported that he 'suspended common household objects . . . from an axle attached to its motor through a door which Tinguely had taken off its hinges and hung from the ceiling of his flat in Basel. He would make these objects rotate at speeds which he could vary with the aid of a rheostat'.[21] The idea of 'translating' (the term is Tinguely's) a form through applied energy into a less material state without changing its shape is central to Tinguely's work. As we have seen, the water mills in the forest were his first experiment with motion. His later experiments with variegated velocities would lead him to the insights that became the philosophical building block of his oeuvre. Rolf Ramstein remembers that during a visit to the artist's quarters, Tinguely showed him three kinetic reliefs: 'There were white or coloured cut-out forms turning at irregular speeds and creating an ever-changing visual tableau. The mechanism was hidden behind a black board and was driving wooden wheels by means of rubber bands.' This description matches exactly the works exhibited in the summer of 1954 at Galerie Arnaud in Paris, which were later named 'meta-mechanical' reliefs (see fig. 10). Ramstein declined to buy one of them for three hundred Swiss francs, even though Tinguely impressed him with the seriousness of his belief that he would be a famous artist one day. From the start, Tinguely trusted absolutely in his own artistic worth.

3-7 Shop-window displays, Basel, 1949-51 ▷

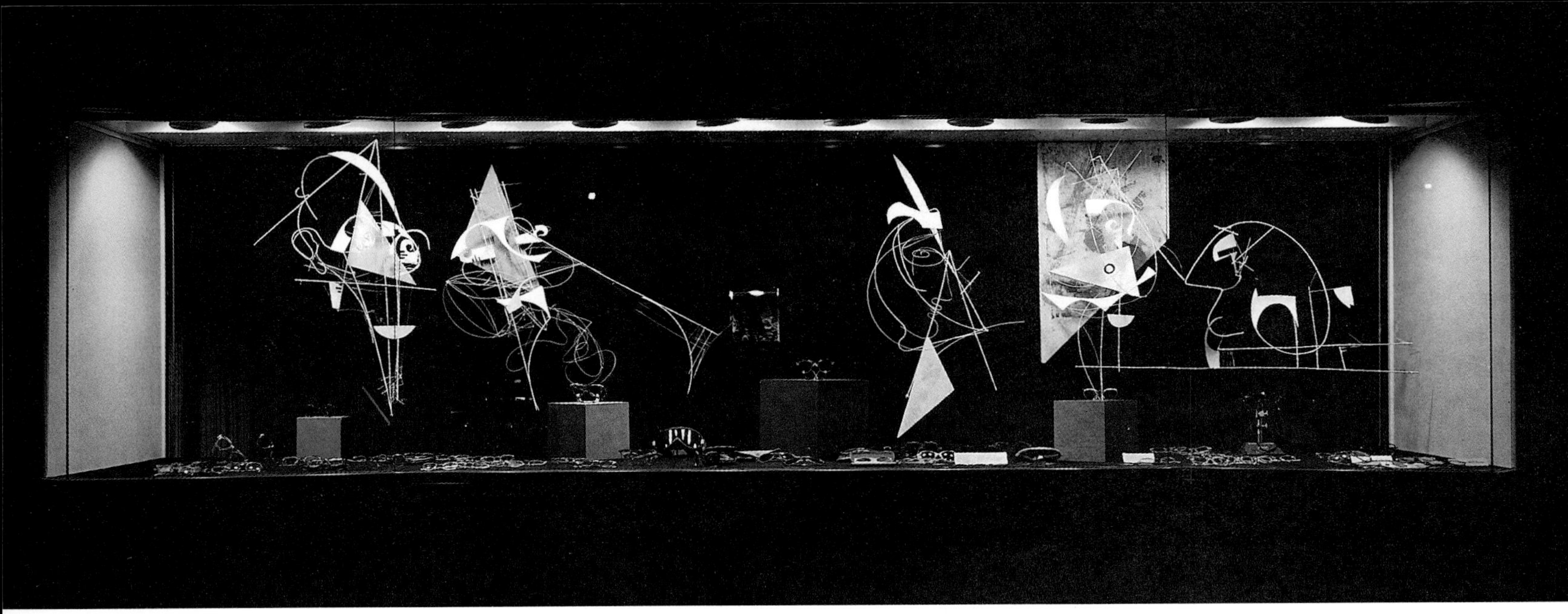

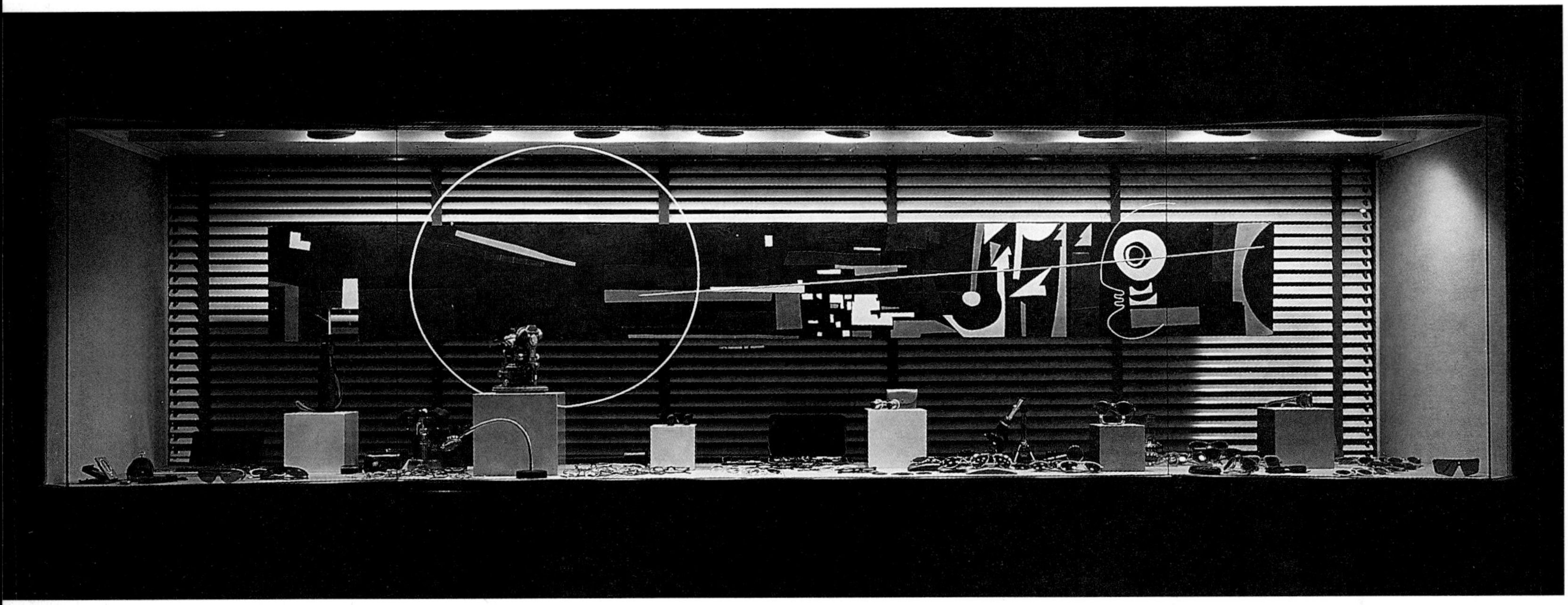

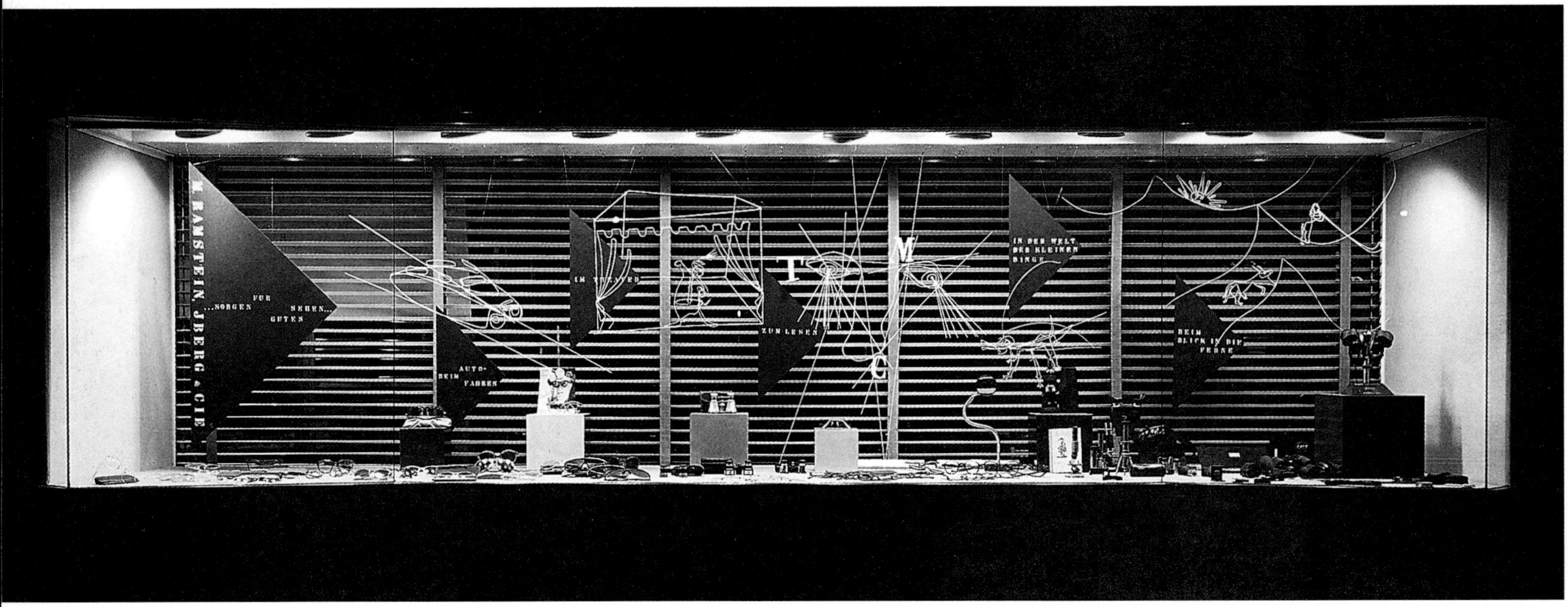
M. RAMSTEIN, JBERG & CIE
...SORGEN FUR GUTES SEHEN...
BEIM AUTO-FAHREN
ZUM LESEN
BEIM BLICK IN DIE FERNE

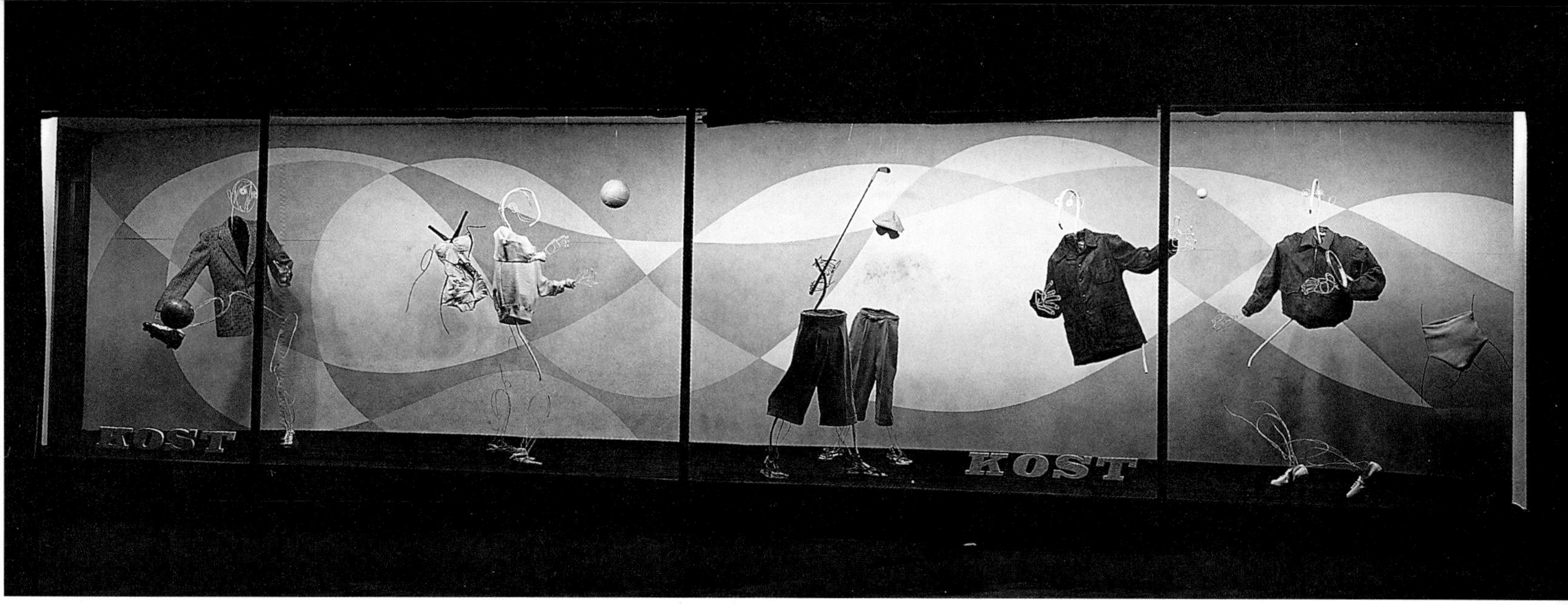
KOST
KOST

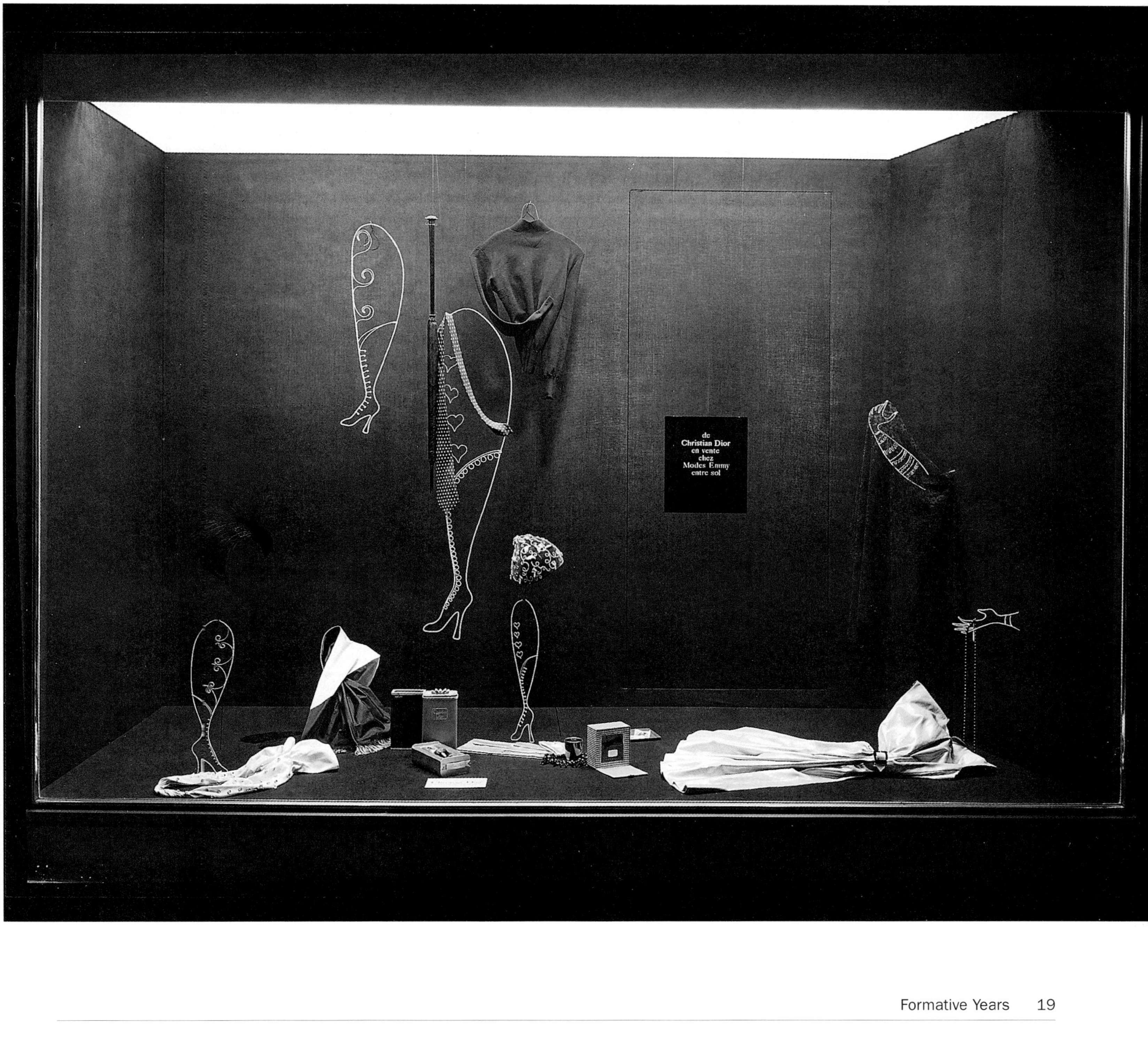
de
Christian Dior
en vente
chez
Modes Emmy
entre sol

'You must steal your own freedom'

1953–57

As a painter, Tinguely had been incapable of deciding when a painting was finished. He escaped from this dead end by adding the temporal dimension to the formal vocabulary of non-objective painting. His artistic sources hark back to the abstraction of Malevich and Kandinsky, Mondrian, Miró and Klee, and to the painted reliefs of the Dadaists Arp and Schwitters. Tinguely found an aesthetic and moral solution to an artistic dilemma:

I was trying to get away from the imperative, the power of these artists, including Mondrian. I began to use movement simply to make a re-creation. It was a way of redoing a painting so that it would become infinite—it would go on making new compositions with the help of the physical and mechanical movements I gave it.[1]

From 1953 to 1959 he worked his way through the formal principles of his predecessors, articulating them anew by making their system part of a temporal process and adding the elements of play and irony.

Tinguely was also familiar with the development of kinetic art. He had read Umberto Boccioni's 'Manifesto of Futurist Sculpture', published in 1912, and the 'Realist Manifesto' by the brothers Naum Gabo and Antoine Pevsner, published in Moscow in 1920.[2] He knew of the paradigmatic kinetic objects such as Marcel Duchamp's ready-made *Bicycle Wheel* (1913), Vladimir Tatlin's project for the *Monument to the Third International* (1920) and Lászlô Moholy-Nagy's *Light Prop for a Ballet* (also called *Light-Space Modulator*, 1923–30).

Crucial to Tinguely's development was Alexander Calder's pioneering art of motion. Ever since Calder had visited Mondrian's studio in 1930 and suggested that the coloured squares tacked on the walls should be made to move, he had been fascinated by the idea of movement. His experiments with motorised works took a direction similar to that Tinguely followed some two decades later. Yet, Calder eventually lost interest in mechanised sculpture. He felt that the inevitable repetition of movement killed the elements of chance, spontaneity and variability: Unlike Calder, Tinguely was not trained as a mechanical engineer and had more freedom to improvise, circumventing machine-like repetition by tinkering with mechanics. His longtime assistant Joseph Imhof, a professional locksmith, still shakes his head in disbelief when he points out the technical liberties, the tricks and stratagems, of the artist. With a twinkle of admiration in his eyes, he admits that the makeshift, sloppy welding, and the haphazard working methods in which he partnered the artist, work. Thus, Tinguely's professional inexpertness worked in his own favour.

In 1953, the twenty-eight-year-old Tinguely moved to Paris with his wife, leaving their three-year old

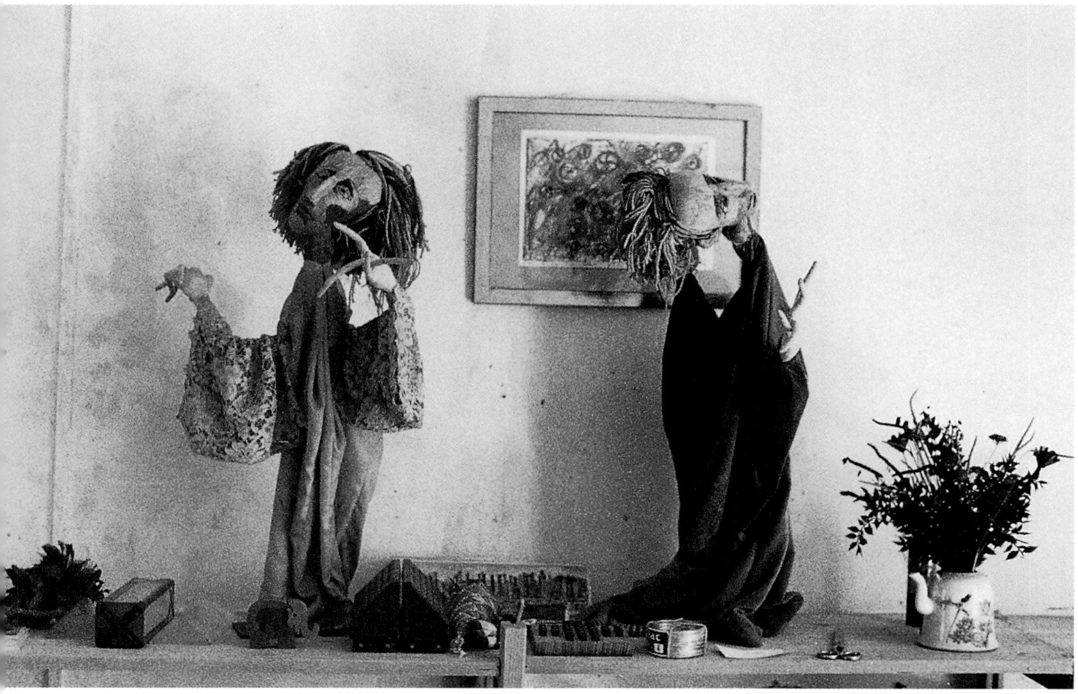

Eva Aeppli, glove puppets

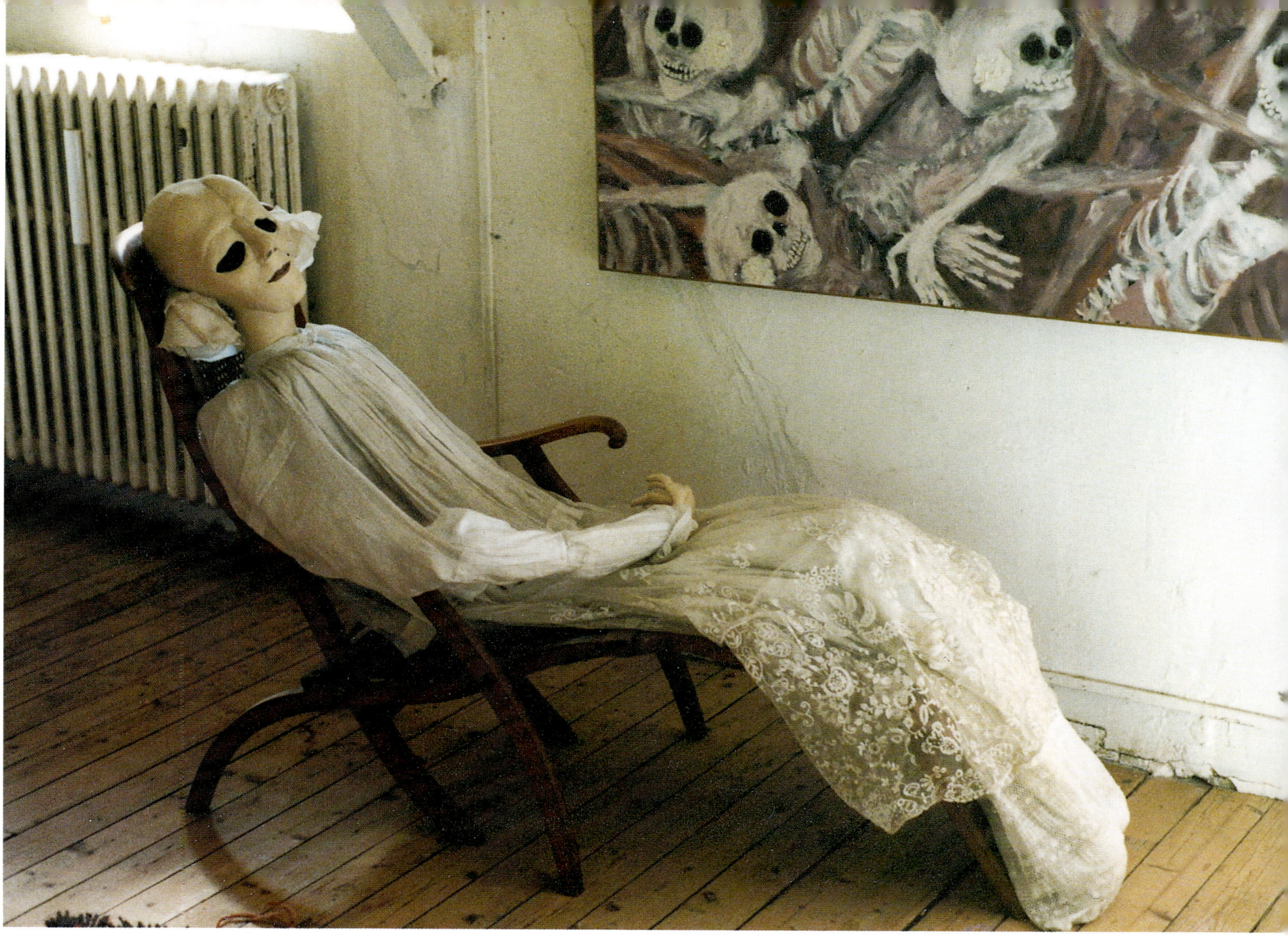

Eva Aeppli, *Toby Turner*, 1973

daughter, Miriam, in the care of Tinguely's parents in Switzerland. Jean and Eva were convinced that they must leave Switzerland, the comfort and prosperity of which they found stultifying. In the fifties, Paris was still the pre-eminent art capital of the world. The Tinguelys lived from hand to mouth, mostly off the meagre sales of Eva's glove puppets (illus. p. 20). The former Waldorf student was talented with a needle and would later create life-size figures that are remarkable as singular reflections of the human soul. Jean worked on a joint project with Daniel Spoerri: an 'auto-theatre' that was to include stage action with or without actors/dancers. The experiment failed—the moment the dancers entered, the entire set collapsed. As he recollected this event, Spoerri pointed out that this was one of Tinguely's rare all-out failures.[3]

Tinguely loved to tell the story that he met Spoerri in the early fifties peddling bananas on the exact spot in Basel where the Dominican cloister housing the famous frescoes depicting the Dance of Death had once stood, a tale that Spoerri vehemently denies. The anecdote is important only insofar as it suggests the complexity of their relationship. Spoerri was singled out by Franz Meyer as one of the personalities who were very important for Tinguely during those years: 'I met Spoerri in Berne when he was a dancer. He also directed first productions in German of Ionesco, Picasso, Beckett and Tardieu in a small theatre in Berne. He was a very active personality and knew many people. He enlarged Tinguely's vision and opened new directions and many different views.'[4]

Tinguely had his first solo show in the book department of Galerie Arnaud. It opened on 27 May 1954 and included 'meta-mechanical' reliefs similar to those the artist had made in Basel (see fig. 8). The gallery published the art magazine *Cimaise*, and it was *Cimaise*'s editor in chief, R. V. Gindertael, who wrote the text of the exhibition leaflet, in which he termed Tinguely's mechanical contrivances *'peinture-automates'*. These automated abstractions, of which an entire series from 1954 was only later entitled 'Meta-Malevich', are reliefs of largely white geometrical shapes cut from sheet metal set on axes in front of black, box-shaped backgrounds. For Tinguely, the colour black symbolised absence, while white represented the imagination, the vital principle. A small electric motor drives a hidden mechanism of wooden pulleys of different sizes linked by a rubber belt. The geometrical forms assemble in infinitely changing configurations because the speed at which they turn is determined by their corresponding pulley—the larger the pulley, the slower the movement. Irregularity of speed is assured by the elasticity of the rubber belt transmitting the movement.

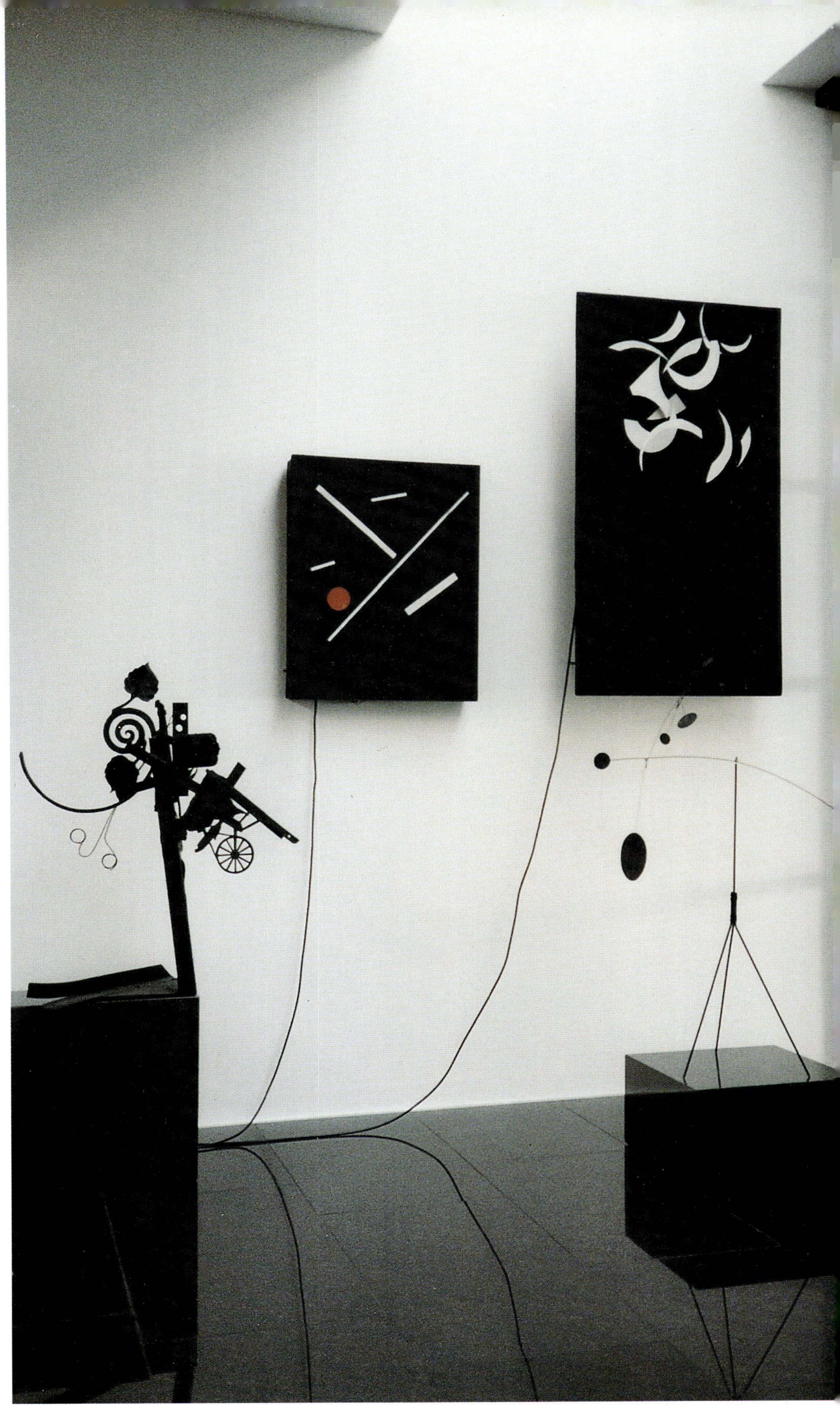

8-9 'Meta-mechanical' reliefs on the wall (left): *Méta-Malevich 'Point rouge'*, 1954; (right): *Spirale éclatée*, 1957

Spirale éclatée, 1957 (view of the back).

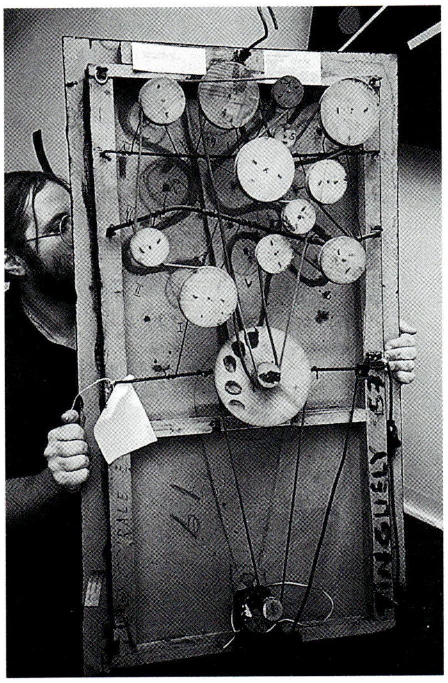

In Tinguely's spidery steel wire reliefs and free-standing constructions, to which he sometimes attached multicoloured cut-outs, the transmission of movement was made an integral part of the kinetic event. These bewitched clockwork mechanisms are wittily subversive of the world-famed precision instruments tooled by Tinguely's fellow Swiss watchmakers. In these pieces, motion is transmitted by means of variously sized wheels whose rims are studded with protruding wires, a type of cogged wheel that meshes with other similar wheels. Hand-driven or animated by a small electric motor—usually the 78 r.p.m. gramophone motor the artist also used in his 'meta-mechanical' reliefs, they move in spasmodic jerks. Their delicate, armature-like skeletons are three-dimensional cousins of Paul Klee's fanciful mechanical inventions, such as *Destruction and Hope* (1916; Kunstmuseum Basel). Both spring from like-minded ironical attitudes.

In July 1954, Tinguely was invited to participate in the Ninth Salon of New Realities, in October he showed again at Galerie Arnaud and in December he exhibited in Milan, at the Studio d'Architettura b24. In the last two shows he included a set of wire sculptures, some entitled *Moulin à prière* *(Prayer Mill;* fig. 11*)*.[5] At the beginning of 1955, the Tinguelys moved into one of the studios of the artists' colony at Impasse Ronsin off the rue Vaugirard, Brancusi's home from 1916 until his death in 1957.[6] Tinguely's work had impressed Pontus Hulten, the Swedish art critic and staff member of the Nationalmuseum in Stockholm.[7] Hulten sought out Tinguely and instigated a lasting friendship. It was Hulten's suggestion to name Tinguely's *peintures-automates* 'meta-mechanical' by analogy with the words *metaphysical*, *metamorphosis* or *metaphor*.

Together with Robert Breer, an American kinetic artist who later became a film-maker, Hulten and Tinguely conceived and submitted the idea of a show on the art of motion to Denise René. The exhibition opened at this leading avant-garde gallery in April

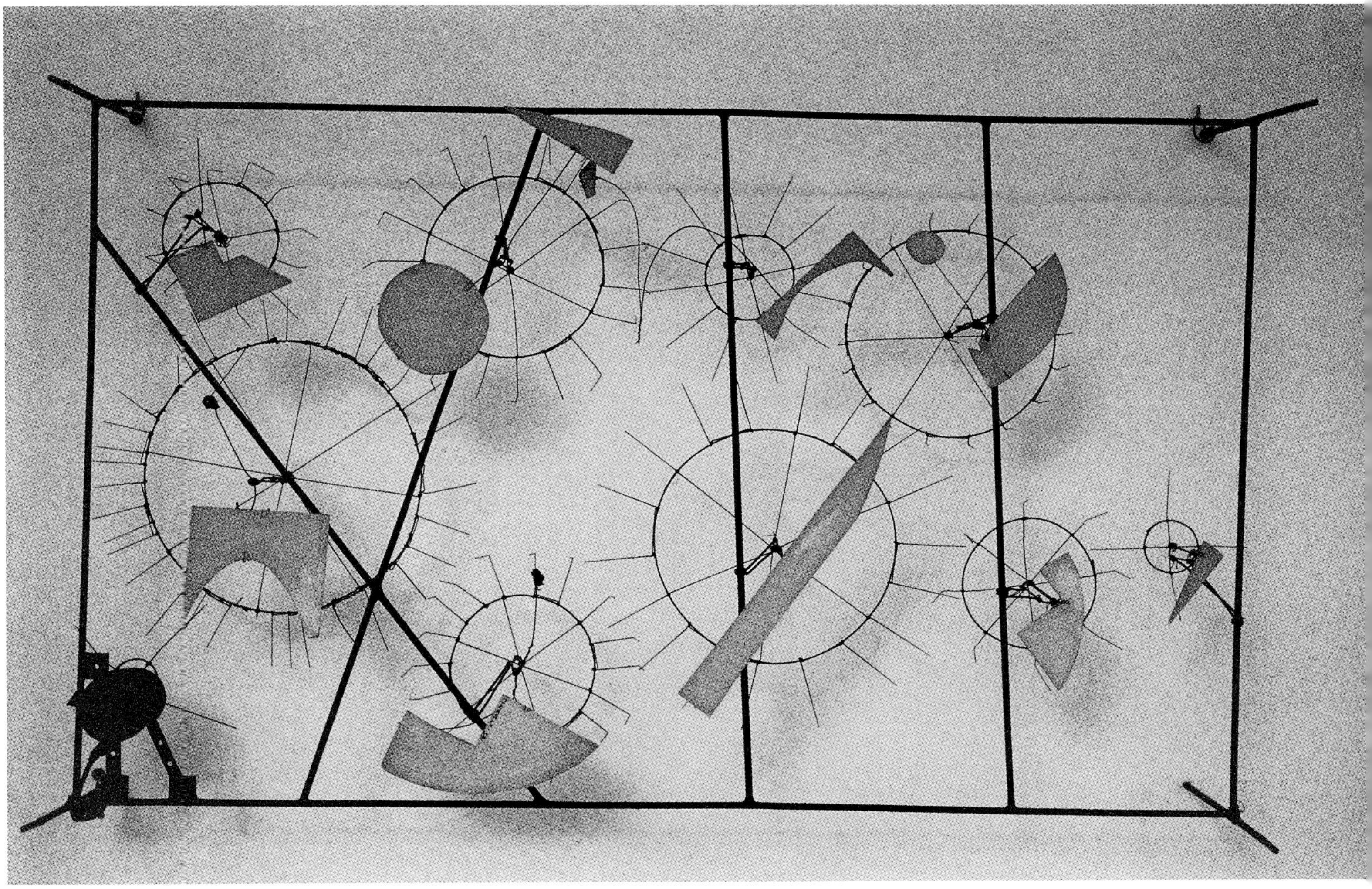

10 'Meta-mechanical' relief *Elément détaché I*, 1954

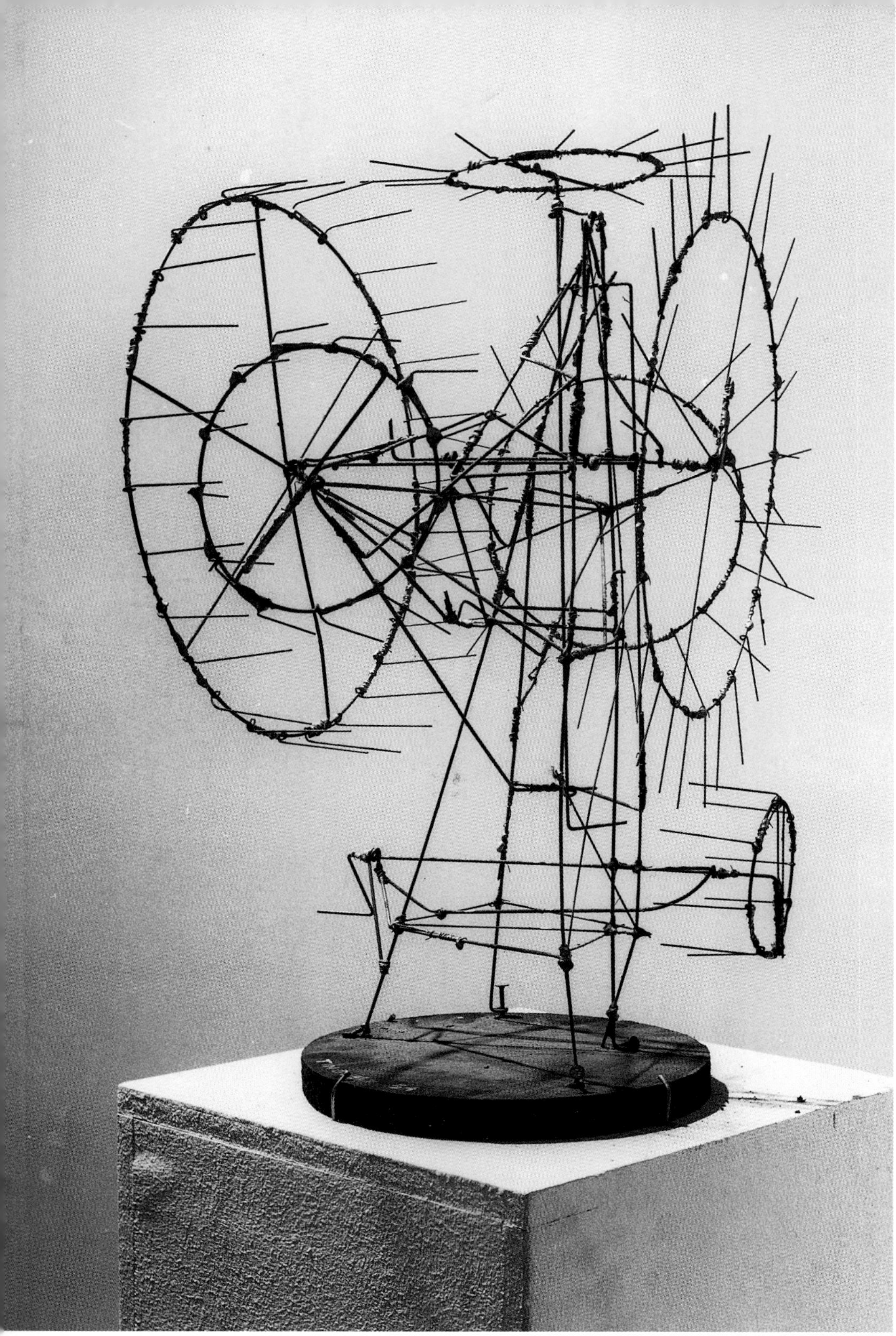

1955 under the title *Movement*. It included works by Duchamp and Calder, in addition to René's regular stable of artists: Vasarely, Agam, Pol Bury, Soto, Jacobsen and the newcomer Tinguely.

For this exhibit, Tinguely worked his way through experiments with real motion done by his predecessors. Two of the reliefs shown included a drawing mechanism and were entitled *Machine à dessiner No. 1* and *No. 2* (*Drawing Machine No. 1* and *No. 2*; fig. 12). These were inspired by works by Duchamp such as *Rotorelief* (first edition, 1935; second edition, 1953) and *Rotary Demisphere* (1925; New York, Museum of Modern Art). Tinguely's *Auto-Mobile* is a Calder-like sculpture that performs a mechanical ballet and moves around the room (fig. 13). His *Volume virtuel No. 1* (*Virtual Volume No. 1*) is akin to Naum Gabo's *Kinetic Construction: Vibrating Spring* (1920; London, Tate Gallery). In both works, rapid movement is perceived as a continuum and also changes the volume of the piece by amplifying it. The show caused quite a sensation, and the public was only too happy to comply with the unusual instructions 'Please touch.'

Relief Méta-mécanique sonore I (*Meta-Mechanical Sound Relief I*; 1955), which he entered in the Salon of New Realities was Tinguely's first work in which some form of random sound played an integral part (fig. 14).[8] Percussive noises are produced by

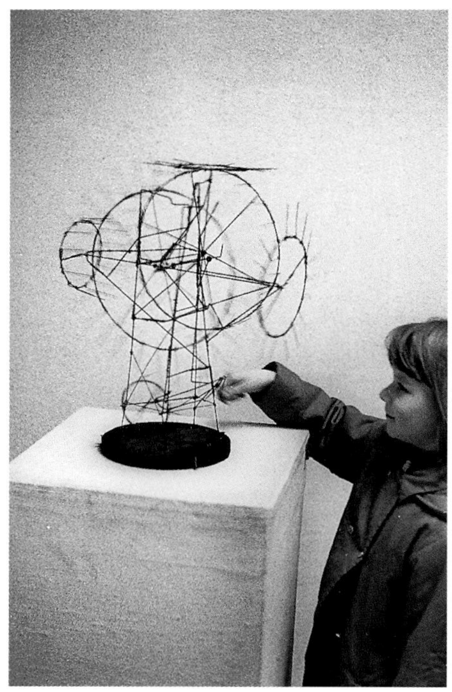

11 'Meta-mechanical' sculpture *Moulin à prière III (Prayer Mill III)*, 1954

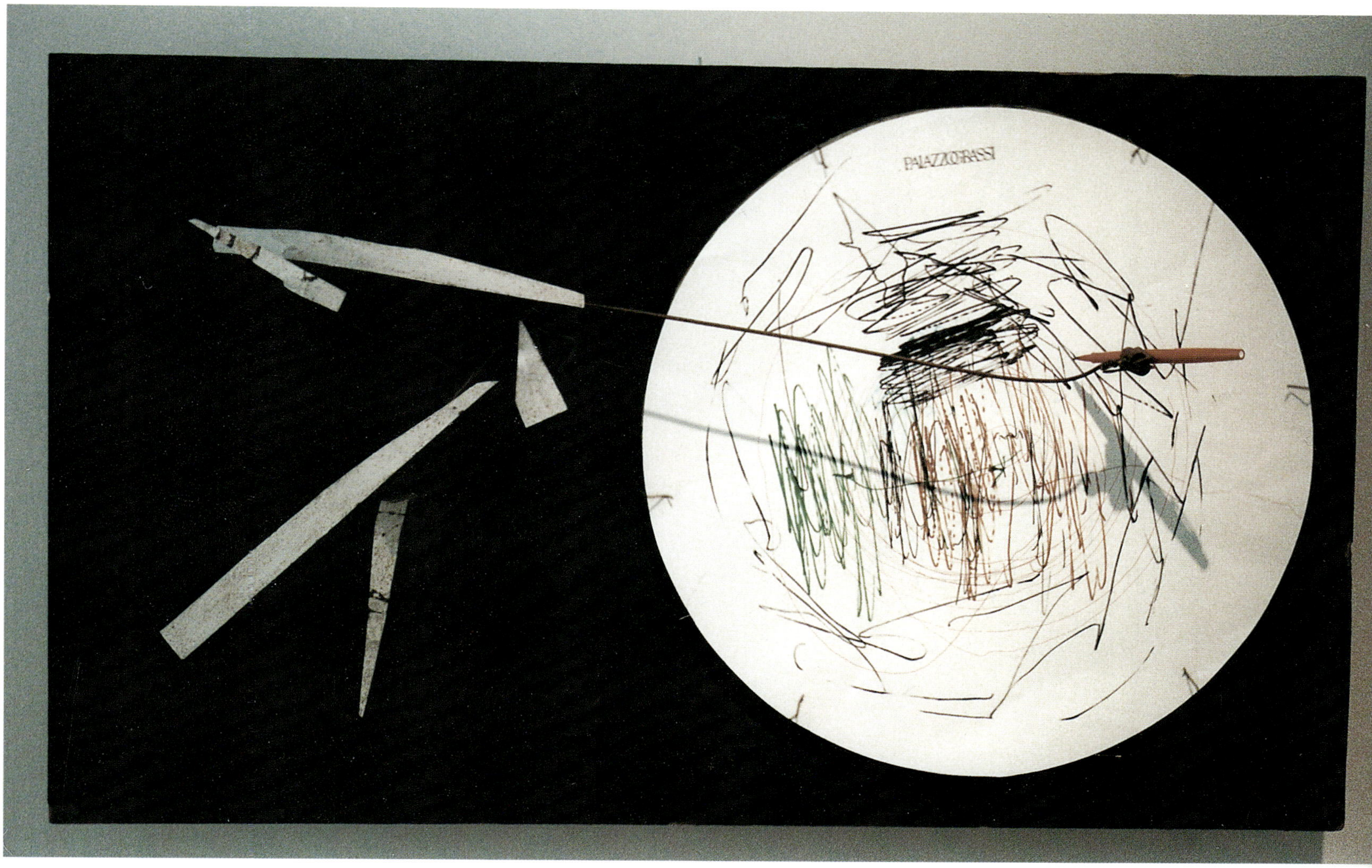

12 *Machine à dessiner No. 2 (Drawing Machine No. 2)*, 1955

little metal hammers striking at irregular intervals ordinary objects retrieved from the trash: glasses and bottles, tuna fish and sardine tins painted uniformly black. As yet only sound resonators, later such objects would become signifiers in Tinguely's work.

Tinguely continued to explore the 'concrete music'[9] elicited from ordinary, non-musical objects, as well as sounds produced by more conventional instruments, including electronic ones such as those found in his monumental musical objects. An example of the latter is *Meta-Harmony II* (fig. 16). These works are elaborations on the possibilities adumbrated in the *Meta-Mechanical Sound Relief*. Beginning in the mid-fifties, Tinguely orchestrated a system of sound imagery, a dramatic aural visualisation that enhanced sculptural motifs. He strove to achieve a particular effect in correspondence with the physical appearance and movement of each work and to increase its emotional impact. Since it is impossible to make a silent engine, the artist exploited the expressive character of sound, using it multifariously, but never as mere décor.

Tinguely was successful and became known internationally. During 1955, he participated in several group shows, and his work was seen in several Swiss cities. He introduced monochromy and polychromy into his reliefs, as well as a greater and more varied number of free-form shapes, and tested the juxtaposition of fixed with mobile elements. He also began to attach motors and wooden pulleys to the front of his reliefs, exposing the hitherto hidden activating parts. The long, narrow polychrome reliefs created at this time were later called 'Meta-Kandinsky' (fig. 15). In October 1956, Denise René invited Tinguely back for a solo show advertised as *Tinguely: Cine-*

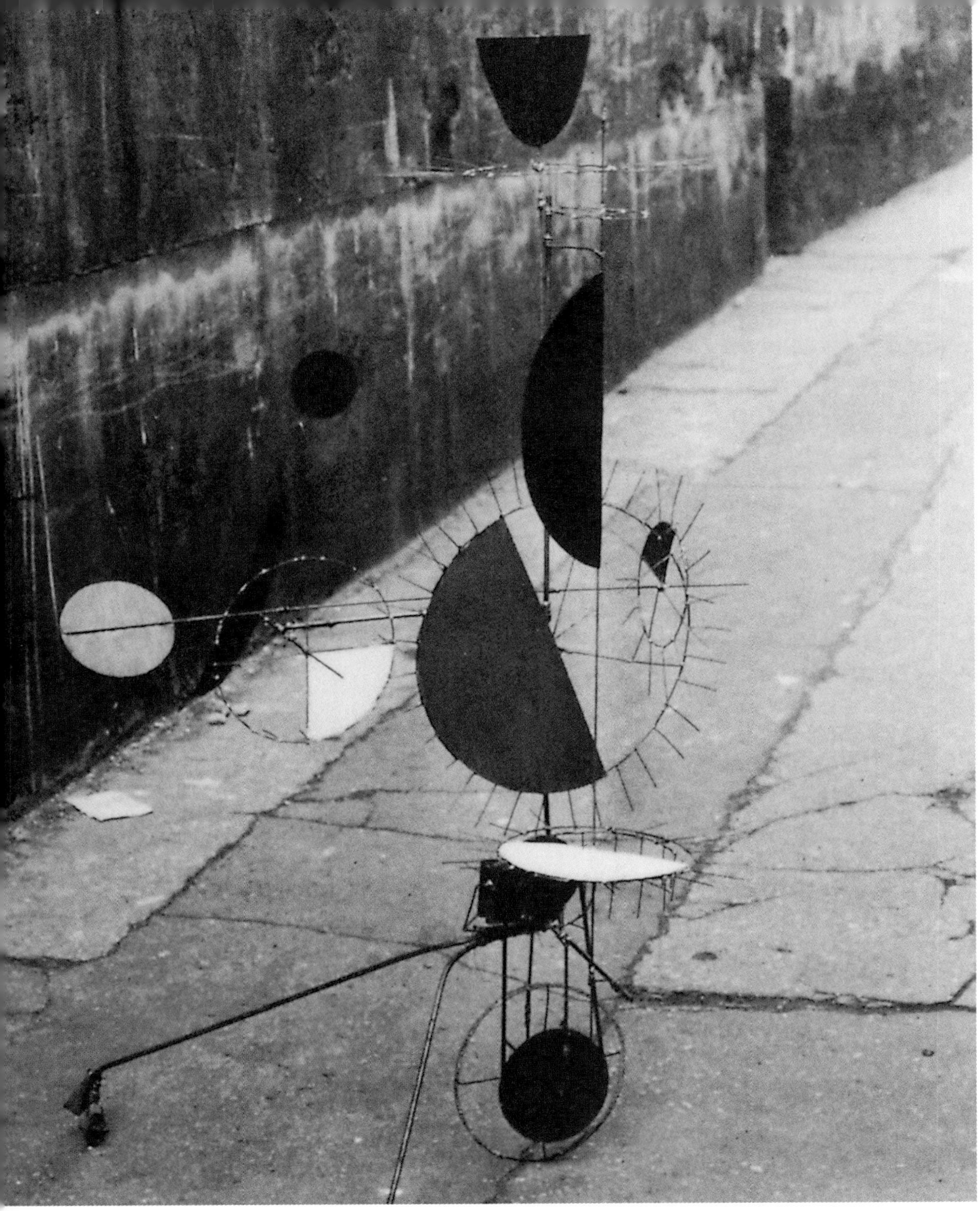

ended up as variations on a well-known theme: Constructivist abstraction.'[11] Tinguely went through a profound artistic crisis which he repressed by devoting all of his energies to women and cars, two subjects that held a continuous fascination for him.

Tinguely prized the act of driving as an experience in which human and machine fuse in an almost erotic fashion, and the driver becomes engine-like in his mechanical precision. He enjoyed fast cars, racing cars and the way cars grant people the freedom to go places, to move, to experience change. For years, Tinguely went to every major Grand Prix race.[12] What primarily engaged him in racing was the fact of its utter absurdity. He himself drove at high speeds and sometimes engaged his passengers in paradoxical arguments about highway safety with

13 *Auto-Mobile*, 1954

14 *Relief Méta-mécanique sonore I (Meta-Mechanical Sound Relief I)*, 1955 (detail)

matic Paintings. Pierre Restany, in a favourable short article on the exhibit in *Cimaise*, wrote: 'Tinguely holds here for certain the elements of a totally original language.'[10]

Despite Tinguely's ongoing artistic evolution, Pontus Hulten reported that in June 1957 he showed works at Edouard Loeb's that were mere variations on what he had exhibited at Denise René the year before: 'It is likely that he felt he had gone up a blind alley. There were, of course, a host of possible ways to develop what he was doing, but they would all have

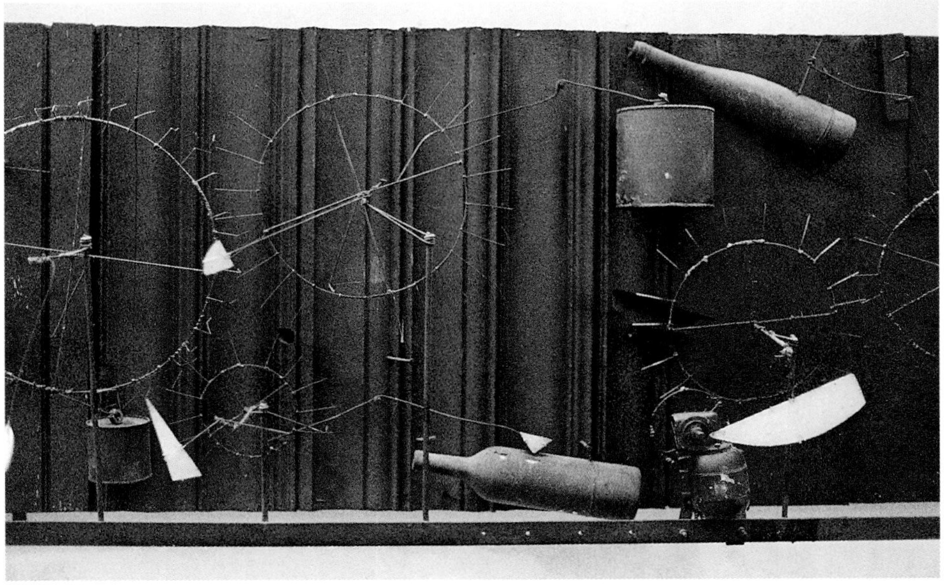

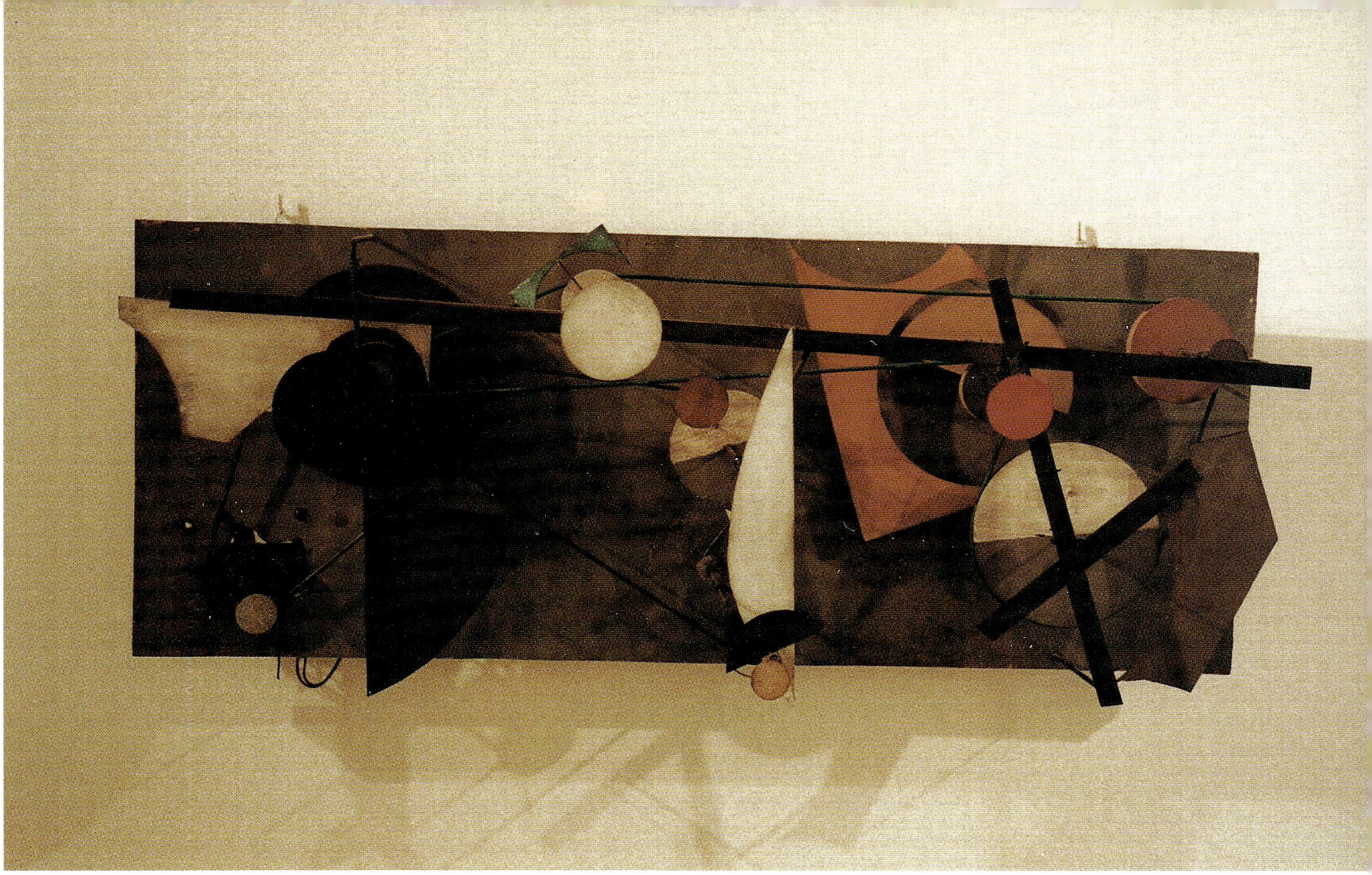

15 *Meta-Kandinsky I (Wundermaschine)*, 1956

such remarks as: 'The quicker one gets off the highway, where most accidents take place, the lesser the risk of getting involved in one.'

In October 1957 Tinguely had a severe automobile accident, in which his car went into a skid and turned over. He suffered a severe concussion, a dislocated hip and a compression of the rib-cage. This close encounter with death was so traumatic that he considered it a turning point in his life. Life's preciousness was suddenly revealed in the face of death. Under these circumstances, Albert Camus's philosophy of the absurd took on a personal meaning. Camus's plea to recognise the absurd and then surmount it by living passionately encouraged Tinguely to enlarge the scope of his own philosophical framework. After the accident, Tinguely's forced withdrawal gave him time to grow intellectually and spiritually and to gather his forces for an artistic renewal.

16 *Meta-Harmony II*, 1979

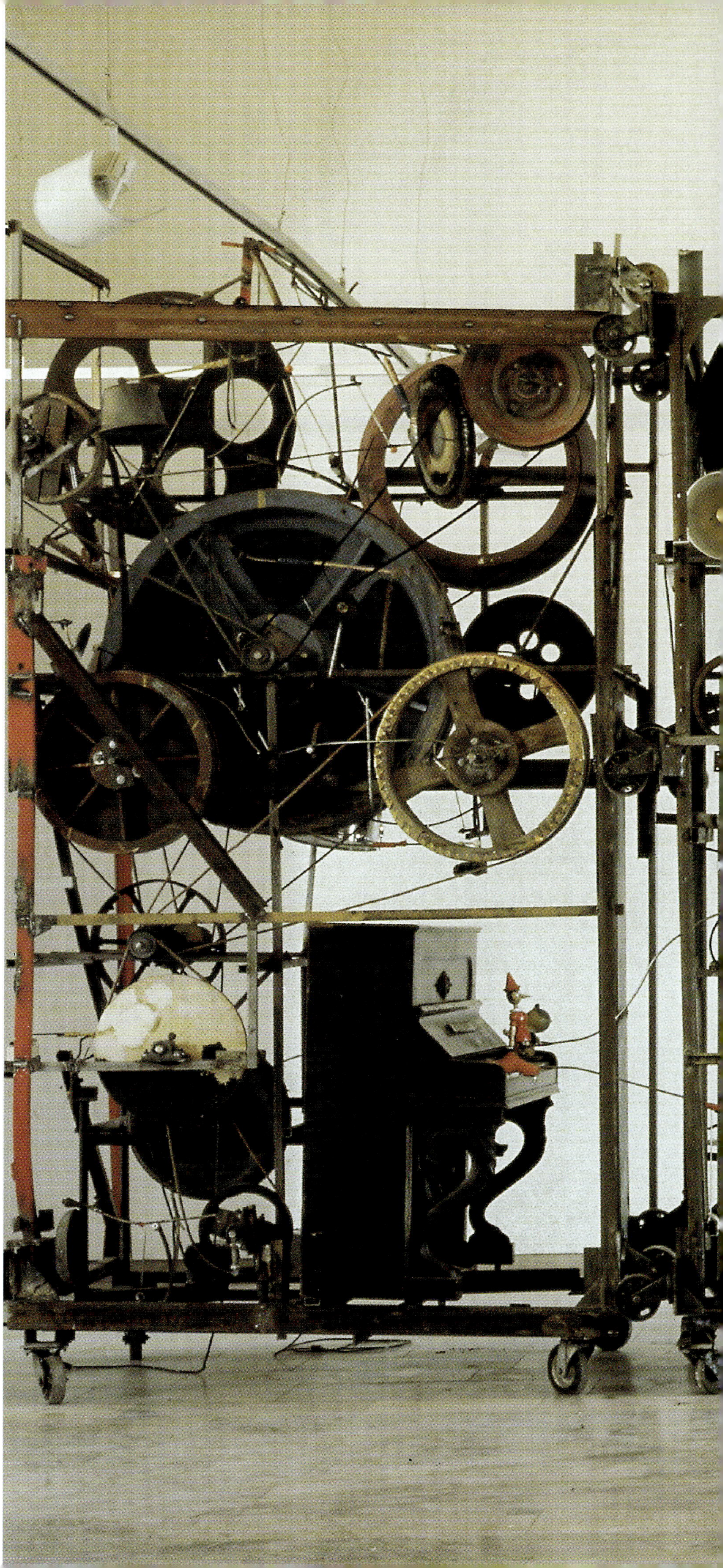

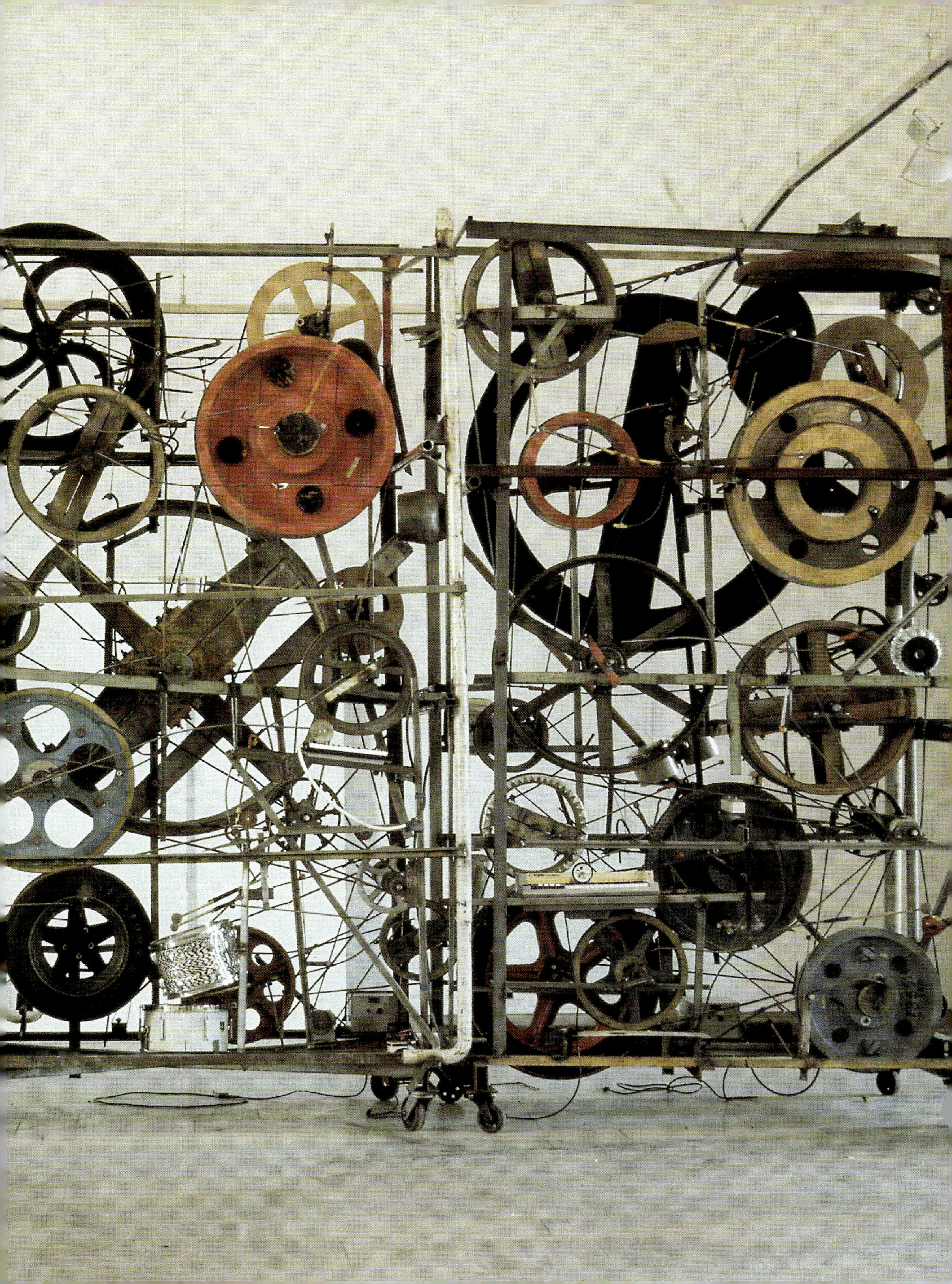

'Everything moves continuously. Immobility does not exist'

1958–59

Tinguely produced little art during the six months following his accident. The turning point was the opening of Yves Klein's exhibition *The Specialisation of Sensibility from the State of Prime Matter to the State of Stabilised Pictorial Sensibility: The Void* at Iris Clert on 29 April 1958. Tinguely had met Klein in 1955 during the presentation of their art to the jury for the Salon of New Realities. Klein submitted one of his early monochrome paintings, which the jury refused to accept. As Tinguely remembered the story, the jury suggested to Klein that he add a splash or dot of a different colour, which would satisfy their criteria. Klein's refusal greatly impressed Tinguely.

At Iris Clert, Klein presented the whitewashed, empty gallery itself as the work of art, that is the art work as a purely spiritual manifestation and the gallery as the locus of transformation. Klein's scenario included two members of the National Guard in full-dress uniform at the entrance as if the *Mona Lisa* were being shown inside. Engraved invitations had to be presented at the door and gave the event an air of exclusivity. Cocktails, tinted with methylene blue, were served. Tinguely wrote enthusiastically to Pontus Hulten: 'They'll all pee blue for one week to ten days, for about the duration of the show. The first opening I've enjoyed!'[1]

Klein's work confirmed Tinguely in his own search for 'dematerialisation'—that is, the question of perceived reality. But what really united them was their understanding of art. Both men wanted to touch—and bring about change in—people. Tinguely also was impressed by Iris Clert's ability to make events out of openings and appreciated her dynamic personality. In Clert's one-room gallery he found the ideal space in which to stage the acoustic-visual event that had its first 'audition' on 9 June 1958 with the title *My Stars—Concert for Seven Paintings*. Tinguely took his experiments with the combined effects of speed and sound a step further in these works, providing them with such characteristic titles as *Le Point radiant* (*The Radiant Point*) or *Volume virtuel*. Each piece is a wooden board concealing a motor. Affixed to the board's surface are a variety of metal cut-outs hiding the sound-making objects. Everything is painted black except for a small white element, the only visibly mobile part within each relief, which creates the visual animation. From a switchboard panel facing the reliefs, the viewer controls the electric impulse for each work independently. That impulse activates the visible mobile part as well as a hidden device that produces a cacophonous sound or furious drumming. Here, Tinguely was exploring the idea of audience-participation art anticipated by Duchamp.

On 17 November 1958, Clert's gallery was once more a locus of transformation when Klein and Tinguely opened their collaborative exhibition entitled *Pure Speed and Monochrome Stability*. Tinguely was in charge of the mechanical aspect, Klein of the pictorial one. Together they created six wall pieces (variously sized monochrome blue discs fixed against the wall and turning at high speeds) and two free-standing sculptures: the *Excavatrice de l'espace* (*Space Excavator*; Switzerland, private collection), which featured a large white twirling disc, and the *Perforateur monochrome* (*Monochrome Perforator*) which spun a diminutive red disc at 10,000 r.p.m. (*La Vitesse totale* [*Total Speed*] is in a private collection, Zurich; the other wall pieces were destroyed.) Clert was at first afraid that the discs would decapitate visitors, but ultimately enjoyed the Dada-like spectacle.[2] Tinguely encountered Klein during a critical phase of his work. Klein encouraged Tinguely in his attempts to emancipate the machine and use it as a medium. More importantly, in Klein Tinguely experienced the naive, unwilling fool, the solemn, quixotic utopist of whom he said: 'For me, Klein was the top nut . . . and that measured simply by the stagnation around him. I was naturally very attracted by him.'[3] In 1958/59, the two friends shared a public commission, Tinguely's first, for which each artist produced several works for a new opera house at Gelsenkirchen, a town not far from Düsseldorf. Tinguely's two large reliefs

Left to right: (back row) Annie de la Celle, Tinguely, Claude Lalanne; (front row) Henri de la Celle, Niki de Saint Phalle and François Lalanne, Château Elyas, 1959

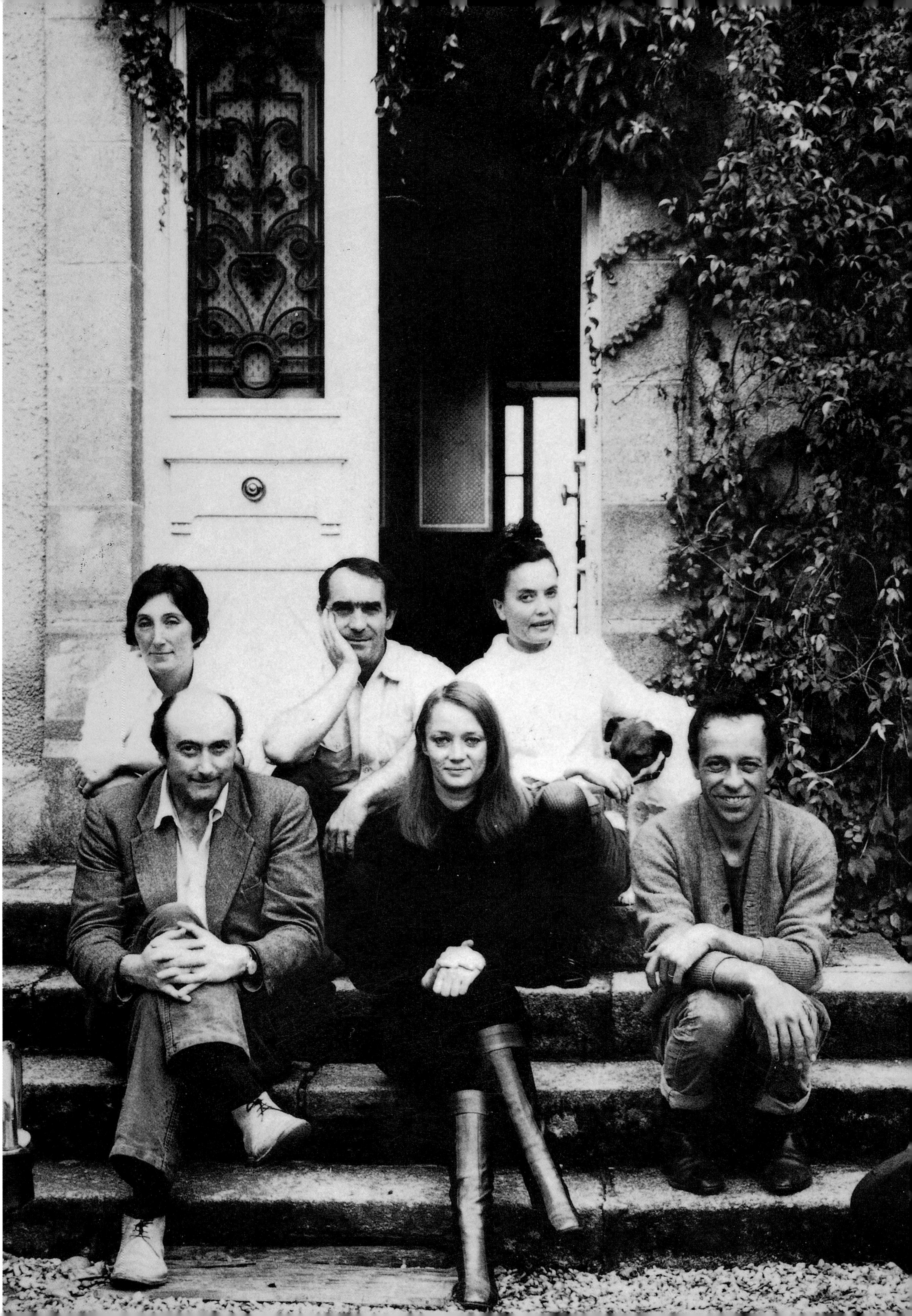

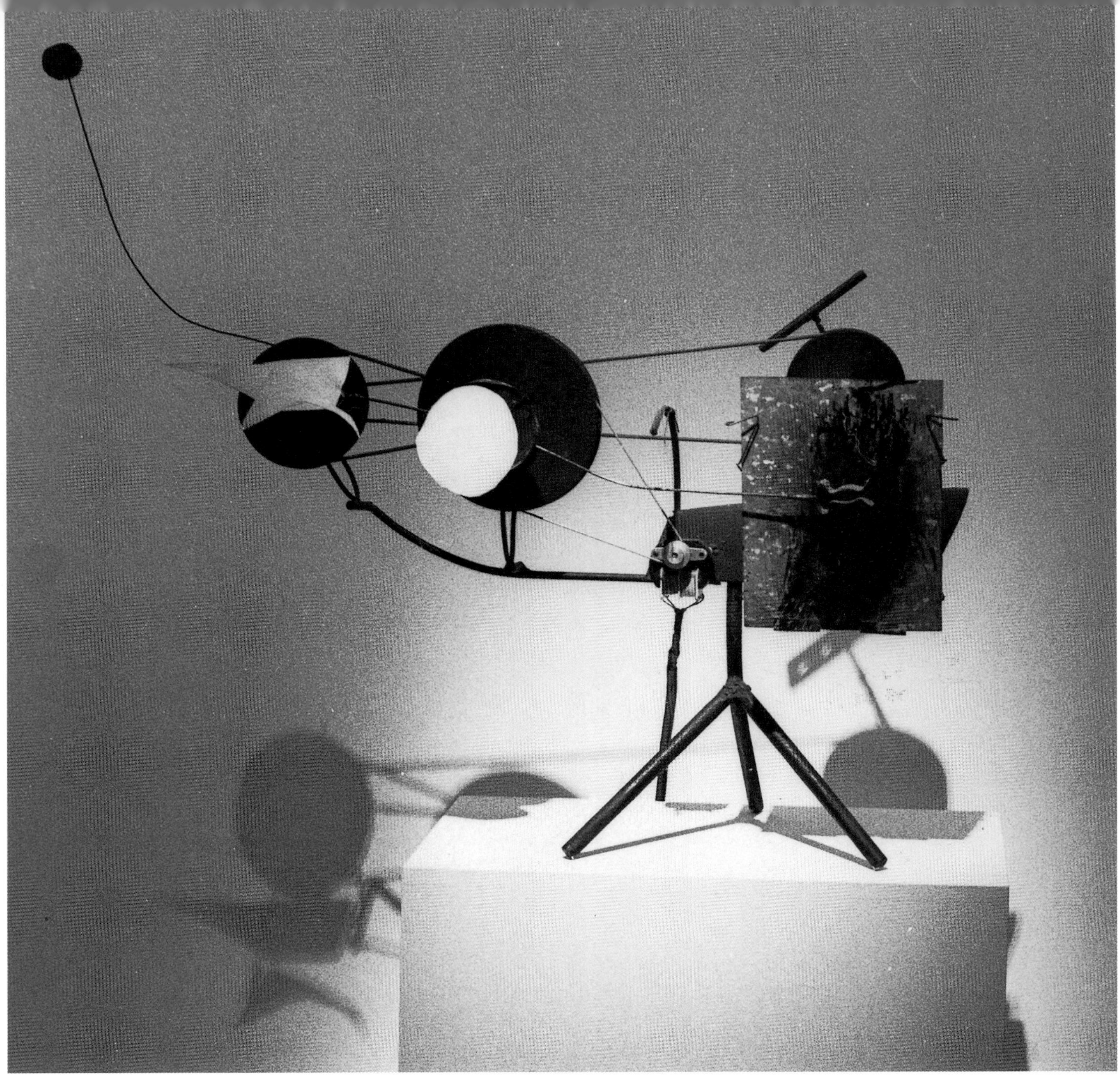

were placed in one of the foyers of the new Musiktheater im Revier. Each of the 1.35-by-4-metre reliefs consists of nearly 30 irregularly shaped flat elements covered with the same grey velvet as the wall and moving at variegated speeds.[4]

During the late fifties, skilled artists and gallery-owners availed themselves of performance-art tactics at exhibition openings, which became extremely useful instruments of propaganda. Iris Clert showed extraordinary flair and know-how in this regard: 'Of each opening I want[ed] to make a feast.'[5] She had convinced the Director of Gaumont cinema newsreels to attend the opening of *My Stars* and to include it in his news reports.[6] Art now began to garner unprecedented publicity, and openings became vaudevillian street-festivals.

In January 1959, Tinguely had his first solo show in Germany, at the Galerie Alfred Schmela in Düsseldorf, where he staged *Concert No. 2*. The highlight of the opening was the simultaneous recitation of three different texts by three participants.[7] The texts were of different lengths, came printed on a piece of paper gathered in a loop and were advanced mechanically on a machine specially conceived by Tinguely for the occasion. The speed at which the texts rolled by

17 Drawing machine, *Metamatic No. 1*, 1959

A drawing machine in the exhibition at the Centre Georges Pompidou, Paris, 1988 ▷

did not make it possible for them to be read in their entirety. Each reader selected how fast and how much he or she would read. The result was an incomprehensible acoustic mix, a concert of words in the best Dada tradition, combining chance with spontaneity. The sound effect came not from individual words, but from the simultaneity of the texts, resulting in a dissonant synthesis.

The Düsseldorf opening had been well publicised and was attended by radio and television reporters, a novelty for Germany. While the show was up in the gallery, the artist wanted to stage a suitable event to publicise his artistic manifesto 'For Statics' by dropping fifteen thousand leaflets from an aeroplane.[8] A photographer was on hand to document the event and fix it in the memory of the avant-garde as one of its touchstones. However, permission to drop the leaflets from an aeroplane was withheld by the police, so the artist had to disperse them from a car.[9] This was the first in a series of events staged by the artist in an effort to reach a wider public, to go beyond the gallery and museum walls.

From the beginning, movement had been a fundamental concept for Tinguely, assuming philosophical dimensions. He formulated his metaphysical concepts in the manifesto dispersed at Düsseldorf:

Everything moves continuously. Immobility does not exist. Don't be dominated by out-of-date concepts of time. Get rid of hours, seconds and minutes. Stop resisting change. LIVE IN TIME—BE STATIC, BE STATIC WITH MOVEMENT. For Statics, for a present taking place in the Present. Resist anxious spells of weakness to halt moving things, to petrify moments and to kill what is alive. Stop continuously setting up 'values' which cannot but break down. Be free, live!

Stop 'painting' time. Stop building cathedrals and pyramids which crumble like puff pastry. Breathe deeply, live in the present: live in time and according to time. For a wonderful and absolute reality!

Tinguely liked to tell an anecdote about a sculptor-friend of his who had carved an abstract form out of a superb monolith of marble. The work, which had taken months to produce, split in two when it was unloaded from a truck on its way to be exhibited. The smallest of faults within this stable, permanent mass was enough to destroy it. Tinguely was fond of quoting Lao-tzu: 'Softness will always overcome hardness—for the tongue, which is soft, lasts—the teeth, which are hard, break.'[10] Or, put in his own words, 'All that is fixed falls to pieces, while all that which is movement, remains. It is to this that my sculptures in movement respond: the movement in stability.'[11]

Tinguely argued against the fixed, which precludes movement and evolution, against established and immutable values, against defined truths. The artist favoured the kind of paradoxical logic that permeates Chinese and Indian thought and was equally inspired by Heraclitus, whose philosophy is the earliest expression in Western thought of paradoxical logic. Tinguely reinterpreted Heraclitus's assertion that all static being is based on deception and that the only unalterable principle is that everything changes. Tinguely's manifesto also reflects his philosophy of libertarian anarchism. For him, 'Be static in movement' was a philosophical exhortation addressed to any individual or society whose goal was duration rather than change, which sought the continuity and solidity of the established order rather than a continuous adjustment and mutuality. Though his gesture had its validity, the statements of the manifesto are so compressed that they verge on the very dogmatism they oppose. The works themselves or the artist's spontaneous verbalising expressed his philosophy far better than the written propagandising of his manifesto.

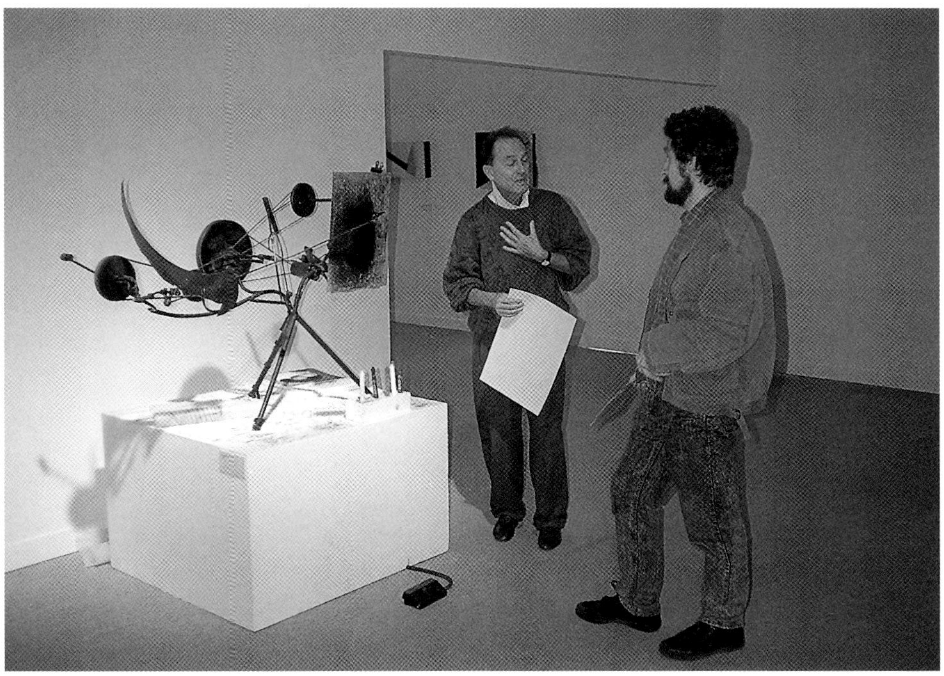

Since the end of the Second World War, abstraction had become the pre-eminent artistic language in Europe and America. Eventually it drove out other approaches and no other styles were successfully exhibited. Tinguely subverted the ideas of the creation of a work of art as a spectacle and of the painter as a heroic showman—both characteristics of action painting as approached by such artists as Georges Mathieu—in his drawing machines entitled 'Metamatics' (see figs. 17-18), which he built during a stay in the spring of 1959 at the Château Elyas at St Priest, Ligoure (Haute Vienne), owned by the collector Henri de la Celle. Tinguely took out a patent on the new works and exhibited them at Iris Clert in July 1959. Here, Tinguely for the first time incorporated the comic dimension as a major element in his work. Another breakthrough occurred in that he began to work more directly with the image of the machine and its functions.[12] The machine and its function became his chosen means of expression.

To use the drawing machines, the viewer took a piece of paper, presigned by Tinguely, clamped it onto the metal support and fixed a coloured pencil or crayon into place. The machine moved like a giant crab or insect, activated either by a switch or by the insertion of a coin into a slot. For three minutes, the arm of the machine moved across the piece of paper, which was also in motion. The result was a 'metamatic' abstraction resembling an Abstract Expressionist painting. Tinguely here involved the spectator actively in the 'automatic' creation of the art work. The tone of the 'Metamatics' was intentionally and unmistakably comic; the show mocked *Tachisme* by mechanically producing a kind of informal art. The machines added a new twist to Duchamp's readymade objects and were quite different from those Tinguely had shown at Denise René in the *Movement* exhibition in 1955, in which he had concerned himself with optical illusions created by motion.[13] The 'Metamatics' represented a major formal breakthrough for Tinguely: as in his more delicate, spatial wire sculptures, he revealed the mechanisms of the machine and began to use them as open-work, structural frames. Thus, the artist ended his 'collaboration' with the father figures of abstraction and embarked on a collaboration with the machine per se.

In 1959, Tinguely began to work with a gas-welding apparatus rather than a soldering iron. This device enabled him to weld heavier pieces of metal. Invited to participate in the first Youth Biennale in Paris, Tinguely enlarged upon the idea and form of the 'Metamatic' sculptures and created a tall *Metamatic No. 17* (fig. 18). This free-standing sculpture, which runs on a petrol motor, draws, cuts the drawings off the moving roll and disperses them via a fan. It moves about, produces noises and smells; in other words, it is Tinguely's realisation of a *Gesamtkunstwerk* and is a spectacle unto itself.

The artist explored the performance-art potential of the 'Metamatics' fully during an evening at the Institute of Contemporary Arts in London on 12 November.[14] This was his first event to incorporate the range of activities typical of happenings. The evening was billed as 'Art, Machines and Motion, a lecture by Tinguely.'[15] This 'lecture' was Tinguely's first serious confrontation with the English language and resulted in a delirious confusion

18 *Metamatic No. 17*, 1959

like that of Eugène Ionesco when he attempted to learn English and, frustrated, ended up writing *The Bald Soprano*. Tinguely's text was immediately and continuously corrected by an English professor and played just slightly out of phase on two tape-players, thus creating hilarious and barely intelligible verbal sound effects. Then, two professional cycling champions took part in a painting competition. Riding a stationary bike attached to a painting machine, the *Metamatic No. 12* (Collection Phyllis B. Lambert), they each tried to 'paint' a one-and-a-half-kilometre-long piece of paper in the shortest period of time. Tinguely had arranged the system so that the paper would land on the audience, engulfing it in an avalanche of instant abstract art. The evening was spiced up with a sexy intermezzo when a gum-chewing beauty in the style of a Playboy bunny demonstrated a hand-operated version of the drawing machine. The 'lecture' thus combined the linguistic absurdities of the Theatre of the Absurd with a satirical pandemonium-like attack on the automatism of informal painting.

In January 1960, Tinguely crossed the Atlantic for the first time to oversee a solo show at the Staempfli Gallery in New York. He intended to build a monumental self-destroying 'Metamatic'; the machine would act out its own demise according to the artist's script. This was to be the first of Tinguely's expendable mechanisms.

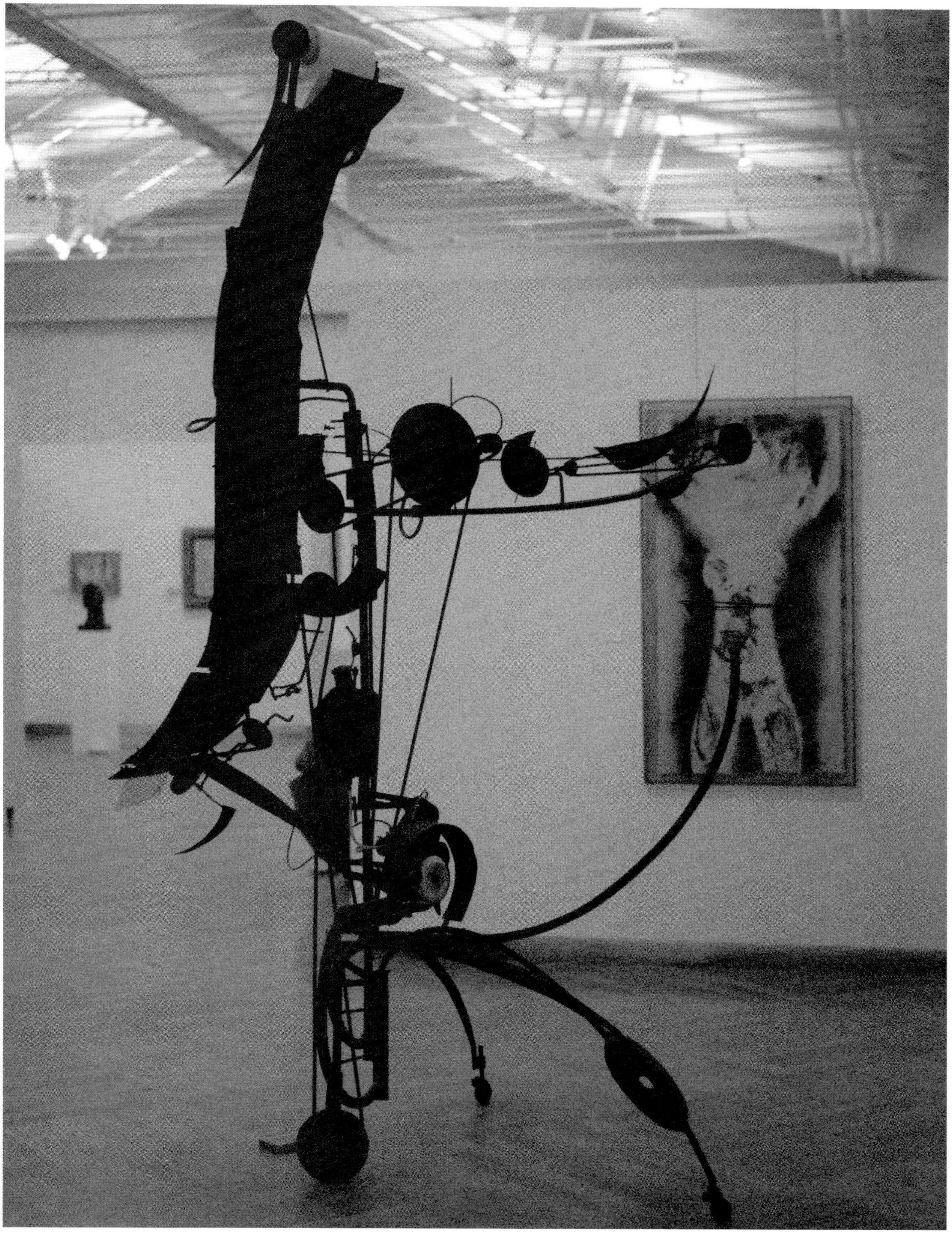

'Art is revolution–revolution is art'

1960

During the Atlantic crossing on the *Queen Elizabeth*, Tinguely drew a great deal. He tried to express his thoughts and ambivalence about New York and to elaborate technical solutions for a work he planned to build there. Since art school, Tinguely had given up drawing for its own sake: 'As an activity in itself drawing didn't interest me—for me it was a way to get closer to the concrete result of the thing, of the dream, of my Fata Morgana. The drawing was only a tool—something I would crumple, fold and throw away.'[1]

Tinguely's reputation had preceded him to New York, and he was able to count on the support of a few influential individuals: the art critic Dore Ashton, who wrote for the *New York Times*; the Dadaist Richard Huelsenbeck, who was his host during his stay; and Marcel Duchamp, with whom he renewed a friendship begun in Paris.[2] Ashton met Tinguely at the pier. He told her immediately of his plans to build a large, self-destroying apparatus, a homage to New York, this city which he had correctly imagined to be 'all those monster buildings, all that magnificent accumulation of human power and vitality, all that uneasiness, as though everyone were living on the edge of a precipice and how nice it would be to make a machine which would be conceived, like Chinese fireworks, in total anarchy and freedom'.[3] Tinguely naturally wished to have his piece at the Museum of Modern Art: 'Dore Ashton and others wanted to find another place. But I needed to do it there, I wanted to do it there. It's a kind of temple; what the Vatican is to God, the MoMA is to art. It is an official place of art. I was against that.'[4]

Tinguely saw museums as sterile domains that fix art in a vacuum and wanted to make a statement against what he called 'recuperation':

> *I wanted something ephemeral, that would pass like a falling star and, most importantly, that would be impossible for museums to reabsorb. I didn't want it to be 'museumised'. The work had to pass by, make people dream and talk, and that would be all, the next day nothing would be left, everything would go back to the garbage bins.*[5]

Tinguely's proposed *Homage to New York* (fig. 20) was to be a playfully spirited confrontation with the role of the museum, and as a happening it had the stuff of myth. Meanwhile, the exhibition at the Staempfli Gallery included four drawing machines and provoked a lively critical debate, since Tinguely's ironic questioning of what was and was not art was unnerving. The show's success helped considerably in persuading the Museum of Modern Art's Director and Administrator to make the sculpture garden available for *Homage to New York*.

The Swedish scientist Billy Klüver, whom Tinguely knew through Pontus Hulten, offered his technical expertise and also functioned as Tinguely's cicerone to America's garbage heaps. In a typical understatement, Klüver said: 'My largest contribution to Tinguely's machine was to visit dumps in New Jersey and pick up bicycle wheels and transport them to the Museum.'[6] Tinguely was also able to rely on Robert Breer, who filmed the event, creating less a documentary than a recapitulation of its spirit.[7] *Homage to New York* began as a large drawing machine and grew into a multipartite structure with about 80 bicycle, tricycle and pram wheels; a bathtub; a piano and a second drawing machine; metal drums; an Addressograph machine; a large bell and klaxon; a child's cart; a piece of the American flag; many bottles, some containing foul-smelling and smoke-producing chemicals; a fire extinguisher; a meteorological trial balloon; and a radio, oil cans, hammers, saws and other odds and ends, driven by 15 motors and all painted white. In his precise notes entitled 'The Garden Party', Klüver estimates that the final structure of *Homage* was equipped with about a hundred different operations, all started by preset time-delay relays so that the machine would function automatically.[8] The work was some seven metres long by more than eight metres high. The art historian Peter Selz said afterward: 'I had no idea how beautiful it was going to be. You had a real feeling of tragedy that that white machine couldn't be preserved somehow', the reaction Tinguely had hoped to provoke.[9] One of the last parts of the machine to be connected was contributed by Robert Rauschenberg: a 'money thrower' that released and

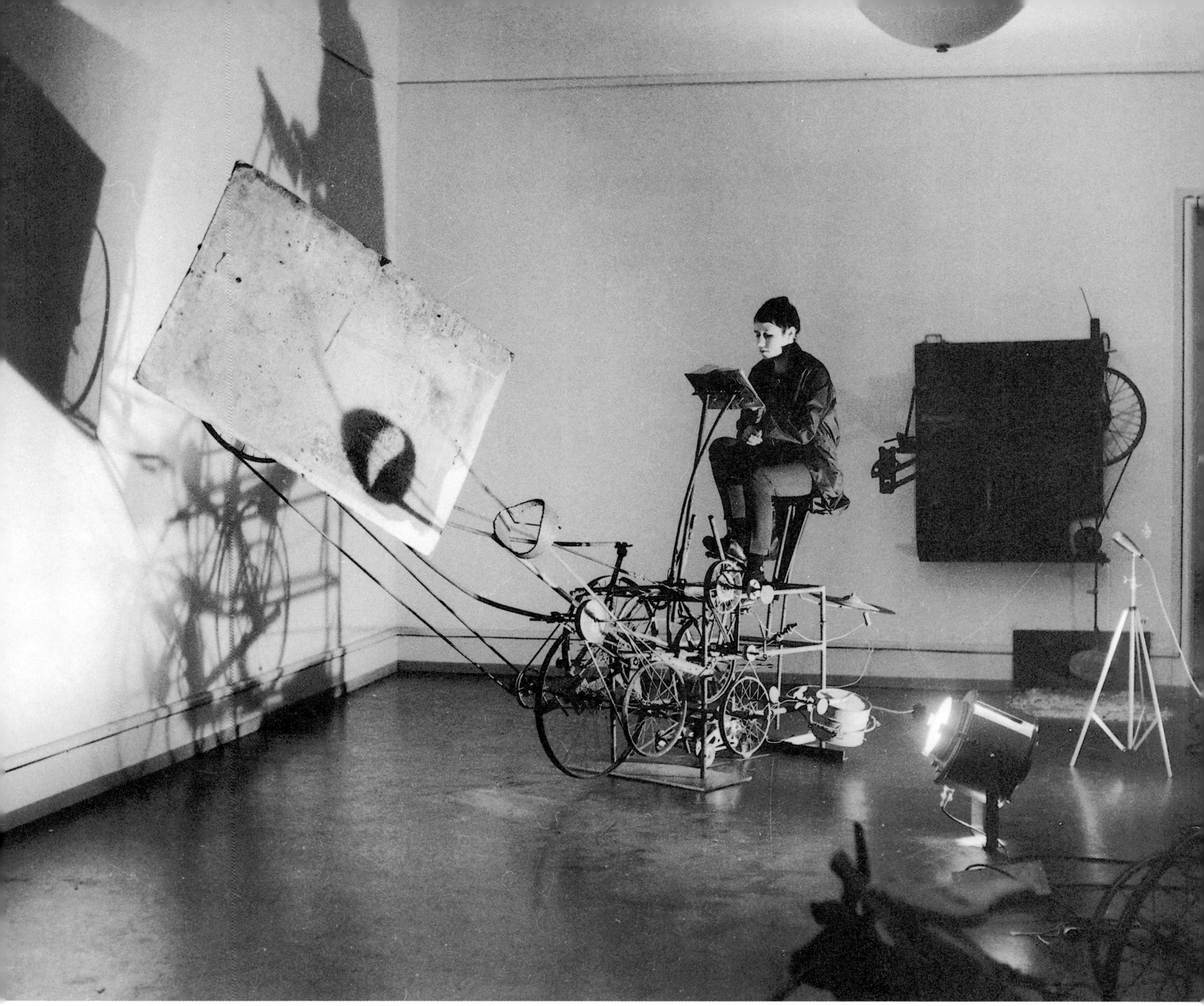

19 *Cyclograveur*, 1960

scattered silver dollars. Rauschenberg recalled: 'I felt privileged to be able to hand him a screwdriver. There were so many different aspects of life involved in the big piece. It was as real, as interesting, as complicated, as vulnerable, and as gay as life itself.'[10]

On 17 March 1960, from 7:30 to 8:00 p. m., Tinguely's explosive *Homage to New York* boogie-woogied to its own tunes towards a chaotic, not so ceremonious seppuku, in a joyous and dynamic celebration of life and death, movement and its antithesis (fig. 20). Journalists defined it variously as a 'gigantic Rube Goldberg cartoon machine come true', 'a multiple super-gadget', 'a katabolic Götterdämmerung of junk and scrap' and 'a bizarre contraption born of Despair out of Impertinence'. One writer reported:

Suddenly, the huge thing was throbbing in an artistic symphony of movement and sound. Within minutes a fire broke out in the shell of an old player piano and three city firemen on hand in case of an emergency snapped to attention with king-sized extinguishers. By this time the guests, kibitzers on top the garden walls and apartment dwellers across the street were enjoying themselves. They cheered the frantic artist and booed and hissed the firemen, yelling to them to 'let it burn'. The indecisive fire fighters finally concluded that safety came before art when the tottering contraption, racked by small explosions,

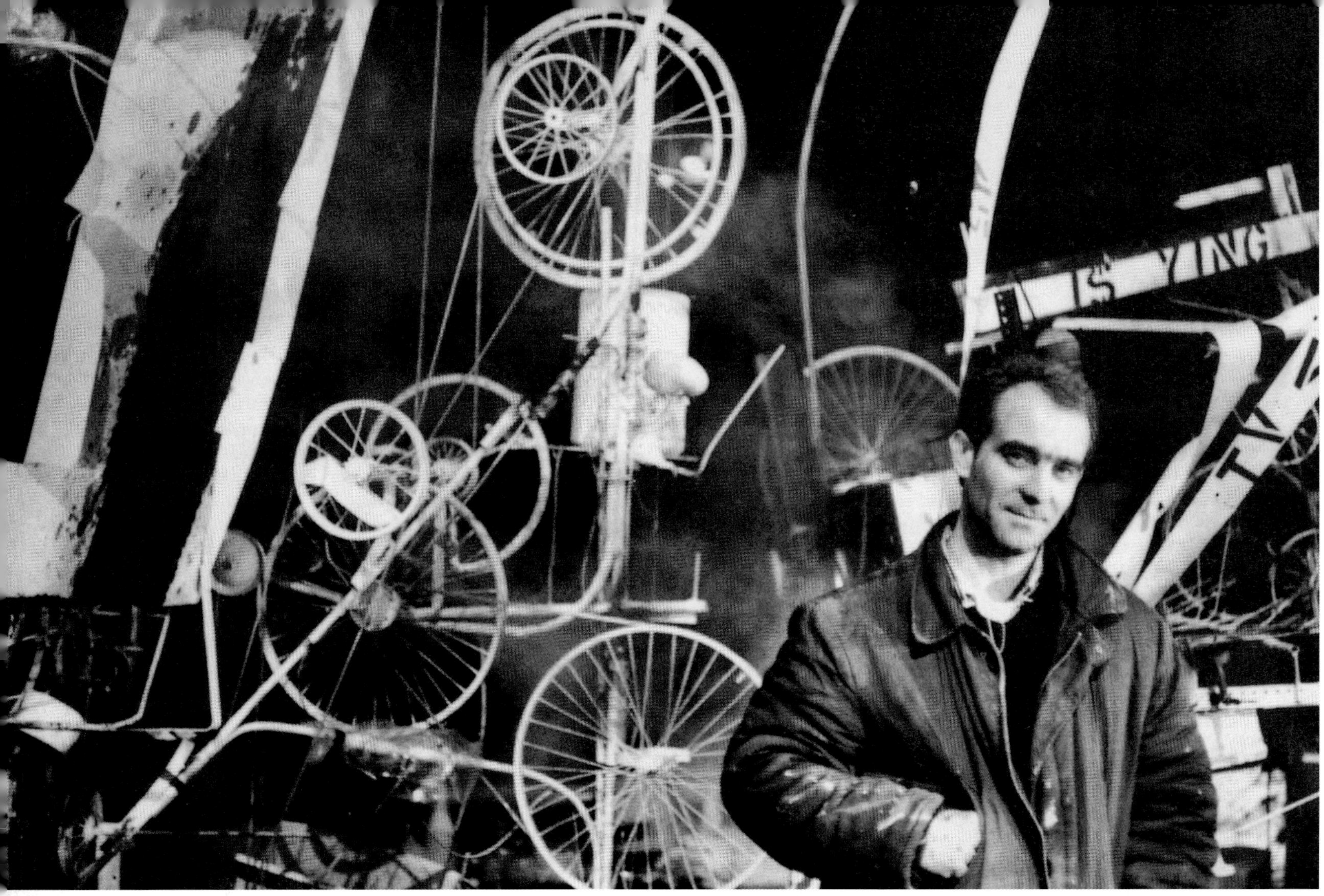

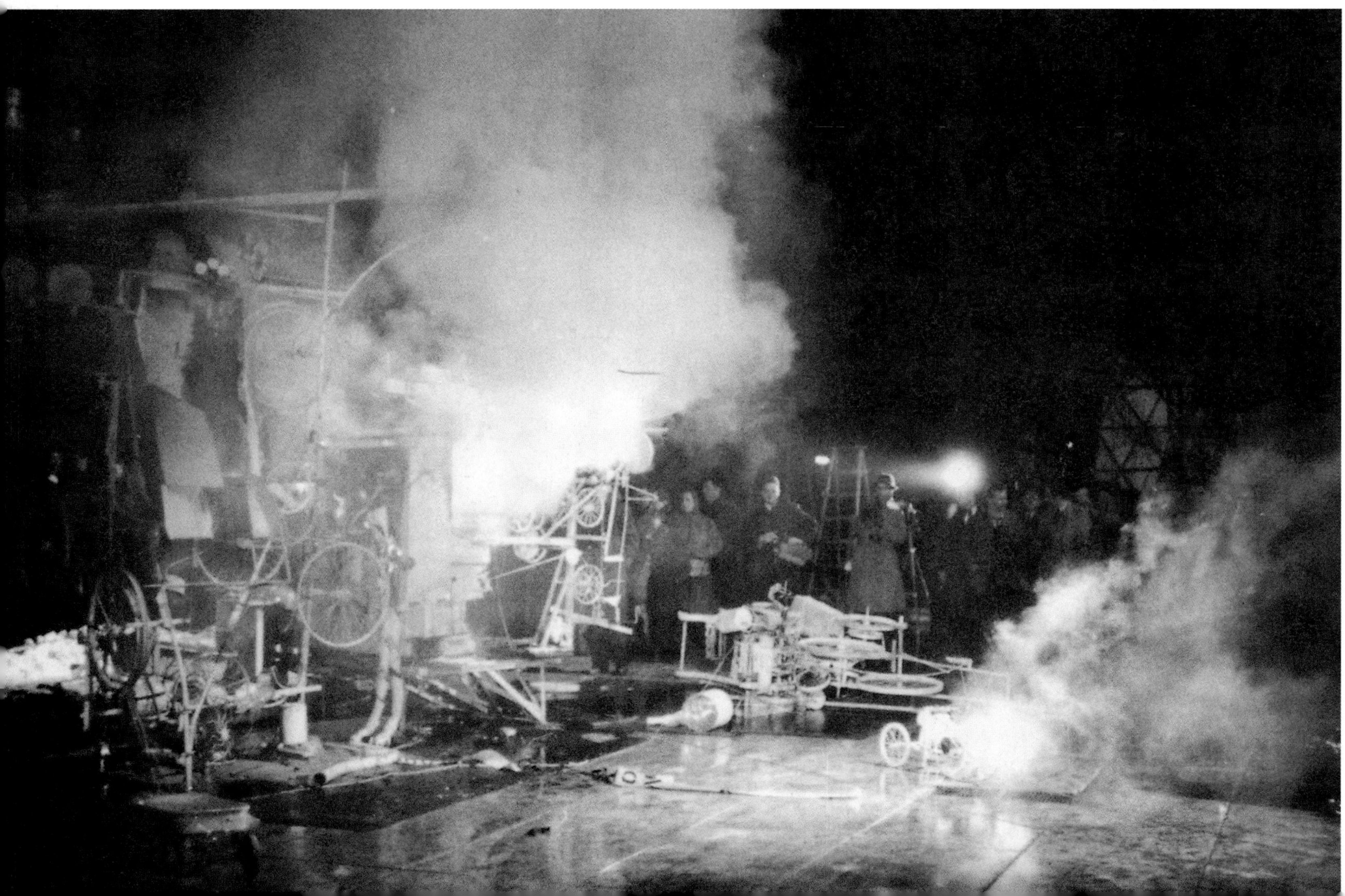

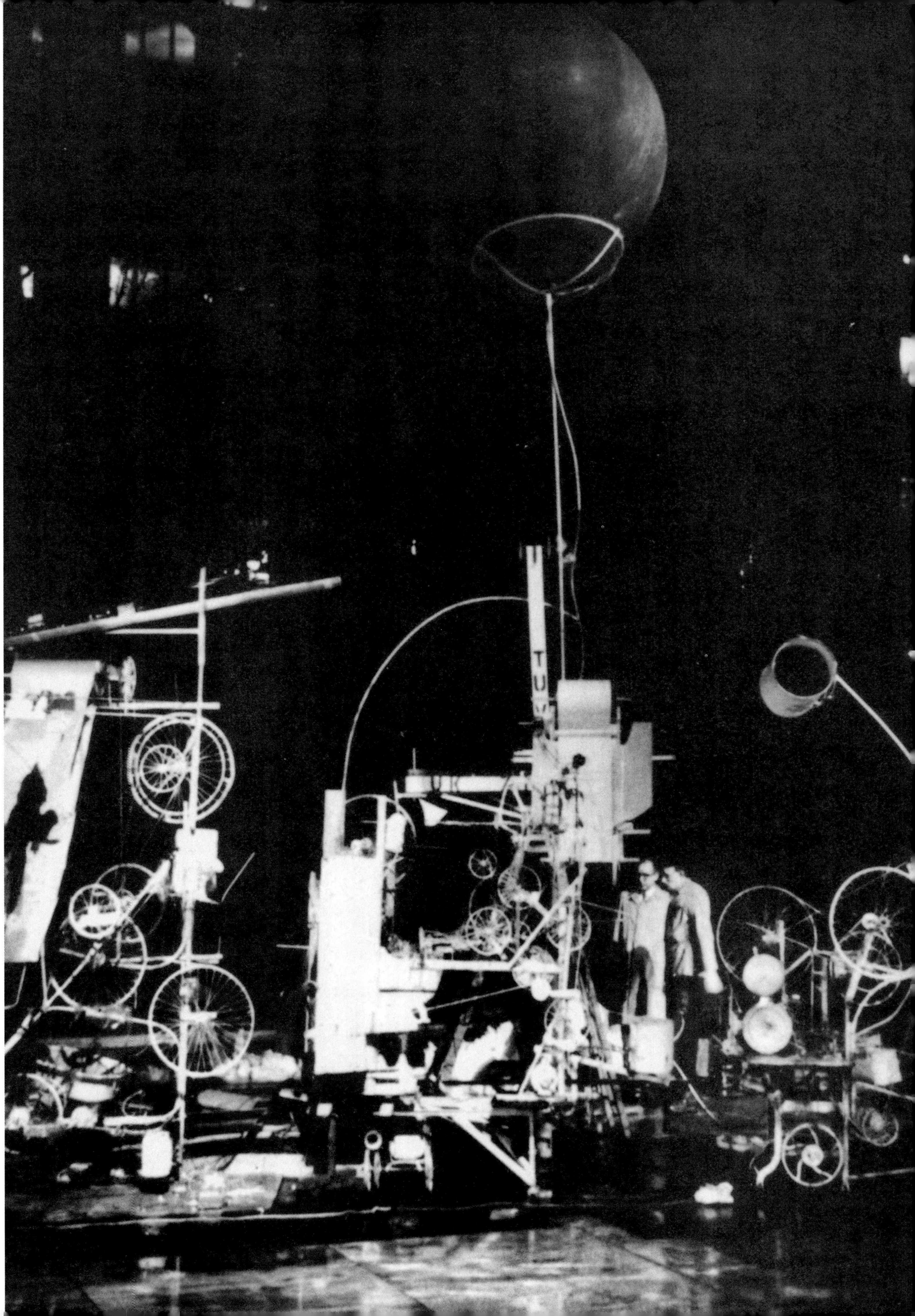

◁ 20 *Homage to New York* in the Sculpture Garden at The Museum of Modern Art, New York, 1960

gave birth to a miniature four-wheel chariot that went scooting across the garden under its own power with its tail section ablaze. When it charged into the onlookers, they turned it around and set it wheeling back toward the firemen.[11]

The self-destroying process of *Homage to New York* involved a number of accidents and failures. Tinguely was delighted by the idiosyncratic behaviour of his mechanism and explained that he had built in two layers of processes to ensure the spectacular effects, calculating that many would not work or work in unpredictable ways.[12] After all, he intended the sculpture to recreate the conditions of confusion and chaos of New York City. He concluded that the piece

remained a good thing because it was purely ideological, without commerce. The only memory is the photo, but the picture guarantees another transformation, because . . . there is also the myth, what people tell who saw it or who didn't see it, or who read and think they saw it or who see the photos and imagine having seen it. There are inevitable transformations. It's a form of treason which takes place, and that's all right.[13]

Back in Paris, Tinguely was bursting with new ideas. In the course of his stay in New York, he had become acquainted with Richard Stankiewicz, John Chamberlain, Bruce Connor, Louise Nevelson and Frank Stella, and had become friendly with Robert Rauschenberg and Jasper Johns. These artists certainly reminded him of Julia Ris's lessons on Schwitters, particularly Stankiewicz's poetic assemblages of bits of scrap iron, plumbing or machine parts. Tinguely had assimilated some of these new ideas in the process of building *Homage to New York*. His use of electric welding equipment permitted the fast, easy joining of metal and the construction of bigger pieces.

Tinguely produced five new works in a few weeks. These were shown in May at the Galerie des Quatre Saisons under the title *Functional Art by Tinguely*. The sculptures were generously sized, open-work assemblages of found objects, mainly bicycle and pram wheels linked by thin metal rods. Cans, pots, pans and other oddments figured as sound resonators and produced a scramble of noises. Formally, the pieces looked like individual sections of *Homage to New York*, except that their surfaces were left unpainted. Henceforth, the machine and its moving parts, to which all sorts of rubbish was affixed, was to become Tinguely's basic medium. Included in the Paris exhibit was a sculpture-making apparatus and a sculpture-destroying device that sawed plaster replicas of Classical reliefs in half. These two pieces were destroyed; only *Cyclograveur*, which also has the art-making process as a theme, and *Gismo* have survived.[14]

Cyclograveur, which is not equipped with a motor, is a sort of stationary bicycle. The viewer was literally made part of the work (fig. 19) as Tinguely, in typical fashion, took a mundane mechanism and turned it on its head. The viewer climbs on top of the structure, and his or her pedalling activates the rusty rubbish attached to the contraption, as well as the arm of an engraving mechanism. The bicycle comes equipped with a multilingual dictionary installed at handlebar height. The *Cyclograveur* is a plaything that liberates the viewer from his or her everyday routine—and from the triviality of cultural experience. A rusty toy car is attached to the *Cyclograveur* by means of a length of wire. A similar small element is featured alongside *Gismo* (fig. 21). Such additions reappear in a number of later works. Richard Calvocoressi sees the origin of these contraptions in the small construction on pram wheels which detached itself from the main assemblage of *Homage to New York*, evoking the image of an animal or child running away from its parent.[15] On another level, one can read these small contraptions—which are usually more grotesque and fanciful than the larger structures to which they are attached— as one does the red nose of a clown: as symbols of nonsense and farce.

Gismo, two metres high and over five metres long, resembles a huge bug on wheeled legs; it curves its tail and extends its long, snout-like frontal protrusion. A helmet, a pot, a pan and other found objects serve as noisemakers. Technically, this and Tinguely's other sculptures that include wheels work by simple mechanical means. An electric motor drives an axle and one or more wheels, and a rubber belt transfers the motion onto a second wheel placed at a distance. Motion is again transferred via the axle to one or more wheels, which in turn are connected to more wheels by other belts. Although the basic working system is easily grasped by anyone, no sooner does one attempt to comprehend the mechanism in its entirety than one realises its intricacies. To be able to grasp the entire sequence of motion, the viewer has to depend on

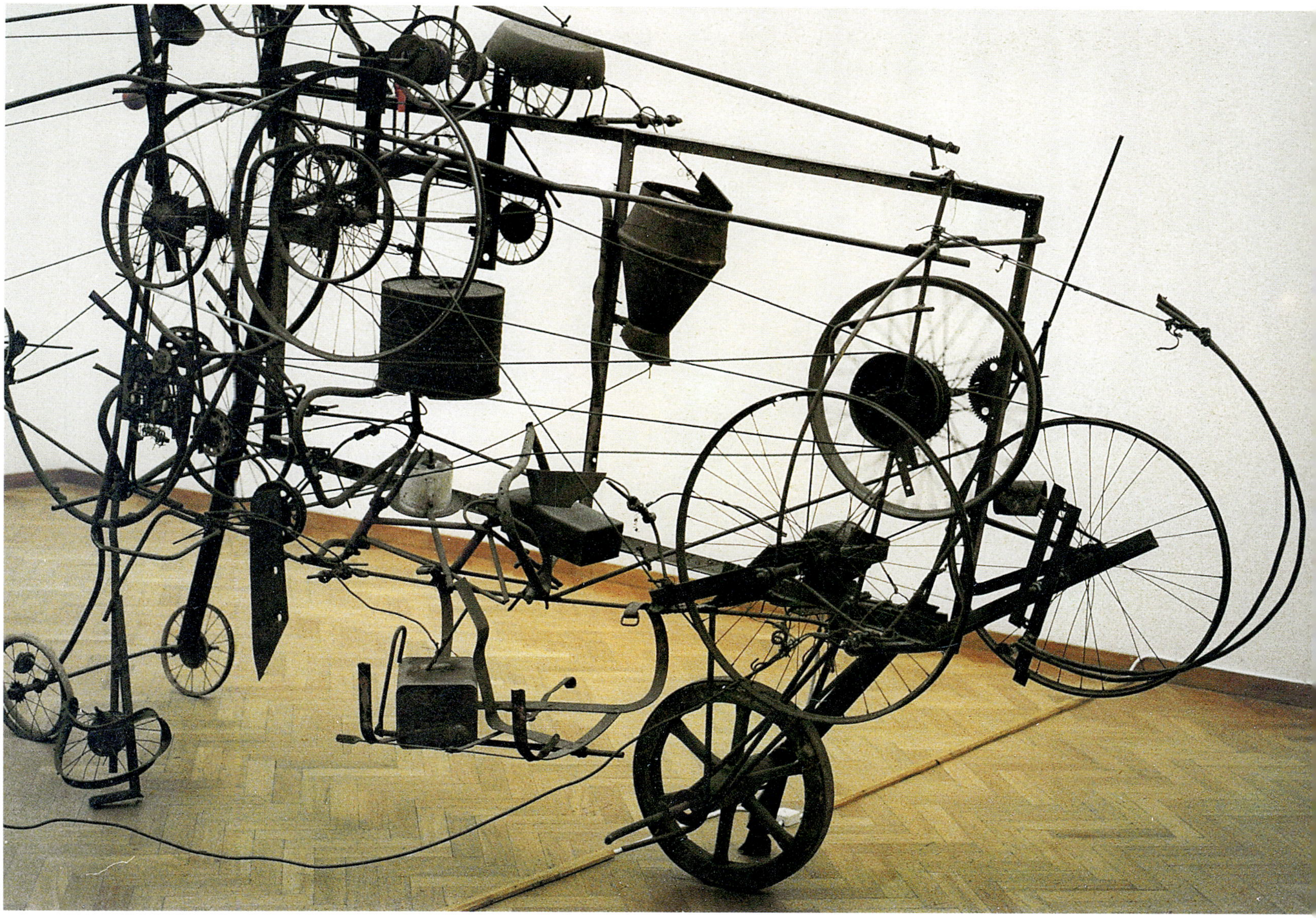

21 *Gismo*, 1960 (detail)

memory as in other sequential arts such as dance, music or poetry.

For the exhibition at the Galerie des Quatre Saisons, Tinguely explored the possibilities of light and shadow by illuminating the sculptures with powerful spotlights. As the shadows of different works overlapped and mixed, their combinations formed a new, two-dimensional work of changing, abstract patterns.[16] The opening of the show on 13 May had a performance-like prelude. Tinguely and his friends pushed, pulled and drove the works of art through the streets of Montparnasse, from his studio at Impasse Ronsin to the rue de Grenelle. This merry parade became known as 'The Transportation' and, true to the spirit of the day, merged art and life by taking art literally to the streets. The parade idea must have come readily to Tinguely, whose experience of the Basel Carnival had deeply marked him, as we shall see.

Since the exhibition at Denise René's in 1955, Tinguely's works had shown evidence of his interest in the art of Marcel Duchamp. As Tinguely explained to Dieter Daniels: 'I am Duchamp-infected; I make ready-made-ism. Julia Ris tormented me with Duchamp, and Hulten too . . . We had to fight for Duchamp at Denise René.'[17] While still in New York, Duchamp had taken Tinguely to Philadelphia to show him his own work at the museum there. Tinguely admired and was inspired by Duchamp's utter detachment in regard to material and artistic success and by his absolute integrity. Technically and ideationally, the

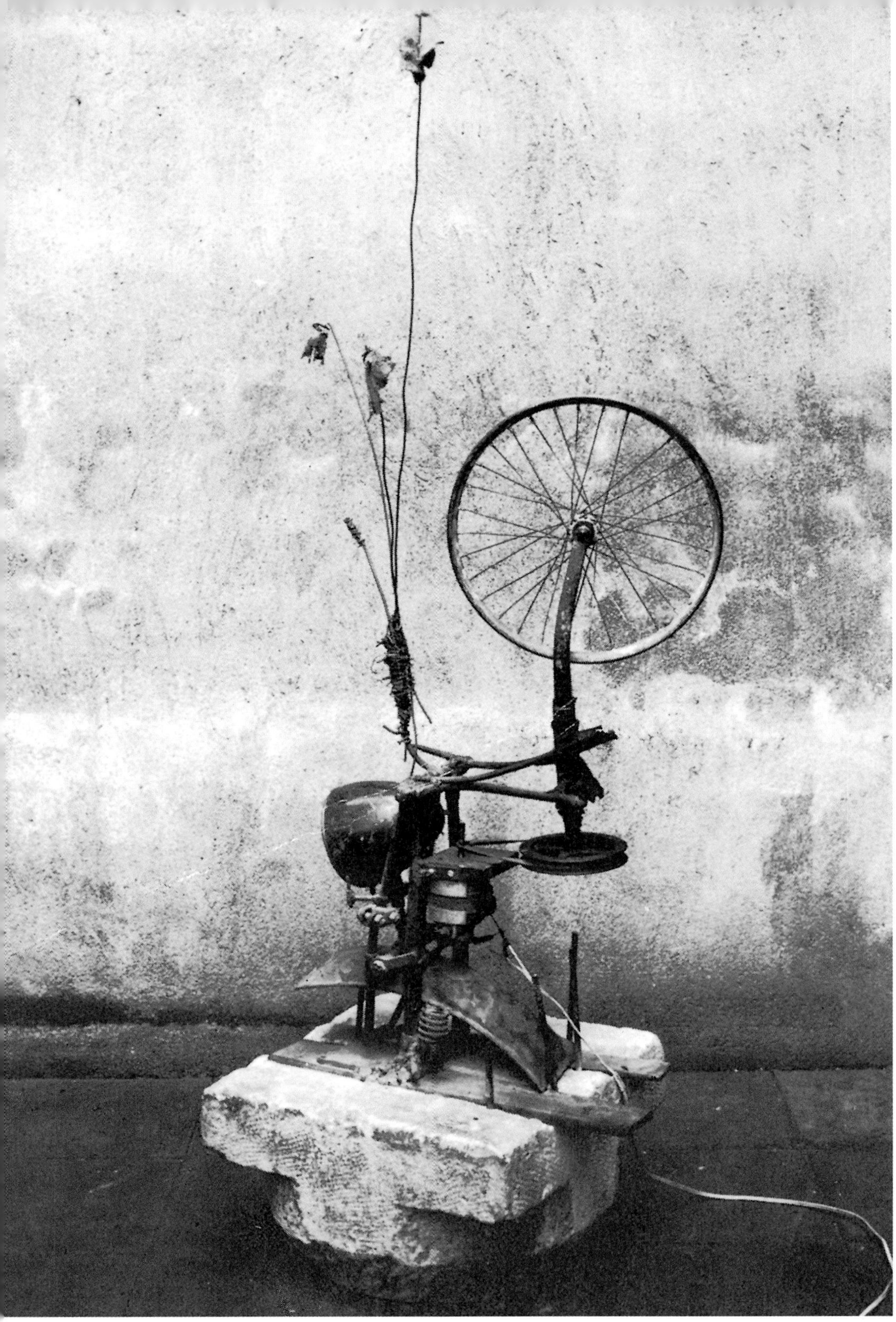

22 *Homage to Marcel Duchamp*, 1960

younger artist built on Duchamp's concept of movement as process and transformation and on the expressive potential of the anthropomorphised machine and of the ready-made, as well as on Duchamp's flair for staged exhibitions. Tinguely also adopted Duchamp's favourite tools: chance and humour. Duchamp said of Tinguely: 'I feel with him a closeness and a rapport that I have felt with few artists. He has that great thing, a sense of humour—something I have been preaching for artists all my life.'[18] For Duchamp, a true ready-made revealed no beauty, no ugliness—there was nothing particularly aesthetic about it. These ideas were liberating to Tinguely and his contemporaries, the Neo-Dadaists and Pop artists in the United States and the New Realists in Europe. What they did not borrow from Duchamp was his idiosyncratic Dada stance, his ironic indifference and ambivalence.

Later in the spring of 1960, Tinguely acknowledged his debt to the man, his wheel and his artistic posture in *Homage to Marcel Duchamp*, which features a bicycle wheel positioned like Duchamp's prototype and made to spin by a motor that also agitates a pedestal taken from Brancusi's studio (fig. 22). Tinguely's *Les Chiottes* (*John*; formerly collection of the artist) was a response to Duchamp's famous urinal (1917; New York, Sidney Janis Collection) consisting of a broken toilet placed on a wooden box with a motor. Unlike Duchamp's pristine, factory-delivered piece, Tinguely's toilet was clearly put to use and misuse and as an object could in no way be cited for its aesthetic qualities. Tinguely was no longer concerned with denying the beauty of art or with substituting good or bad taste with indifference. He was declaring life itself to be art. This discarded mundane object represents life at its most basic, scatological level. *The John* is not exclusively masculine, as is Duchamp's urinal, but is universal. By adding a motor and a couple of noisemakers and by setting the toilet on a platform, Tinguely elevated it into an uninhibited poetic realm. Much later, in 1987, Tinguely acknowledged Duchamp's continuing relevance when he gave a urinal peopled by plastic Smurfs a prominent place in his encyclopaedic *Big Meta-Maxi-Maxi*, the last in the series of 'Meta Harmonies' (figs. 23, 66). The added cartoon characters subverted and rejuvenated the ready-made, wiping it clean of its weighty load of theoretical discourse.

Tinguely's interests and concerns were shared by the New Realists (a term coined by Pierre Restany in 1960),[19] a heterogeneous group whose members employed a variety of expressive means. The New Realists were united in their opposition to everything that caused art to be exclusive and élitist and embraced the 'new reality' of contemporary industrial and urban culture and appropriated its products. Like the Neo-Dada, Pop, Fluxus and Arte Povera artists, the New Realists believed that any material could legitimately be used by an artist, no matter how unconventional or banal. Tinguely additionally pointed to the expressiveness and beauty of the non-material, by working with sounds as well as light, fire, water, smoke and fireworks. The New Realists were far from being a closely knit group, and some of them were ambivalent about the identification. They agreed with Tinguely, who said:

I received the label 'New Realist' although I don't have anything to do with it. The true New Realists are Daniel Spoerri and Arman. Even Yves Klein did not really belong there. But we formed this group in Paris that Pierre Restany linked to Dadaism. This I had long ago discovered for myself. I had always been infected by Dada. My disposition for Dada was a natural talent.[20]

As he attributed equal value to all things, Tinguely in fact can be called a secular pantheist. Without naming Heraclitus, Tinguely based his manifesto on the former's philosophical framework. Heraclitus justified both the totality of process and a belief in the all-inclusiveness of the universe, in which everything participates in that process, thus eliminating any justification for hierarchies. Thus, discrimination is sacrificed in favour of eclectism, and the artist can take garbage and turn it into something poetic. In Tinguely's words, 'There is no good and no evil'.

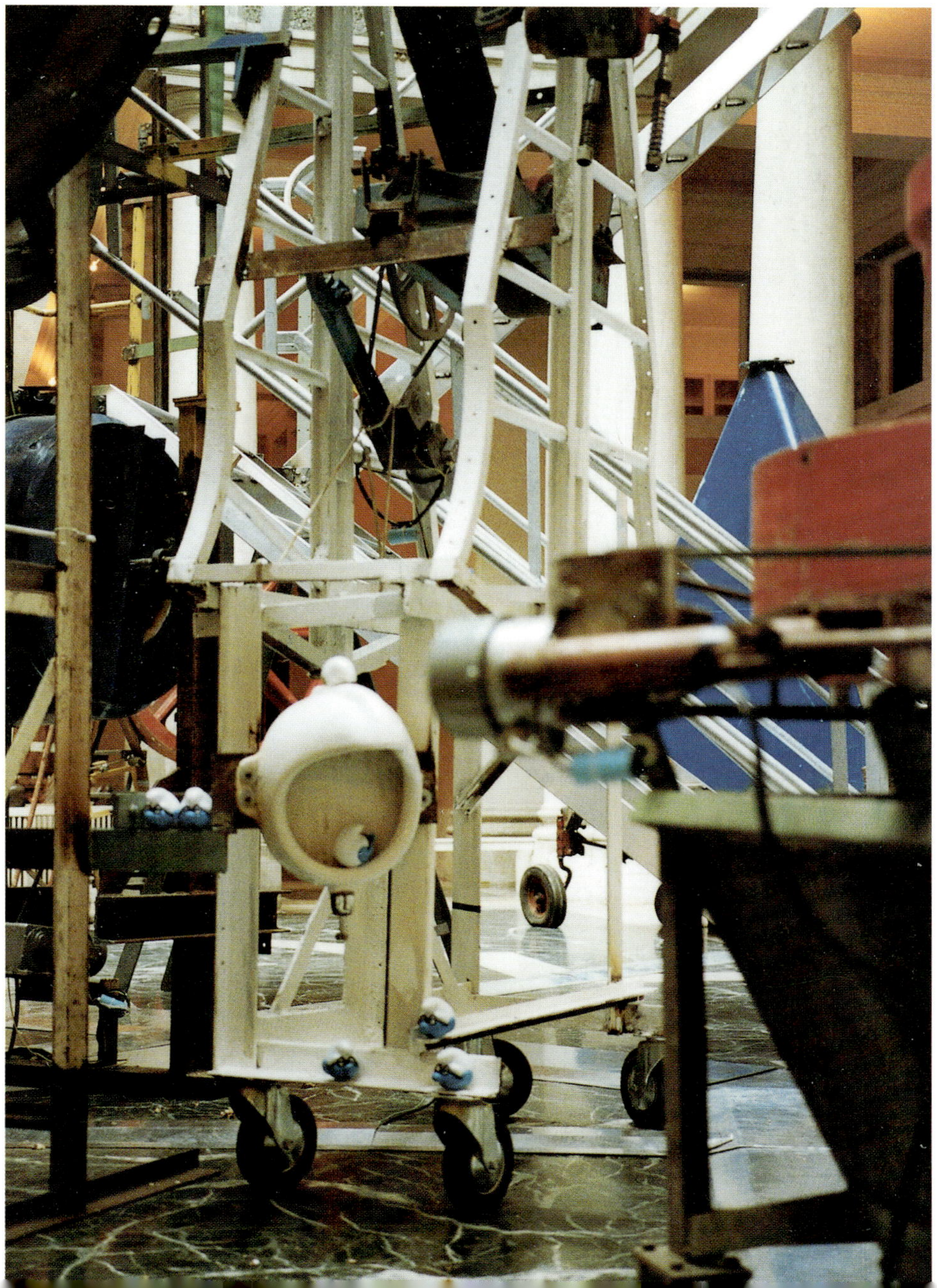

23 *Big Meta-Maxi-Maxi*, 1987
(detail; see plate 66)

'In my work, somehow art is not art'

1960

In the course of the spring and summer of 1960, Tinguely continued to produce a plethora of new sculptures. These were shown in exhibitions at Krefeld and Berne, both of which opened in September. The show at Krefeld's Museum Haus Lange opened first and included *Homage to Marcel Duchamp* among 25 new works. Johannes Cladders, later Director of the Krefeld museum, remembers vividly the strong impression made by Tinguely's machine art. In it he saw the merging of two things: one was the unconventional procedures Tinguely shared with the Abstract Expressionists and the everyday materials and subversive attitude that linked him to the Dadaist tradition. The other was the breaking away from these traditions to make something absolutely positive, using a medium that was close to the pulse of contemporary civilisation. Cladders felt that Tinguely's approach was tremendously liberating.[1] His positive approach to the recycling of the old, his playful irony and his forward-looking philosophy of movement and change struck a particularly strong and congenial chord in a country emerging from a difficult past and still rebuilding itself from the ruins of war.

At Haus Lange, Tinguely developed an exhibition technique that would not change fundamentally over the years. As always, his priority was communication. The new work was built principally from parts of bicycles, tricycles and baby carriages, incorporating scrap metal and other oddments collected from dumps and junkyards. In the case of special finds such as radios, typewriters, a refrigerator or computer parts, the artist explored the formal aspects of these orphan materials. While in the early works, motion qualified geometric compositions with the meaning embedded in motion and sound, in some of the new works exhibited in Krefeld and Berne, symbols shifted to encompass elements extraneous to both. Simultaneously, these heterogeneous objects also served the artist well in his pursuit of an ever more expressive vocabulary of motion.

As a matter of fact, Tinguely operated rather like a *bricoleur*, a term used by Claude Lévi-Strauss for someone who will make do with whatever is at hand:

> *[. . .] The elements are collected or retained on the principle that 'they may always come in handy' . . . He interrogates all the heterogeneous objects of which his treasury is composed to discover what each of them could 'signify' and so contribute to the definition of a set which has yet to materialize.*[2]

Tinguely remained an avid scavenger of new and old junk and scrap, which he accumulated in his different studios and factory halls. For example, it is conceivable that when he came upon a length of hose, he was inspired to make his first water sculpture.[3] The *Fountain*, which premièred in the park of Haus Lange,[4] was assembled from a variety of metal wheels on a tubular framework with a motor. Arm-like extensions held and moved about three nozzled hoses. The water drew an ever-changing abstract design as it was pushed through the variegated nozzles, which were themselves in constant motion. Gaston Bachelard's description of fountains as 'form perpetually renewed in the midst of process itself'[5] fits all of Tinguely's similar creations admirably. Franz Meyer recalled that 'this was a time when everybody was reading Bachelard, whose personality corresponded so well to the feeling of this period'.[6] In addition to the visual display, Tinguely explored the auditory quality of water in this and many subsequent works. Another novelty of the show in Krefeld was the do-it-yourself plan that Tinguely published for the occasion with detailed instructions for making a 'meta-mechanical' relief similar to his 'Meta-Malevich'. Fifty of the plans were numbered and signed by the artist. Tinguely recognised the constructions now known as 'Maschinenbild Haus Lange' as his original work if the execution was accurate.[7] This multiple was the last of its kind.

Tinguely's other museum exhibition opened on 24 September 1960 at the Kunsthalle, Berne. There, Director Franz Meyer included him in a group show with Bernhard Luginbühl and Norbert Kricke. Of the two dozen assemblages on view, only two had been exhibited before. The Berne public had never seen anything like these works before and was not prepared for their elemental quality. The pieces shared the mood of Beckett or early Ionesco, with a feeling of irrationality and of energy going to the edge and turning things upside down. Meyer remembered: 'When the people came and looked at it, they were like children. Some of them may have been angry too. But most of them were happy. And then, they went home and on the street, started thinking: that's not art! I remember terrible articles in the paper.'[8] The artist's parents visited their son's first exhibition in Switzerland. His mother wrote him: 'Your father was very angry that people can make money out of stuff like that . . . I can't understand how someone as intelligent as you can make such foolish things.' Tinguely was fond of quoting this letter and counted it among his greatest accolades.[9]

Tinguely chose his works for the Berne exhibition with the flair of a cultural anthropologist. Characteristic of his subsequent method, he took into account not only the specifics of the exhibition halls but also their placement within a larger geographical and political structure, as well as the cultural and psychological make-up of the viewers. Tinguely chose to show *Cyclograveur* and *Appareil à faire les sculptures* (*Apparatus for Making Sculptures*) in Switzerland rather than at Krefeld because the Swiss public had the background to read the language that informed them: the ancient carnivalesque tradition of Basel and its grotesque assemblages of old oddities on carts.[10] Being neither simplistic nor cryptic, Tinguely's art allows his viewers to congratulate themselves for picking up his clues. He also helps his public along with his titles, which by that time he had begun to select with increasing care and wit. The Bernese public saw a chaotic assemblage of scrap iron on wheels that looked like the junk collected by a vagabond. Then called *Vehicule stable* (*Stable Vehicle*), it was stable only within Tinguely's metaphysical logic. He later changed the title to *Marilyn* (fig. 24), establishing an amusingly sarcastic connection between this heap of rubbish and America's glamour queen in a tribute as irrational as the idolatry of stardom itself. At times, Tinguely would select several titles for a single work or adopt the title given by someone else, his public or a collaborator. He often used puns or chose titles for a specific public, as when he named a tall, tower-

24 *Marilyn*, 1960

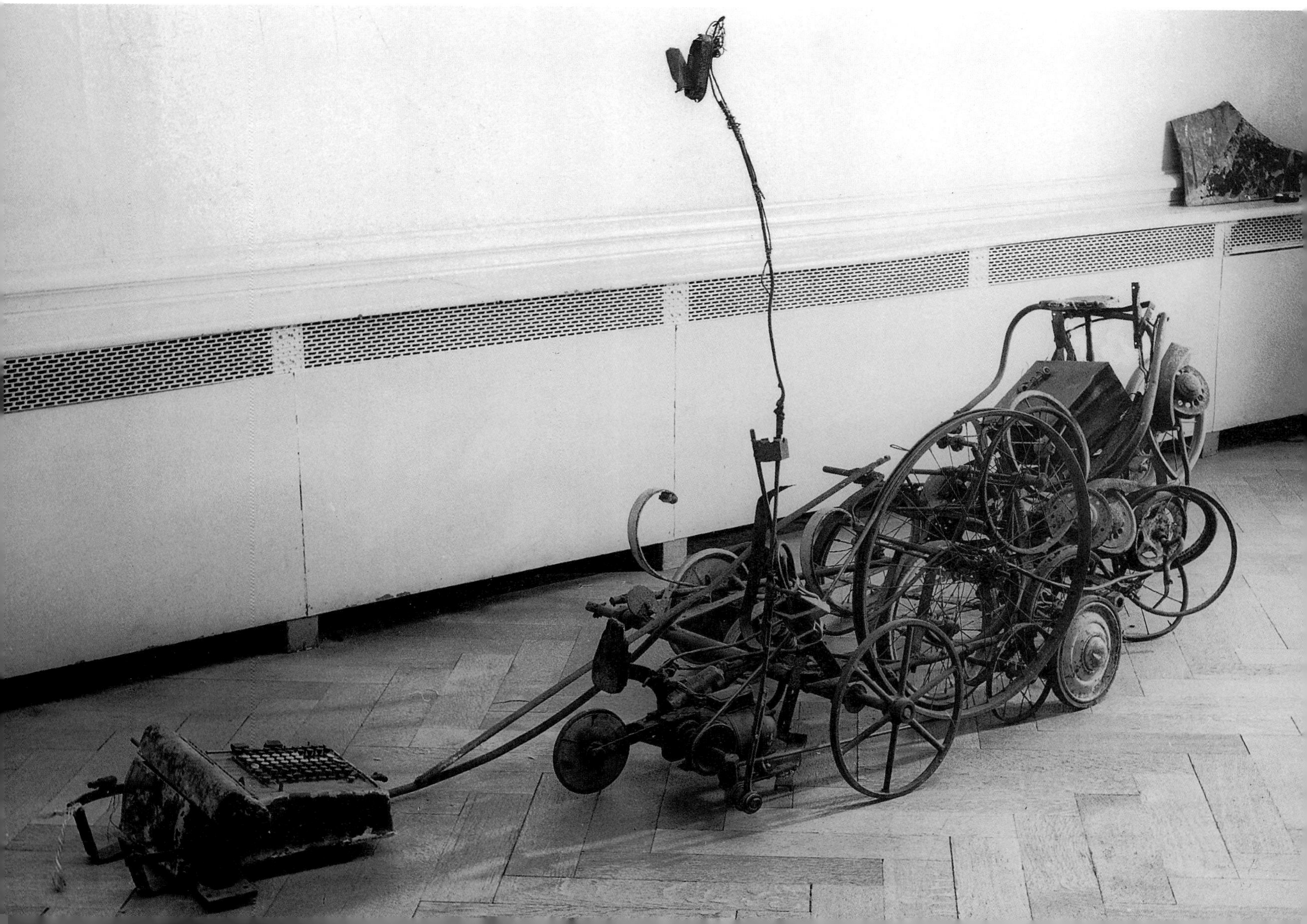

like assemblage at the Kunsthalle *Zytgloggeturm*, after a famous 12th-century Bernese landmark.

Like *Si c'est noir je m'appelle Jean* (*If It's Black, My Name is Jean*), a work he created in order to play out a difficult or painful experience in order to master it, *Scooter (fig. 25)*, exhibited at Krefeld, features a helmet that serves as the support for a child's scooter (Antwerp, Collection S. Perlstein). The front of the vehicle is damaged, and one wheel is missing, so only the back wheel turns. The precariousness of the toy's balance on top of the helmet adds to the sense of its fragility; it is as if the viewer is in the presence of a war invalid. Compared to the work exhibited at Berne, this is a subtle, nearly silent reference to war. The helmet serves as the pedestal in a work that has the dignity of a memorial to suffering in general, to childhood and its injuries in particular.

Two works exhibited at Berne were likely to have been inspired by Tinguely's private life. *La Jalousie I* (*Blind I*; formerly Collection Felix Handschin)[11] is a curtain of wooden beads suspended from a metal track with a motor. At rest it resembles the door hangings common in countries with warm climates and implies their dual function of concealing and revealing. In motion, the nervous jiggles of the strands can be seen to suggest the emotional state implied by the title.In *Matrimonial Self-Portrait*, the self-directed irony is scathing (fig. 26). The piece recreates in its nerve-racking noise what must have been a rather tense domestic atmosphere in the last days of the artist's marriage to Eva Aeppli. She and Tinguely separated in 1960.

The woman who took the place of Aeppli was to be an equally strong, challenging partner. Niki de Saint Phalle, born in 1930 in Neuilly, had spent her youth in New York. Having begun to paint as part of a therapeutic treatment, she found that she could express her innermost feelings through art. However, she also found her existence as an artist to be irreconcilable with a happy family life. Having decided to leave her husband and two children in order to pursue her ambitions as an artist, she became ill with hepatitis: 'This had nothing to do with Jean, we were not together then. I really felt strongly that I had to take my destiny into my own hands. I was ambitious, I wanted to confront this male-dominated world, I wanted to conquer.'[12]

In de Saint Phalle's ongoing search for her own identity, she began to dwell on the idea of the feminine, giving form to the universal female roles: the bride, the mother in all her aspects as the life-giving or life-consuming force, the saint and the prostitute, as well as such archetypal figures as Eve and Mary. While Eva Aeppli's imagery concentrates on the head, de Saint Phalle shows us and affirms the body. Both women mastered their existential conflicts through their artistic creations, thus transforming their frailty into creative strength; married to Tinguely, both women helped him exorcise his own demons of revolt through the poetic language of art. Tinguely has included both women in his work. An exceptional collaboration developed between him and de Saint Phalle. He increased her self-confidence and spurred her on by saying, 'The dream is everything; technique is nothing'.

This is how, in 1984, in front of a large Parisian audience with a twinkle of mischief in his eyes and in the best 'Tinguely style', he described his meeting with de Saint Phalle in 1955:

She visited Brancusi and came also to my studio next door. I showed her a sound-making relief—the disorganisation of order or the organisation of chaos—it's an arrangement of pulleys which activates a percussion system, the instruments being old tuna and sardine cans and discarded bottles making lovely sounds. And Niki, a very beautiful girl, told me something atrocious. She said I should put feathers on my machine. I wasn't happy—I didn't understand it then.

And in a confiding tone, he continued to describe the beginning of their romance:

Eva was getting tired of me. She had found someone else and had decided to divorce me, but could not leave me just like that. The two women actually made a deal and it worked: Eva attached me to Niki, while she would eventually marry the gentleman Niki introduced to her as a better suited partner than the man she first had in mind. So that's how I ended up with Niki in my bed. It was wonderful, and that's when I began a substantial battle. When I met Niki, she

25 *Scooter*, 1960

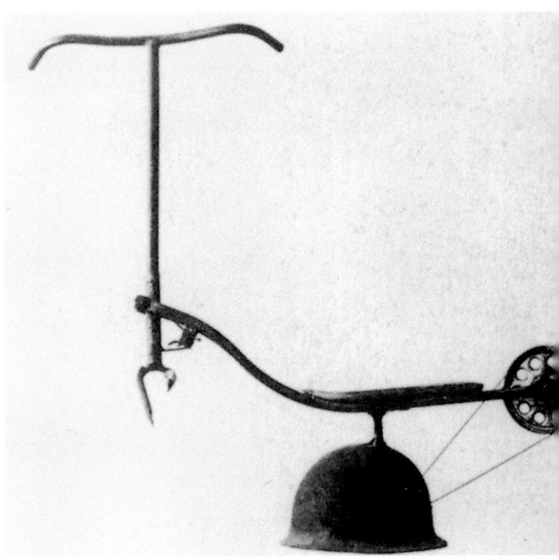

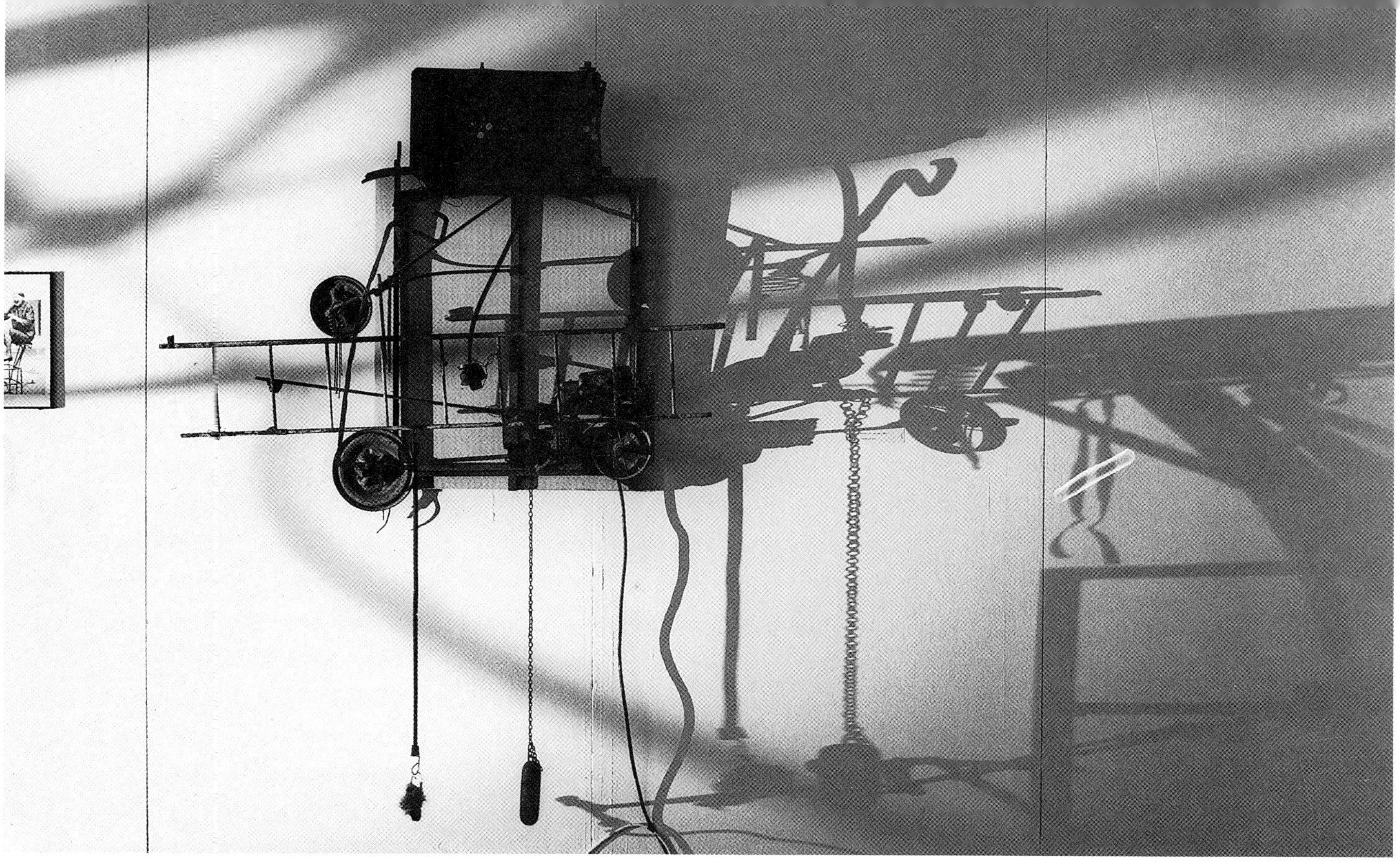

26 *Matrimonial Self-Portrait*, 1960

was terribly combative and aggressive. She carried a knife and a loaded pistol in her pocket. She was extremely skinny when she came to see me, and she had, like Eva, self-destructive tendencies and suffered from depressions. Once again, I had to counteract a self-destructive propensity, and I must have had a beneficial influence on her and was able to help her channel these aggressive inclinations.[13]

From 1960, the two artists lived together, first in Tinguely's studio at the Impasse Rousin. The bond between Jean and Niki developed over the years —each recognised and appreciated in the other the extraordinary artistic impulse and passionate embrace of life. Their partnership remained constant—their affair of the heart was tumultuous. I asked de Saint Phalle how the collaboration came about:

Our works are complementary—we are opposites that come together. We have a rapport that is unique in the history of art . . . My colours and his machines, my overt symbolism and his more abstract symbolism. We worked in separate studios, but at one time, at Iolas's, my exhibition arrived while Jean's was leaving. And there, we saw our things together, and it was beautiful. That's when we decided to do something together.

In their artistic collaboration the two artists found each other to be provocative counterparts. He helped her in the technical execution of her ideas, beginning with the reliefs for her shooting actions, then moving on to her monumental walk-in sculptures such as *Golem* (1972; fig. 47) and *The Dragon* (1973) and, above all, the remarkable *Tarot Garden* in Garavicchio, begun in 1979. De Saint Phalle named her collaborators the 'All-Star Swiss Team' with 'General Jean, Colonel Rico Weber and Colonel Seppi Imhof and Paul Wiedmer'. Their help in the construction of the metal framework for her architectural sculptures was crucial. According to de Saint Phalle's wishes, Tinguely installed several works within the *Tarot Garden*, among them *Tower of Babel* in 1985 and, in 1987, *Injustice*, a machine for de Saint Phalle's *Justice* figure. De Saint-Phalle compared the rules of the game between herself and Tinguely to ping-pong. As in the actual game, the one provoked the other to do bigger and crazier things.[14]

'... and anyway, the definitive is provisional, and chaos is order'

1961

Tinguely was back in New York in April 1961 for his second solo show at the Staempfli Gallery. This exhibition, including many objects from the Berne show, confirmed his reputation as the poet of mechanised ephemera: 'Wonderful Luna Park objects on the move, jiggle, and whoop. Joy and dementia!', wrote one critic,[1] while another commentator focused on the absurd dimension of the work, seeing in Tinguely the 'Dr. Coppelius of Existentialism; his eclectically powered Dreckmobiles are equivalents, transmitted in motor behavior, of the insights and outcries of Ionesco or Beckett, with a nod to the New York of Rauschenberg and Cage.' The same writer concluded that 'Tinguely's machines are like an entangled meeting between Jacques Tati and Kafka; their switch-on passage from the astatic to the ataxic is a sure and athletic seizure of the absurd pathology of contemporary deportments'.[2]

Two of the sculptures shown at Staempfli were chosen by William C. Seitz for his momentous *Art of Assemblage* exhibition that opened in October at the Museum of Modern Art. In this overview of assemblage, Seitz was an unbiased observer of an international phenomenon. Each of the contemporary artists was represented by two works.[3] At the time, an international artistic entente and exchange seemed possible to such artists as Tinguely and Robert Rauschenberg. At their first meeting, in 1960, they had immediately felt great sympathy for one another, sharing sparkling wit and acute intelligence. While their means coincided, their aims differed, however. The American avant-garde did not place any value judgement on American culture, but embraced it. Although the European avant-garde also embraced the real world, they maintained an ironic and critical attitude towards it. Tinguely wielded humour not only as a neutraliser of aesthetic questions but also as an instrument for positive criticism. Between 1960 and 1962, he and Rauschenberg participated in a number of exhibitions and collaborative events together with other American and European artists.[4]

On 20 June 1961, Rauschenberg and Tinguely joined David Tudor, Jasper Johns and Niki de Saint Phalle in their first multimedia theatrical collaboration at the Théâtre de l'Ambassade des Etats-Unis in Paris. The performance was known as *The Concert*.[5] In the simultaneity of several individual and equally important multimedia elements and sensory stimuli, this wordless performance paralleled American developments in non-literary theatre; indeed it was very close to John Cage's theatrical concepts. A few days later, the same artists showed together in an exhibition entitled *New Realism in Paris and New York*, organised by Pierre Restany and Jean Larcade at the latter's Galerie Rive Droîte in Paris. The show also included Klein, Arman, Hains, Bontecou, Chryssa, César and the Americans Chamberlain and Stankiewicz.[6] Another New York painter made the trip to the French capital: from October to the following July, Larry Rivers and his wife, Clarice, were next-door neighbours of Tinguely and de Saint Phalle in the Impasse Ronsin. Rivers had known Yves Klein in New York and reports that all of them became very close: 'Since that time, there is in my work a lot of things which come from this disrespect which Tinguely had in relation to things and objects'.[7] *Disrespect* as in *disillusionment* and an ambiguous response to, and critical dialogue with, contemporary reality marked Tinguely's fundamentally humanistic approach.

The *International Exhibition of Art in Motion*, the first major international survey of kinetic art, opened on 10 March at the Stedelijk Museum, Amsterdam, under the title *Bewogen Beweging*. Pontus Hulten, now the Director of the Moderna Museet, Stockholm, collaborated with Directors Willem Sandberg and Knud Jensen and enlisted the help of, among others, Billy Klüver and Daniel Spoerri. Seventy-two artists were represented with over two hundred works. Tinguely contributed a restrospective of 28 pieces. The exhibition, which featured a survey of the origins of kinetic art, from the Futurists to Calder, was hugely successful and broke all attendance records in Amsterdam. The public was

27 *Baluba No. 3*, 1961

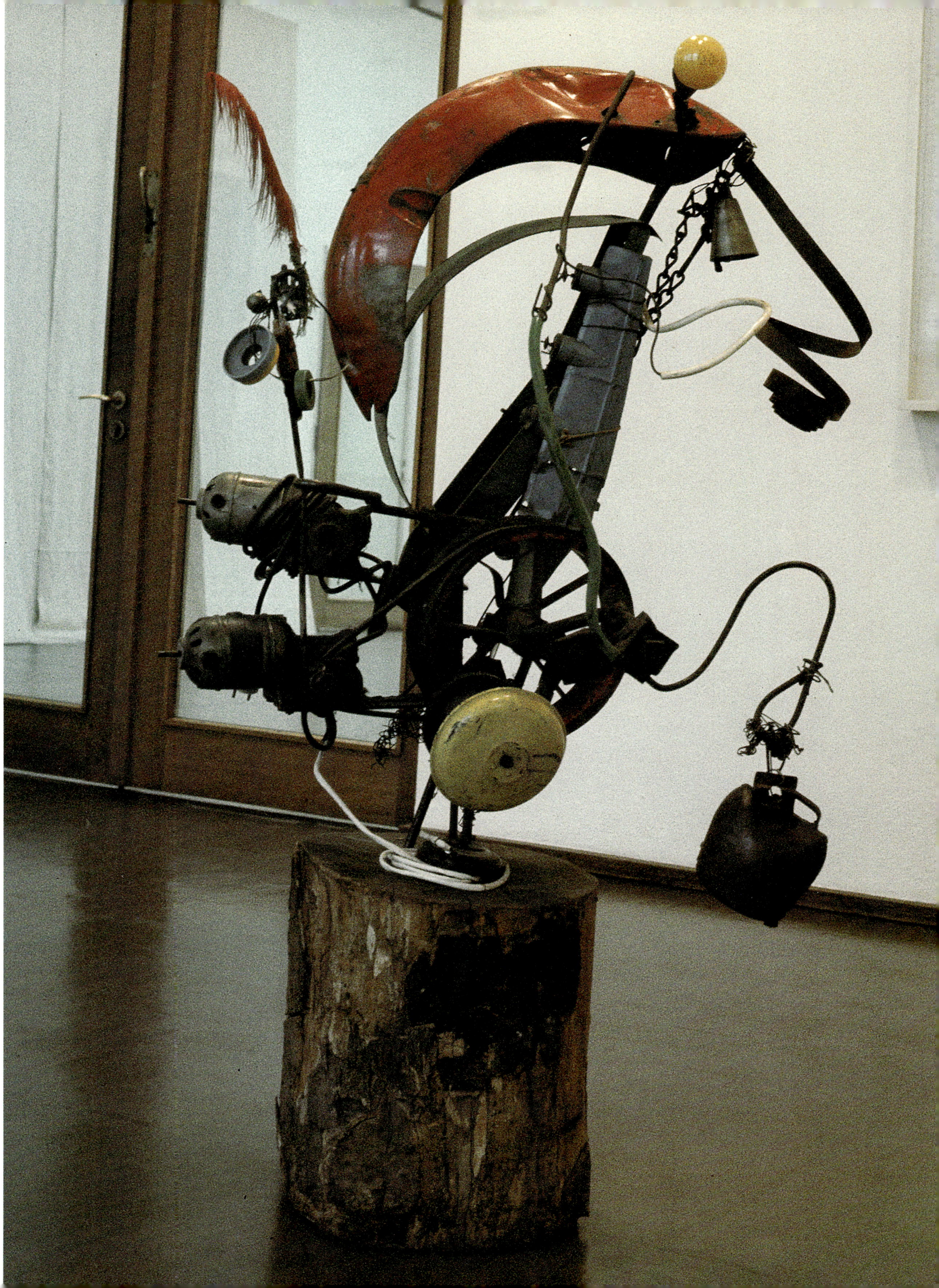

delighted that it could touch everything; the press was not all favourable, as can be gathered from a headline reading 'Circus in Arts and Crafts'.[8]

A serious division occurred among the contemporary artists included in the show—between the neo-Dadaists and those inclined to Constructivism. Tinguely's status of primus inter pares was a thorn in the side of the Constructivist faction. They had some cause to believe that the organisers had turned the exhibition into a virtual solo show of the Swiss. Over the entrance, Tinguely had installed an eye-catching, 15-metre white machine; in the entrance hall, he had placed the large *Metamatic No. 17*, which had already made history at the first Paris Youth Biennale; and in the garden pool he presented the seven-and-a-half-metre water sculpture first shown in Krefeld. Besides, Tinguely's noise-making mechanisms seemed to occupy more than the space in which they were placed—their clatter literally prevailed over the whole show.

George Rickey denounced the neo-Dada bias of the exhibition in an article in *Arts Magazine* in which he criticised Tinguely for having induced abandon in the visitors and for having established a 'boiler-shop mood' which overpowered the 'quieter and far more significant works' that required contemplation.[9] Feeling sabotaged by Tinguely's work, Rickey and others vented their frustration in a prank: they 'counter-sabotaged' and silenced *Metamatic No. 17* by replacing its regular fuel with beer. Arthur Secunda concluded in his comparison of the two motion sculptors:

We need not take sides for there is at least a little bit of each of them in all of us. It is not a question of mechanism versus nature which separates the two, but simply a matter of which aspects of one or the other the artist has selected of emphasis. And it is this psychic editing that gives each artist's work a meaning peculiar to itself.[10]

The *International Exhibition of Art in Motion* opened under the heading *Rörelse i Konsten* at the Moderna Museet, Stockholm, on 16 May, and its arrival was celebrated with an elegant dinner dance for over four hundred guests and unintentionally misfired fireworks set off by Tinguely from a boat. Tinguely built two new works for the occasion: *Narva*, 'a monster machine' (France, private collection), and *Miramar*, rechristened by the public *The Ballet of the Poor* (Switzerland, private collection). These pieces heralded the 'Balubas' (see fig. 27), Tinguely's most extreme art of junk and ephemera. *Miramar*, a hanging sculpture, was described by Hulten:

Nine levers hung from camshafts, which were hidden by an intermediate ceiling. When the machine was switched on, the levers tore at a tangled heap of junk and rags, a dirty nightdress, an artificial leg wearing a red sock, a washing-up bowl, coffee-tins and lengths of film. After the machine had been running for a certain time, this collection of jumble suddenly exploded into violent, spastic jerks.[11]

In August 1961, Tinguely and de Saint Phalle travelled to Spain. Marcel Duchamp had invited them to participate in a celebration honouring Salvador Dalí. The 'bull' they contributed for the fiesta at the arena of Figueras was introduced as the 'Toro del Fuego', a creature of imposing dimensions. Gilded and glorious and bravely suicidal, it surrounded itself in clouds of thick smoke and, spurred on by its inner pyrotechnics, finally blew up. At the opening of *Bevaegelse i Kunsten* at the Louisiana Museum, Humlebaek, Tinguely's pyrotechnical performance benefited from his past experience. It was more explosive and carefully staged. (The artist, a landlubber, had nearly drowned on the job in Sweden.) On 22 September, he unleashed an 'auto-destructive-dynamic-and-aggressive monster-sculpture' entitled *Study for an End of the World No. 1*. The bucolic park setting between the museum and the sea provided a peaceful backdrop for Tinguely's machines—five large and some smaller ones. One shot a broken doll into space in celebration of the Russian astronaut Yuri Gagarin. Tinguely worked mostly with scrap materials and plaster together with dynamite and fireworks. Here, as in *Homage to New York*, he gave the structures a uniform appearance, applying whitewash and wrapping certain parts in aluminium foil. Tinguely's preparatory sketches include the sequence of events with notations that sound like stage directions: 'Overture: little smoke. Opening allegory, atmosphere of farce: Dove of peace, Pram, Siren, Rocking Horse, Sewing Machine, Gagarin, much smoke. Centre: classical, serious jokes: the 5 symbols of nature. IV: aggression. V: terror and fear. VI: atmosphere of parody, burlesque'.[12] Knud Jensen, the founder and Director of the Louisiana Museum, will never forget the event's stormy aftermath. The dove, which as the 'opening allegory' was meant to fly away, died during the apocalyptic doings, and Tinguely was found guilty of having caused the bird's untimely end. He was given a suspended sentence of two month's imprisonment which, after much effort on Jensen's part, was transmuted into a hefty fine.[13]

This incident brings to mind the death of the bird in *An Experiment on a*

Bird with the Air Pump (1768; London, National Gallery), depicted by Joseph Wright, of Derby. Wright's experiment was a success; a vacuum was created which caused the bird's death. Tinguely's experiment 'failed' because the bird died accidentally. Tinguely equated the destruction of the machine with the idea of freedom, while for positivists of the Enlightenment the efficiently functioning machine symbolised that same freedom. For Wright, the death of the bird was a necessary sacrifice for scientific progress.[14] Tinguely's mechanism represented the loss of faith in progress as perfection. While his bird symbolism recurred, he never used a live animal again, however.

During this period, Tinguely began his series of 'Baluba' sculptures, which look as if the *Ballet of the Poor* had come down from the ceiling and been transformed into High Art by being set on oil barrels or other pedestals (fig. 27). Informed by the same ideas as Tinguely's expendable art made around the same time, these sculptures appear nearly as transient as their self-destructing counterparts. Tinguely explained:

> *I drew immediately in space with the materials themselves. It was very simple. I always used the same motor (Lilliput), with a reduction unit that always turned at the same speed, I think about one hundred r.p.m., and those hundred turns had to be tortured in a thousand different ways.*
> *I made tests, I pulverised those motors and I assembled the most disparate materials. That's how the 'Balubas' happened.*[15]

La Folie (*Folly*), one of the first (Stockholm, Collection Eva af Burén), set the mood for the other 'Balubas.' Characteristically, these works depend entirely on movement and sound for their effect, but their essence is not the process of motion but motion and sound as expressive means. The junk Tinguely assembled was mostly abstract to begin with or else it was transformed into an abstraction of colour and sound by speed—hence the analogy with the trance-like frenzy of tribal dancers, with ringing bells, shaking toys, fluttering feathers and rattling rubbish. Tinguely sympathised with the efforts of the Balubas, a Bantu tribe led by Patrice Lumumba in the 1960 Congo war. The wild choreography of the 'Balubas' set to a noisy musical score was a salute to those Congolese freedom fighters. Yet the primitivism of these pieces was given a singular twist by Tinguely. Like bizarre but loveable hoboes, these assemblages endear themselves to the viewer with their nonsensicality, the better to launch their subversive attack. They poke fun at colonialism and deride the idea of art as a commodity.

'Don't stew in your own juice'

1962

In 1962, Tinguely was in Los Angeles for a show at the Everett Ellin Gallery when a producer for NBC asked him to stage an event for *David Brinkley's Journal*. For *Study for the End of the World No. 2*, Tinguely chose a location in the Nevada desert, near the test site used for detonating nuclear bombs and the gambling town of Las Vegas, where millions of dollars are 'blown up' daily. Since the event, which took place on 21 March, played only for the cameras, he could build as expansively and destroy as violently as he wanted to:

The material conditions of the desert are magnificent. I worked all in extension, in breadth. There was no need for vertical extension. The only big thing was a refrigerator, charged with a good quantity of explosives and stuffed with feathers. When it exploded, the feathers covered everything in a snow of burning feathers, producing a most spectacular effect. I had been carried away with explosives. They are freely available in each hardware shop.[1]

When his most ambitious sculpture-event did again not go off exactly as planned, the artist simply quipped: 'You can't expect the world to end the way you want it to.'[2] The Russian newspaper *Izvestiya* reported the happening as 'the realised fantasies of a mentally disturbed person, the notions of an insane [*sic*] who can only be subdued in a strait-jacket. But Tinguely is at large.'[3] Here as elsewhere, the artist cultivated the paradoxical and safeguarded the absurd. When asked if his creations were elaborate practical jokes, Tinguely answered:

These things are serious for me. Absurdity can be carried a long way, and when it's carried far enough, its effect is to make conventional values ridiculous, cut them down to size, cast some badly needed doubt on this 'wonderful age' we're living in. 'Century of the Common Man!' Man today is ill-treated, humbled as he has never been before. I take the noise and blood and brutality and make a work of art of them. That makes them doubly ironic, to be raised to the level of art. I feel a tremendous relief that the whole thing is going to be destroyed, because it's like a lunatic end to everything monstrous in the world.[4]

The fact that such mechanisms as *Study for the End of the World No. 2* did not last allowed Tinguely to play out their ultimate dramatic possibilities. From Los Angeles, Tinguely and de Saint Phalle went to New York, where they stayed at the Chelsea Hotel, Mecca for the European and American avant-garde at the beginning of the sixties.[5] They met Kenneth Koch, a poet and playwright, and decided to stage an event together with Robert Rauschenberg. Rauschenberg secured the collaboration of Merce Cunningham to direct the project. De Saint Phalle remembers that Koch wrote a piece that featured a Jean Tinguely, a Robert Rauschenberg, a Niki de Saint Phalle, and he wanted them to play their own roles. As de Saint Phalle described it, 'It was called *The Construction of Boston*. Bob should bring the weather, Jean should bring architecture, I should bring art. But we all had our own ideas and dreams: Jean was hooked on the idea of being Mae West and my folly was to be Napoleon.'[6] Tinguely reminisced:

I wanted to be Mae West. I had to read lines, but my English wasn't very good. No matter, I dubbed myself with Henry Geldzahler. We were smoking cigars and we dressed up like hookers, with hoop skirts and feathered hats. I began to build a wall on the stage. We carried the cinder blocks in with wheelbarrows. I was a split personality. An actress was playing my spirit. Henry Geldzahler was my voice, I was myself too. It was organized schizophrenia. The wall was getting higher and higher. ['The tits were hanging out, and the feathers were flying everywhere', added Niki]. It was sexy, sensational, we were builders, and the wall kept getting higher. On top of the wall was the spirit of Tinguely singing. The audience saw the wall getting higher. They got scared, five tons of cinder blocks, they panicked and some left.[7]

Rauschenberg had constructed a set looking like a furnished apartment in which two dancers from Cunningham's company went about their daily routines, which included being rained on by a rain-making contraption. Tinguely's cinder-block barrier between spectator and actors was a literal visualisation of the problem of communication in the theatre. The entire performance, on 4 May, did not last longer than 15 minutes. John Wulp, then Director of the Maidman Playhouse, a plush off-Broadway theatre on West 42nd Street where the piece was performed, gave an entertaining account of the event:

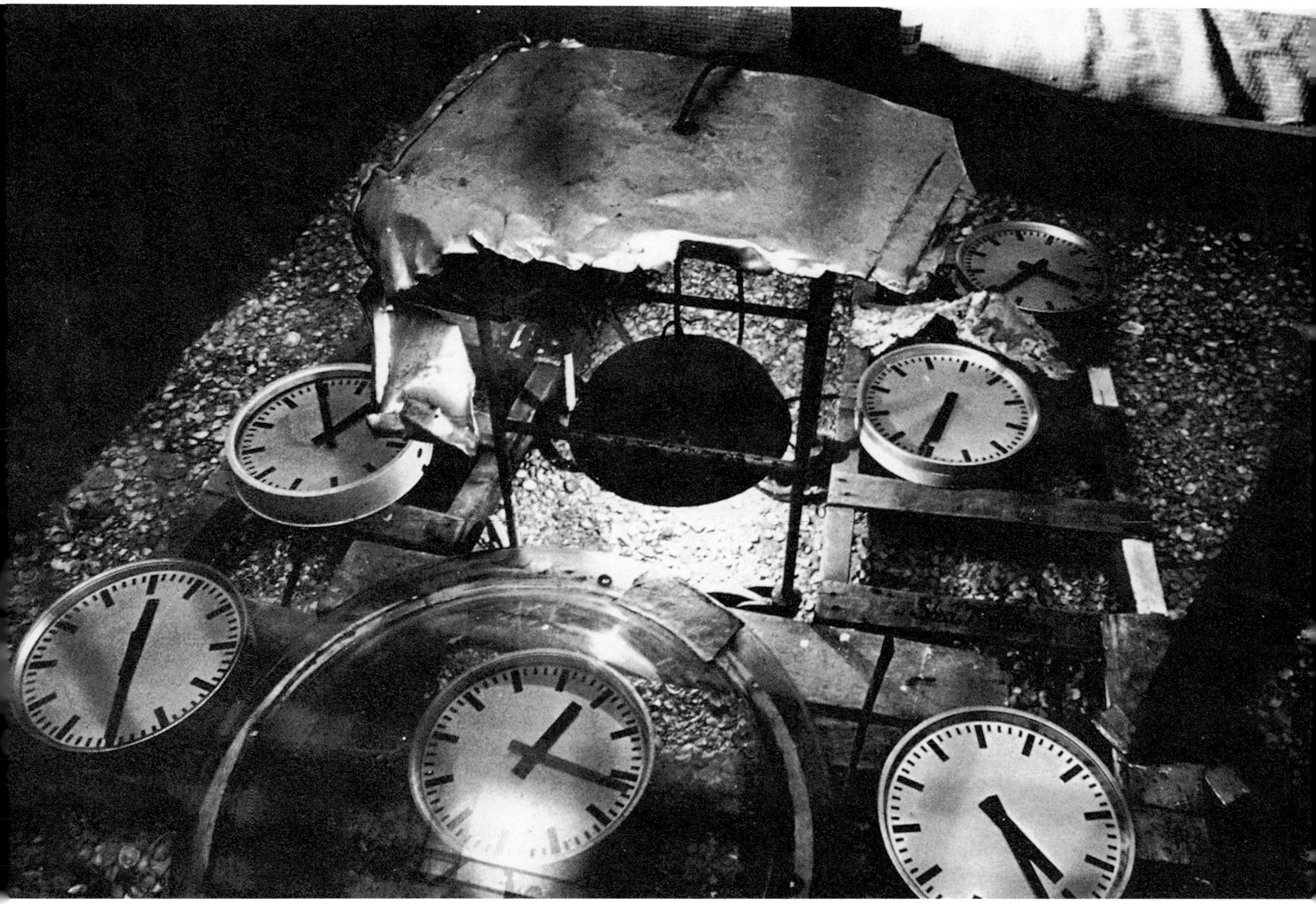

28 *Dylaby*, installation by Robert Rauschenberg (see plate 29)

29 *Dylaby*, plan of installation at the Stedelijk Museum, Amsterdam, 1962, by Robert Rauschenberg, Niki de Saint Phalle, Daniel Spoerri, Per Olof Ultvedt, Martial Raysse and Tinguely ▷

No one was quite sure when The Construction of Boston *had been completed. As soon as Jean Tinguely ran out of cinder-blocks and it was no longer possible to see or hear any of the performers, the house lights were turned on. There was a moment of stunned silence. A few people clapped, some booed.*[8]

The show was a huge success. People had lined up to buy tickets, which had sold out almost immediately. The press was there, Marcel Duchamp was spotted in the audience and Senator Jacob Javits and his wife attended, even though they had to make do with standing room. Although it was both profitable and hugely entertaining, Tinguely argued against a repetition of the event, reasoning that a great deal of its success was due to its novelty.[9]

Another occasion to collaborate with Rauschenberg in 1962 came with the *Dylaby* project (see figs. 28-29) at the Stedelijk Museum, Amsterdam (30 August–30 September). *Dylaby*, short for 'dynamic labyrinth', was conceived as a temporary collaborative work of art, but was not so different from a one-night stand, with 'sets' designed by the artists and the audience featured as actors. When Willem Sandberg offered Tinguely the ready-made setting of the Stedelijk, the two agreed on a general proposal, and Tinguely suggested participants. Rauschenberg, de Saint Phalle, Daniel Spoerri, Per Olof Ultvedt and Martial Raysse accepted. The exhibition was organised within three weeks; materials were obtained from the flea market and from

DYLABY

I daniel spoerri
1 zoemer
2 fietswiel
3 schuimrubber vloer
4 draaibare zuilen
5 schuine vloer
6 fietsbanden
7 marmer
8 blitzlicht
9 oude kleren
10 bed
11 kippengaas
12 schuine vloer
13 rolschaats (tinguely)
14 fietswiel
15 paspop
16 brandweerhelm
17 draaischijf
18 rubberdraden
19 beweegbare wand
20 "tableau piège"
21 warm paneel
22 natte spons
23 closetpot
24 hagedis op sterk water
25 rood licht
26 ketting
27 vochtige wand
28 groene lamp
29 nooddeur
30 microfoon
31 matras

II per olof ultvedt
A gedesynchroniseerde radio (tinguely)
1 ingang
2 buffet
3 stoel
4 hobbelpaard
5 gebroken stoel
6 contra gewicht (rieten been)
7 deur met kippengaas
8 cyther
9 fietswiel
10 dienblad met aluminium servies
11 aluminium pan
12 ruimte met contra gewichten
13 mangel
14 fauteuilrug
15 gong
16 niet gebruikte meubelen
17 uitgang

III daniel spoerri
1 stoel
2 theekastje
3 beeld
4 lamp
5 schilderij

IV martial raysse
1 jukebox
2 badstoel met baadster
3 meisje met parasol
4 groen gras met vruchten
5 bad met plastic dieren
6 bonte vloer
7 zwarte tegels
8 meisje met zwaan
9 strand
10 strandspelen
11 de rand van het strand
12 zee in het zuiden

V niki de saint phalle
1 diplodocus lentus
2 tyrannosaurus rex
3 hoofdenzuil
4 raket
5 kathedraal
6 paspop
7 wolkenkrabber
8 vrouw met grote slang
9 en 10 mechanieken voor het monster en verfzakjes (tinguely)
11 geweer
jean tinguely
12 machine/sculptuur
13 "hommage à anton müller"
per olof ultvedt
14 doorloop met spoken

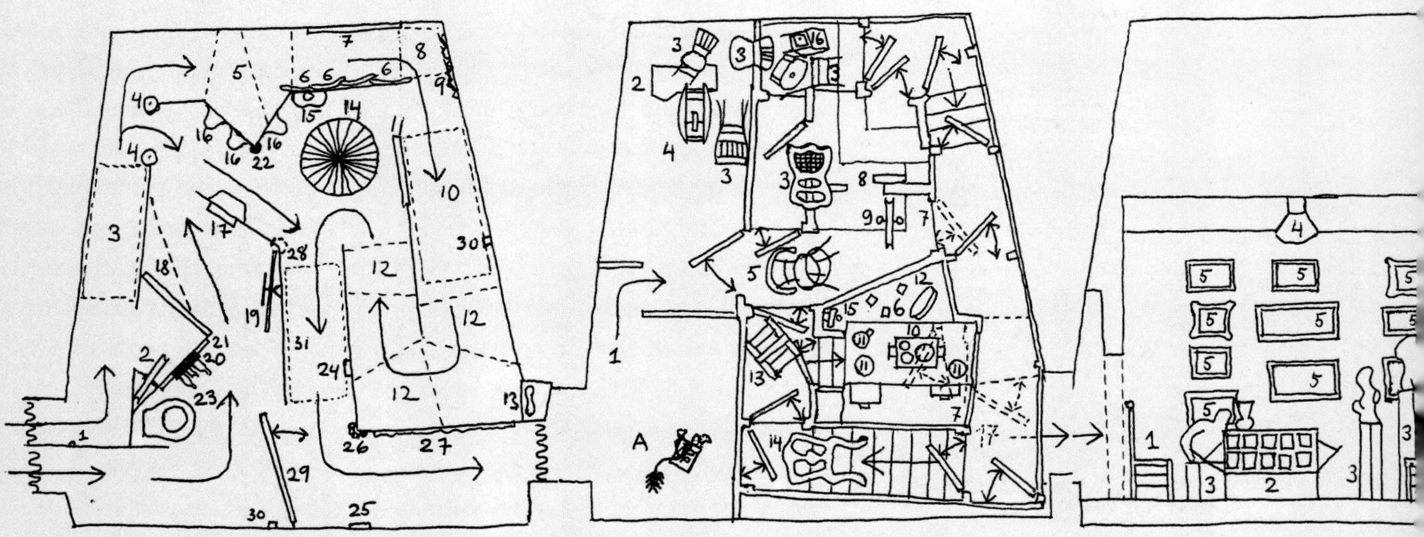

I II IIII

VI robert rauschenberg

1 deur
2 canvas met coca cola bord
3 lamp
4 bad met water en luchtpomp
5 stukken van een vliegtuig, autoband, etc.
6 laag ding met licht en zes snel-draaiende klokken
7 fietsframe
8 tafel op wielen
9 tuin
10 witte wegmarkering
11 schelpen
12 grond
13 hout

VII jean tinguely

1 grote ventilator
2 kleine ventilator
3 luchtstroom
4 ballon
5 knappende ballon

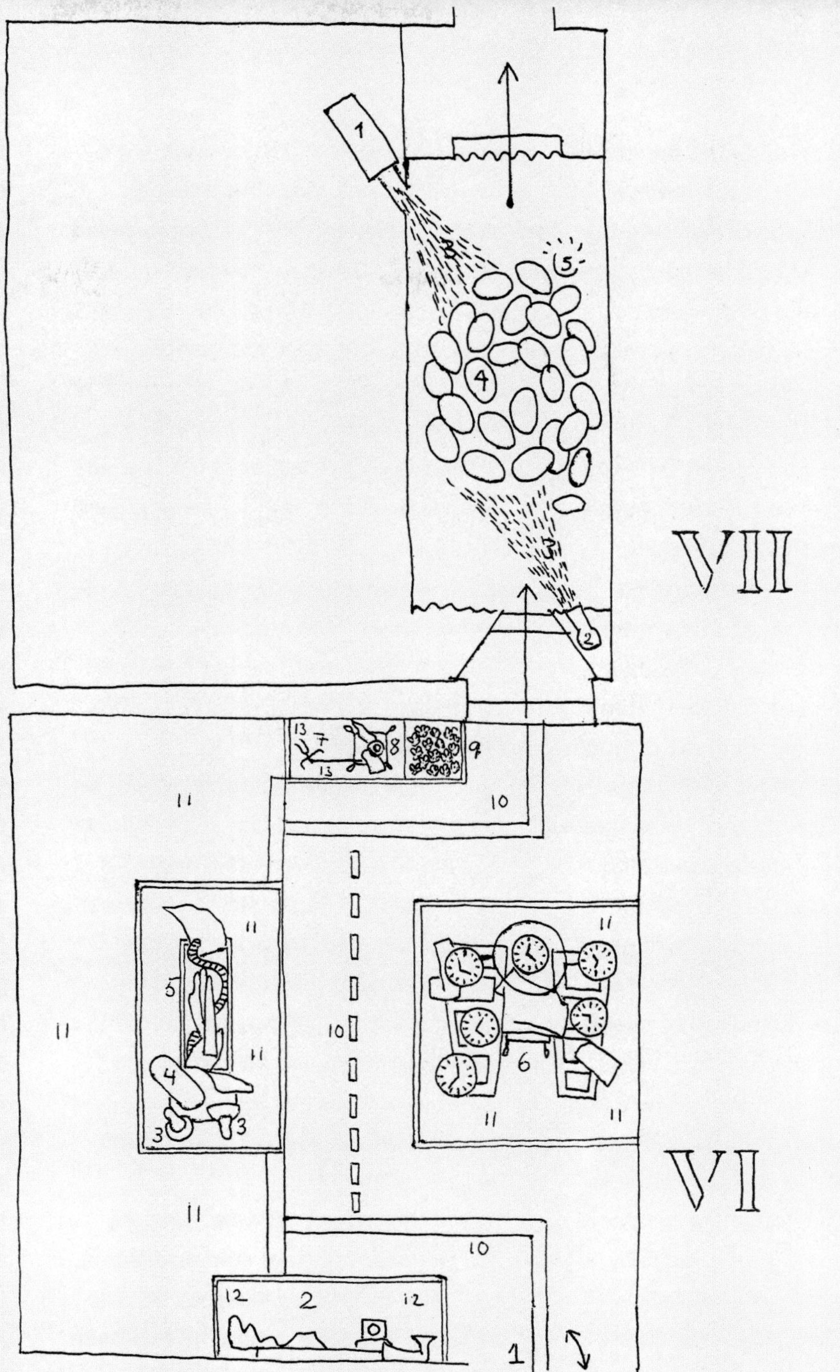

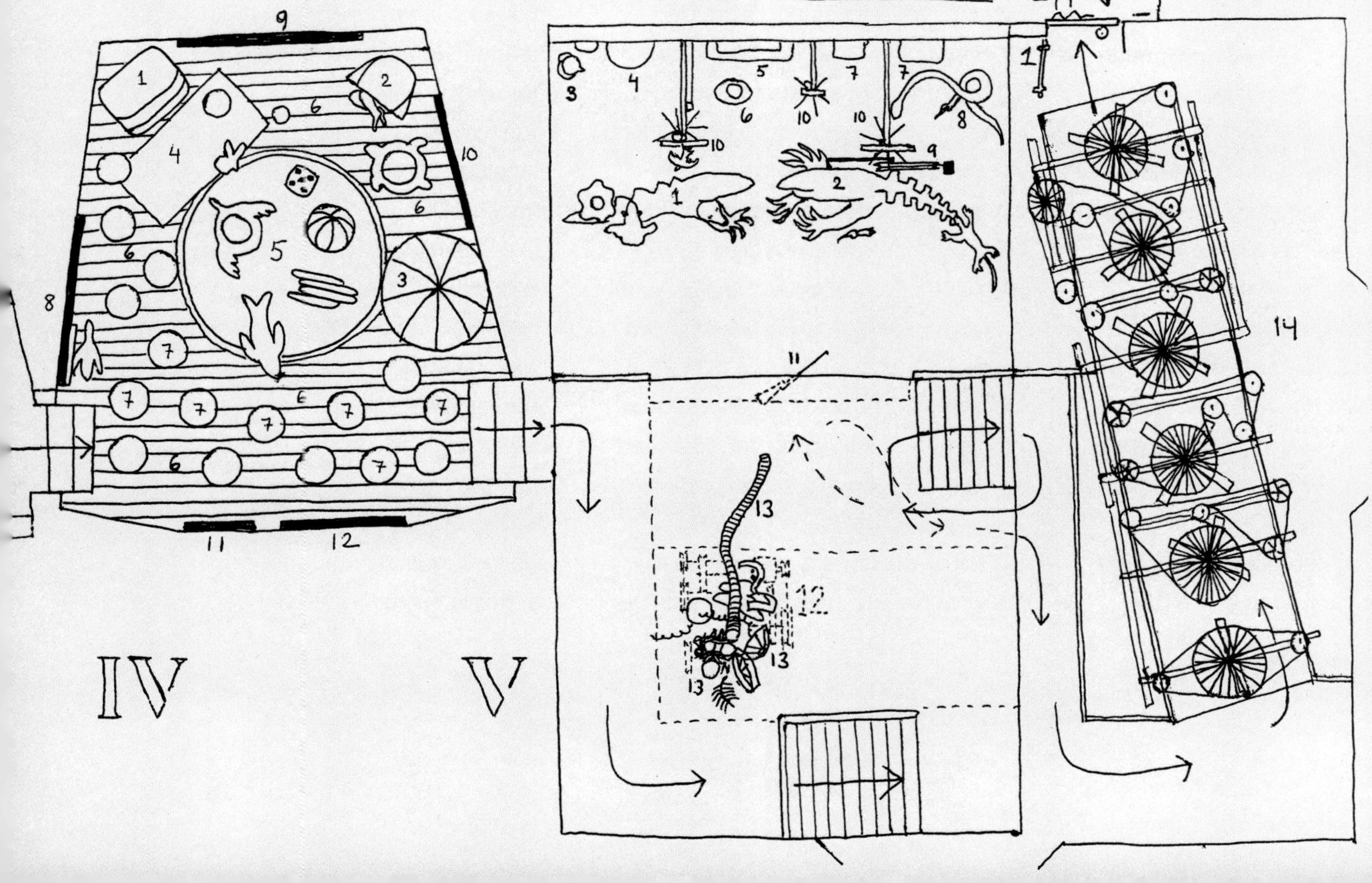

scrap-iron dealers, and after the show most of them ended up as garbage. Ad Petersen of the Stedelijk reported that Tinguely, who was the principal organiser and co-ordinator of the event, took it upon himself to help out with material and technical problems.[10]

The artists turned the suite of rooms into seven completely different environments that confronted viewers with multiple sensory experiences. First, visitors felt their way through Spoerri's shady labyrinth. They were then further confused by Ultvedt's environment, which was filled with Rube Goldberg-like machinery made of wood, including animated chairs. This was followed by an upside-down version of a room by Spoerri, which was exited through the ceiling. Then, viewers arrived in *Raysse-Beach*, with its neon signs, jukebox, water-filled inflatable swimming pool and plethora of plastic toys. The next space, Room V, was shared by Tinguely, de Saint Phalle and Ultvedt. Tinguely contributed a 'Radio' sculpture and a 'Baluba'-type contraption that he dedicated to the memory of Heinrich Anton Müller, a mentally disturbed man who built fantastic machine-like structures. A bunch of rods garnished with an array of junk, including bits of fur and old rags, suddenly burst into a wild dance, activated by a concealed mechanism.

De Saint Phalle, with Tinguely's help, built a shooting gallery which Ad Petersen described as a large white relief with aggressive prehistoric monsters. In front of the relief, small bags filled with paint hung from a string that moved. Visitors fired guns at these targets, and, whenever a bag was hit, paint splashed onto the relief: the hostile act turned into a creative one. Next, Ultvedt had devised multiple turnstile machinery, from which the visitor emerged into Rauschenberg's room filled with three-dimensional caged combines. One of them included six clocks. Tinguely's tunnel of balloons was the last room. Here, visitors were confronted by a mass of moving balloons playfully barring their exit in a birthday party-like apotheosis. The collaboration of *Dylaby* did not proceed without problems. Gallery owner Ileana Sonnabend seemed overprotective of Rauschenberg and interfered between him and the others.[11] Though Rauschenberg and Tinguely continued to see one another, *Dylaby* was their last collaboration.

Just before the *Dylaby* event, on 6 June, Tinguely had lost a collaborator and friend when Yves Klein died of a heart attack in Paris: 'When I was told that he had died, I was very suspicious. I thought it was one of those extraordinary things he used to put over on us. Because he had always talked about two things: he talked about levitation, and he talked about just vanishing.'[12]

Throughout the year, Tinguely had several important solo exhibitions, beginning in January in Basel, at Galerie Felix Handschin, where he had been presenting works since 1958. On 11 September, Felix Handschin conveyed a group of guests to Baden, a renowned Swiss spa, for a special kind of cocktail party, where most of the drinks were served by Tinguely's fountain sculptures. These were formally and ideationally related to the 'Baluba' sculptures, with water replacing such things as feathers. For one critic, the majestic natural environment was distracting. As it happened, he described as an alternative the very conditions under which Tinguely would later work with similar fountains to animate a town square in Basel: 'The water-spraying things would have a totally different effect in a sterile, barren environment of concrete, in a bleak, paved square, in modern, stern surroundings—and one should produce them once under these conditions.'[13]

Throughout 1962, Tinguely pushed ahead with his experiments with transient media, such as fire, water and sound. The results of his interest in sounds transmitted by radio were presented in New York at the Alexander Iolas Gallery from 27 November to the end of December. His free-standing 'Radio' sculptures such as *Radio WNYR* and his relief-like 'Radio' drawings were devised so as to tune in and out of stations from one end of the radio band to the other (fig. 30), thus creating a kind of universal and simultaneous collage of sounds.[14] Tinguely's 'Radio' works involve chance to produce volume and select stations, since sounds are picked up by the dial, which is turned by a mechanical device. The result is a jumble of words and musical sounds interrupted by silence and a crackling buzz between stations. The bits and pieces of dialogue audible through the 'Radios' are just as nonsensical as the manipulation of sentences by 'anti-theatre' dramatists such as Ionesco and Beckett.[15] Tinguely demonstrated what John Wideman recently observed about language, that it is both 'carnival and minefield'.[16]

Since his departure from Switzerland in 1953, Tinguely's star had risen rapidly. His critical success was assured by such articles as Calvin Tomkins' 'Profile' in the 10 February 1962 issue of *The New Yorker*. Commercial success followed, with major contemporary galleries vying for his work. As always, he remained independent, his relationships with dealers

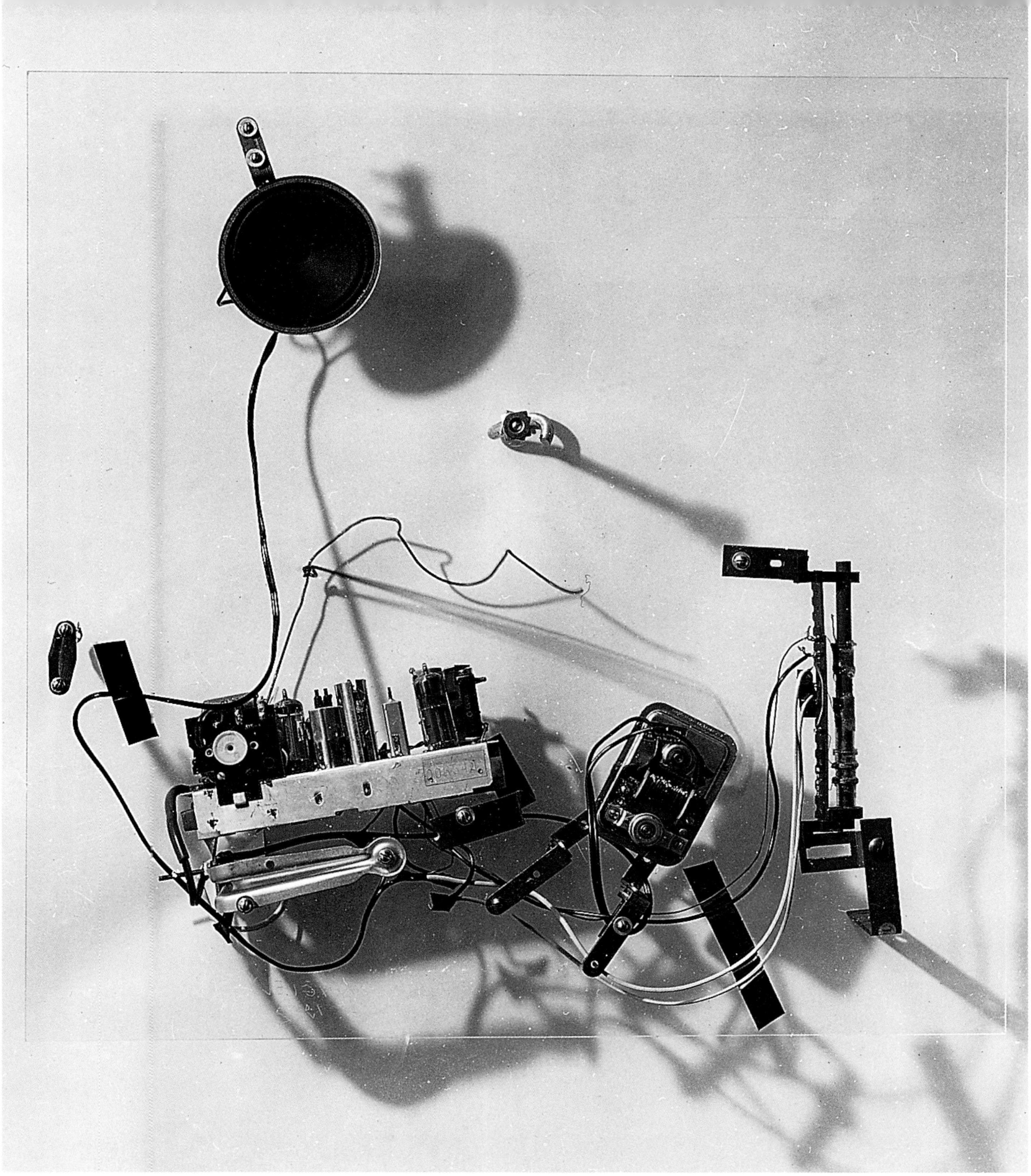

30 *Radio WNYR*, 1962

based more on congeniality than on contracts. The monetary value attached to his work was on the rise. But prosperity was not among his priorities, and he shared Niki de Saint Phalle's healthy opinion of price tags: 'labels which show only where the fashion is; and fashion changes'.[17] What writers noted in 1962 about Tinguely's lack of interest in material goods and dread of ownership remained true: The only evidence of his prosperity at the time was a luxurious new sedan equipped with safety belts; in later years, it would be latest top-model Mercedes.

'I don't have to think about what to do; I just do it'

1963–65

The Minami Gallery in Tokyo invited Tinguely for a solo exhibition that opened on 20 March 1963. He had arrived in Japan some weeks previously with only a few sculptures to complement the works built on the spot in the gallery. Hiroshi Teshigahara documented Tinguely's creative method on film. One of the sequences traces the making of *The Bamboo's Swan Song* (fig. 31), from the estimating of the necessary wall space with a long bamboo stick (which gave the work its title) to the final changes Tinguely made to the wire hooked around a small ball until it dangled perfectly. The artist is observed combining precise, quick gestures and rapid execution with a meticulous attention to seemingly minor details: 'One has to resolve the problem beginning with the upper end, on the spiritual-poetic level, work from the top to the bottom, not the other way around—otherwise the result would only be a heap of animated junk.'[1] In Japan as elsewhere, Tinguely sensitively mirrored his cultural environment. For example, the Japanese love of golf prompted *The Monument for a Golf Player* (Geneva, Galerie Bonnier); the ball's precarious position mimics the winning stroke in an actual game.[2]

At the end of March, Tinguely was back in Los Angeles, where he prepared another exhibition, this time at the Dwan Gallery. Although Tinguely had mostly been using reconditioned motors, Virginia Dwan changed that when she took him to a large hardware

31 *The Bamboo's Swan Song*, 1963

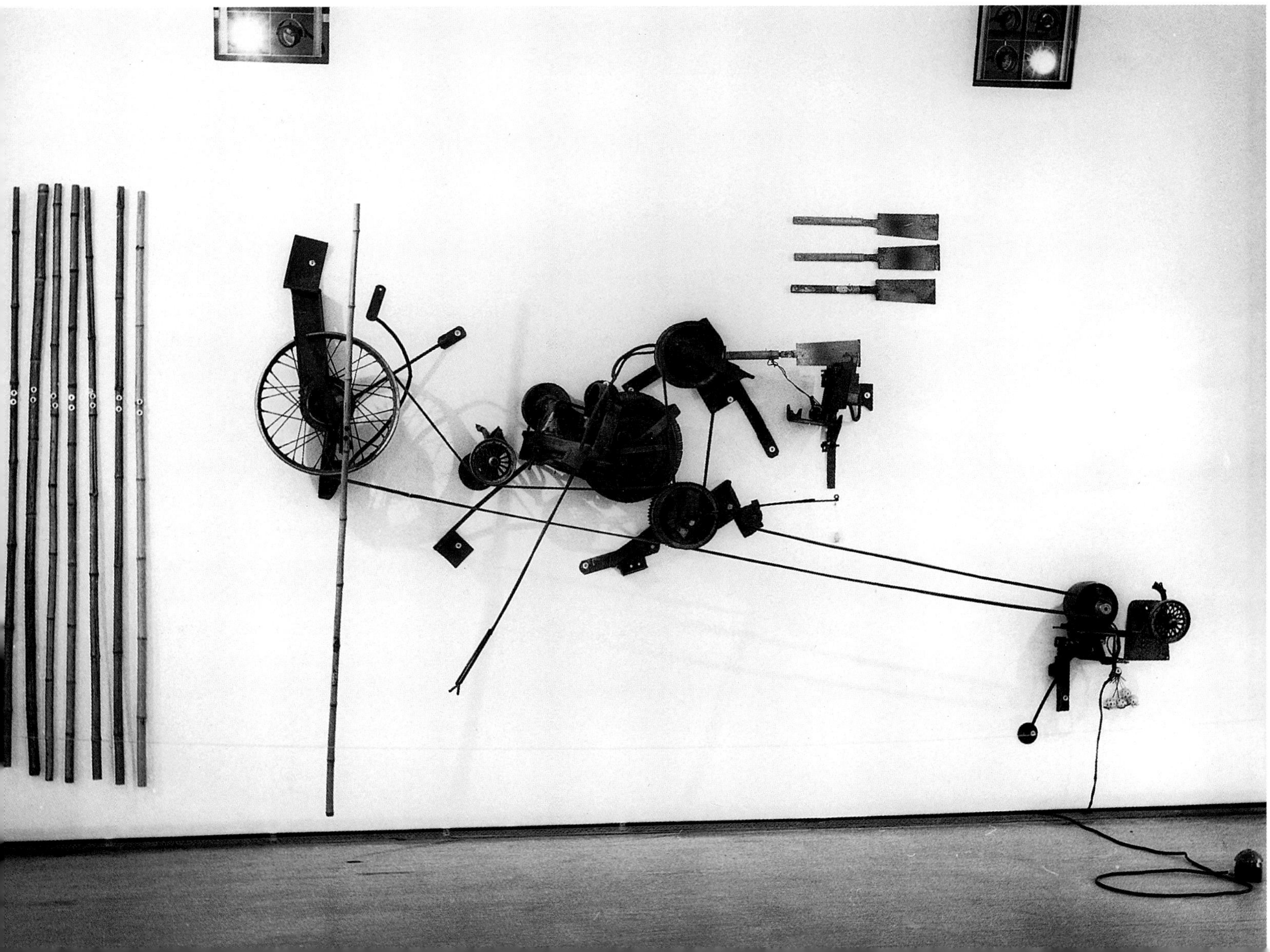

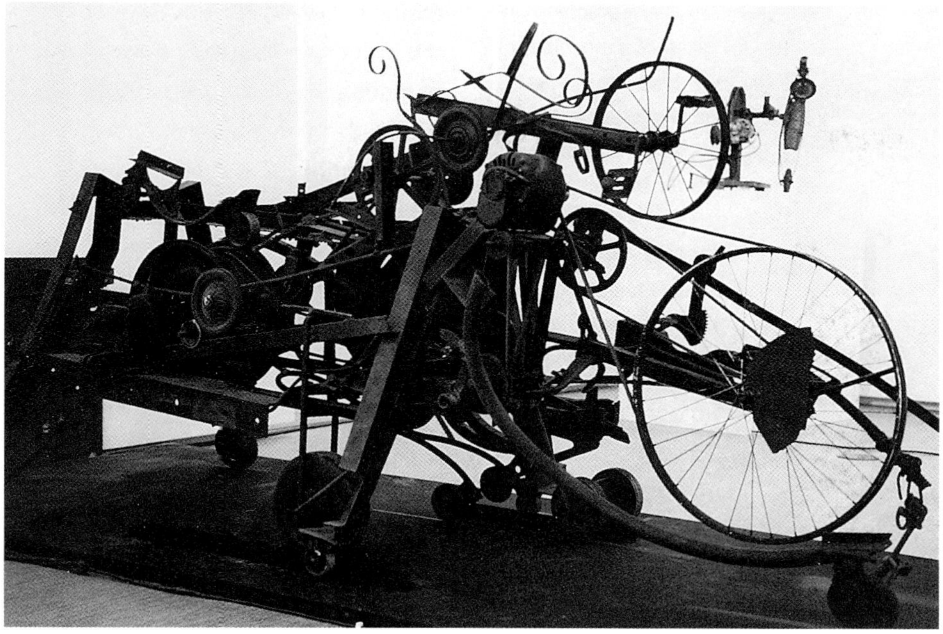

32 *Hannibal I*, 1963

store: 'I would find him thrilled by motors the size of a baby, cradling them with a tender yet also devilish expression of, "Am I maybe allowed to have this new motor?" written all over his face.' She observed that Tinguely chose motors that were much too powerful for the weight of his sculptures, so that the works had to be bolted down to keep them from taking off, the smaller ones to tables, the larger ones to walls: 'Jean became very involved with motors, and their power communicated to him so that the sculptures he built were a kind of appendage to that power.'[3] *Hannibal I* is a complex bulk of assembled wheels that noisily and forcefully stretches its trunk and tusk like an elephant intent on tearing down the wall to which it is attached (fig. 32). The title is paradoxical in its reference to the Carthaginian general who crossed the Alps using elephants, given that the sculpture is an image of impotence and waste of power. To counterweight the power of the motors he preferred, Tinguely began to employ heavier pieces of metal and to adjust motion and sound to match these materials, their weight, flexibility, stiffness or resistance. The forms became fewer, simpler and more compact. The result was a work such as *Hong Kong*, which has a stately elegance and integrity of form. Though Tinguely continued to use found objects, he was shifting away from the idea of junk imagery, and for the first time since 1960 painted all his sculptures a matt black in what he referred to as 'the pre-eminently anti-New Realist gesture. No more New Realism, no more found objects'.[4] This was a way of cancelling out the aspect of assemblage and of emphasing sculptural form as a whole. Motion and sound became less erratic and more controlled. The Los Angeles exhibition was praised by a critic as 'Tinguely's best show to date, for in it he shows a concern for formal considerations equal to his interest in expressing the human situation'.[5] The artist realised more fully what he had begun in Los Angeles when he returned to Europe and began work on his first public commission, a giant machine for the 1964 Swiss National Exhibition in Lausanne.

The Swiss National Exhibition, held every 25 years, presents a panorama of the achievements and activities of Switzerland in the economic, industrial and cultural fields. The 1964 theme was progressive, rational modernism. The organisers of this important Swiss fair commissioned Tinguely to build the signal tower and official symbol. Tinguely built his controversial *Eureka* (fig. 34) and became instantly famous. The work occupied him until the following spring. He made numerous drawings to help him grasp the mechanical complexities involved in this monumental construction and learned much about technology from the workmen who assisted him.[6]

Eureka has imposing dimensions (780 x 660 x 410 cm). Its base, embedded in concrete and formed from three straight and one double C-shaped leg, supports a multi-leveled platform of seven independent mechanisms, each powered by its own motor and each with its own vertical and horizontal rhythms. Sounds punctuate these movements. The sculpture expands and contracts its volume as it goes through its motions, lifting its saucer-hat up and down and pushing smaller, wheeled contraptions backwards and forwards along its flanks. In September 1993, I stood in front of *Eureka* in the company of a German art historian. Beforehand I had asked at the tourist office about the machine's running time. As we strolled along the lake towards the Zürichhorn, where the work now stands, I remembered my initial encounter with it 30 years earlier. *Eureka* had been the first contemporary work to leave an indelible impression on my consciousness. As I began to describe it to my companion, we came upon the sculpture itself, standing in front of a leafy backdrop, itself a mighty scrap-iron tree-thing. My companion asked why it had not been placed in front of the Kunsthaus instead of here, where it seemed exiled. I described the difficulties encountered by Dr Walter A. Bechtler, the industrialist and patron, that had resulted in the sculpture's being placed here, following extensive polemics, rather than near Rodin's *Gates of Hell*. We walked around the sculpture. My companion compared it to the fossil of a nineteenth-century industrial plant. We were just about to begin an argument about Romanticism when *Eureka* interfered noisily, right on time! The scrap-iron hobgoblin worked its decorous magic, thwarting our clever analysis. The whole performance took 15 minutes.[7] The fact was that the ideas *Eureka* reflected were simply too subversive to be acceptable to the majority of art lovers, especially in 1964. Tinguely remembered that the French Swiss never accepted the work's title:

They always called it 'Tinguely's machine'. To them it was the synonym of a machine for performing gratuitous acts, the useless machine which somehow represented the discovery of non-develpoment, non-productivity. The Swiss hesitated for the first time about progress and capitalism! That was in 1964 and the French-Swiss immediately reacted to the philosophical meaning of the machine, while the German Swiss looked at 'Eureka' carefully (which doesn't mean they understood it properly), but they were less sensitive to its essence. 'Eureka' was obviously a title meant to deceive: positive, beautiful, correct. In fact it's a joke.[8]

At the end of 1963, the studios at the Impasse Ronsin in Paris were demolished, and Tinguely, together with several other artists, had to relocate. He and de Saint Phalle found a suitable residence in the Fontainebleau region: the former bar and dancing hall called Auberge du Cheval Blanc in Soisy-sur-Ecole. Orchards surround the building, and Tinguely became involved in the cultivation of flowers, his favourite being sunflowers.

During 1964, Tinguely had five solo shows, two in Switzerland, two in Germany and one in Paris.[9] The last, a retrospective at Alexandre Iolas's Gallery, included two large new works: *Eos* and *Chariot M. K. III*. Both inspired a series of similar sculptures on the theme of Sisyphus and evolved out of the artist's experiments with new types of motion and the different techniques explored in *Eureka*. *Eos* and the 'Chariots' such as *Chariot M. K. IV* and *Chariot No. 8* mimic intimate human activities. In their endlessly repeated to and fro of a bent form poking against a more contained body of wheels, the viewer witnesses a bedroom drama that proceeds in virtual silence (see figs. 33, 35). The apparatus, painted a uniform black, is lighted so that it is seen in sharp silhouette, playing itself out in shadow on the wall behind it. Explained Tinguely: 'I wanted people to be at first shocked by the machine itself, to make big monsters, scorpions, bizarre things—and I came to make mechanisms that make love.'[10]

The exhibition at Alexandre Iolas was acquired in its entirety for the Museum of Fine Arts, Houston. The museum Director, James Johnson Sweeney, recalled how this purchase came about:

33 *Chariot M. K. IV*, 1966

Stills of *Chariot M. K. IV* in motion

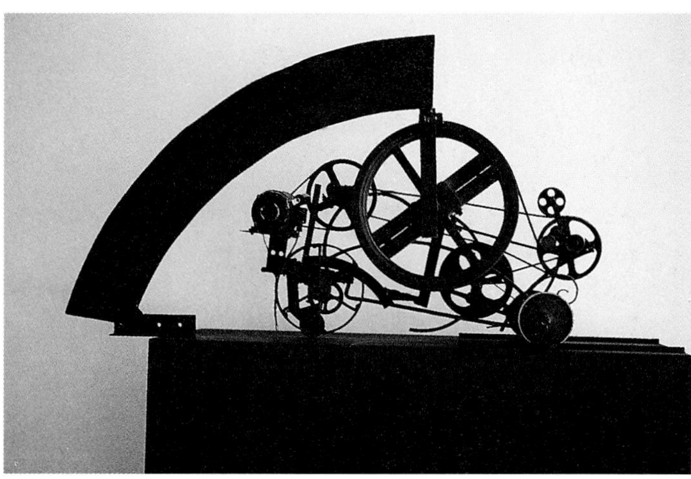

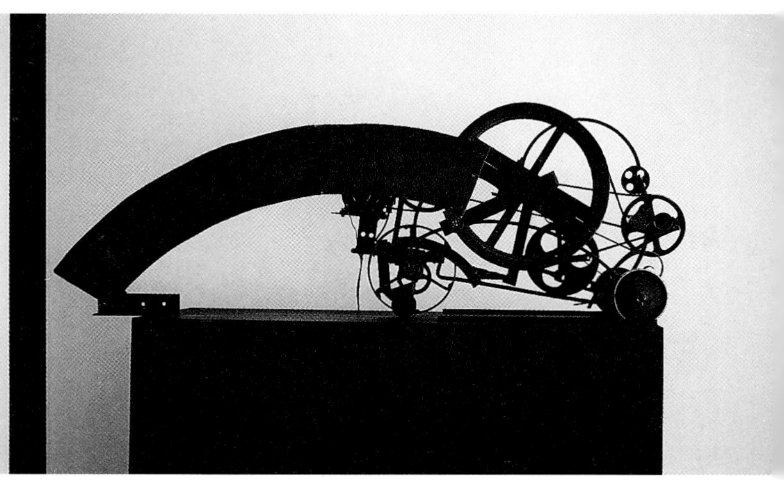

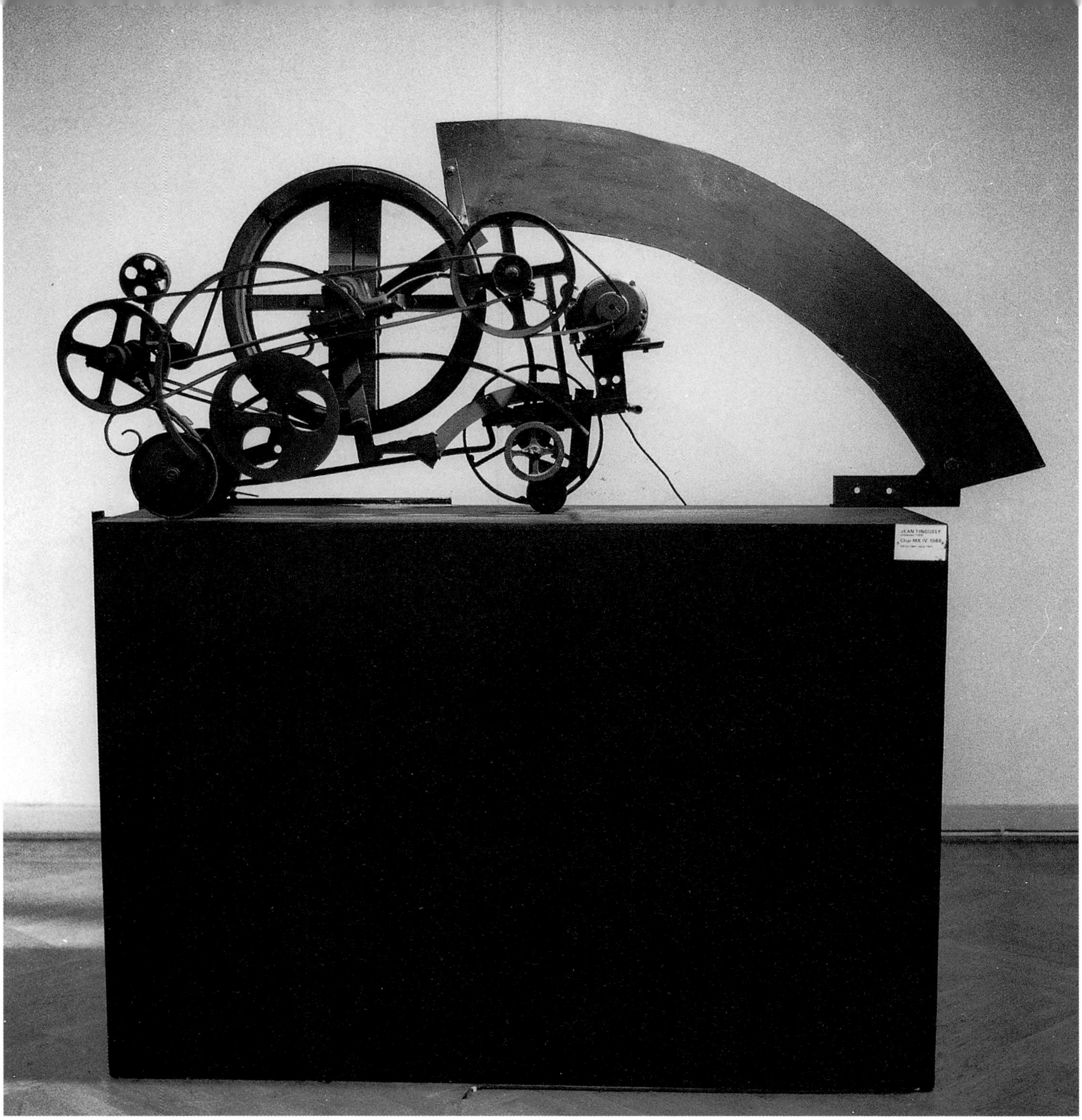
JEAN TINGUELY
Char MK IV 1966

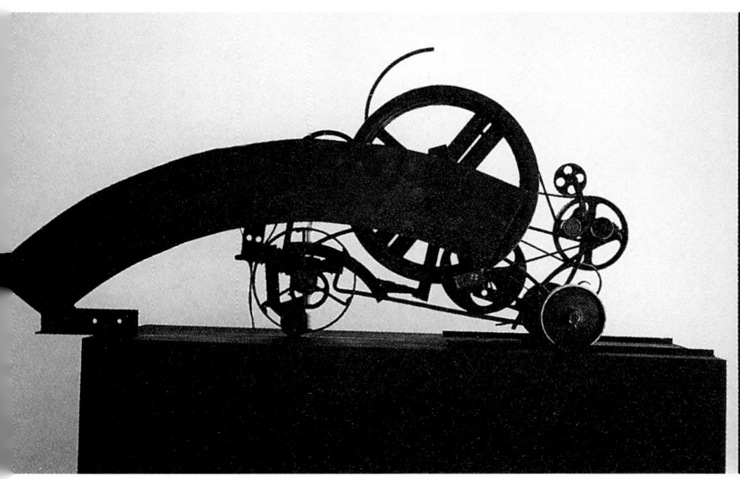

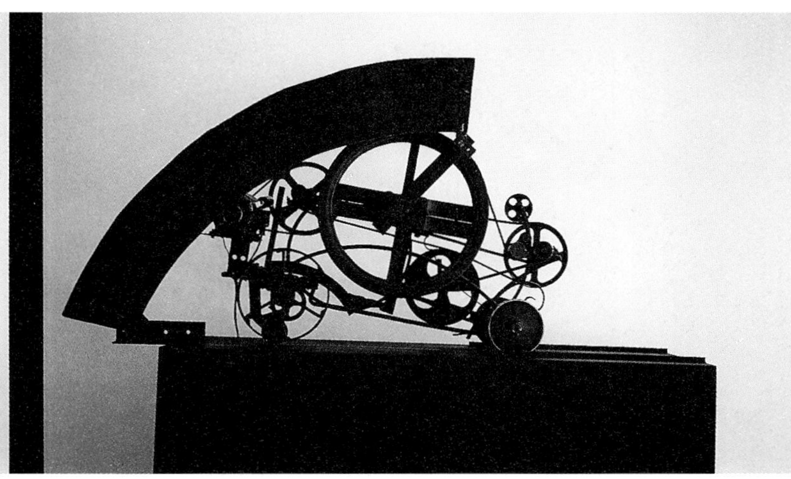

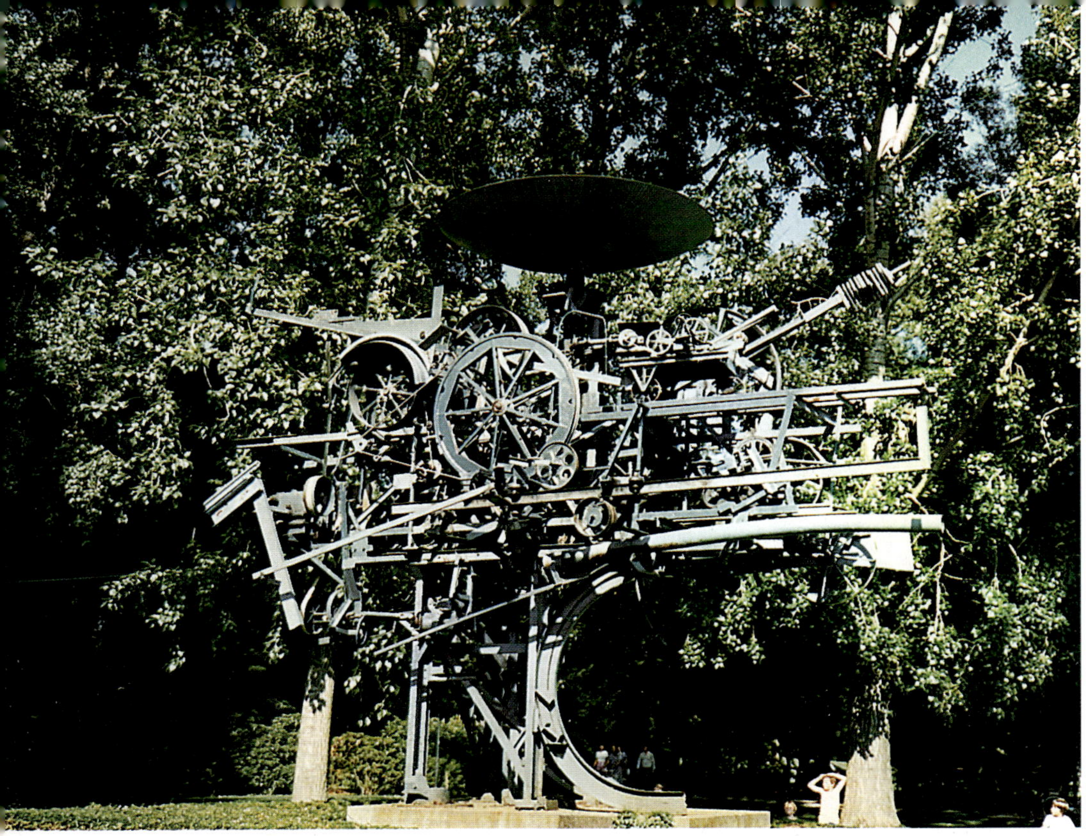

34 *Eureka*, 1964

I was taxiing down the Boulevard St. Germain when throngs pouring into a gallery blocked our way. I hopped out and inched my way in to find the reason for such excitement. It was Tinguely. It represented 10 years of the artist's explorations, a cross-section of his work—not just a single expression. It was the sort of selection a museum should offer to represent a sculptor's efforts and acievements.[11]

When the works were exhibited in Houston, the press commented favourably on the new acquisitions as an 'enviable collection of a contemporary sculptor of international importance' and called Tinguely 'a creative talent of great originality and sensitivity.'[12]

For a show at the Musée des Arts Décoratifs in Paris, where he exhibited with sculptors César and Roël d'Haese, Tinguely presented a monstrous, chain-rattling work, *Chariot-Meta I.*[13] Through this machine, he evoked the dangers inherent in the abuse of power, in the spirit of Goethe's poem entitled 'The Sorcerer's Apprentice'.

Tinguely's absolute devotion to his means of expression was a struggle against their opposite:

But now it's as though this monster of stability were pushing me, pushing me toward a certain point in myself where I will have to end all these experiments and experiences—or, rather, where the experiences I've had will have to be reconciled as one and the same. I feel that in a way I am almost condemned to be myself, integrally and totally, and this sometimes fills me with despair.[14]

He always openly acknowledged his allegiances and his adoption of forms and techniques. These were structural rather than mimetic appropriations, never intended to mould a fixed style, but to avoid a fixed identity. Olle Granath called this method 'collaboration'.[15] Tinguely's continuous seeking out of collaborations with his contemporaries was also a tactic to escape from the 'monster of stability'.

At the end of 1965, Tinguely was in New York for a large show at the Jewish Museum entitled *2 Kinetic Sculptors*. He and Nicolas Schöffer had been singled out by the Director, Sam Hunter, as the two most original motion sulptors of the day. Tinguely's contribution of 41 sculptures was complemented by over 20 drawings.[16] For the show, Tinguely built a large machine at the Southampton studio of Larry Rivers. Inspired by a store-window mannequin Rivers had used for his piece *Murder at B. Altman & Co* and entitled *The Dissecting Machine* (fig. 36), the work is a kind of 'bachelor machine' nodding in the direction of Duchamp's masturbatory contraptions. Similar to Surrealist objects in that it involves a 'doll' in a dramatic, slightly pornographic and perverse narrative, the machine contains spikes, nails and other threatening elements. Tinguely dismembered the clothing dummy and impaled it on a chair-like stake assembled from cast-iron parts and welded scrap. Three enormous saws attack the limbs, and a huge drill aims at the grinning head coquettishly turned sideways. One writer observed: 'Since it is the spectator himself who sets the thing going he can hardly dissociate himself from the nuance of cruelty it cheerfully implies. And it rather cleverly makes the point that there is no real gap between the vicarious enjoyment of cruelty and the act itself.'[17] Tinguely's torture device is reminiscent of his friend Edward Kienholz's pathetic abortion scene *Birthday* (Beverly Hills, Collection Mr and Mrs Frederick R. Weisman), in which a female figure is impaled on an operating table. Kienholz's narrative is grounded in reality, while Surrealism's fiction of dreams and the unconscious is based on an exchange between the subjective and objective worlds. The *Dissecting Machine* partakes of both sensibilities.

Tinguely's art is formally, ideologically and psychologically opposed to the impersonal, sleek, corporation-sponsored constructions of Schöffer. However, both artists had an interest in the performance aspect of their machine art; both emphasised the notion of time and ephemerality rather than matter. Sam Hunter believed that

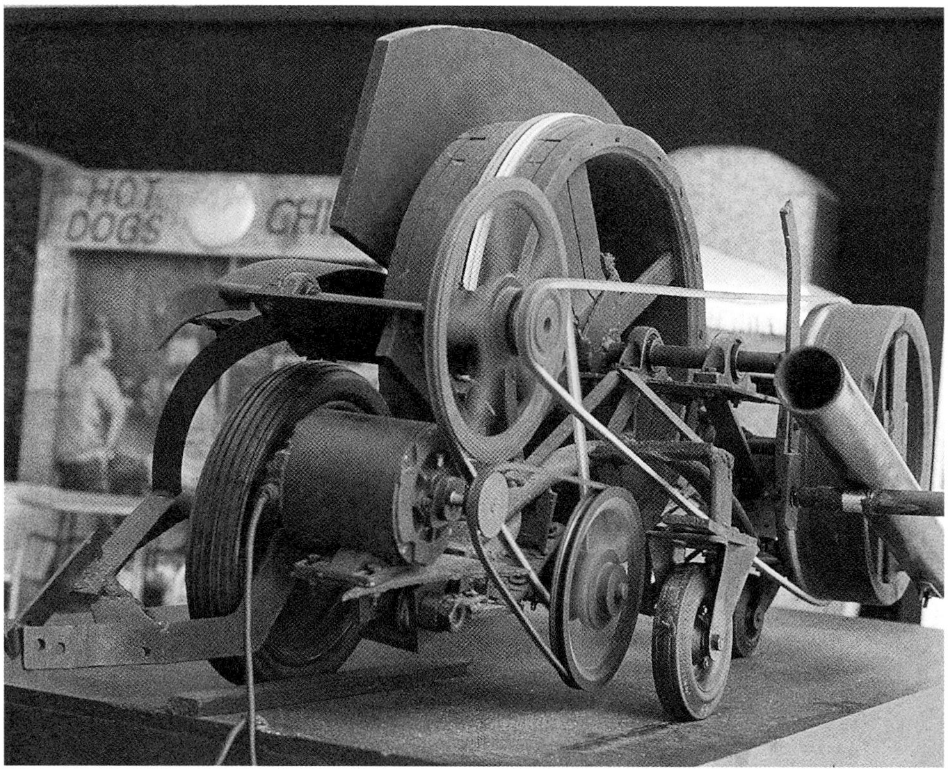

35 *Chariot No. 8*, 1968

Chariot No. 8 (view of the front)

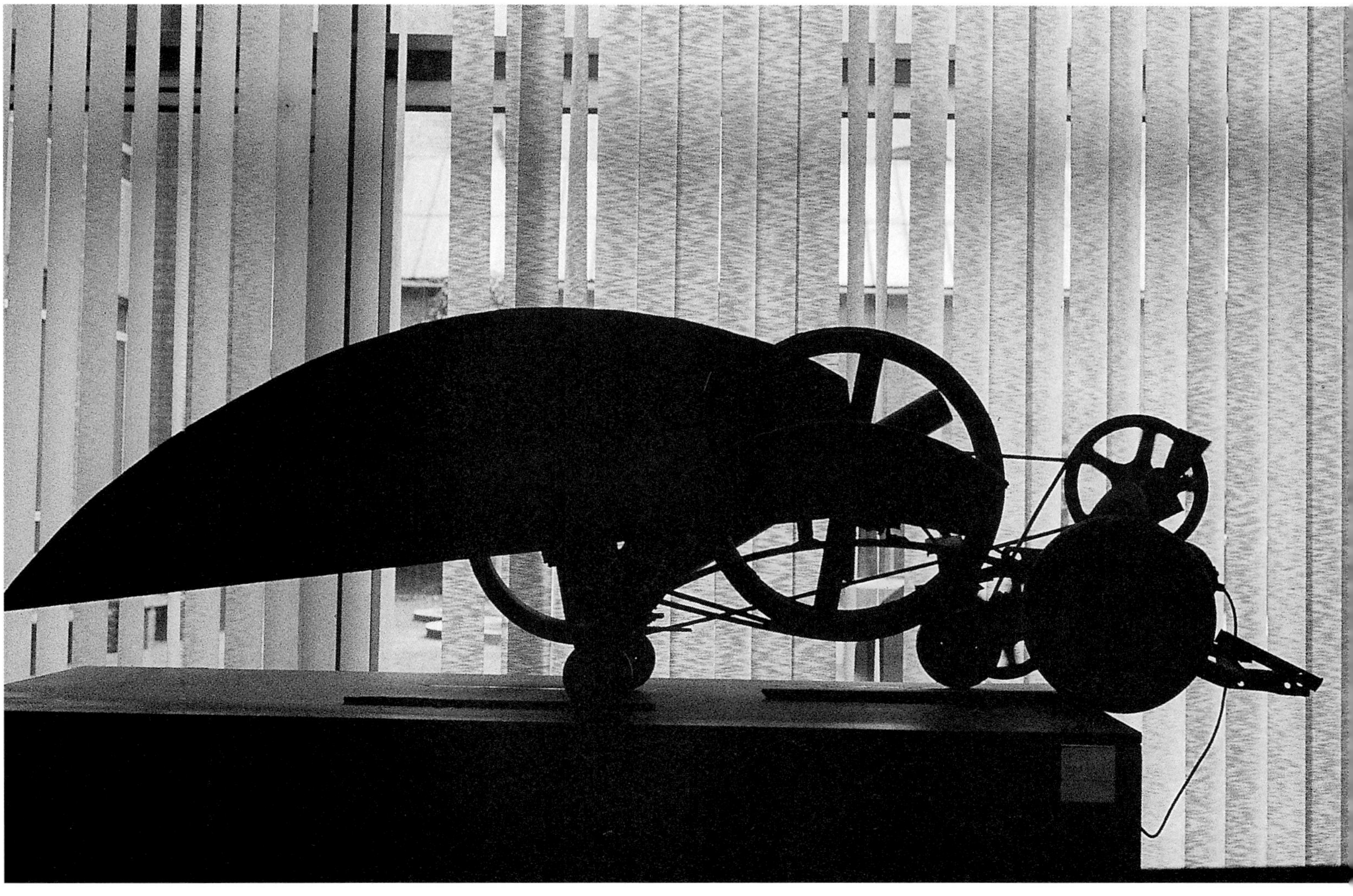

both views of the machine were essential: 'Tinguely's inspired humor and irony in the face of the dilemmas posed by the machine age... [and] Schöffer's assurances that the technological environment can be mastered through art.'[18] This opinion was not shared by Hilton Kramer, who criticised Tinguely's work for its lack of formal invention, calling it a 'second-hand vocabulary' and dismissing his humour as 'now already dated and tiresome'.[19] Since Kramer rarely admires art work that objectifies existential dramas, his negative reaction to Tinguely's work is not surprising.

On 22 December at the Jewish Museum, Tinguely and de Saint Phalle collaborated again with Kenneth Koch on a one-night, one-act spectacle entitled *The Tinguely Machine Mystery* or *The Love Suicides at Kaluka*. It 'starred' three Tinguely machines, *Attila*, *Odessa* and *May Fair* (locations unknown).[20] The play, a murder-drama, featured poets John Ashbery, Kenward Elmslie and Arnold Weinstein. Larry Rivers played a corpse that was resurrected as a police chief, his wife, Clarice, appeared as an Elizabethan princess who flirted with Larry, and a detective was played by Sol Solomon. The art dealer Alexandre Iolas and the artist Kiki Kogelnik were cast as a pair of suicidal Japanese lovers. The painter Jane Freilicher impersonated the city of Odessa. De Saint Phalle, dressed in black leotards, was billed as the 'Spirit of Night', and Tinguely acted the part of another Japanese lover. Morton Feldman had composed music for the occasion which merged with the clattering, clacking chorus of Tinguely's machines for the grand finale. The event was described by Grace Glueck as 'a ragout of Gilbert and Sullivan, 18th-century opera, Keystone cops and charades. Its crosscurrents had crosscurrents and its subplots had subplots'.[21] Although the experiment was once more an enormous public success, it was the last such event in which Tinguely himself performed. Thereafter, he was involved with theatre as a set designer, at Paris's Théâtre des Champs-Elysées in the following year (for a new ballet by Roland Petit, *In Praise of Folly;* see fig. 38) and in 1972 for Werner Düggelin's production of Jacob Bidermann's *Cenodoxus* at Salzburg (fig. 58).

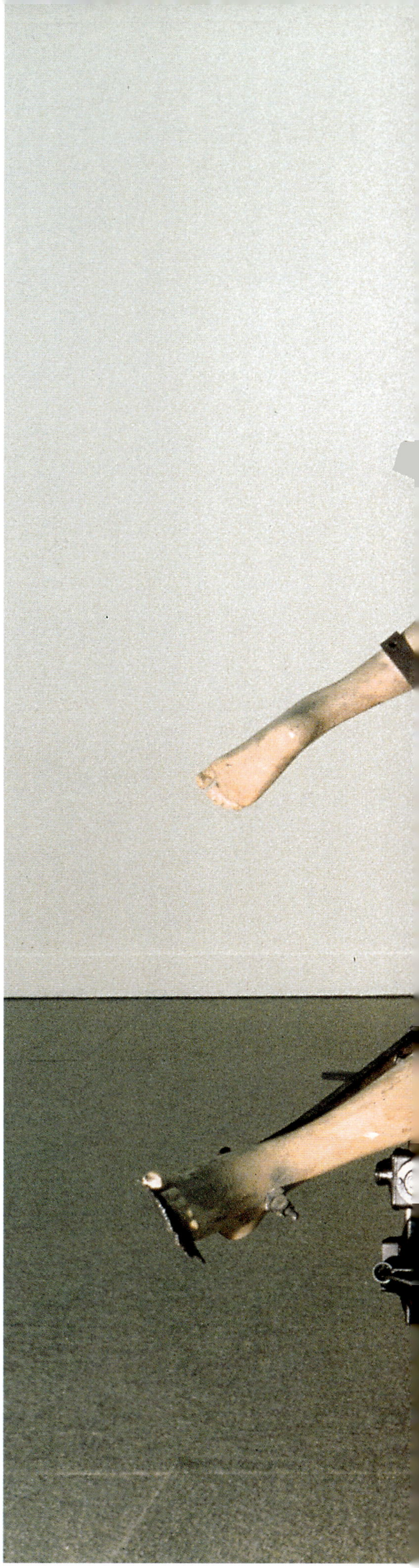

36 *Dissecting Machine*, 1965

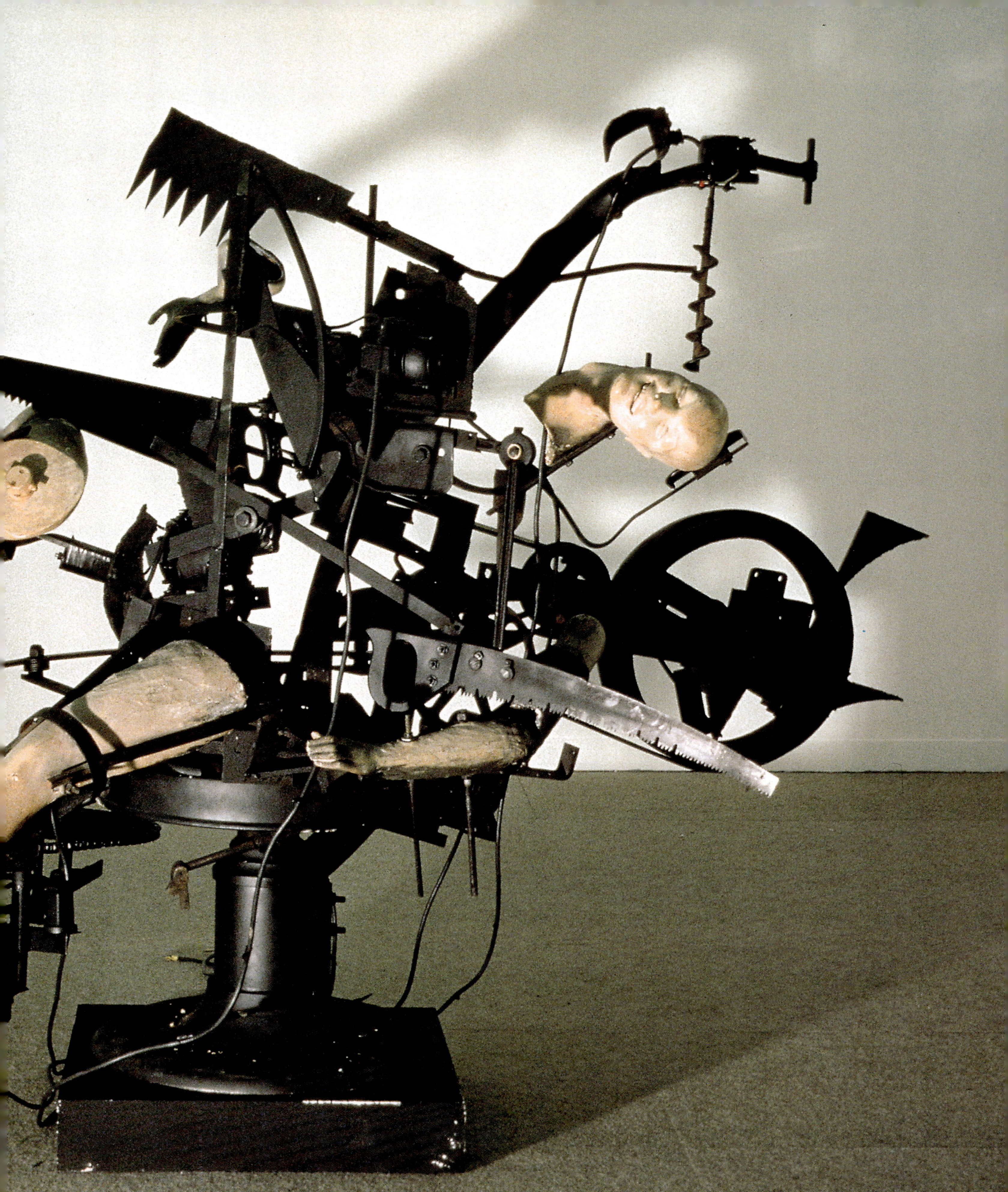

'After all, it's the woman in a man that makes him a poet'

1966–70

For the overture to Roland Petit's *In Praise of Folly*, named after the work by the philosopher Erasmus, Tinguely built a machine propelled by a pedalling dancer (fig. 38). The relief was lightweight, so that it could be raised easily. The framework was built of aluminium, and the wooden wheels were specially cut from narrow planks. All of the elements were painted black. Gutters built of wire tipped and tilted over as a ball passed through them, a guillotine-like aluminium form slashed the air, and the wheels, with their variegated spokes, rotated slowly. The elegant choreography of this mechanical ballet was sharply silhouetted against a brightly lit white backdrop.[1]

Pontus Hulten invited Tinguely and de Saint Phalle to Stockholm together with Per Olof Ultvedt, Claes Oldenburg and Martial Raysse for a collaborative improvisation to be shown from June to September 1966. When the latter two artists cancelled, it was up to de Saint Phalle, Ultvedt and Tinguely to come up with an idea. In the end a proposal of Hulten's excited their imaginations. He suggested building a construction in the shape of a 'Nana', one of de Saint Phalle's female figures. It took the three artists and a number of volunteers recruited by Hulten five weeks of hard work to finish the construction, which they christened *Hon* (Swedish for 'She') and subtitled *A Cathedral*.[2] One of the volunteers was Rico Weber, a Swiss art student who became the assistant, collaborator and friend of de Saint Phalle and Tinguely.

Hon was a gigantic pregnant female figure with huge breasts who reclined on her back with her legs wide open (fig. 37). Arriving at the museum, visitors felt like Gulliver arriving in Brobdingnag. The female giantess was entered through the 'portal of life', with traffic controlled by red and green lights. From there, the public could explore her corpus from belly to bosom. The sculpture, like a zeppelin, had a three-level, solid steel armature. Wire mesh shaped the outer shell, which was covered with an envelope of multi-layered pieces of treated fabric. De Saint Phalle had painted the whole figure in brilliant colors. Inside one of the breasts was a soft-drink bar com-

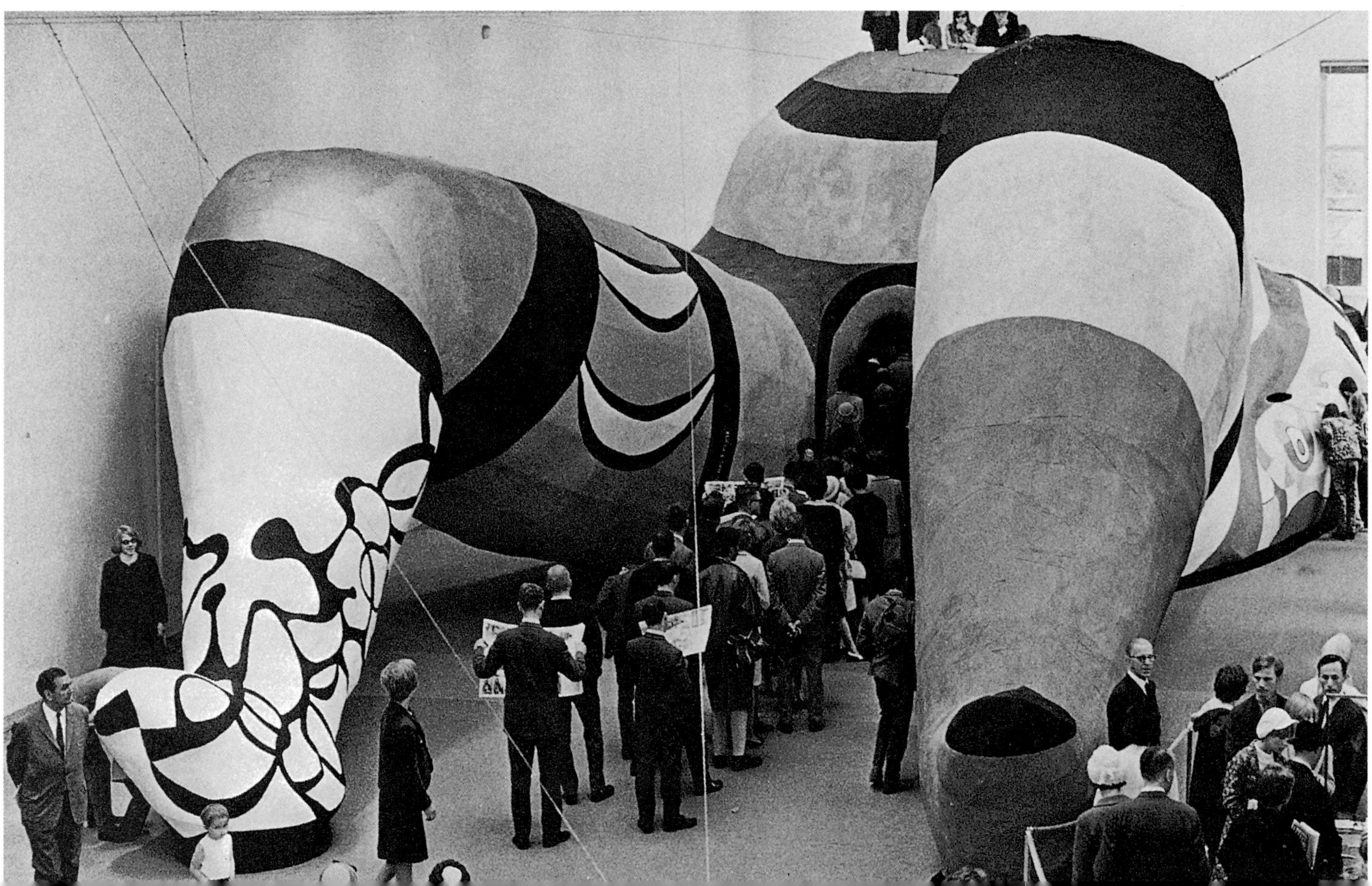

37 *Hon — A Cathedral*, at the Moderna Museet, Stockholm, 1966, by Niki de Saint Phalle, Per Olof Ultvedt and Tinguely

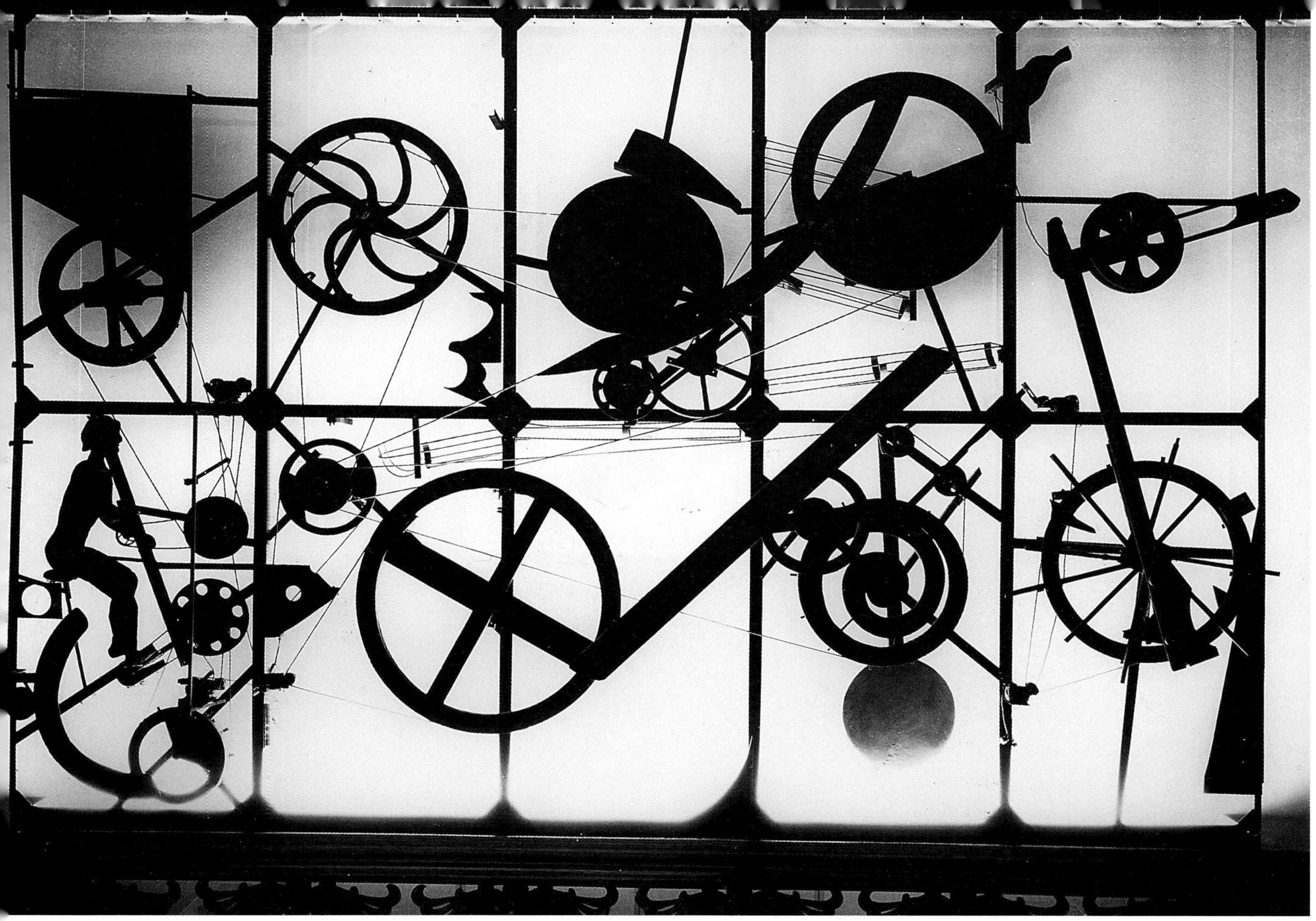

38 *In Praise of Folly* mechanical stage curtain, 1966

plete with automatic drink dispenser and barman. A bottle-crushing mechanism disposed of garbage. The navel-terrace offered a panoramic view, and the movie theatre showed Greta Garbo's debut in film, consisting of a short and daring swim. *Hon*'s left leg was intended for lovers whose conversations were broadcast through hidden microphones to the crowd at the bar. Art viewing was quick and cheerful as visitors tobogganed down one thigh past a gallery of fakes. There were hostesses, as in Disneyland, and a public phone, in addition to a number of mechanisms that Ultvedt and Tinguely contributed. Their whirring and clanking mingled with the solemn sound of organ music by Bach. *Hon* had a huge body and not much of a head and lasted only as long as the period of the exhibit, a paradoxical counterpart to Egyptian or nineteenth-century gigantism.[3] De Saint Phalle recalled: 'She was like a grand fertility goddess reclining comfortably in her immensity and generously receiving thousands of visitors which she absorbed, devoured, and gave birth to again.'[4] Indeed, *Hon* corresponded to the aesthetics of carnivalesque-grotesque realism as described by Mikhail Bakhtin: 'Contrary to modern canons, the grotesque body is not separated from the rest of the world. The stress is laid on those parts of the body that are open to the outside world, that is, the parts through which the world enters the body or emerges from it.'[5] Inevitably, his intentions were misread, with particularly unenlightened attacks coming from Swiss critics who had only seen the press release. They decried the work as 'pure pornography', a 'monstrous obscenity', as heralding 'the age of the swine'.[6]

Tinguely's later collaborative works, such as the permanent *Head* (fig. 46) and the temporary *Crocrodrome* (1977; fig. 53), share many features with *Hon*. In 1970, he built *La Vittoria* (*The Victory*; fig. 39), a masculine counterpart of *Hon* (fig. 37).

Tinguely realised the cultural importance of people at play, of feasting and of merry-making. He was a great instigator of feasts, of those moments when the individual merges with the group and when people live moment-

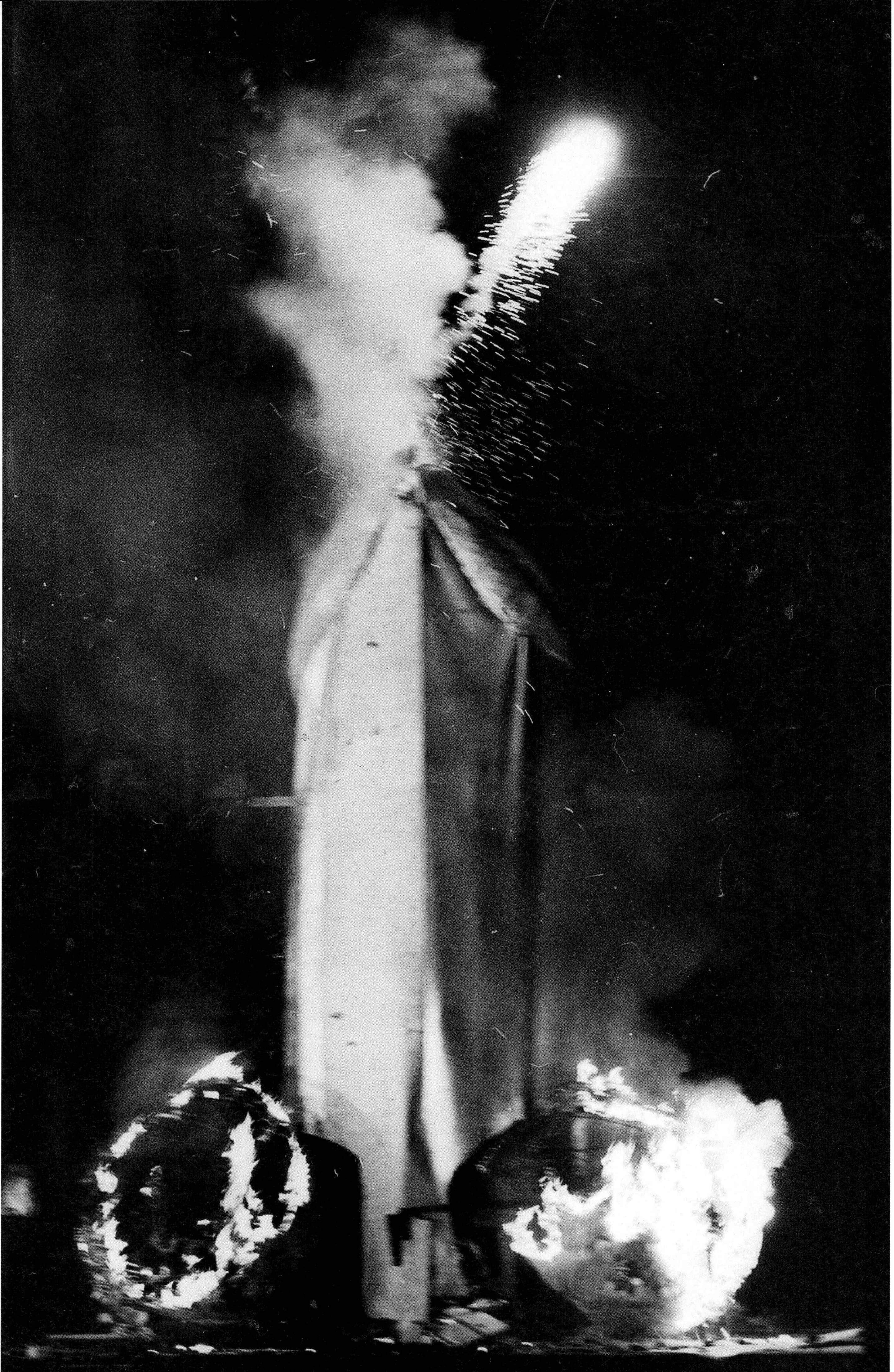

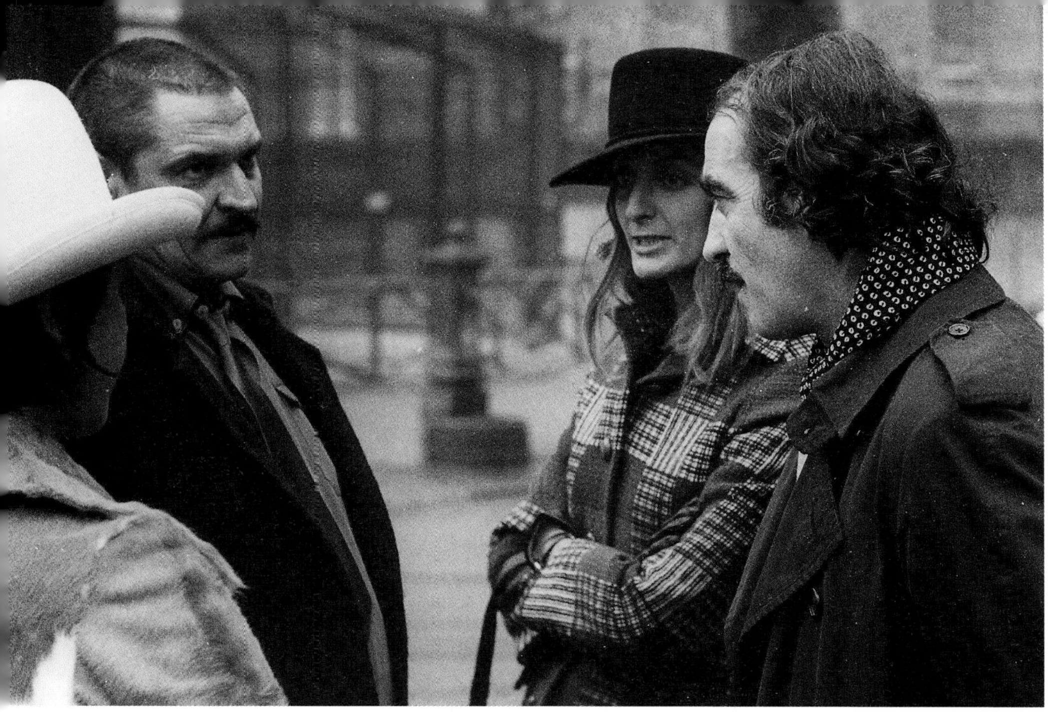

Tinguely with Micheline Gygax and Ursi and Bernhard Luginbühl, Milan, 1970

◁ *The Victory* during self-destruction

39 *La Vittoria (The Victory)* in the Piazza del Duomo, Milan, 1970 (the covered sculpture before the happening) ▷

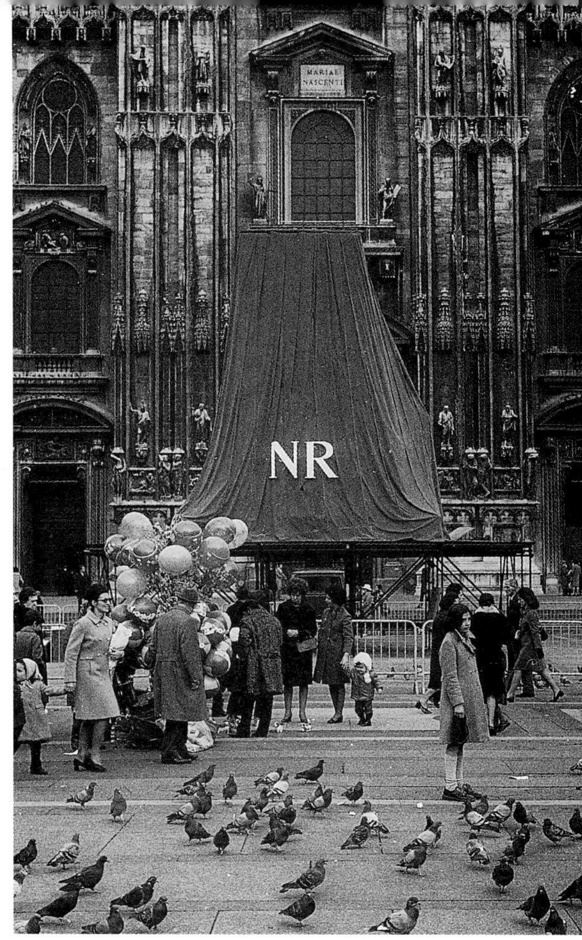

The Victory starting to self-destruct

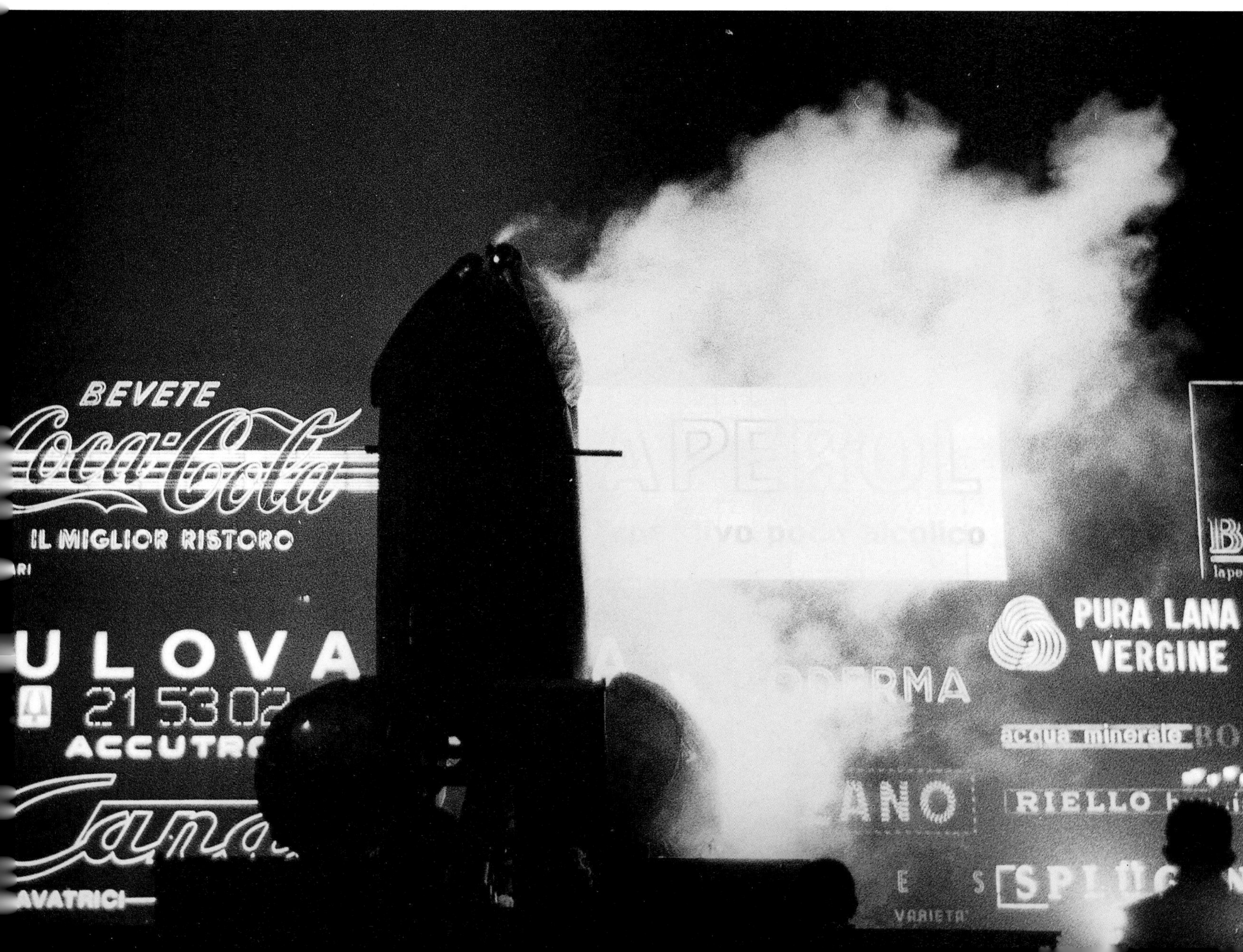

arily in parallel worlds with parallel systems. In November 1970, he built *The Victory*, a temporary sculptural spectacle in the form of a monumental penis (fig. 39). Tinguely's contribution to the 10th-anniversary celebration of New Realism, this image harked back to the phallic revelries of the Dionysiac festivals, when the penis was worshipped as a symbol of regenerative power. Tinguely emphasised the Dionysiac theme by decorating the testicles with gilded plastic grapes, bananas and pine-cones. In our culture, sexuality has been eroticised and associated with the cult of radical individualism. Agricultural societies however, relate human sexuality to the fruitfulness of the earth, and it was in this spirit that Tinguely placed his fertility symbol in the Piazza del Duomo in Milan. His image of masculine potency burned itself out, literally and metaphorically, in 30 minutes. The destruction of *The Victory* was the symbolic killing of New Realism as well as a spectacular auto-da-fé.

Tinguely intended this work to be a satire on masculine enterprises—the patriarchal Catholic Church, rifles, cannons, pistols, knives and missiles, as well as attempts at space travel.[7] By affixing the logo *NR* for (*Nouveau Réalisme*) onto the cardinal-red curtain draped over the scaffolding built around the phallus, he evoked the letters *I. N. R. I.* (*Iesus Nazarenus Rex Iudaeorum*) on the cross of the Crucifixion. Tinguely also chose the lacy façade of Milan's Duomo to serve as his backdrop, implicating the Catholic Church in his spectacle. Tinguely's act was in keeping with the spirit of such old ecclesiastical customs as the

Tinguely installing *Requiem for a Dead Leaf*, Montreal, 1967

40 *Requiem for a Dead Leaf*, 1967

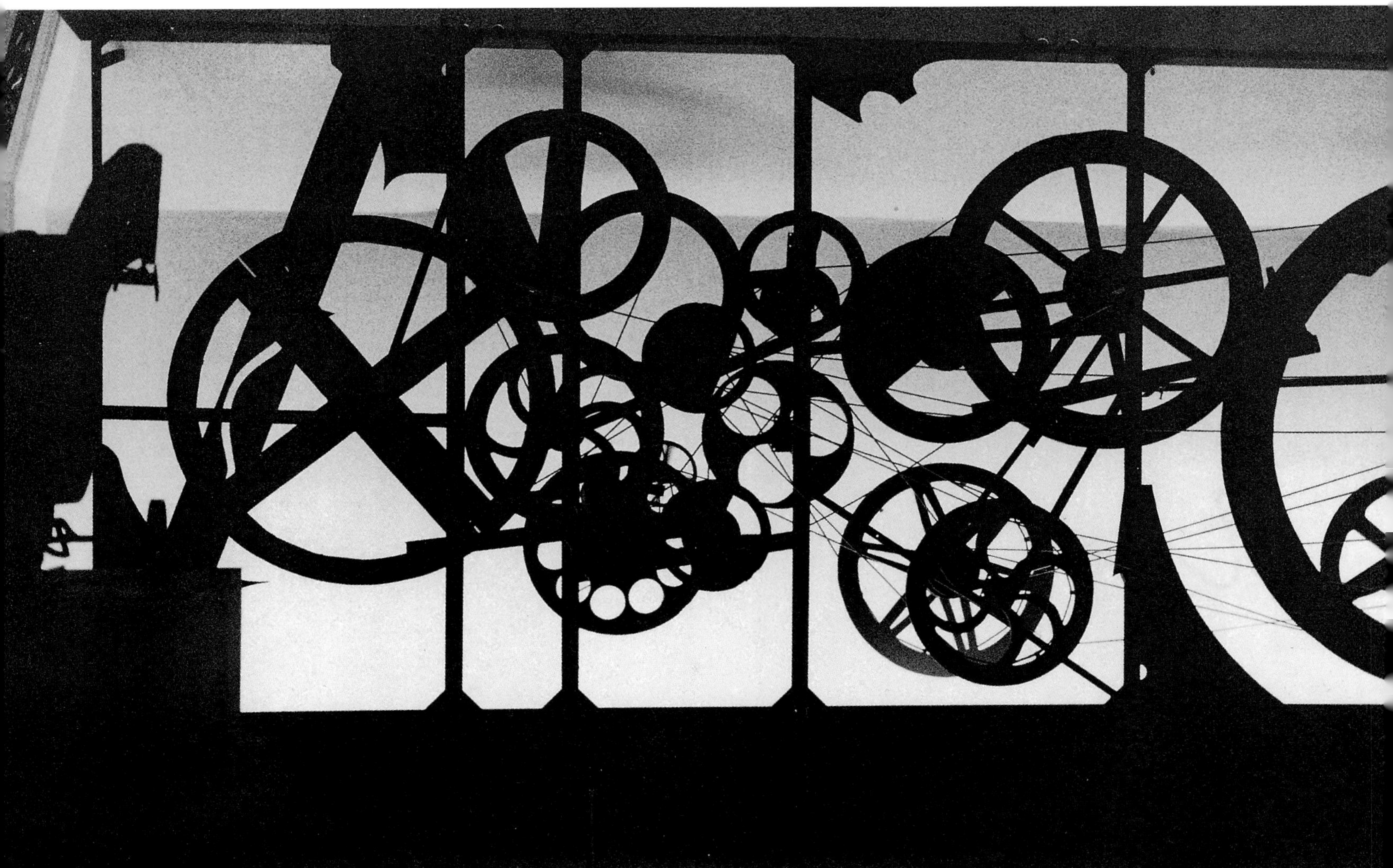

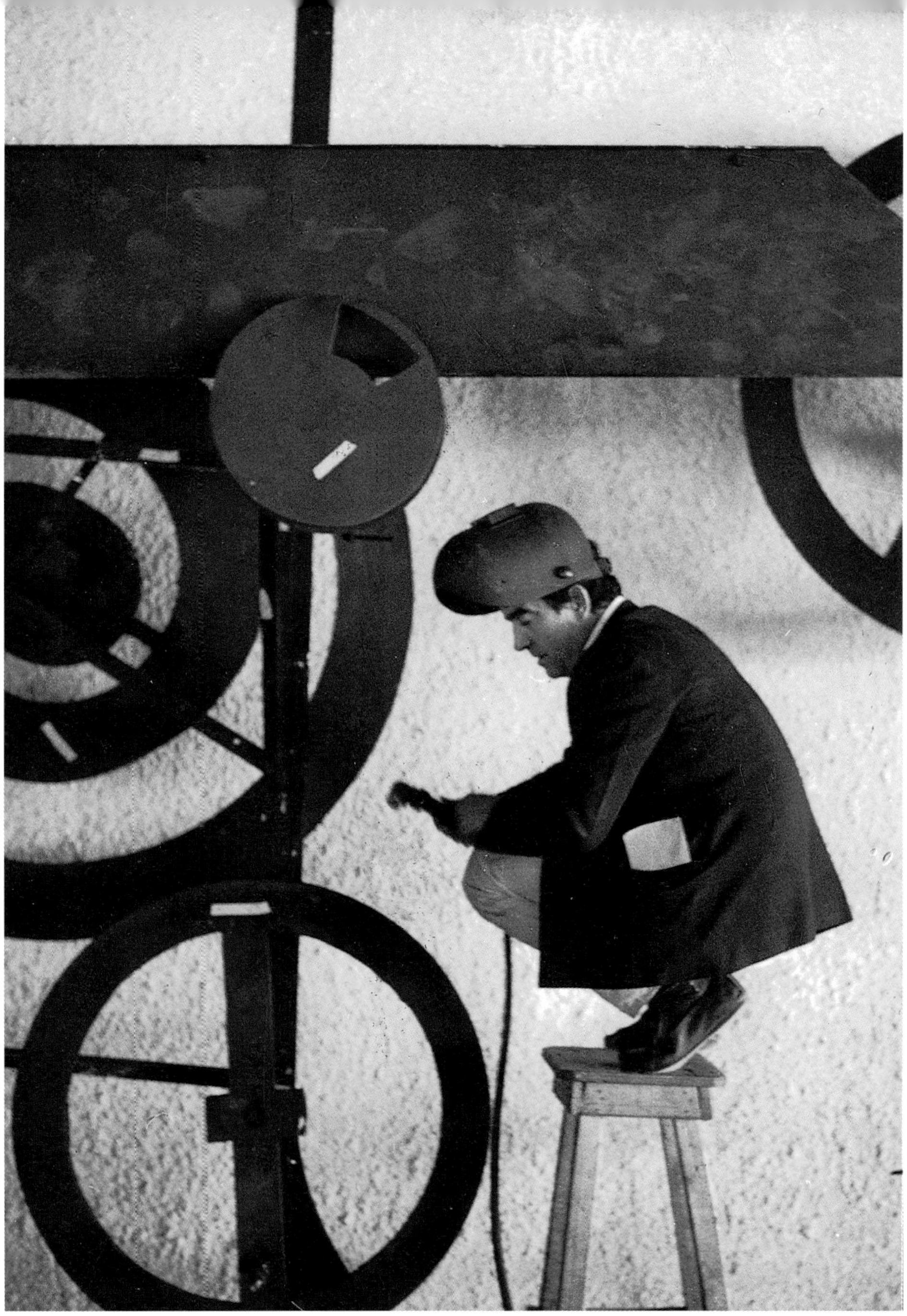

ideas for an official commission he had just received from the government, this time for the Swiss Pavilion at the 1967 World's Fair in Montreal. He said that he planned to build into it the motion of a train.[10]

In April 1967, Tinguely and de Saint Phalle were in Montreal. At the Swiss Pavilion, Tinguely assembled a long relief entitled *Requiem for a Dead Leaf*, 'a farcical title, and anti-title', as he put it (fig. 40). The combination of large wheels and a couple of connecting bars indeed resembled the driving gear of a steam locomotive. The work was in some aspects similar to the relief built for *In Praise of Folly* with its silhouetted, black geometric forms and wheels for the most part fabricated by the artist out of lightweight materials. In the later relief, Tinguely employed fewer moving parts. The noise was lessened, and what the piece lost in playfulness it made up for in solemnity. Motion originates at one point only and spreads via rubber belts from one set of wheels to another, from left to right, resulting in the bottom right corner in the rotation of a metal leaf painted white. The artist stated:

> *[The white leaf is] the only psychological element. I always have in my machines a human factor. I do not want to make movement for the sake of movement. I want to bring the machine back to man. I like geometric forms, but I prefer my relief with the leaf, a small interrogation mark. I like the strange aspect, that which doesn't fit the expected.*[11]

Feast of Fools, with its irreverent juxtaposition of the sacred and the obscene. His work suggested the carnivalesque-grotesque spirit of the inverted world, in which deviance is part of festive behaviour. As with Tinguely's other sculptures made to be destroyed, this one satisfied what Michael Gibson called 'the infantile joy of destruction [that] outrages an instinctive desire for permanence'.[8] The Milanese authorities buried the affair in their own way—Tinguely's spectacle went virtually unnoticed in the press. For them, it should not have taken place, therefore it had not taken place.[9]

Between 1 October and 12 November 1966, Tinguely had his first solo exhibition in Zurich, at Gimpel & Hannover Galerie. The works in the exhibit, all dating from between 1965 and 1966, included a number of anthropomorphic and zoomorphic sculptures. These were statuesque and vertical, and their movements were erotic. At the opening of the Zurich show, Tinguely discussed his

In addition to the commission from the Swiss government, Tinguely had been solicited by the French authorities to submit a proposal together with de Saint Phalle for a work to go on the roof of the French Pavilion. Their proposal for a collaboration was accepted

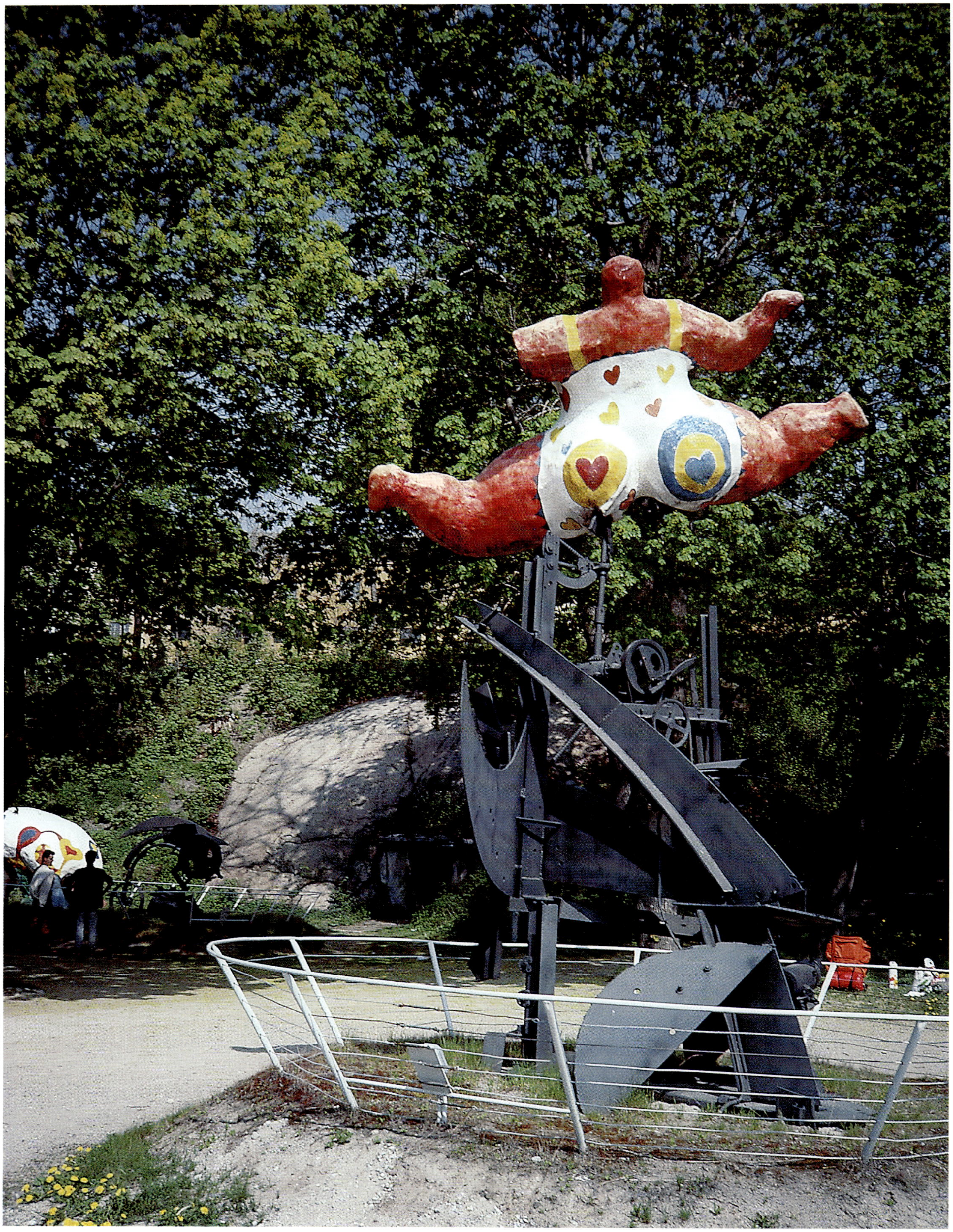

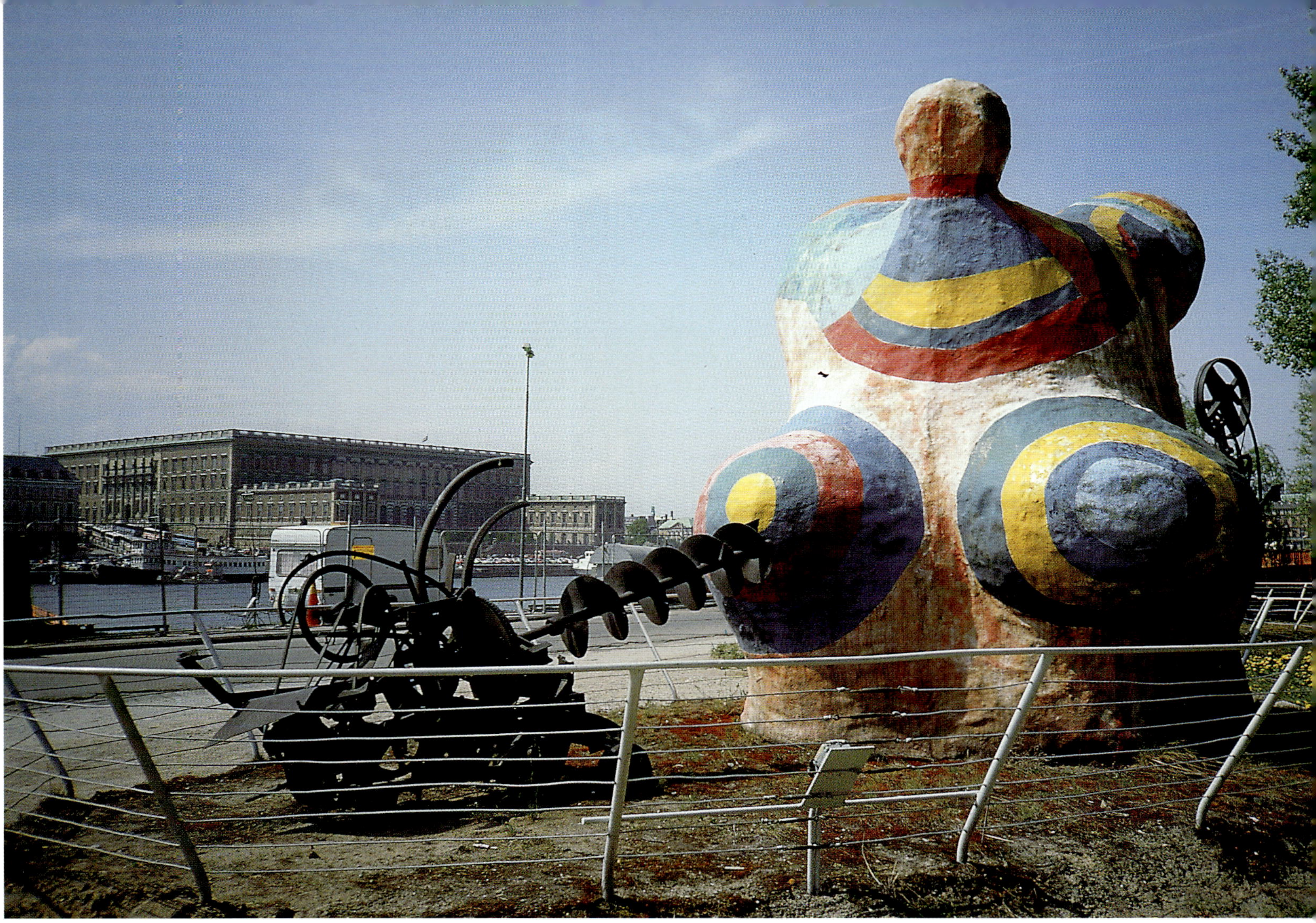

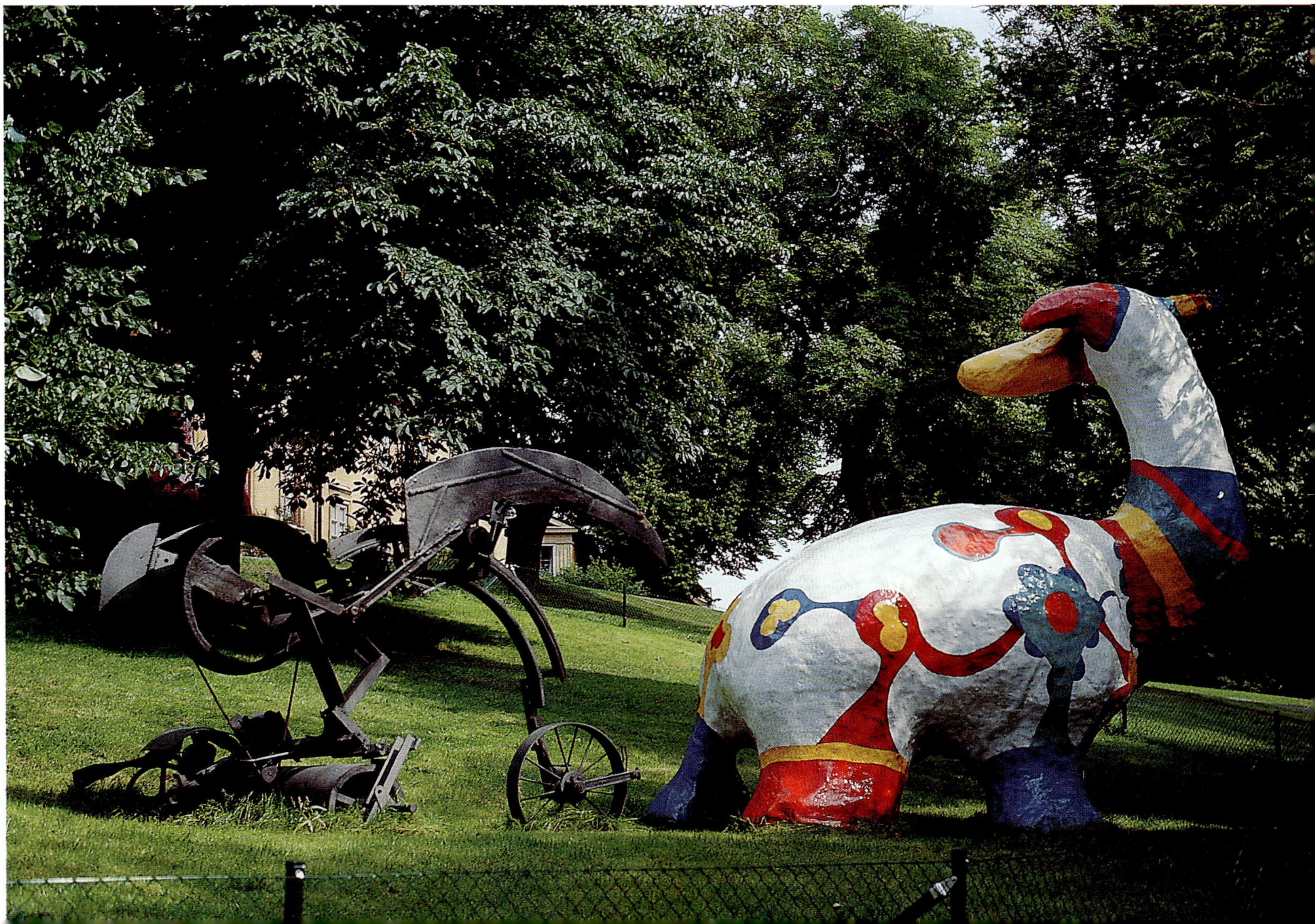

41 Jean Tinguely and Niki de Saint Phalle, *The Fantastic Paradise*, 1966-67, from a group of 9 figures

◁◁ *The Pierced Nana* and *The Machine*

◁ *The Fat Nana* and *Drill*

◁ *Gentle Creature* and *Rotozaza*

Tree-Nana and *Madwoman*

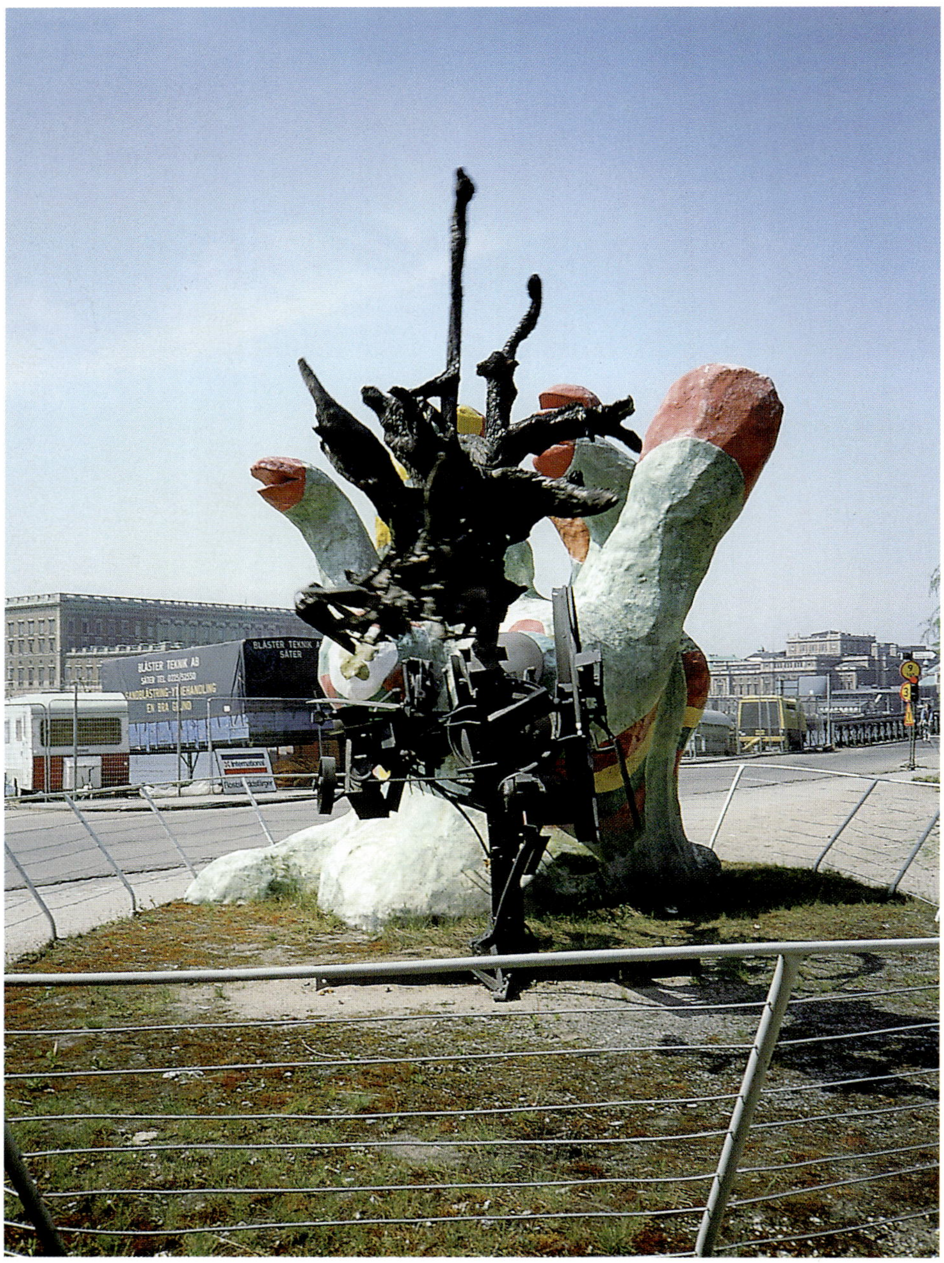

and they built *The Fantastic Paradise* (fig. 41).

De Saint Phalle created six overblown creatures in polyester painted in cheerful lollipop colours to interact with Tinguely's six black iron and steel mechanisms. Three more figures by de Saint Phalle completed the ensemble: the *Flower* the size of a tree, the athletic *Nana* standing on her head and the *Bather*. Another *Nana* was impaled on a spike and rotated to be admired from all sides like a trophy by a sort of giant weathervane that Tinguely contributed. *The Fat Nana* confronts Tinguely's *Drill*, a huge spiral aimed at her considerable buttocks, which are painted like targets. Tinguely's *Madwoman* caresses the breast of a bosomy *Tree-Nana* with a disc and teases it with a number of pitchforks while madly wiggling its own large, tree-root tail. Tinguely's *Rasputin*, a chariot on rails driven by a profusion of small and large wheels, is engaged in the conquest of *Baby Monster*, de Saint Phalle's elephantine dragon. Her chubby *Gentle Creature* is pushed on its rump by the wing-shaped part of Tinguely's *Rotozaza* and is 'expelled' in a rather gentle fashion from this 'paradise'. A giant *Bird* stands still while a towering machine, *The Pecker*, has it all wrong and pecks upwards. *Fantastic Paradise*, a fresh look at an old theme, the Garden of Love, is as erotic as an eighteenth-century fête galante. At the close of the Montreal fair in November, the exhibit was shipped to Buffalo, where the two artists set up their sculptures in the courtyard of the Albright-Knox Art Gallery. From Buffalo, the exhibition was moved to New York City and then to Stockholm, where it was installed on the island of Skeppsholmen in May 1971. On that occasion, Tinguely completed the *Paradise* with a *Fountain of Youth*, a water sculpture to connect the two bathers. In 1989, the ensemble was moved again, to a site next to the Moderna Museet.[12]

During an interview with Alain Jouffroy the year before, Tinguely had talked about his project to build a large machine with a complicated mechanism, a machine that would 'play with people, that [would] take care and touch the public'.[13] *Rotozaza I* premièred at Alexander Iolas's Paris

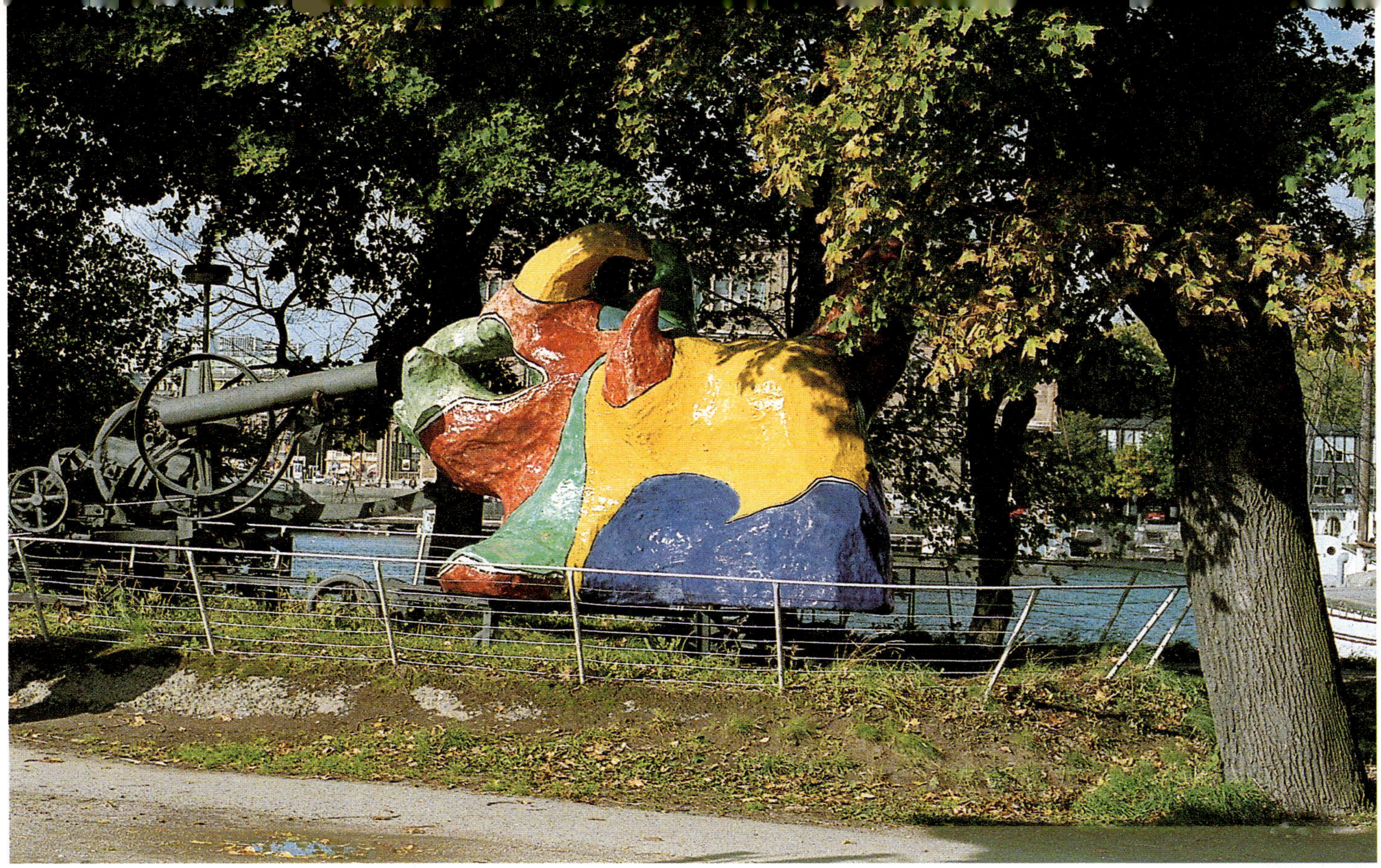

Rasputin and *Baby Monster*

gallery on 9 June and was the main attraction among the 20 sculptures included in the travelling museum exhibition of Tinguely and Bernhard Luginbühl's works.[11] *Rotozaza I* is a voracious ball-eater that has to be fed by the viewer (fig. 43). Balls disappear into its elephantine trunk only to be thrown back at the viewer, who becomes part of the machine's ceaseless and furious play while being encouraged to release excess energy. Tinguely communicated his view of life by requiring the viewer to play a part in an absurd predicament, thereby perhaps discovering more dangerous Rotozazas in his or her own life.

Tinguely's show of 17 works in Lucerne included *Rotozaza I* and a new work, *Hannibal II* (fig. 42). As in *Requiem for a Dead Leaf*, the mechanisms suggest the driving gear of a steam locomotive. In fact, in this machine the heavyweight engine is linked to a smaller one that actually moves on tracks and manoeuvres like a train. All parts are again painted a matt black. The main 'chariot' is covered with a big hood cut from a sheet of metal. Its body is an intricate combination of variously sized wheels. The thick, long chain dangling from its side and a tube like the barrel of cannon are motifs of bondage and war; they establish a mood of threat and aggression. The smaller 'chariot' is linked to its 'Mother' by a connecting rod attached to one of the larger wheels. It carries on its platform a version of Tinguely's erotic 'Eos' sculptures: a long, crescent-shaped piece of metal repeatedly poking at the air. The chaotic aspect of *Hannibal I* and the first of these 'Chariot' mechanisms, *Marilyn*, has given way to clearer forms and a slower, more limited choreography of movement. *Hannibal II* is larger and heavier and the pointless repetition of its movements seems particularly obsessive and impotent. Although at the time it seemed impossible to integrate such an attention-grabbing object into a public collection, *Hannibal II* was the first major work by Tinguely to be purchased by an institution in his home town. In 1971, while it was on exhibition in the foyer of the Komödie, its sounds became the jumping-off point for the pianist Jürg Wyttenbach, who improvised music to accompany them. The public, who had been invited to bring their instruments, joined in.[15] On loan from the Verkehrsverein Basel, *Hannibal II* has made its home at the Kunstmuseum in Basel since the late 1970s; its noisy machine life is viewer-controlled.

On 13 October 1967, the Basel *National-Zeitung* published Tinguely's article 'Art is Revolution'. The article, which included his Düsseldorf manifesto of 1959, was otherwise less didactic than his earlier tract, corresponding to the non-linear, poetic verbal style that was the linguistic equivalent of his machines in motion. In the text, he described an idea:

I would love to decorate the windows of the Globus store. I would build a really marvellous machine, something like a scorpion, a proud, black monster—and there would be a conveyor that would bring two or three thousand teapots a day to the machine with mechanical reliability, complete regularity (one every 80 cm), and whoops and crash, the tea-pots would be neatly destroyed, annihilated, for weeks on end (until the shop would be bankrupt). And there would be a man in the window as well, an old Chinese, who would sweep up the bits and tip them tidily through a slot in the wall at one side, put there specially for the purpose.[16]

Tinguely realised two versions of the shop-window project. The first, *Rotozaza II*, was built and demonstrated at New York University's Loeb Student Center on 11 December 1967. The occasion was an international congress of futurologists entitled 'Vision 67: Survival and Growth: The Second World Congress on Communications in a Changing World'. About three hundred participants attended the three-part event, entitled *Confrontation*. The programme featured two films by François de Menil, a documentary of the building and destruction of *Hon*, and *The Tragic Destiny of Lorenzo Bandini*, a film about a racing-car disaster. Third on the program was Tinguely's systematic beer-bottle smasher.[17] Charlotte Willard reported what was clearly the highlight of the evening:

Beer bottles were suspended on a line and were dragged up on the trough till they were brought under the hammer. The hammer went bang, the bottle was shattered with a great explosion of foaming beer and glass (a screen in front of the operation protected the audience) to much applause and laughter. There were groans when the beer bottles escaped the hammer, applause when they did not. Not that anyone was anti-beer, but rather they were for smashings.[18]

Tinguely then escorted to centre stage an elderly Chinese man equipped with a broom and a dustpan who attempted to clean up the mess.[19] Clarice Rivers made an appearance, chanting to the accompaniment of a trombonist 'Too many telephones; too many cars; too many cigars; too many guns; too much of everything'. Excluded from her litany was 'too much sex,' which her husband, Larry Rivers, portrayed on stage, 'wearing a golden phallus and doing push-ups imitating the act of love. Love against destruction?' Willard wondered.

42 *Hannibal II*, 1967

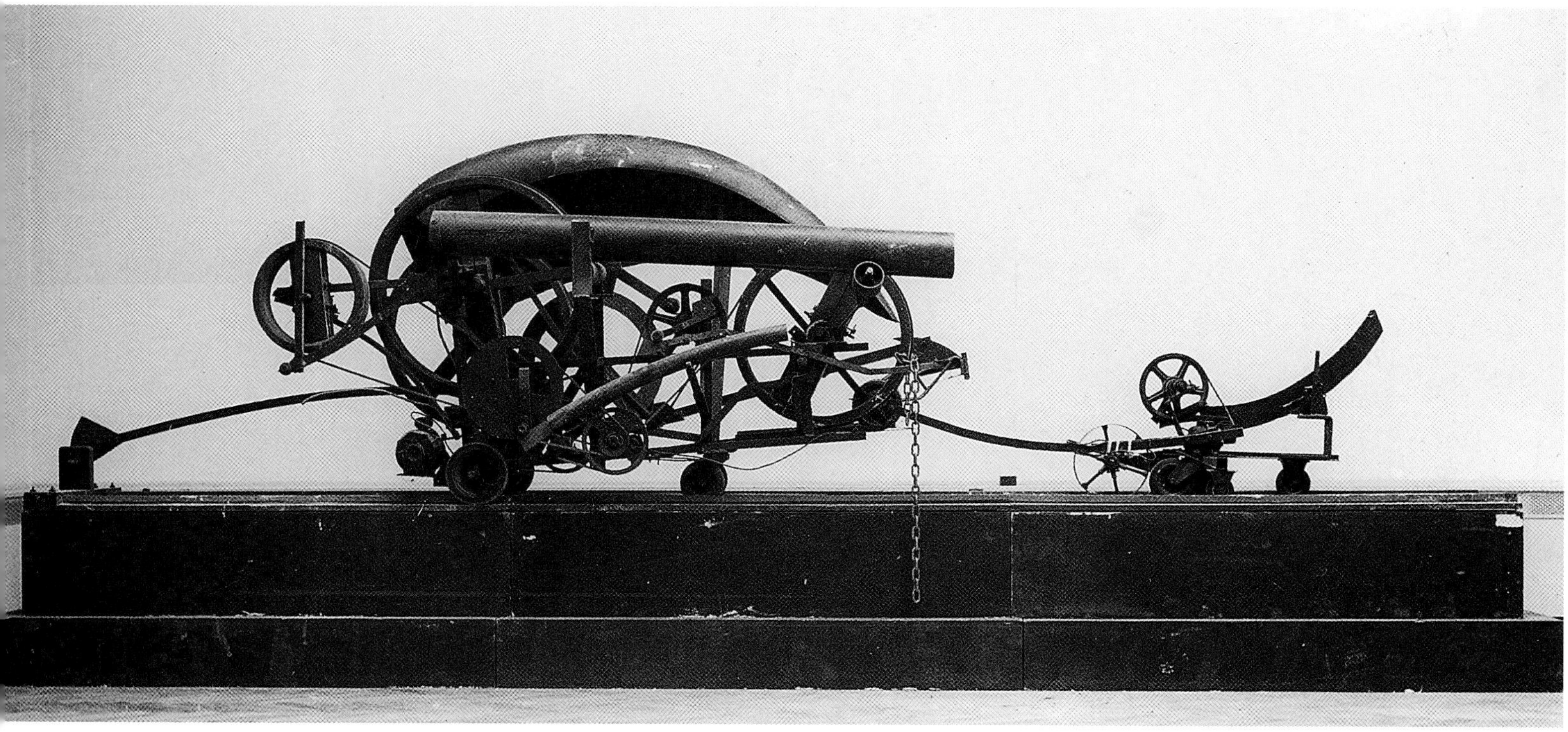

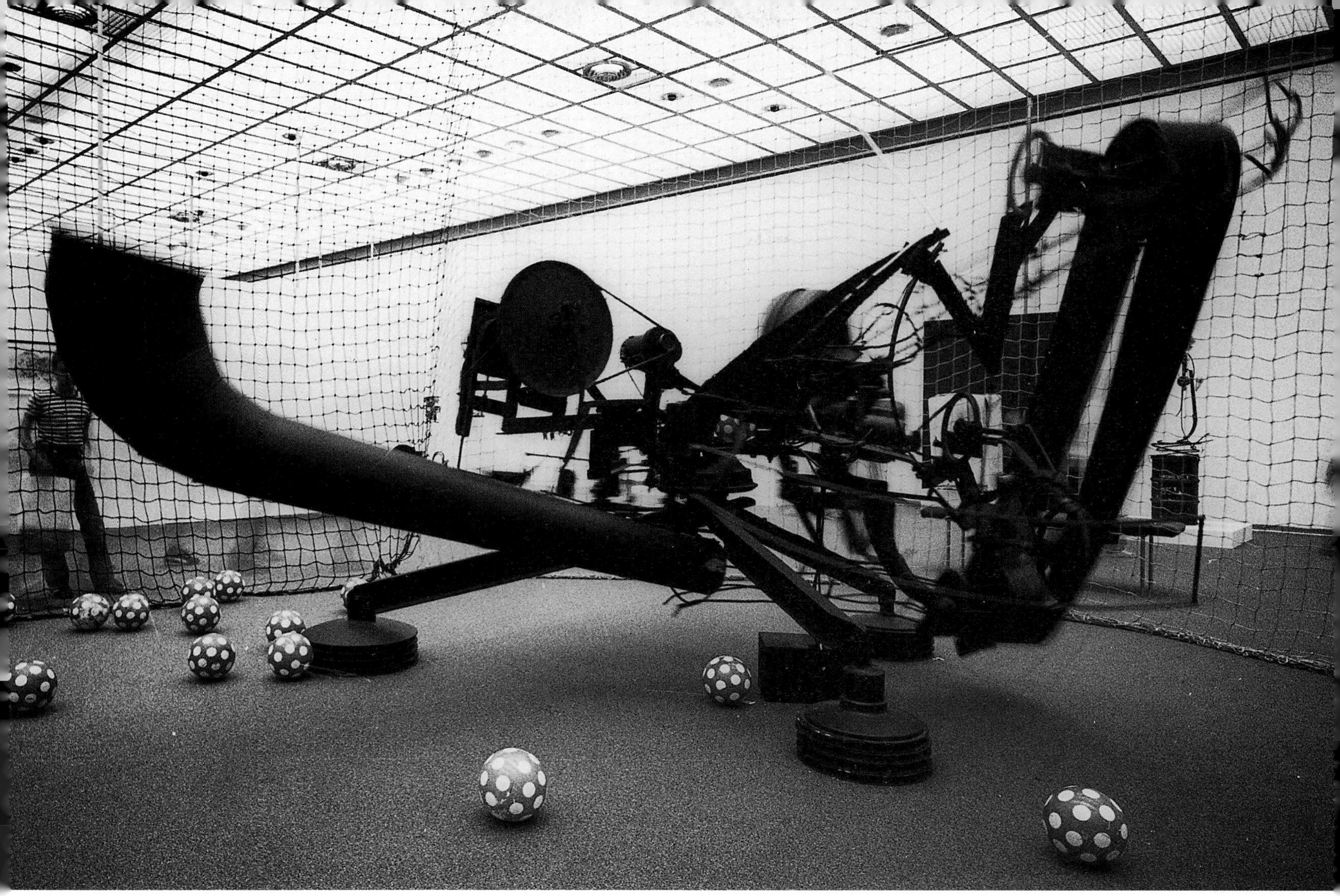

43 *Rotozaza I*, 1967

Tinguely situated the 'problem of consumerism ... at the point from which goods are distributed, namely the supermarkets and the department stores, and that's why I wanted to build my machine in a display window of a large store'.[20] *Potozaza III*, built in October 1969, destroyed approximately 10 plates per minute while it operated in the windows of the Loeb department store in Berne. Tinguely would have preferred the mechanism to crush examples of Switzerland's finest industries, such as watches or the teapots mentioned in his article or straw boaters, like those worn by Maurice Chevalier, objects that combined consumerism with romanticism. He wanted something associated with bourgeois ceremonial behaviour, but such alternatives were too costly. Victor Loeb, an enlightened art collector whom Tinguely had finally won over to the project, searched for suitable goods to be destroyed. He even tried to buy defective stock from one of the leading Swiss porcelain manufacturers. However, the manager refused to sell even defective plates when he learned that they would be smashed publicly by an artist's contraption. Ambassador Dr Paul P. Jolles remembered that Loeb, after great difficulty, finally acquired a sufficient stock of plates, and about twelve thousand were smashed by the machine's huge hammer.[21]

'Dreams are the best organisers'

1968–74

Between 1968 and 1974, Tinguely participated in numerous thematic exhibitions in Europe and North America,[1] and in 1969, he returned to Japan to participate in the 'International Sculptors' Symposium for Public Space' in Osaka. During his two-week stay in October, he built the 'Chariot'-type *Cenotaph for a Kamikaze* (fig. 44).[2] Technically and formally, the work is similar to *Hannibal II*: a main body of assembled wheels covered by a hood runs on tracks, with its appendage straining at the leash. However, here the metal is unpainted and rusted, the hood is broader, more turtle-like, and the wheels appear to have been assembled in a more haphazard fashion. Animal-like, the sculpture crouches on a low podium, ferociously extending and contracting its members. The deep rumbling clatter and scraping noises add to the impression of brutal aggression and stubborn fanaticism. *Cenotaph* is also similar to the 'Meta' sculptures such as *Meta II* (fig. 45), commissioned for Tinguely's first solo retrospective in Paris, at the Centre National d'Art Contemporain (12 May–5 July 1971).[3] Such works seem to incarnate the machinery of war that tramples dreams of freedom. Tinguely agreed with Gaston Bachelard, who had written that science is often blamed for faults whose roots are not in the will to know but in the will to evil, a will always ready to seize arms.[4]

In the late sixties, Tinguely began to spend more time in Switzerland, as he had met and fallen in love with Micheline Gygax, a Swiss writer, with whom he had a son, Milan, in 1973. Through the good offices of his car-racing friend Joseph Siffert, in 1968 Tinguely acquired L'Aigle Noir, an old farmhouse that had been a bar in Neyruz, a small village near Fribourg. Its barn, a spacious, unheated room attached to the main house, served as his studio. This remained Tinguely's home base, together with Milan and Micheline, until his death. Tinguely's marriage to Niki de Saint Phalle, actually a good-bye present, took place

44 *Cenotaph for a Kamikaze*, 1969

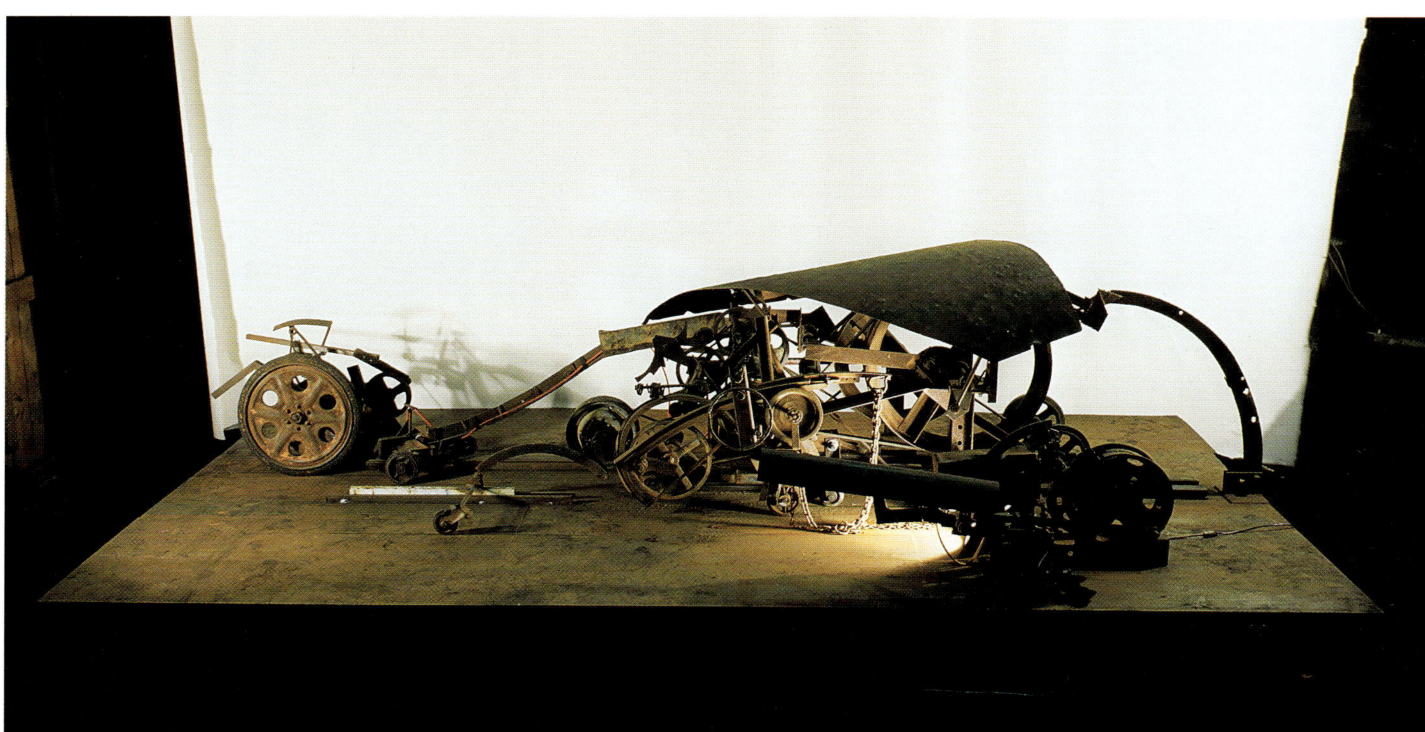

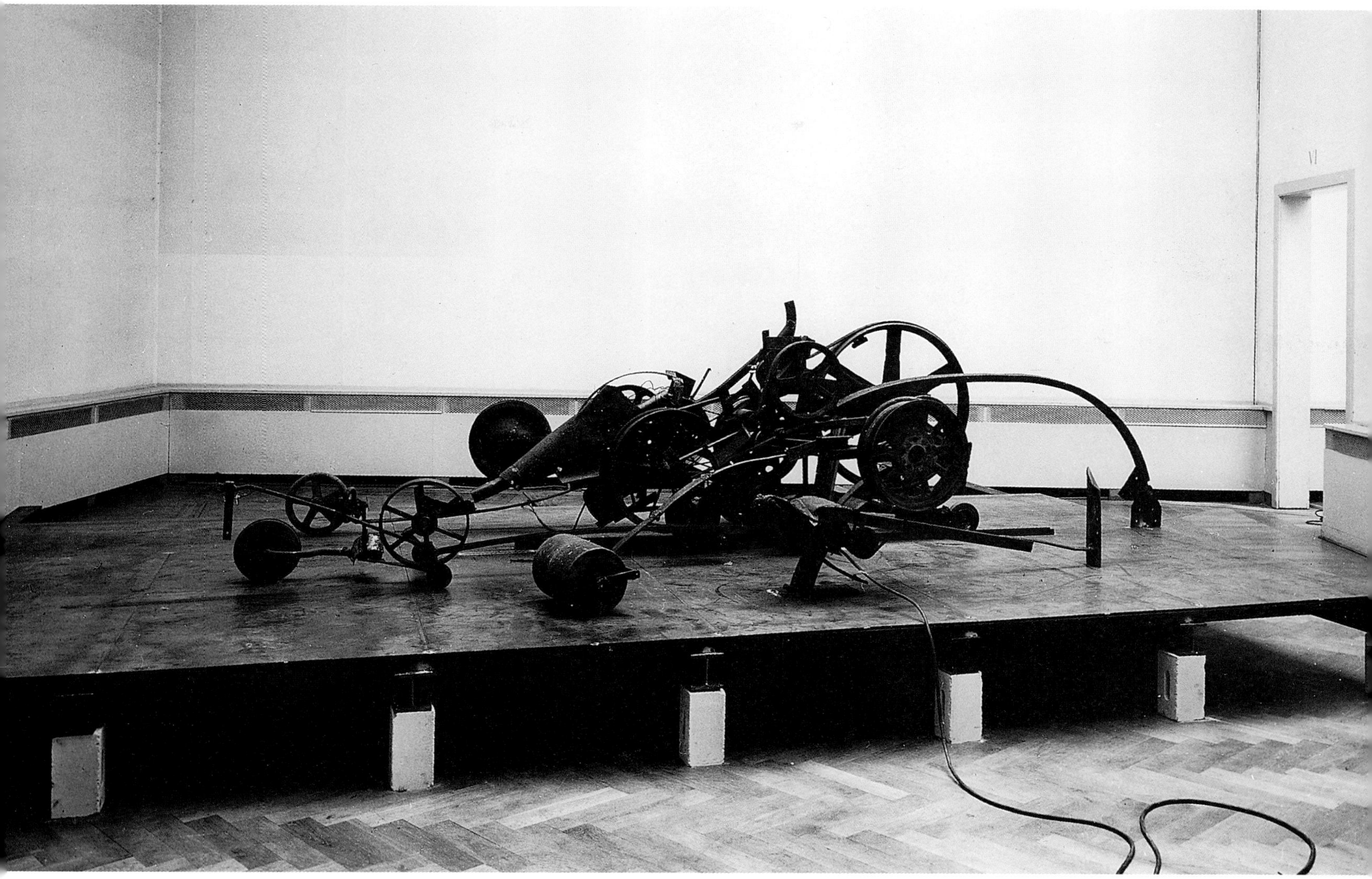

45 *Meta II*, 1971

in Soisy-sur-Ecole in 1971 and was an official seal of their partnership. The two artists remained close and continued to collaborate on major projects.

During the summer of 1968, Tinguely and Bernhard Luginbühl conceived a large-scale project, the *Gigantoleum—Cultural Station*, which combined the ideas of similar but unexecuted collaborative projects.[5] Having presented a maquette and written proposal to the President of Berne, Luginbühl noted wryly: 'Our project got stuck in the thick fur of the Bernese bear.'[6] Tinguely did not abandon the idea of a monumental collaborative work, however, one in which '[n]othing was for sale, nothing was for dealers or for museums'.[7] One day, Tinguely surprised Luginbühl with the news that he was building the head of a giant who was buried up to his shoulders in the ground and that de Saint Phalle had prepared a model of the face.

The *Head*, also called *Monster* or *Cyclops* was Tinguely's most ambitious undertaking (fig. 46). It was erected over a period of several years, intermittently, like a cathedral, unknown except to a few intimates. The construction site had about it something of a medieval *Bauhütte*, with strenuous physical work being accomplished by simple ropes and pulley and dogged moral devotion. Luginbühl, together with his entire family, contributed actively in the beginning, and Tinguely also 'borrowed' Luginbühl's assistant, the Swiss artist Paul Wiedmer. Rico Weber also continued to help him, but the sheer monumentality of the task made it necessary for Tinguely to look for a professional locksmith. Joseph Imhof of Solothurn answered Tinguely's advertisement in a Swiss newspaper, which called for a 'competent locksmith and card-player'. Imhof did not realise that his life would henceforth be radically changed. The lovable, humorous 'Seppi', as he was called by 'Jeannot', became the factotum of the Tinguely enterprise.

In 1986 Tinguely took me to see *Head*. Having entered the forest, he continued to drive for a few minutes along the road, turning left suddenly and parking the car. Following him on foot through the underbrush, we could not detect any sign of the work except for a wire fence that blocked the passage. A few more steps, and we emerged into a small clearing. And then we saw it. The sculpture overwhelms not by its monumentality—it peaks at the level of the forest and in a friendly embrace accommodates several trees that grow through it—but because it is so fantastical. From where we stood, the most astonishing sight was a French railway carriage hovering at the height of the treetops as if lifted and placed there by the hand of a giant. It seemed precariously connected to *Head* and as fanciful as a clown's hat. Tinguely explained that it was intended to house the *Windows*, a group of sculptures by Eva Aeppli in memory of the millions of Jews deported in similar freight-cars. The *Head's* features, moulded in concrete, were somewhat hidden behind a scaffolding that added to its mystery. One could make out a single eye, a nose, an open mouth and a long tongue. Then Tinguely and Imhof opened the first in a series of heavy metal doors, one of which was made by Luginbühl,

46 *Head*, 1971-94, at Milly-la-Forêt, near Paris, by Tinguely, Niki de Saint Phalle, Bernhard Luginbühl, Daniel Spoerri, Eva Aeppli, Rico Weber, Joseph Imhof, Paul Wiedmer, Jean-Pierre Reynaud, César, Arman, Larry Rivers, Jesus Raphael Soto and others

Head (under construction)

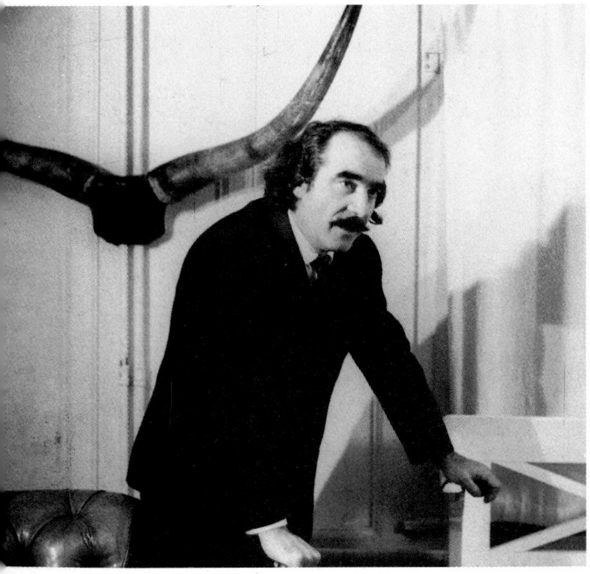

Tinguely at Bernhard Luginbühl's home, Mötschwil, 1971

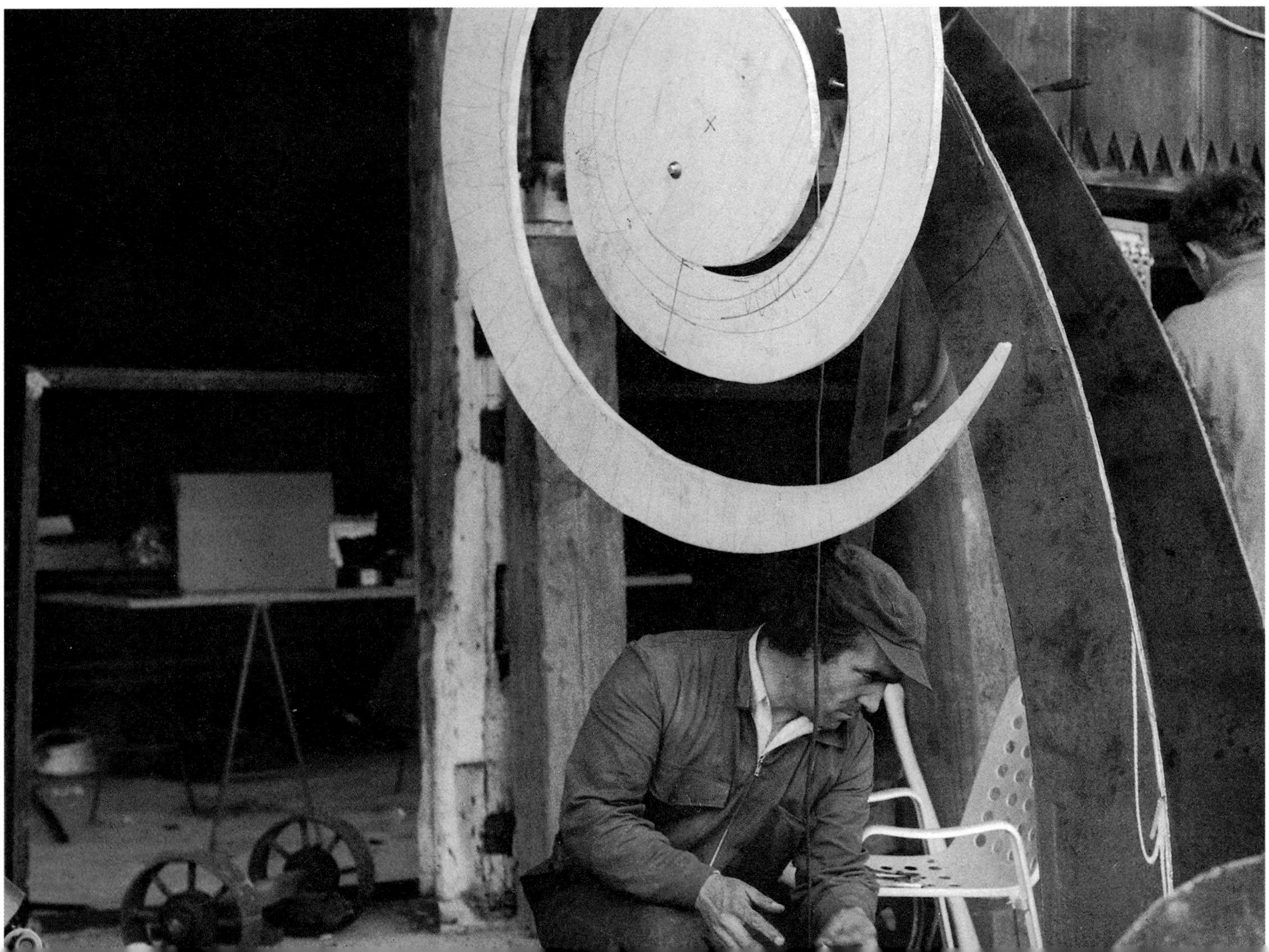

Tinguely in his studio, Neyruz, 1969

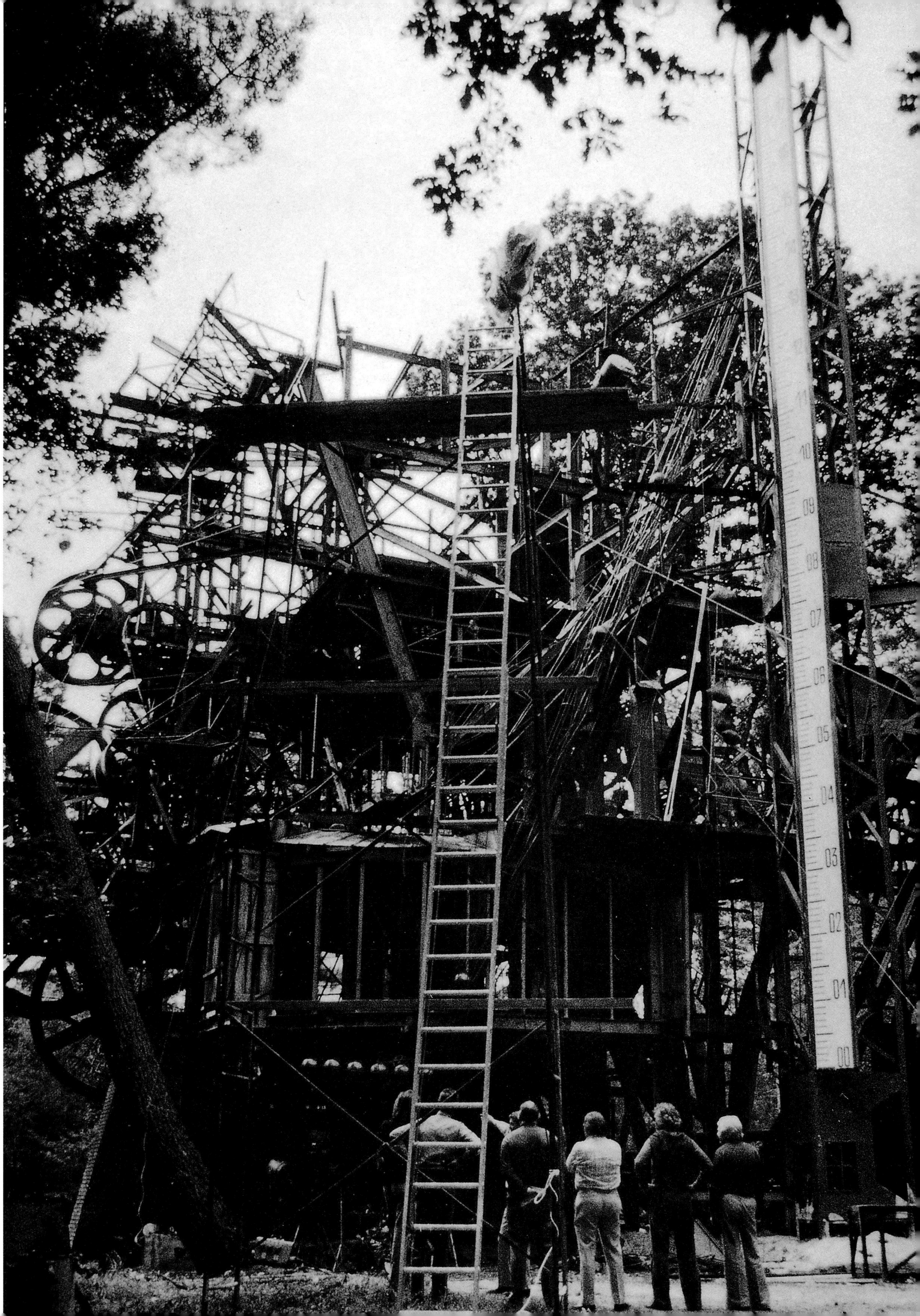

and we began to climb the stairs. I felt simultaneously like a child about to climb up into a huge tree house and as if I were penetrating a sacred precinct. We climbed up and down on stairs small and large, of metal and concrete, some leading nowhere, some onto or into balconies, hallways and rooms. The perception of *Head* as a mysterious, nearly impenetrable fortress changed as we took possession of it. It became a familiar thing, a playground to be explored, walked through, climbed upon, slid out from and ridden on, Utopia made real.

Head is multifaceted, formally and symbolically. As an exaggerated part of the human body emphasising the orifices, it is a carnivalesque-grotesque creation. The monstrous mouth is wide open; its thick, long tongue licks the earth. Big nostrils complete the bulbous nose. One huge petal-like ear built by Luginbühl directs its ocular antenna towards the sky, while the other aims its hearing aid, a discarded air-conditioner vent (from the Centre Georges Pompidou) to the ground, seeming to listen in on the business of the earth. *Head* is equipped with living quarters and a small theatre and is animated throughout by a 'Meta-Harmony'. Metal balls speed down an elaborate gutter that runs through the entire structure. Like thought impulses or life-giving blood running through arteries, the balls' thunder is the pulse of invigorating animation. The unexpected surprises the visitor at every turn. In the small theatre, the chairs suddenly start to move up and down, like the horses of an old-fashioned carousel. Luginbühl's gigantic pinball machine *Tell* awaits players, while de Saint Phalle invites the visitor to slide out of the mouth and down the tongue-chute, which ends in a refreshing pool of water, a joyful 'cultural baptism'.

A square pool, on top of the sculpture, is a homage to Yves Klein. Tinguely recalled that '[Klein] would spend insane amounts of energy to convince some fellow that the earth was flat and square. And they believed him. He had such fire, such force, in conversation, he marshalled so many proofs of an unrecognisable metaphysical character, that the idiots would leave feeling sure he was right.'[8] The image of the world reflected in the pool on top of *Head* is indeed flat and square.

In the latter half of the seventies, Tinguely and Imhof turned *Head* into a fortress in their increasingly complex efforts to outsmart vandals. Because of continuous break-ins and a fire, the planned installation of a number of significant art works by

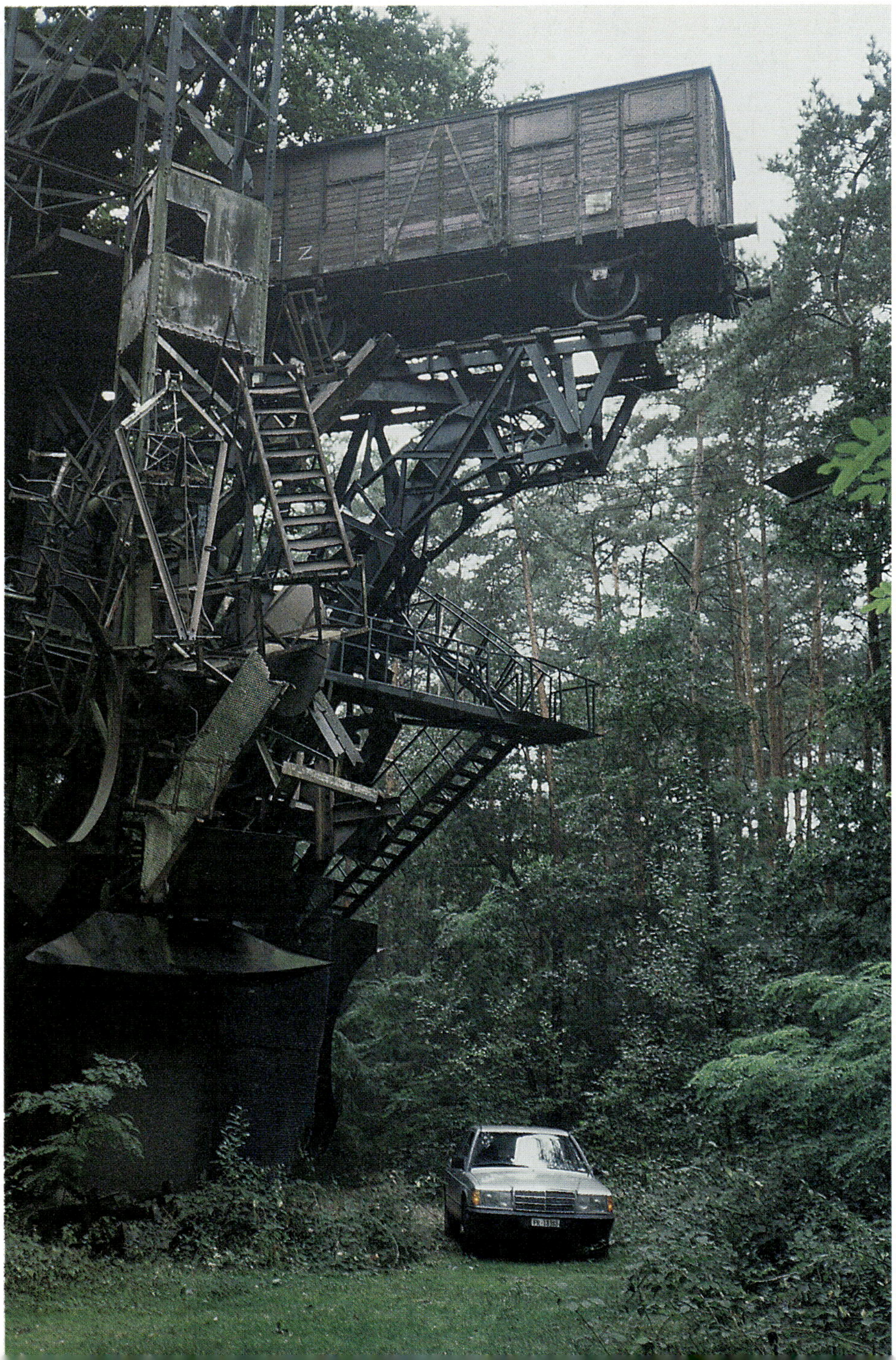

Head (overall view) ▻

Head (the railroad car)

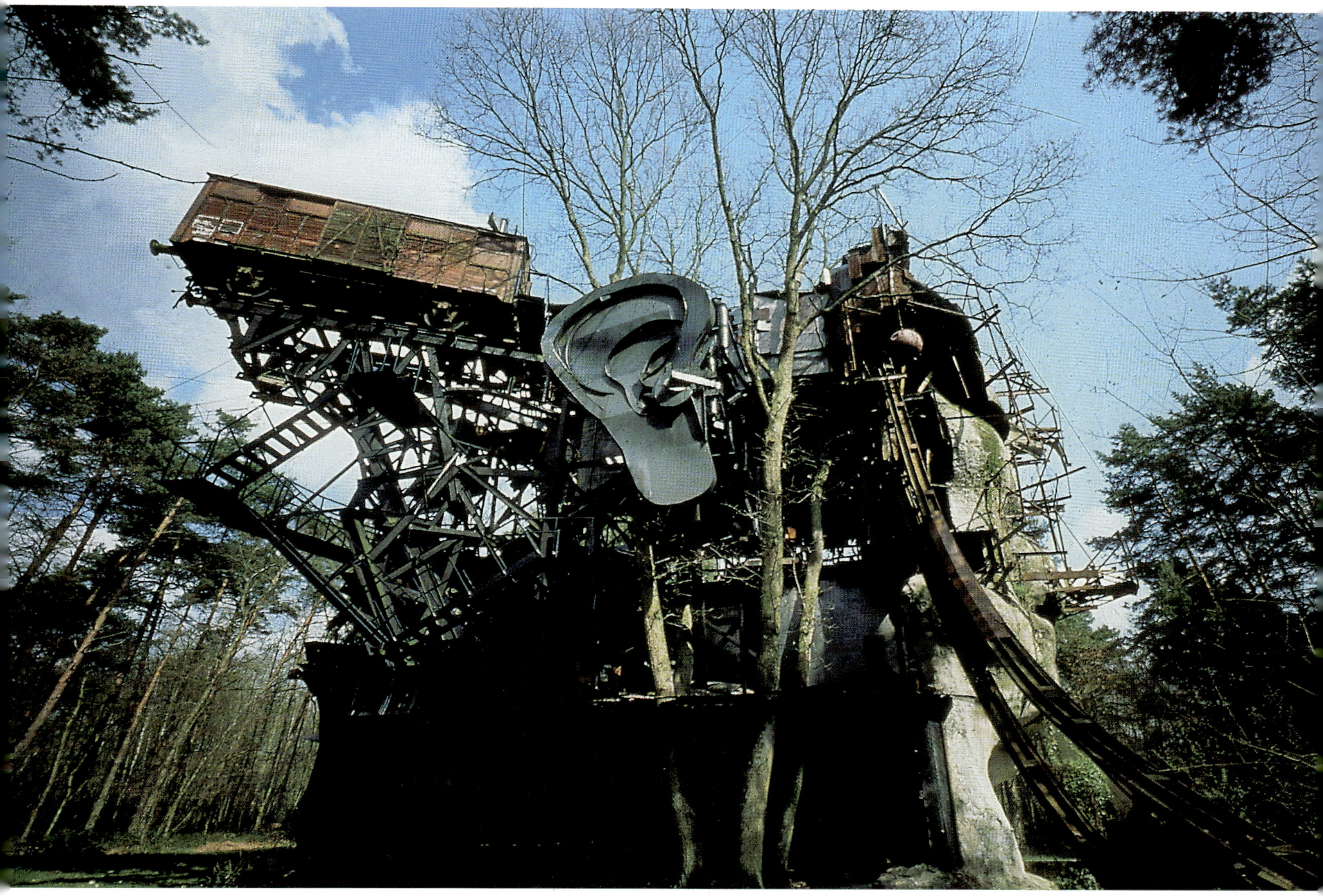

Aeppli, Arman, César, Jean-Pierre Raynaud, Larry Rivers, Jesus Raphael Soto, Daniel Spoerri and others had to be postponed. *Head* entered what de Saint Phalle described as its 'Sleeping Beauty' period. In 1987/88, two events changed the destiny of the sculpture. Tinguely and de Saint Phalle offered it to the French State, and it was officially accepted. In January 1988, ready to embark on a new fantasy, Tinguely purchased an abandoned factory in the bucolic countryside near Gruyère. This inspired him to finish *Head*. De Saint Phalle suggested that the face be covered with a layer of mirror mosaic, and Tinguely agreed. This reflective skin now covers the entire face, making it disappear magically into the surrounding environment. In 1994, the work was made accessible to all by bus from the Centre Georges Pompidou. In a time when our experiences are determined by an artifical world of images created by electronic means, Tinguely became increasingly more concerned with the sensual experience one has when directly confronted with a work of art.[9]

While work on *Head* was in progress, Tinguely and Rico Weber contributed to two of Niki de Saint Phalle's projects conceived specifically with children in mind. The first, made in 1972, was a monumental play-sculpture, *Golem* (fig. 47), for a park in Jerusalem. This squat and horned but benevolent monster is a sort of giant toboggan. Tinguely and Weber also made the iron structure for de Saint Phalle's *Dragon* at Knokke in Belgium. A particularly accommodating pet, it offers its hollows as children's quarters, complete with kitchen and bathroom.

Another collaborative event, which Tinguely staged with his friend Luginbühl, paradoxically twisted the motif of destruction. It took place in

Head (the pool)

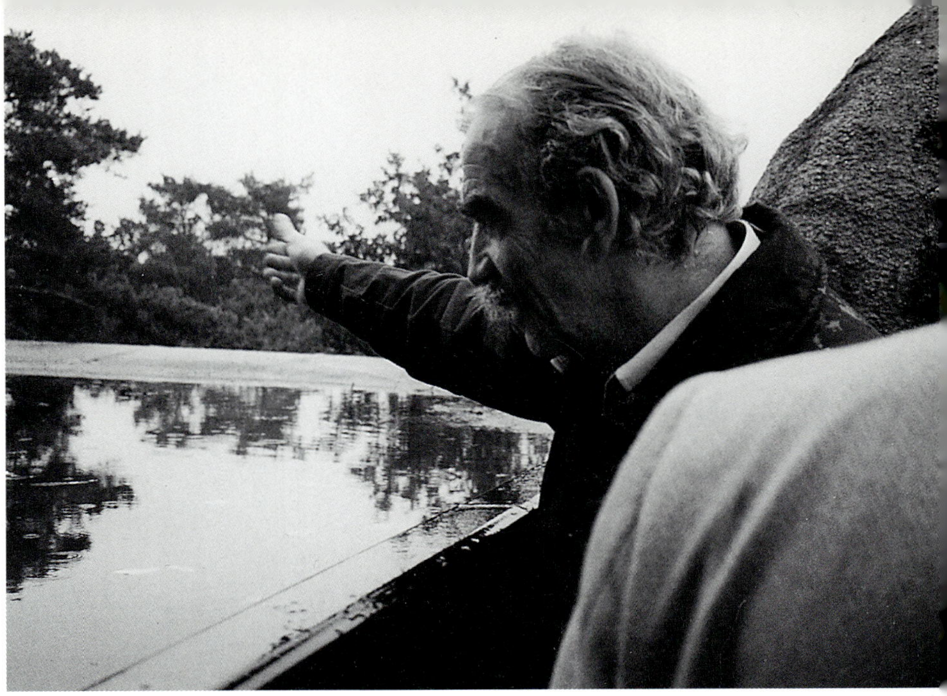

the garden of the Kornfeld gallery in Berne on 4 December 1972, St Barbara's Day. The two artists aptly saluted the patron saint of artillerymen with an event that included the firing of several cannons. These weapons, affectionately named Celio, Fata Morgana, Greta Garbo and the like, produced

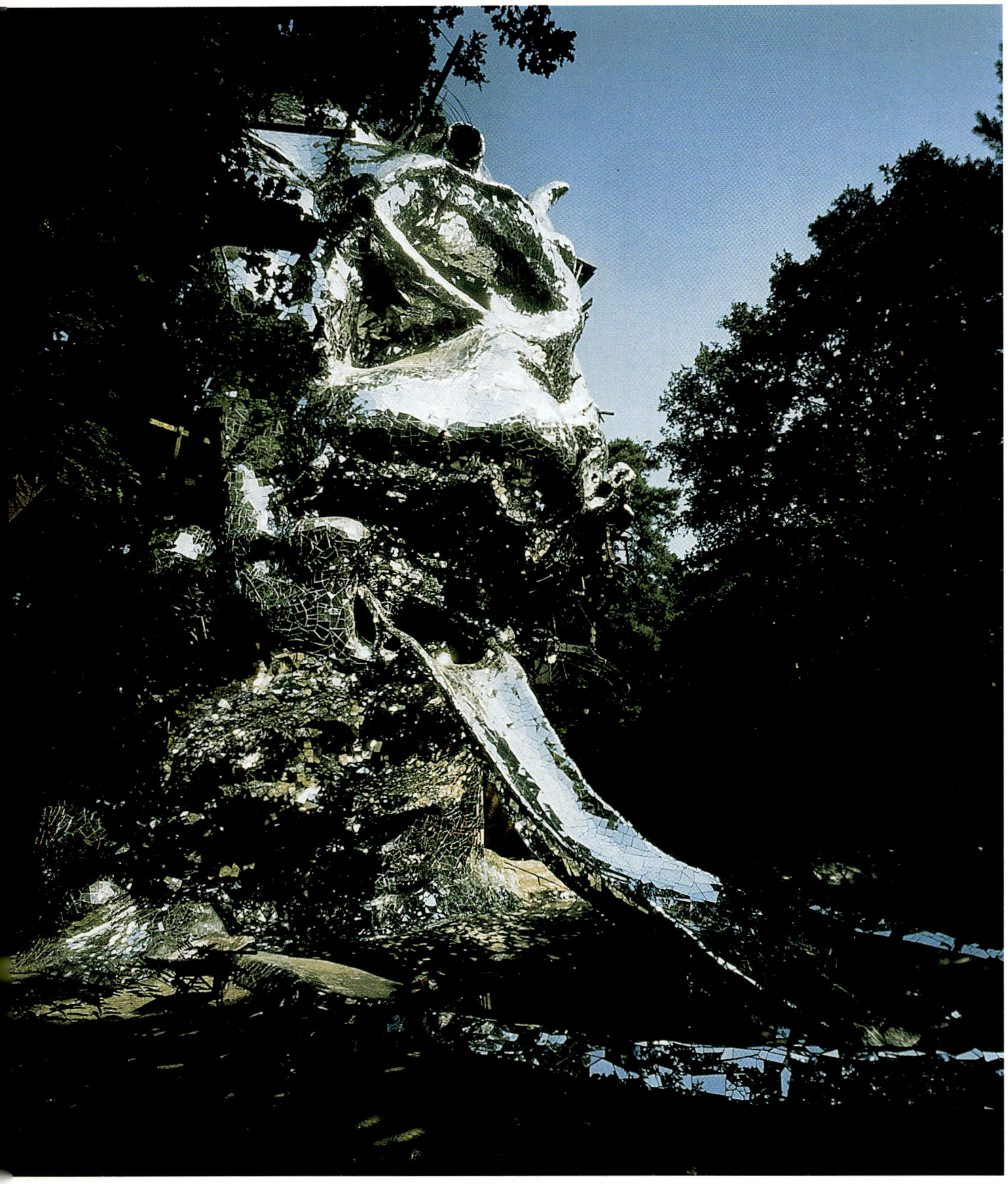

thunderous booms and sooty smoke. With Frau Holle, loaded with nothing more offensive than poultry feathers, the artists succeeded in covering the entire garden with a kind of 'snow' in an action that whimsically re-canonised the former saint.

In 1972, the first monograph on Tinguely, written in German by Pontus Hulten, was published.[10] *Jean Tinguely: 'Méta'* covered the artist's activities up to 1972, the text being complemented by nearly a thousand photos. Reminiscent of Duchamp's 'portable museum', the 1941 *Box in a Valise*, the Tinguely book-object had a cover designed by the artist. The decoration for the end-papers was provided by one of the drawing machines of *Homage to New York*, and the book included a recording of sounds from that event.

Late in 1971, Tinguely had been asked to create a monumental free-standing sculpture for a glass-enclosed civic centre in Columbus, Indiana, then under construction by the architect

Head (mirror-mosaic work of the face)

Cesar Pelli. Besides the generous fee, the city's proximity to Indianapolis and its world-famous race-track won Tinguely over: 'Columbus was the best situation I ever had. I was free to dream, and it was good for me to step back, to get away from Paris and Switzerland. The city's machine and electric shops and most of all the huge scrap iron yards were inspirational . . . in a situation like that it is possible to go beyond oneself.'[11] Tinguely's work was intended to be the 'great magnet, a focal point such as the old town clock . . . a place for people to meet and greet one another';[12] *Chaos I* accomplished this goal.

Tinguely built *Chaos I* between 1973 and 1974 (fig. 48) in the old City Power House from scrap metal and

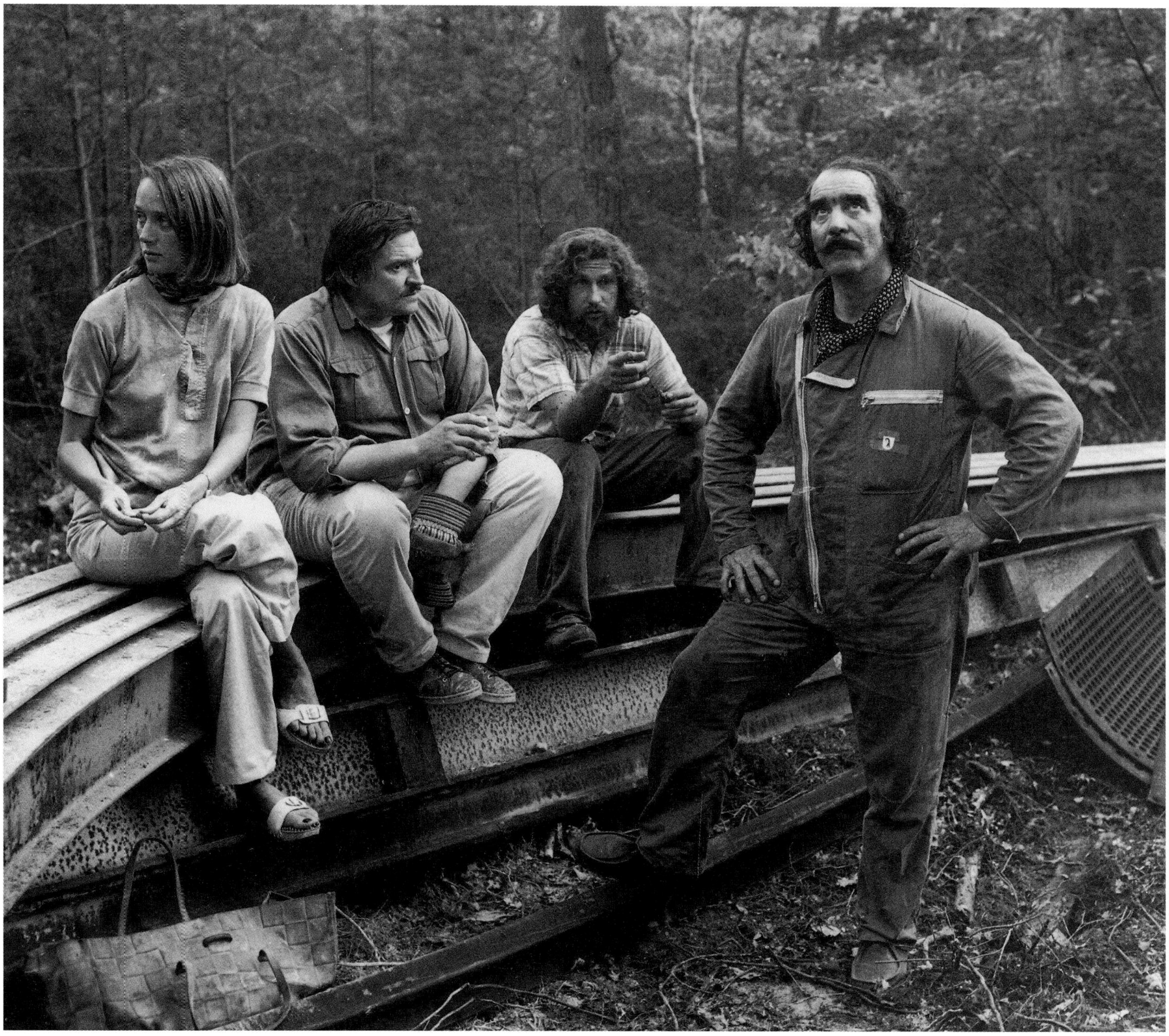

Niki de Saint Phalle, Bernhard Luginbühl, Joseph Imhof and Tinguely during construction of *Head*, Milly-la-Forêt, 1971

new materials. People recognise in it many aspects of southern Indiana life, from antiquated farm equipment, to an assortment of old wheels to the up-to-date technology for which the city's major company, Cummins Engine Company, is known. Local craftspeople and engineers helped Tinguely achieve a new level of mechanical sophistication. The sculpture, about thirty feet high and estimated to weigh seven tons, rotates almost imperceptibly on its square base and is surrounded by a round, shallow pool, an aesthetically pleasing solution to the problem of security. Singly or in concert, 12 motors activate its different parts, and 24 programmed combinations of movements can be used to control the sculpture's day. Tinguely wanted it to mirror the city in motion, and in fact it does:

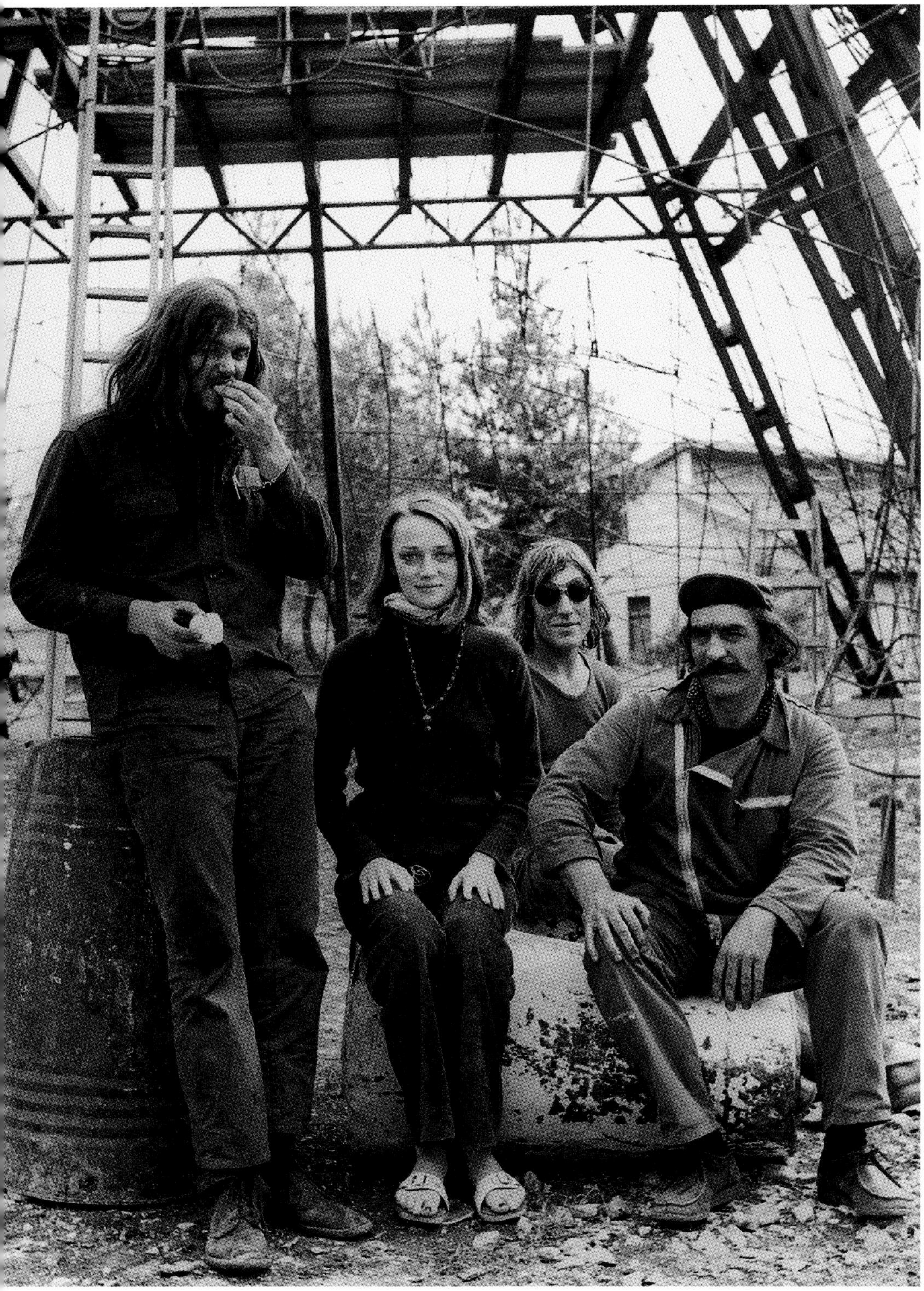

It will start very slowly in the morning, like the city getting up, and begin moving faster and faster until it reaches a crescendo at noon. Then it will quiet down for an afternoon rest, and build up again the same way until 6, when everybody's going home and the city is at its busiest. It will quiet down again for dinner, then keep getting busier until 10 p. m.[13]

Chaos I is subtitled more explicitly *Dr Jekyll and Mr Hyde.*[14] The work is Janus-faced, at first relatively unchaotic in appearance (in direct contradiction to its principal title) and then wildly chaotic. Within it, Tinguely combined different types of works developed over the years. There are, welded onto long sticks, an orange-yellow doughnut, a blue-white triangle and a square mirror. These garnish the sculpture like giant ice lollies; they are also the only continuously moving elements. More noisily, eight steel balls clink and clank as one after the other rumbles through a gutter cage resembling a giant marble-track. The cage encircles the upper part of the sculpture, like a roller coaster, in a figure of eight. The small wagon suddenly detaches itself from the upper part of the trunk and rattles back and forth over a short length of

47 Niki de Saint Phalle, *Golem*, 1972, Jerusalem ▷

Rico Weber, Niki de Saint Phalle, Paul Wiedmer and Tinguely during construction of *Golem*, Jerusalem, 1972

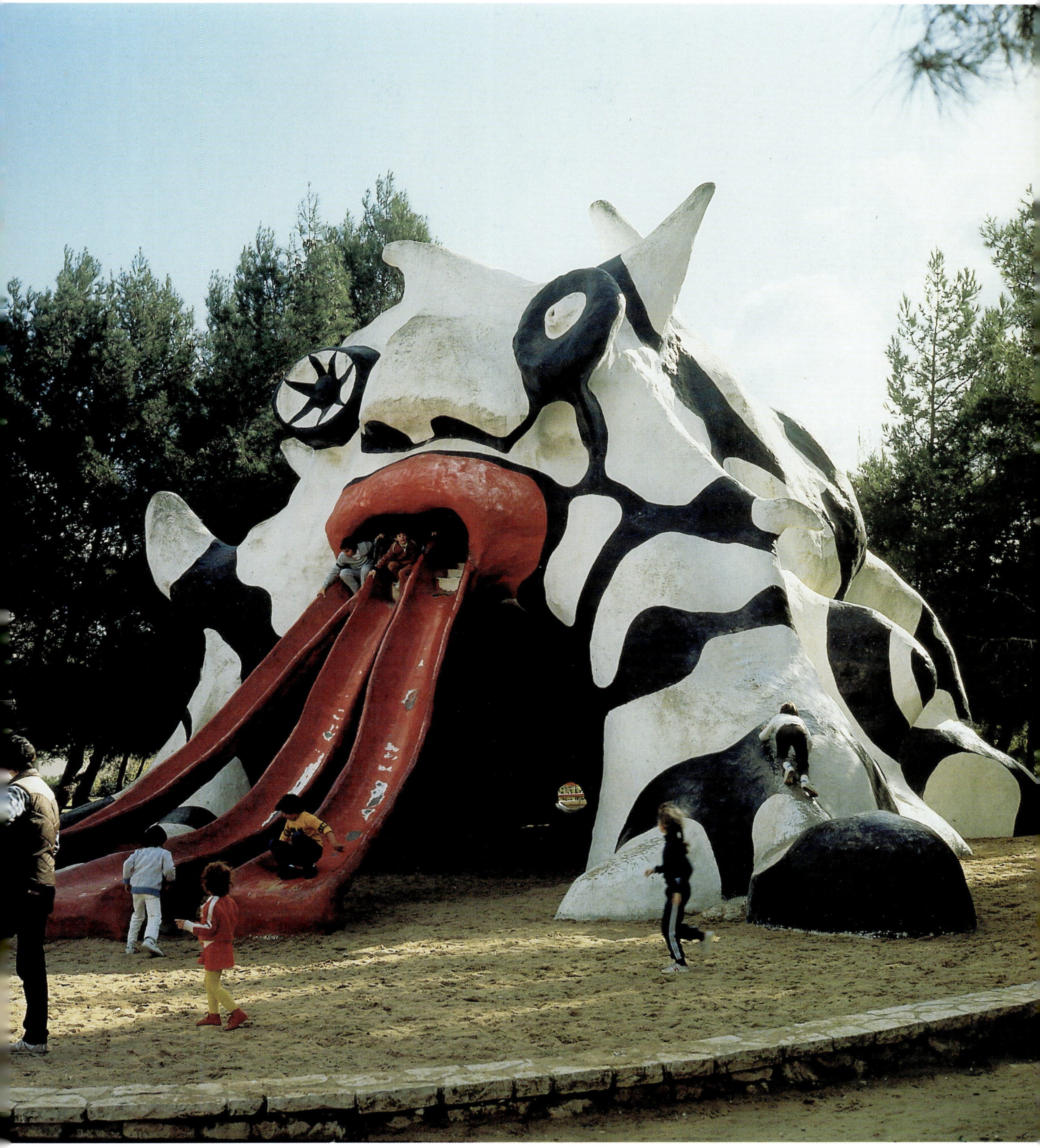

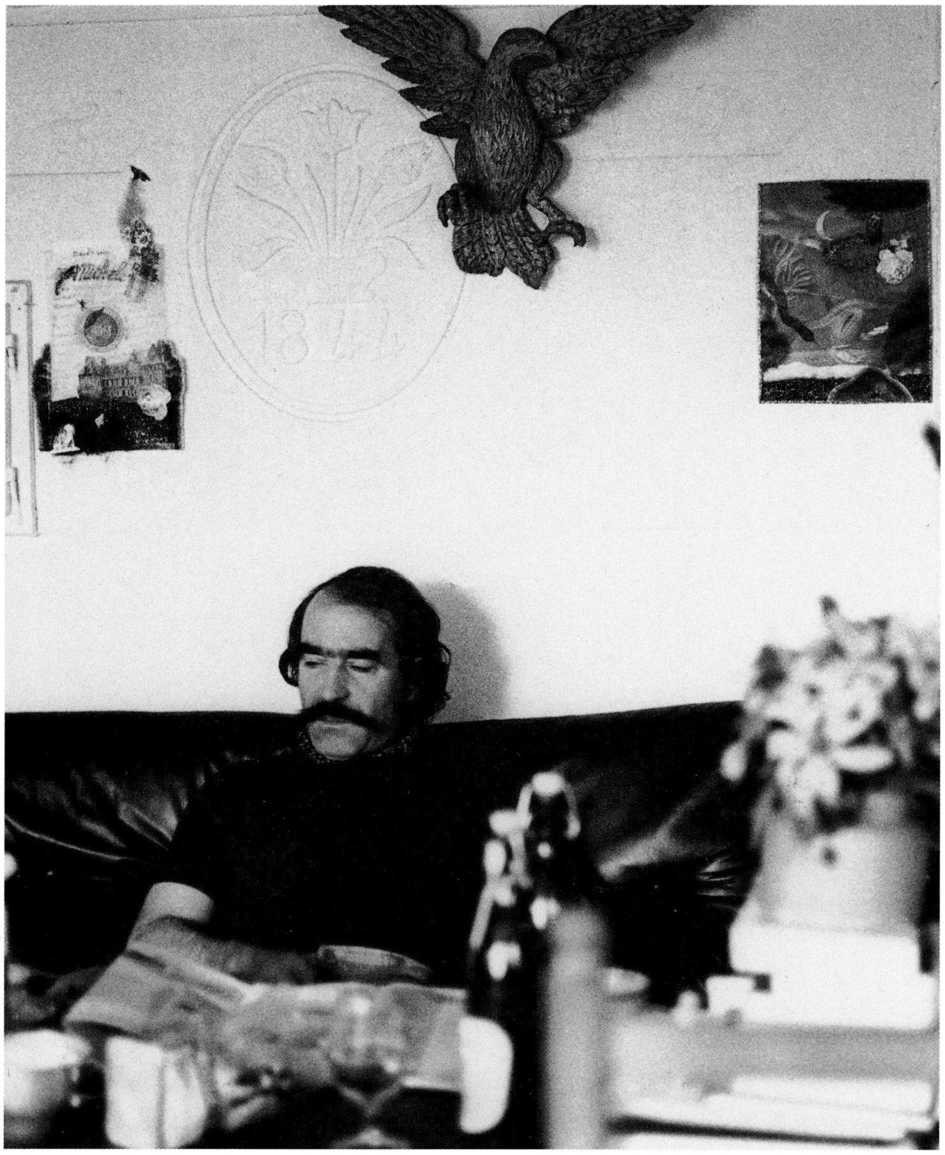

such as drills, spanners, hammers, saws, shears and the like—in other words, the tools of his own trade were made into art.

At home in Neyruz, 1974

track. Tinguely meant this 'lousy, ridiculous piece of assembled junk' to have a derisory function, in contradistinction to the rest of the sculpture, which is 'serious and very well constructed'.[15] Even more nonsensical is a cowboy boot that either Rico Weber or Joseph Imhof had forgotten near the spiral. Tinguely remembered that when he removed the boot, people noticed its absence, so he replaced it. The essential thing, said Tinguely, was that everybody should have fun with his machine.

At the end of 1974, just after he had completed *Chaos I*, Tinguely felt the need to work on a smaller scale. The result was exhibited at Galerie Bischofberger, Zurich, under the ironically witty title *Débriscollages*, a pun on the words *débris* (debris, waste), *bricole* (petty job) and *collage*. The show's catalogue was designed to look like a Sears mail-order catalogue. Tinguely had assembled 15 objects from the treasury of an efficient 'do-it-yourselfer': electric and non-electric tools

48 *Chaos I*, 1973-74

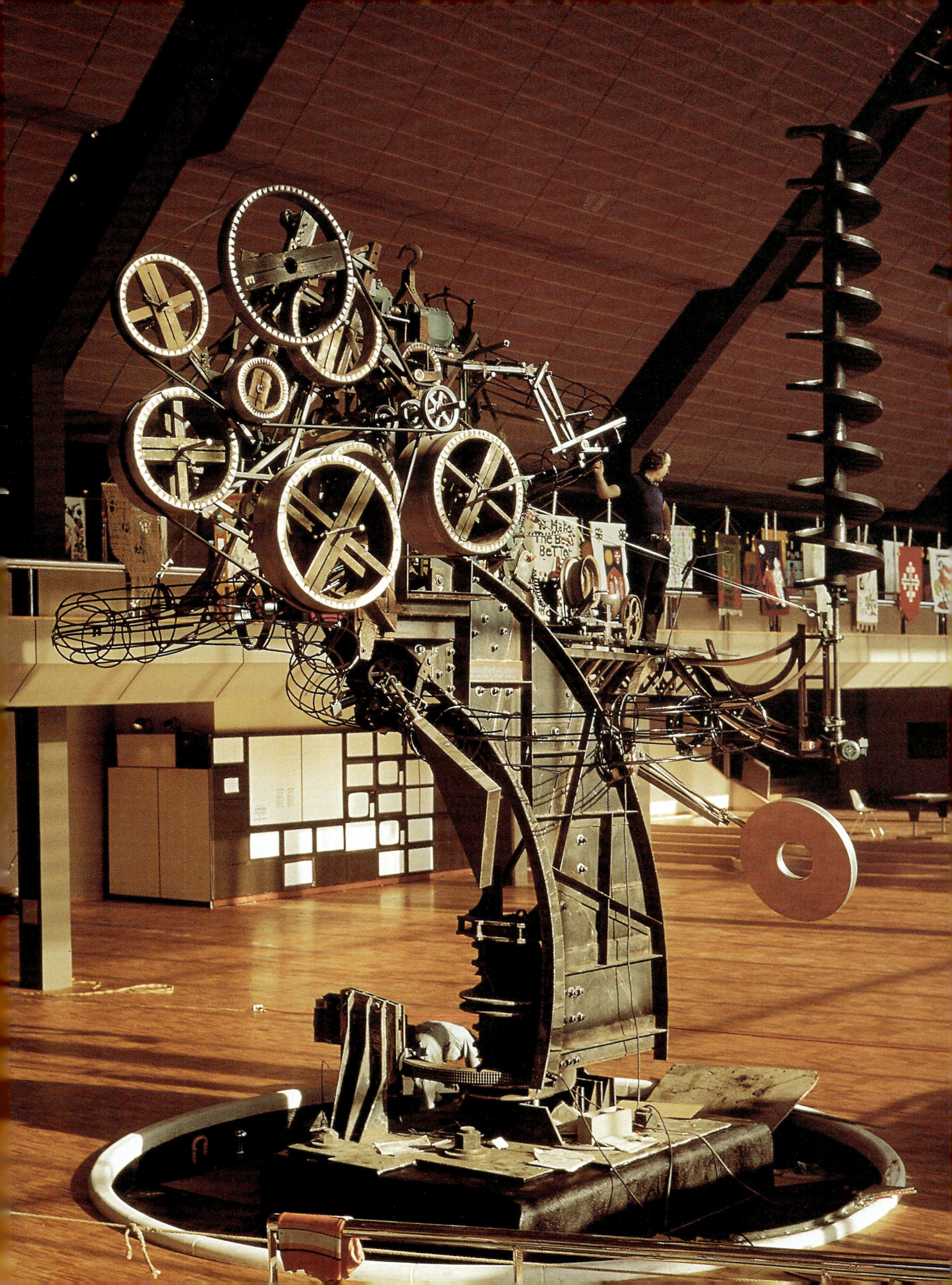

'It's hard work to make people enjoy life'

1974–88

In 1974, Tinguely joined one of Basel's Carnival *Cliques*, the dissident and idiosyncratic *Kuttlebutzer*. Carnival, an interweaving of play and culture,[1] had been important to the artist since childhood. Mikhail Bakhtin, a pioneer in exploring humour in folk culture, observed that Carnival is both counterpart and parody of official feasts, celebrating a temporary suspension of hierarchy, privileges and law and order. This levelling of rank and liberation from everyday rules of behaviour and speech forge a sense of fraternity.[2] The age-old seasonal revel had been kept substantially alive in Basel, where Tinguely had grown up and lived until his 28th year.[3] The organising *Cliques* were structured like social clubs, each including a vanguard, a major-domo, drummers, piccolo players, sometimes wagons, carts or cart-like objects called *Requisits* and, most importantly, a lantern of substantial size on which the theme of each year was made explicit in artful paintings. The yearly theme could be anything that lent itself to humorous satire and determined the entire appearance of the *Clique*, including masks, wigs and costumes. For Tinguely, the Basel Carnival was an event that marked the artistic vision of a lifetime; in his earliest memories of it, he was simultaneously terrified and fascinated, but as an adult he often supplied his *Clique* with material and built props and masks. Conversely, he recycled objects from the Carnival in his assemblages. Such objects were left in a corner of his atelier until one day, an element or costume inspired him and became a signifying element within a new sculpture.

Carnival and other celebratory objects derive their power from the very fact of their impermanence—like Christmas trees, for example, they are used and then discarded. Objects created for Carnival are indeed 'useless', non-functional in the conventional sense, just as Tinguely's machines are 'useless'. As the anthropologist Roger D. Abrahams has pointed out, usually the language of art and that of festive celebrations are actually opposites. The arts exalt permanence—the creative act is memorialised and the object valued as such—while festive celebrations honour the transitory qualities of life.[4] Tinguely is therefore an exception, since some of his major works were ephemeral, and this transience was the core of their expressive metaphors. In fact, Tinguely's artistic method and the creative process of Carnival are analogous. For both, the modus operandi is assemblage. Everyday things are torn apart and pieced together again in new forms in a process of recombination. This is why, for Tinguely, Carnival was a

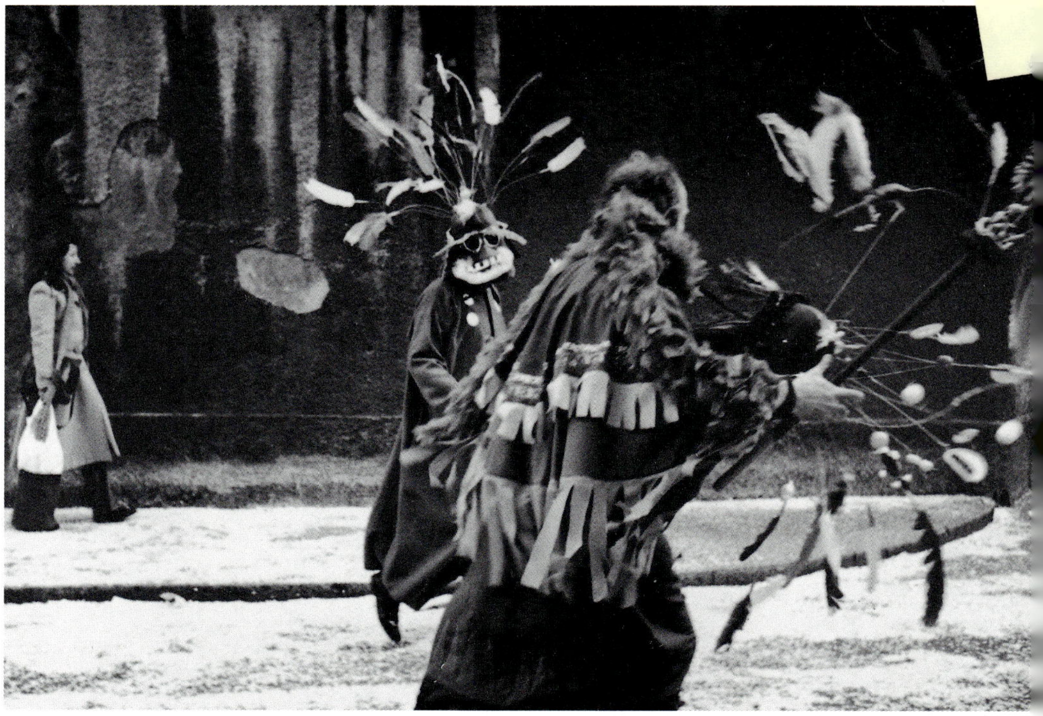

Tinguely with the *Kuttlebutzer Clique* at the Basel Carnival, 1976. The Carnival theme that year was 'Indians'

Tinguely at the Basel Carnival, 1988, in his 'down-and-out' costume (see plate 76)

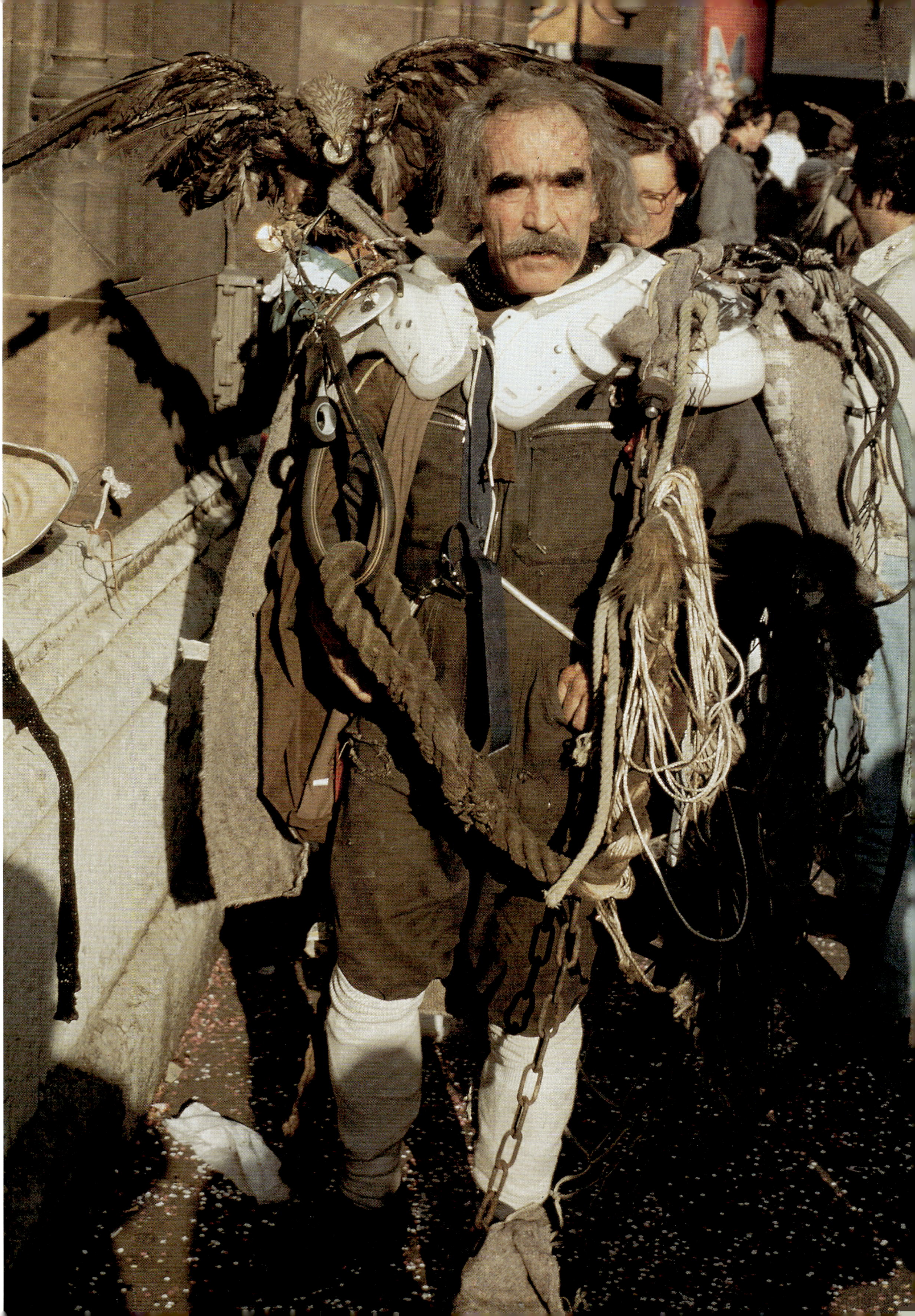

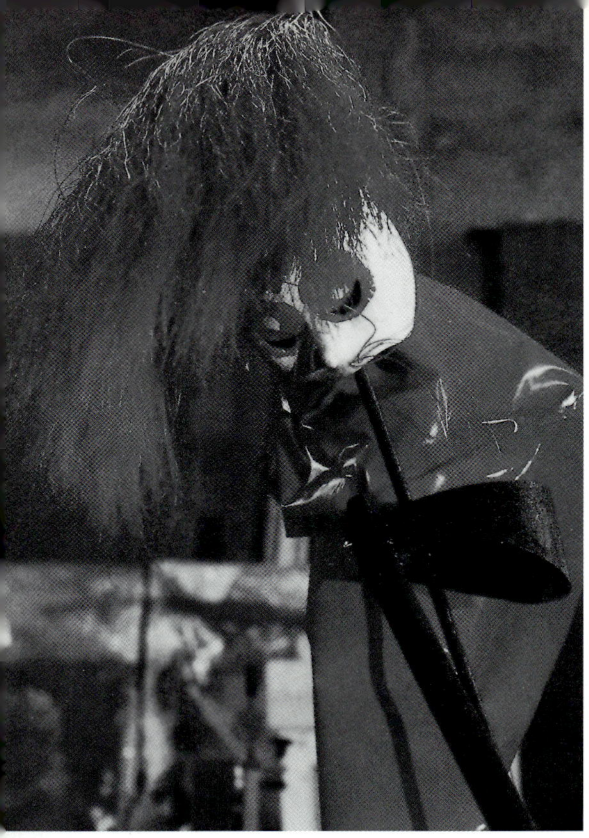

49 *Ludwig Wittgenstein*, 1988 (detail)

The *Kuttlebutzers* at the end of Carnival, 1988. The theme that year: 'Bankruptcy and the Resurrection of the KAFKA AG', Galerie Klaus Litmann, Basel

formal, aesthetic and ideational paradigm.

In 1974, the *Kuttlebutzer* chose the Carnival's organising committee as a target for satire. The *Kuttlebutzer* had come to resent what they perceived as the committee's over-regulation of the festival and, in true Carnival fashion, staged the committee's funeral, parading in mournful white masks, dressed entirely in ceremonial black with black hats and umbrellas. Behind them they dragged a hearse-like *Requisit* in which was hidden some fireworks and other special effects that Tinguely had prepared. Once in front of the committee, the hearse began to unleash smoke and other noisy and nauseating effects and 'buried' its members under soot and ashes.[5] This was a typical Carnival action—to bury so as to revive, to kill the old so as to resurrect the new.

In 1976, the *Kuttlebutzer* agreed to Tinguely's proposed Carnival subject, 'Indians'. The artist designed and built the masks for the drummers, the lantern and the *Requisit*. Believing the traditional way of life of the American Indian tribes to be an embodiment of freedom, he connected them symbolically with the spirit of freedom alive in Carnival. The *Kuttlebutzer* decided upon a mock-religious subject in 1977. Tinguely, it was reported, was so immersed in the role of a blessing priest that he unceasingly swung an incense burner as if Basel that year was in particular need of exorcism.[6] In 1985, Tinguely designed and built the masks, the lantern and the *Requisit* for the *Kuttlebutzer* military theme. The following year, the *Kuttlebutzer* named themselves a corporation, the KAFKA AG (for Kuttlebutzer Autonome Fasnachts Kommer-

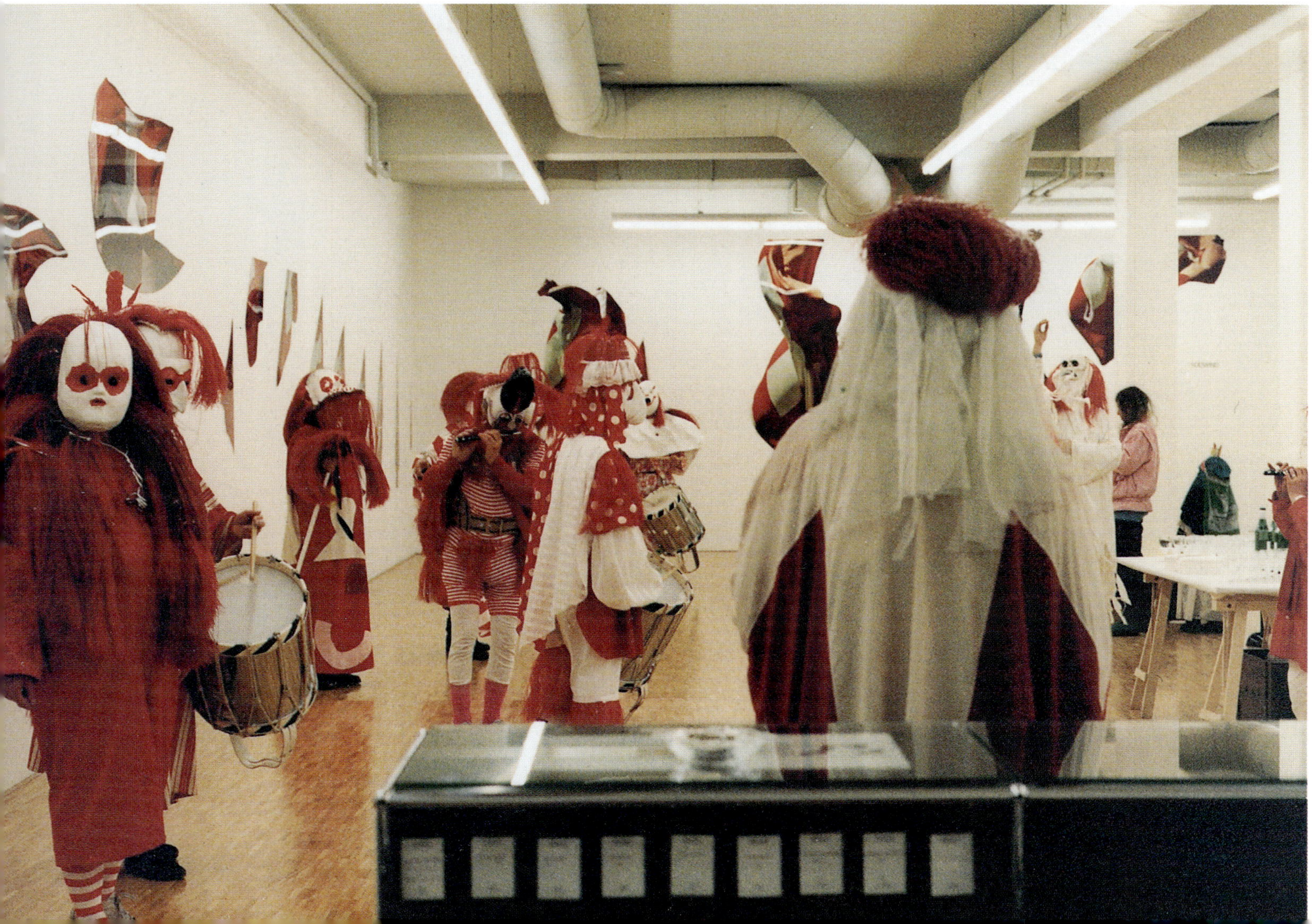

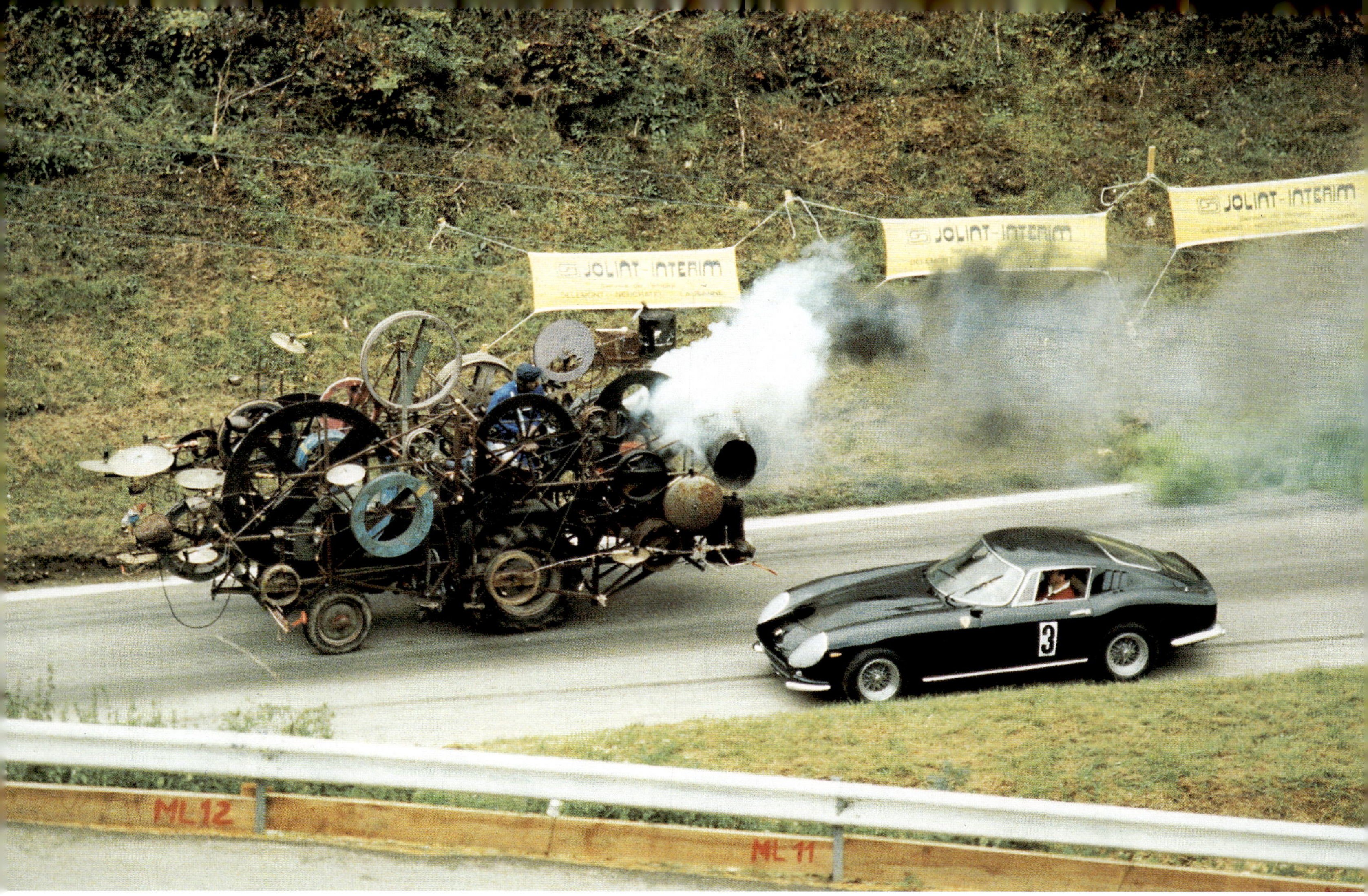

50 *Klamauk*, 1979, at Côte St Ursanne-Les Rangiers, 1981

zialisierungs AG), and in 1988, KAFKA AG declared bankruptcy. Its members played out the company's demise over a period of three days. Tinguely's mask and costume did full honour to those who are down and out (illus. p. 91). His trashy outfit was a conglomeration of rags, nets and chains, he bore a bird of prey on his shoulder and his mask's fantastical protuberance thumbed its nose at a new type of takeover 'fool'. The *Clique*'s resurrection, with its members clad in the heraldic colours of Mother Helvetia, red and white, was celebrated in Klaus Littmann's gallery. Tinguely resurrected one of the red and white masks in a sculpture entitled *Ludwig Wittgenstein* (fig. 49).[7]

Carnival's form of play had been of enormous consequence to Tinguely's persona and his work for years. As early as 1960, he had taken his art to the streets of Paris. The same ideas are expressed in a work of 1979, *Klamauk*, again an apparatus on wheels. This time, Tinguely started with a real tractor and transformed it into a festive object (fig. 50). *Klamauk* is a kind of *Requisit* that would fit right into the Basel Carnival, producing its own *Guggemuusig*, the cacophonous sound created by unruly musical *Cliques* who reflect in sound the topsy-turvy nature of Carnival. The tractor supports a complex relief of wheels whose motion activates hammers and metal sticks that bang on big and small bells, a variety of cymbals and even a rusty oil barrel, also releasing fumes and smoke. The piece recalls *Gismo* of 1960 (fig. 21), nearly as chaotic in appearance. When *Klamauk* appeared on the streets of Solothurn, its rumpus was especially enjoyed by people who saw its parallel in their own local Carnival. The work even poked fun at the speed and slickness of racing cars when it participated from start to finish in an automobile race held at Côte St Ursanne-Les Rangiers in 1981. On 4 September 1991, Joseph Imhof drove *Klamauk* behind Jean Tinguely's hearse, the only non-solemn noisemaker in a procession with the importance of a state funeral. Together with the *Kuttlebutzer Clique*, who played unmasked except for the major-domo as Death, the piece represented the carnivalesque with all its meanings.

In 1963–64, a new theatre had been built in Basel to replace a building that was demolished. Set at a considerable distance from the street, it left a large gap that proved particularly difficult to shape into a harmonious public place. It was thought that a fountain, with its traditional association as focal gathering point, would accomplish the task. Fortunately, a sponsor was found to donate the fountain, and Tinguely was chosen to create it.[8] There is no seating in the immediate vicinity of the fountain, yet passers-by

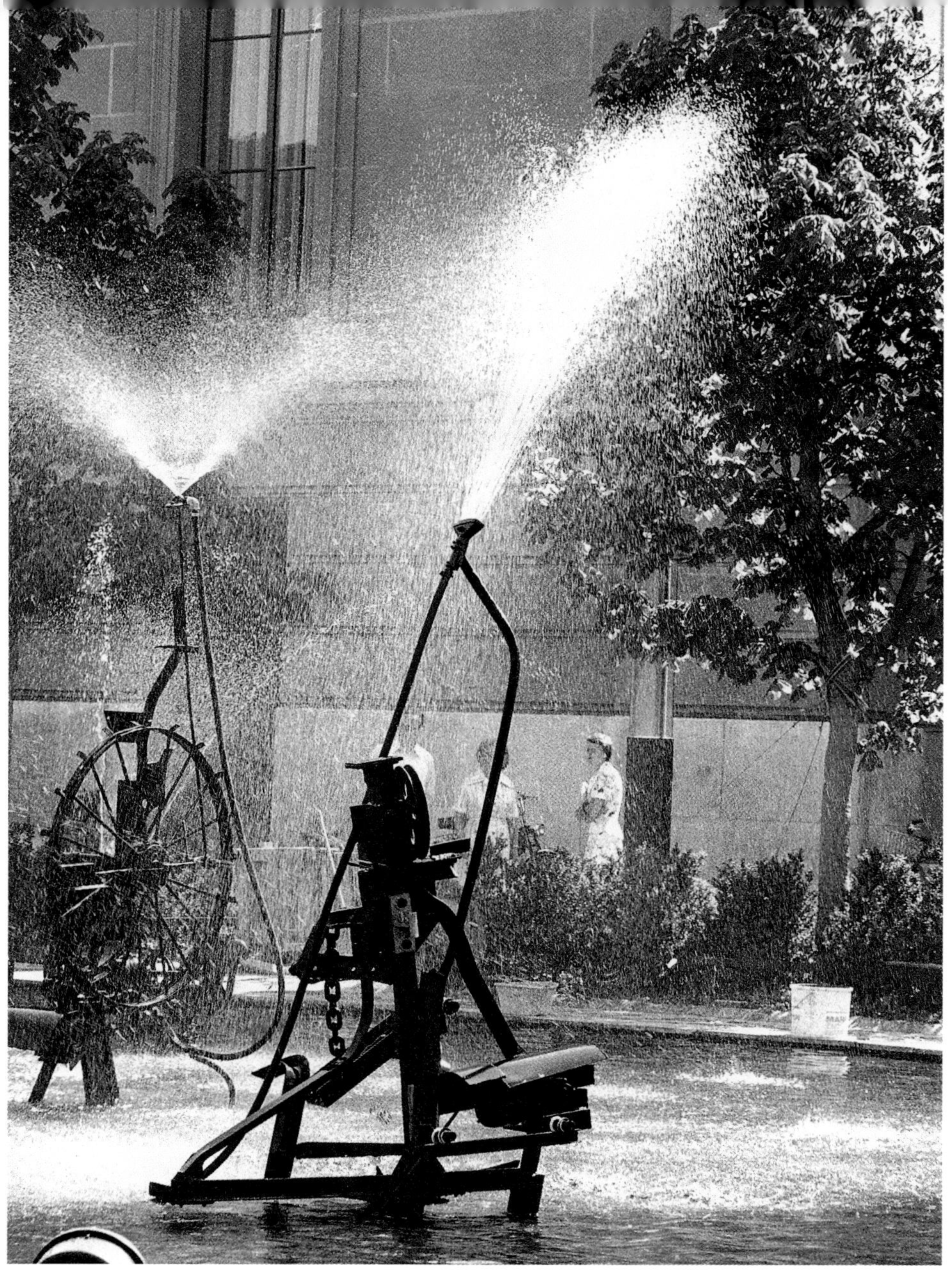

51 *Fasnachtsbrunnen (Carnival Fountain)*, 1977

Dr Wäädel (The Wagger)

Dr Suuser (The Whistle) ▽

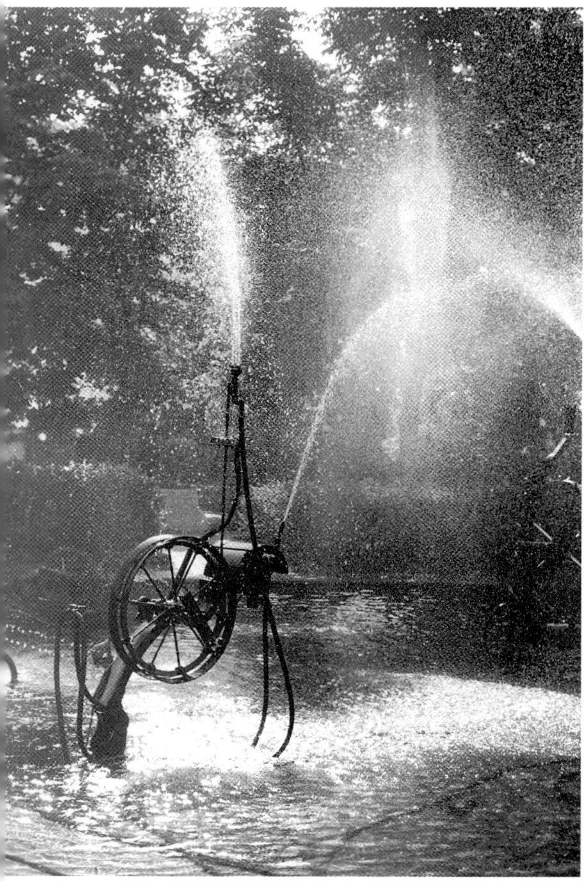

stop, observe, sit where they can and walk around the basin, enchanted by the sheer beauty of this hydrokinetic display. Tinguely achieved nothing short of a miracle, transforming this ill-conceived space into a major point of attraction by building the *Carnival Fountain*, one of the most beautiful modern fountains in existence, now known popularly as the *Tinguely-Brunnen* (*Tinguely Fountain*).[9] The programme for its inauguration reads like a multimedia spectacle. It occurred at night and included the *Kuttlebutzer* in seafaring costume, playing the newly composed 'Fountain March' and providing a fittingly carnivalesque touch. Then, members of the Basel ballet, dressed in prisoners' striped suits, joined in a playful interaction of bodies, machine-sculptures and water. Braving the inclement weather, Tinguely himself made a paradoxical entrance on a camel, thus associating himself and his situation with this exotic creature.

The *Fasnachtsbrunnen* (*Carnival Fountain*) consists of 10 individual works distributed evently within a shallow pool (fig. 51). The sculptures, nearly uniform in size, were assembled in part from scrap iron Tinguely had gathered from the demolition site of the old theatre. For his waterworks he used a sophisticated array of nozzles

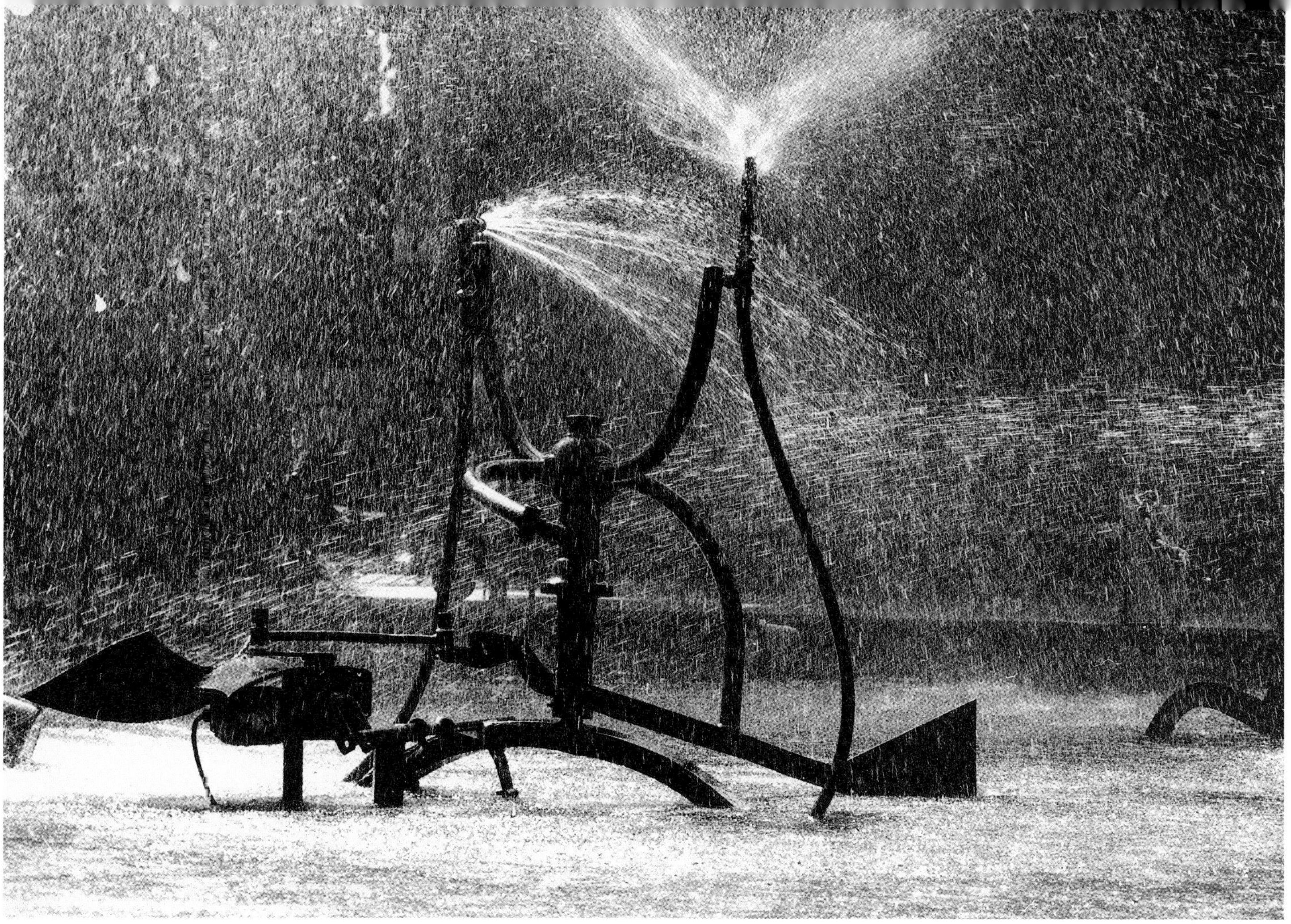

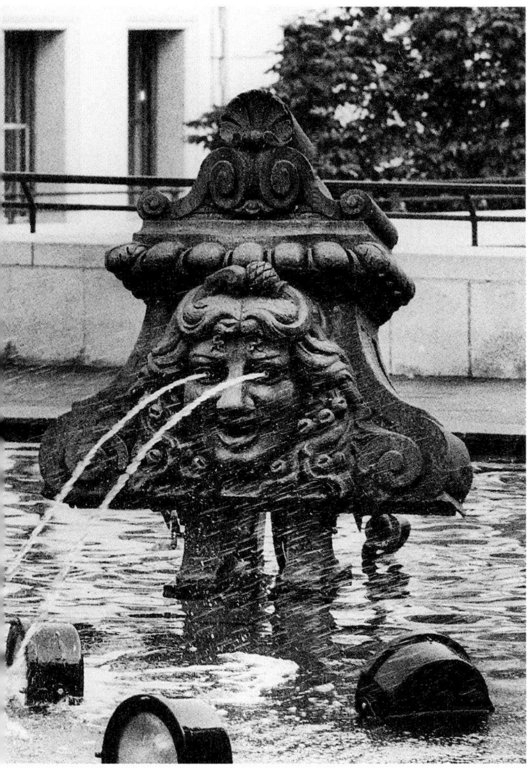

Dr Theaterkopf (The Theatre Head)

D' Spinne (The Spider)

Carnival Fountain (overall view) ▷

designed to create a vast range of visual and auditory effects. Though small and squat, *dr Spritzer* (*the Squirter*) epitomises self-assertiveness and aggresiveness. Its powerful jet hits the surface of the pool sharply with a regular, march-like pulse. Almost as fast-paced is the lower jet of *dr Suuser* (*The Whistle*),[10] which waves as energetically and authoritatively as the baton of a major-domo controlling his *Clique*'s musicians. The two additional sprays play out a complex pattern of interwoven sounds and rhythms.
Dr Seechter (*The Sieve*) tries over and over again to strain something, lowering its shallow vessel into the water and lifting it out again. *D' Fontääne* (*The Fountain*) is the simplest and most elegant of the objects. A large wheel is mounted on a tripod and moves a long tube slightly up and down. The motion resembles that of the flame-bearer's arm as he runs across the stadium to open the Olympic Games. The cloud of water droplets that emerges from the nozzle forms a watery fan that dissolves into the air and creates a multitude of rainbows. *D' Spinne* (*The Spider*) turns slightly on its central axis, sprays water from its two horn-shaped protrusions and shovels water with its feet.
Dr Theaterkopf (*The Theatre Head*) is a replica of one of the masks of the comic muse Thalia that decorated the façade of the old theatre. Paradoxically, though she is laughing, tears pour in a strong jet through her eyes as she rocks back and forth. Thus, she also symbolises Melpomene, the tragic

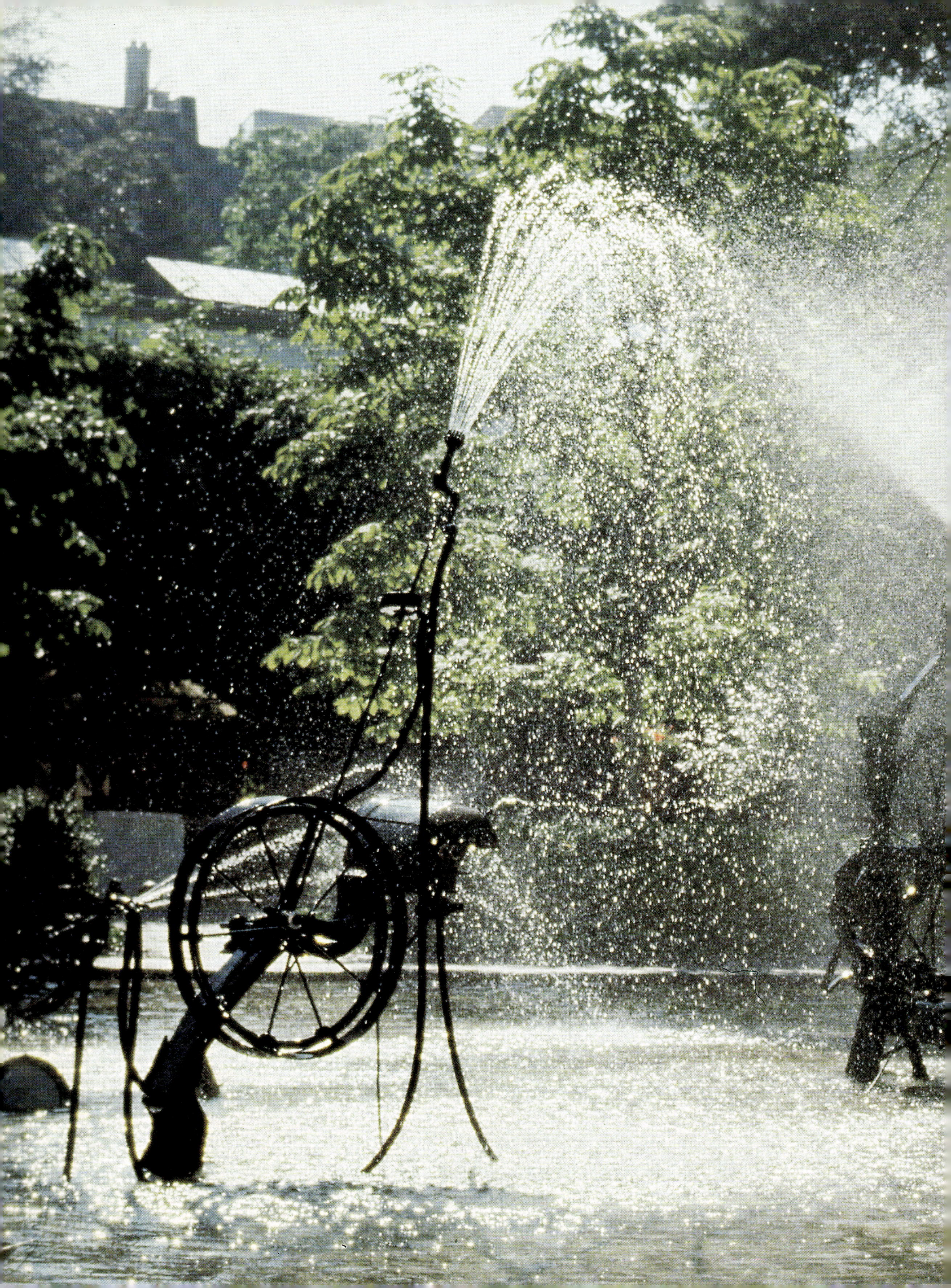

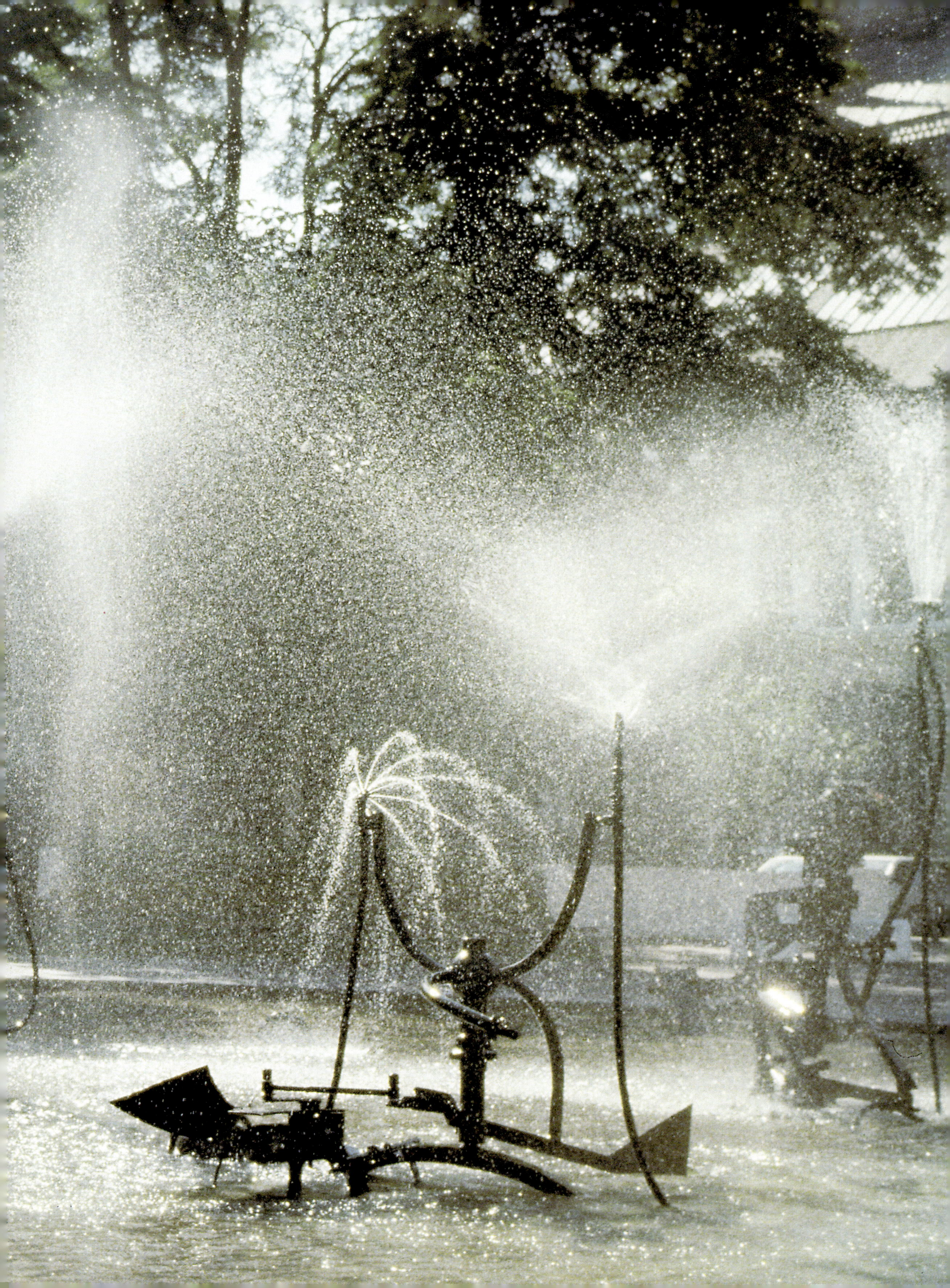

At work on the *Carnival Fountain*

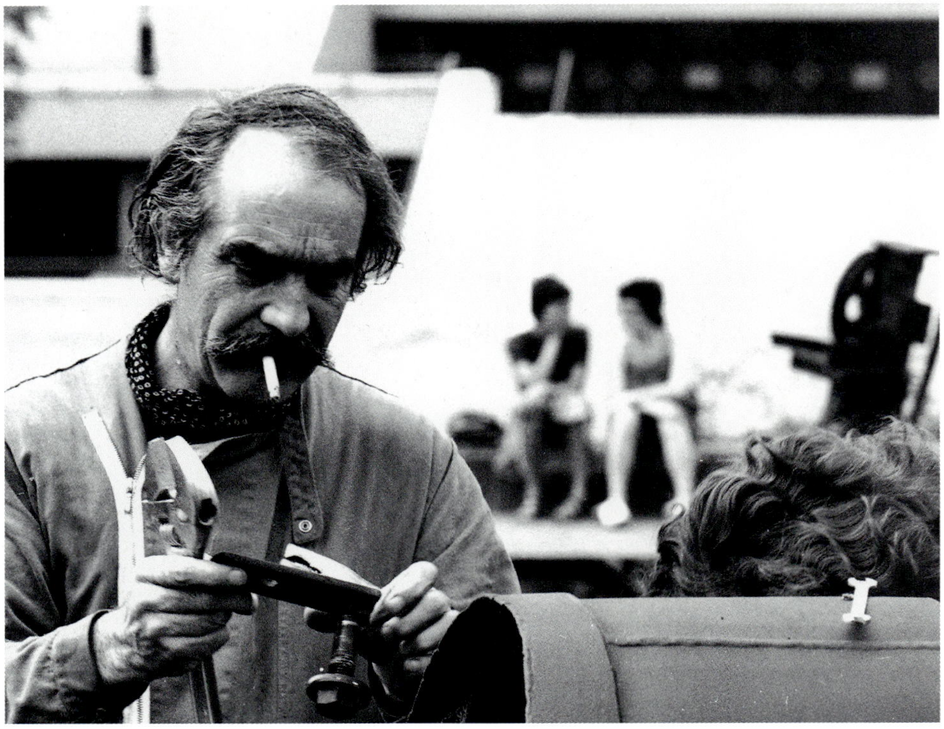

Dr Spritzer (The Squirter)

Dr Schuufler (The Shoveller) ▽

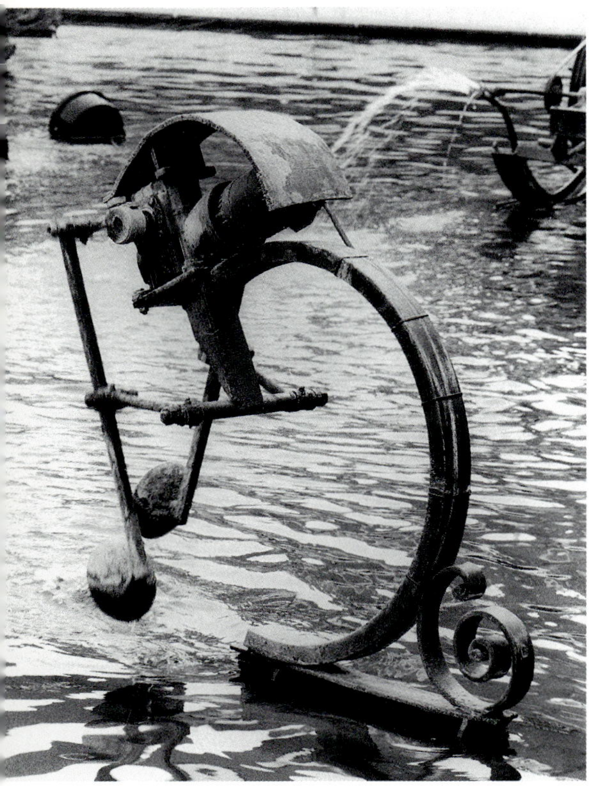

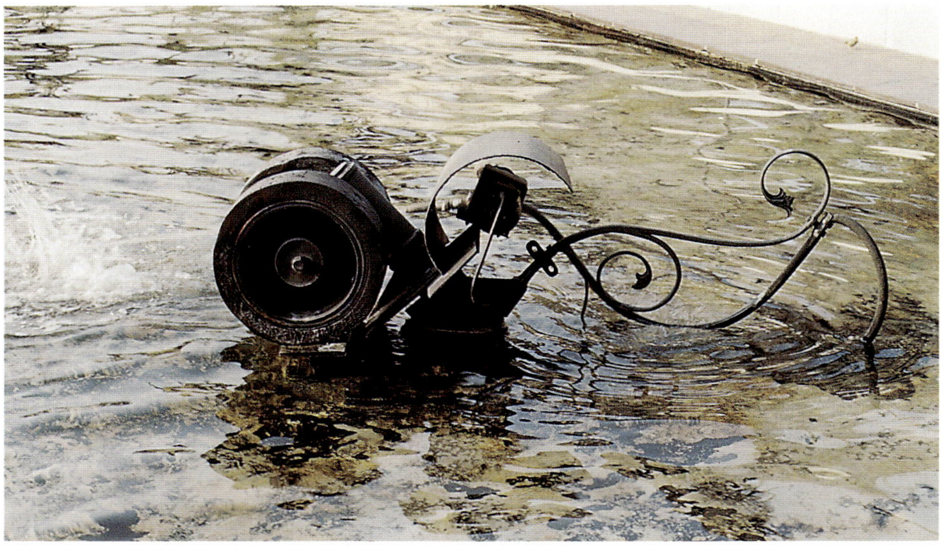

muse whose mask is also present in theatres, but is absent from this watery stage.

Dr Waggler (*The Rocker*) has multiple wheels that turn at different speeds and activate a hoe. This absurd handyman relentlessly digs the water, which naturally eludes it. *Dr Wäädel* (*The Wagger*) is the least graceful of the sculptures, an image of something shattered. The sombre note is balanced by a powerful jet of water pushed through a fine nozzle towering over and veiling the sorry remains below. *Dr Schuufler* (*The Shoveller*) is another absurd toiler defeated in advance in his labour. Small scoops fixed to two arms push and shovel the elusive fluid without results. Finally, *Dr Schildchrott* (*The Turtle*), the smallest of the sculptures, was added in 1983. A powerful jet of water originates from underneath a curved metal shell. It animates one corner of the basin, and its jet connects it diagonally to the other side. This piece completes the visual and auditory network created by the jets of each sculpture. The sprays and jets extend the works in an everchanging web of gestural abstraction.

Fashioned from old debris, the sculptures and the water itself represent change and transition. Each of the figures has its own idiosyncrasies, and each participates equally in a harmo-

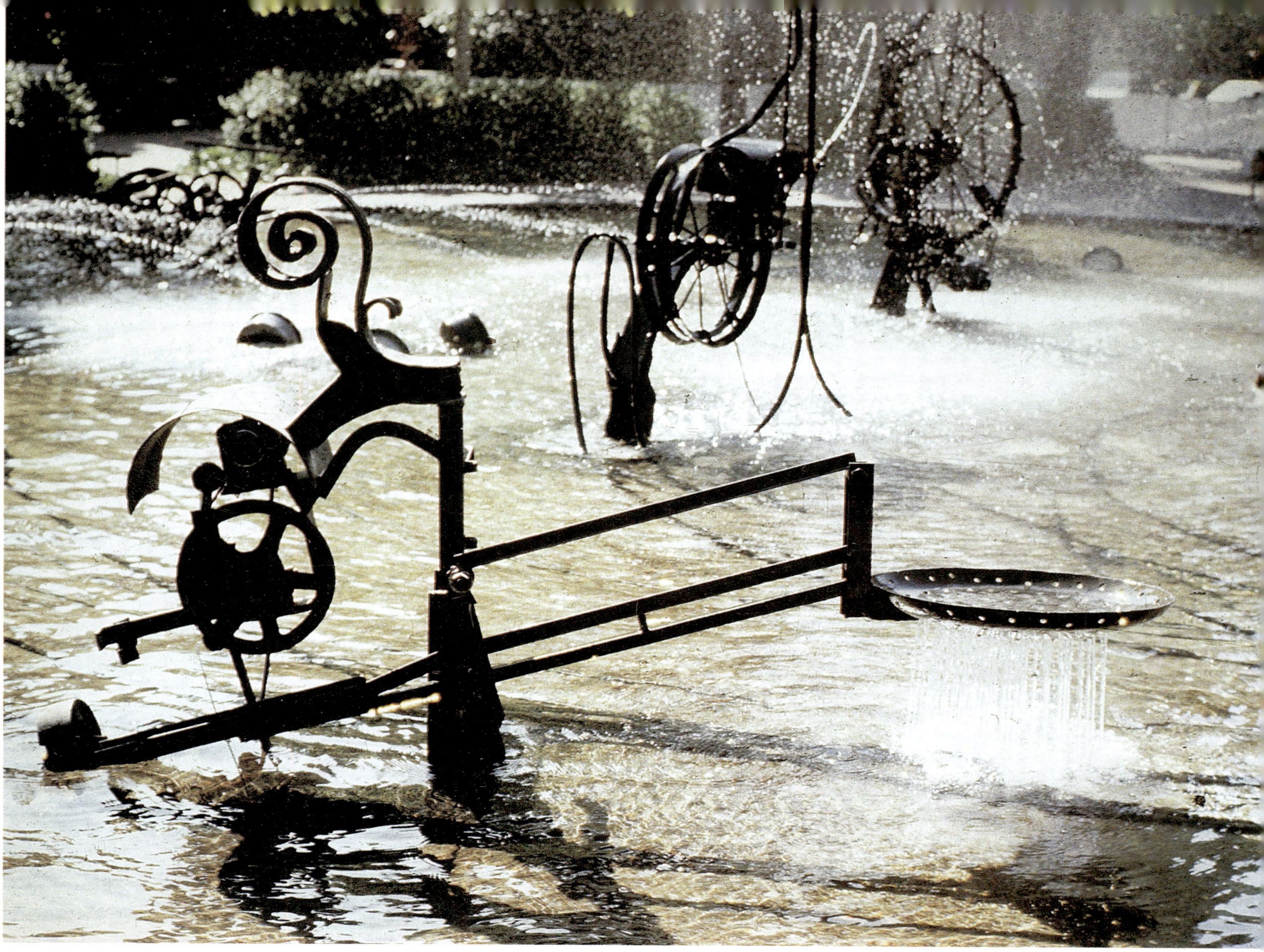

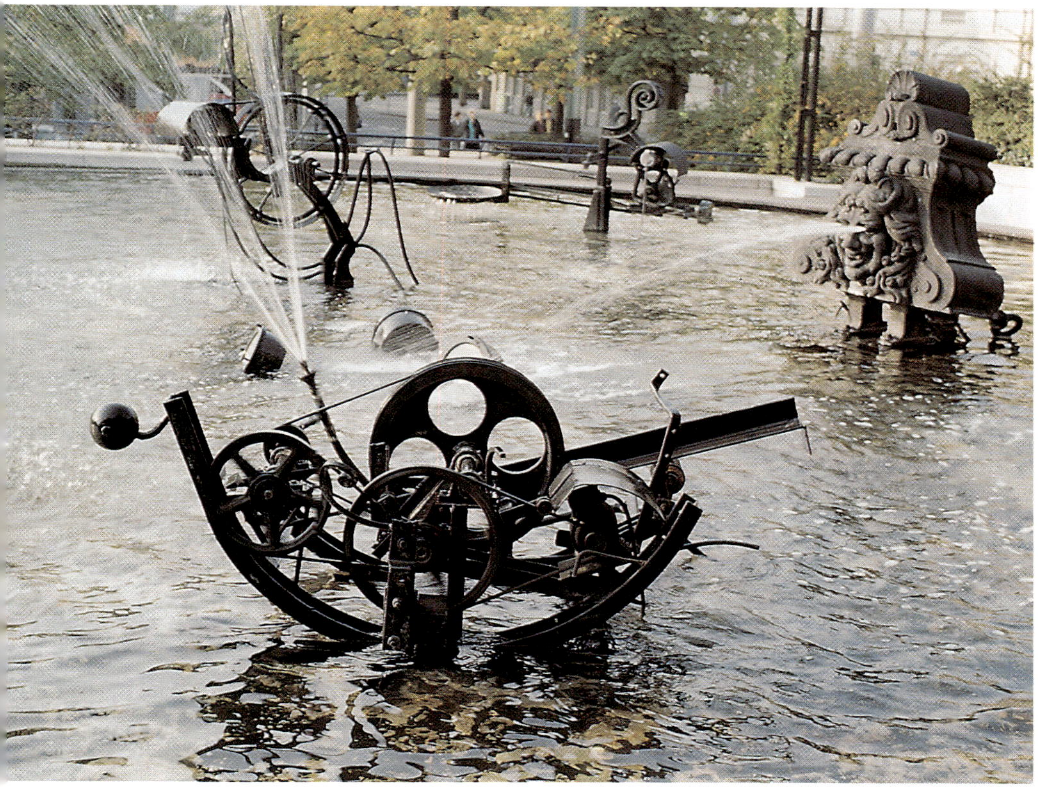

Dr Seechter (The Sieve)

Dr Waggler (The Rocker)

nious symphony of movement and sound. Like *Guggemuusig*, they make variegated sounds, and like a *Clique* at Charivari,[11] each figure acts out its subject. The fountain celebrates the suspension of hierarchy. Here, each one of the objects is 'unique and its own', a salute to both Carnival and the spirit of true freedom as described in Max Stirner's *Der Einzige und sein Eigentum*.[12]

In 1983, 'A fountain begot another fountain', said Pierre Boulez (fig. 52). Boulez believed that only Tinguely's magical waterworks could bring life to the desolate plaza named after Igor Stravinsky and situated above Boulez's Institut de Recherche et de Coordination Acoustique/Musique in Paris.[13] Tinguely accepted the commission under the condition that Niki de Saint Phalle would collaborate with him. He felt that her colours and shapes were necessary together with his black mechanisms to create a harmonious visual flow between the futuristic and brightly coloured Centre Pompidou on one side and the grey Gothic façade of the church Saint-Merri on the other. The technical difficulties of the site were considerable. To reduce weight, Tinguely's sculptures were built of aluminium and de Saint

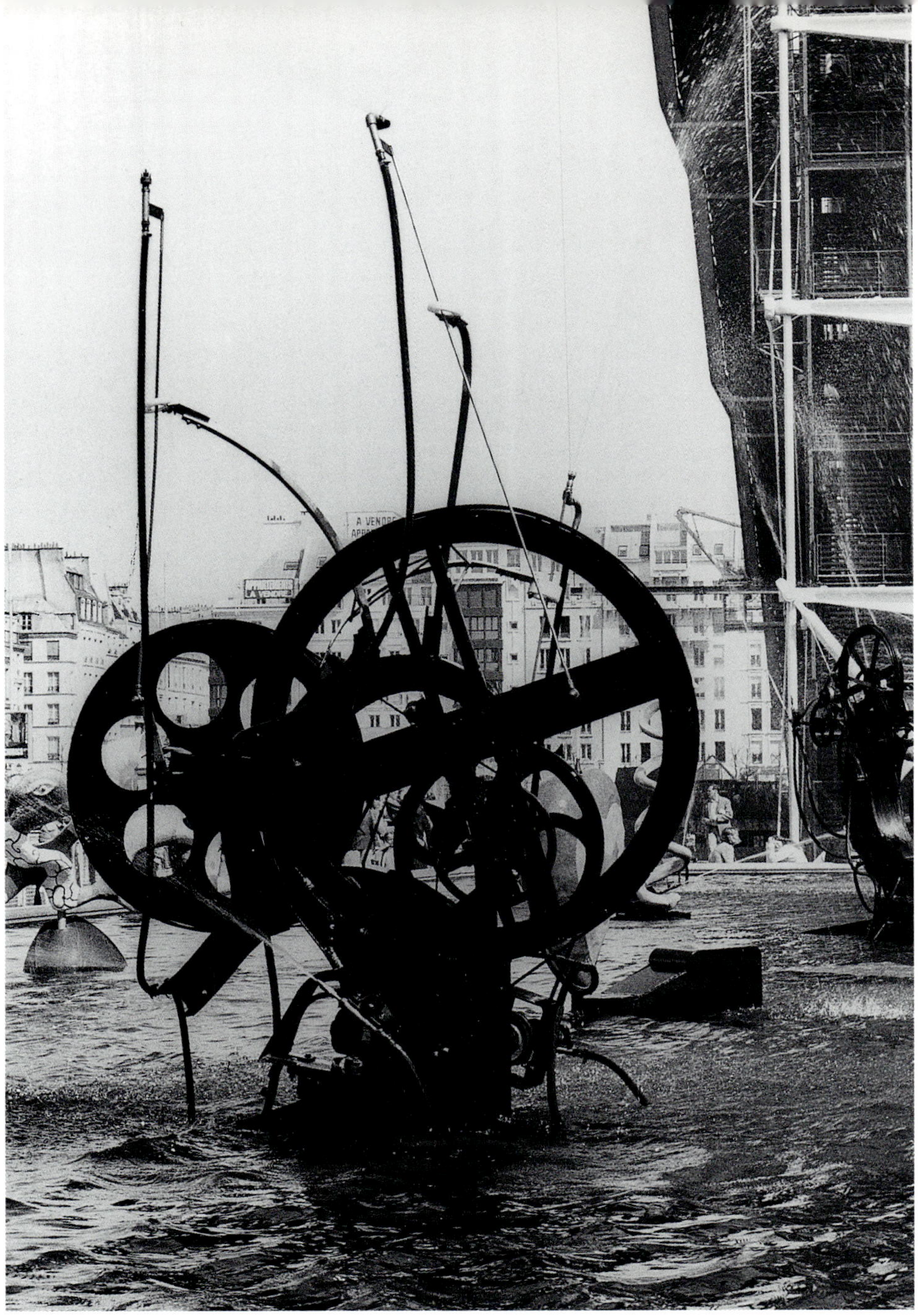

52 Tinguely and Niki de Saint Phalle, *Stravinsky Fountain*, Paris, 1983

Ragtime ▷

Life and *Snake*

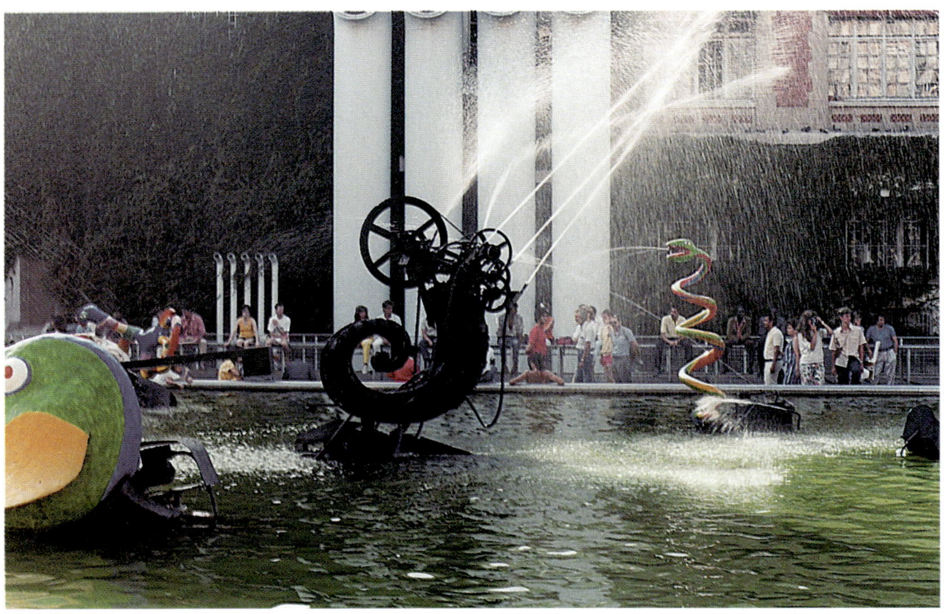

Phalle's of lightweight fibreglass and polyester, and the water level of the basin was made as shallow as possible. Stravinsky's dazzling music so closely associated with dance and with Russian folk tunes and fairy tales provided the two artists with a rich thematic repertoire. The fountain is similar to the brightly coloured page of a Russian children's book, and in the spirit of the composer's orchestration, the sound of the water forms syncopated patterns that emanate from the sculptures in a dazzling variety of ways.

Tinguely's *G Clef*, motionless, makes sound by means of its two low sprays. The three large wheels of *Ragtime* turn into one another; their choreography is enhanced by five jets that create a throbbing rhythm in a fitting tribute to Stravinsky's early American jazz-inspired pieces. *The Fox* similarly evokes the burlesque tale of three barnyard creatures around which Stravinsky composed his chamber opera of 1916–17. The sculpture's rapidly rotating barrel bristles with spikes and slashes and whips the water. The composer's *Rite of Spring* is evoked by a work Tinguely entitled *Life*. Its abundance is symbolised by a cornucopia whose horn is filled with wheels that move several gushing hoses about. *The Diagonal* and *The Frog* reach out with their two powerful jets, while *The Spiral* rotates and churns the water. *Death* is a helter-skelter assemblage of metal bars, tubes and odd shapes topped by a skull-like mask which de Saint Phalle transformed into a nozzle, a playful reminder of life's transience. The fountain also honours Serge Diaghilev, Stravinsky's associate. De Saint Phalle's *Fire Bird*, crowned in gold, dominates the fountain by size and placement in homage to the ballet of the same name, scored by Stravinsky for Diaghilev's Ballets Russes in 1910. Like a Madonna of Mercy, *Fire Bird* appears to protect the assembly under its cloak, magically woven by myriad water droplets emanating like an aura from the bird's crown. *The Nightingale*, of Hans Christian Andersen fame, is another legendary bird that inspired Stravinsky to write two scores and de Saint Phalle to create a colourful creature that dips one of its wings into the water. Other components of the fountain include *The Clown's Hat*, *Love*, *The Siren*, *Heart*, *Elephant*[14] and *Snake*. The 16 sculptures that make up the *Stravinsky Fountain* occupy a basin twice as large as the one in Basel. Again, dialogue and cohesion are created by the

G Clef and *Fire Bird*

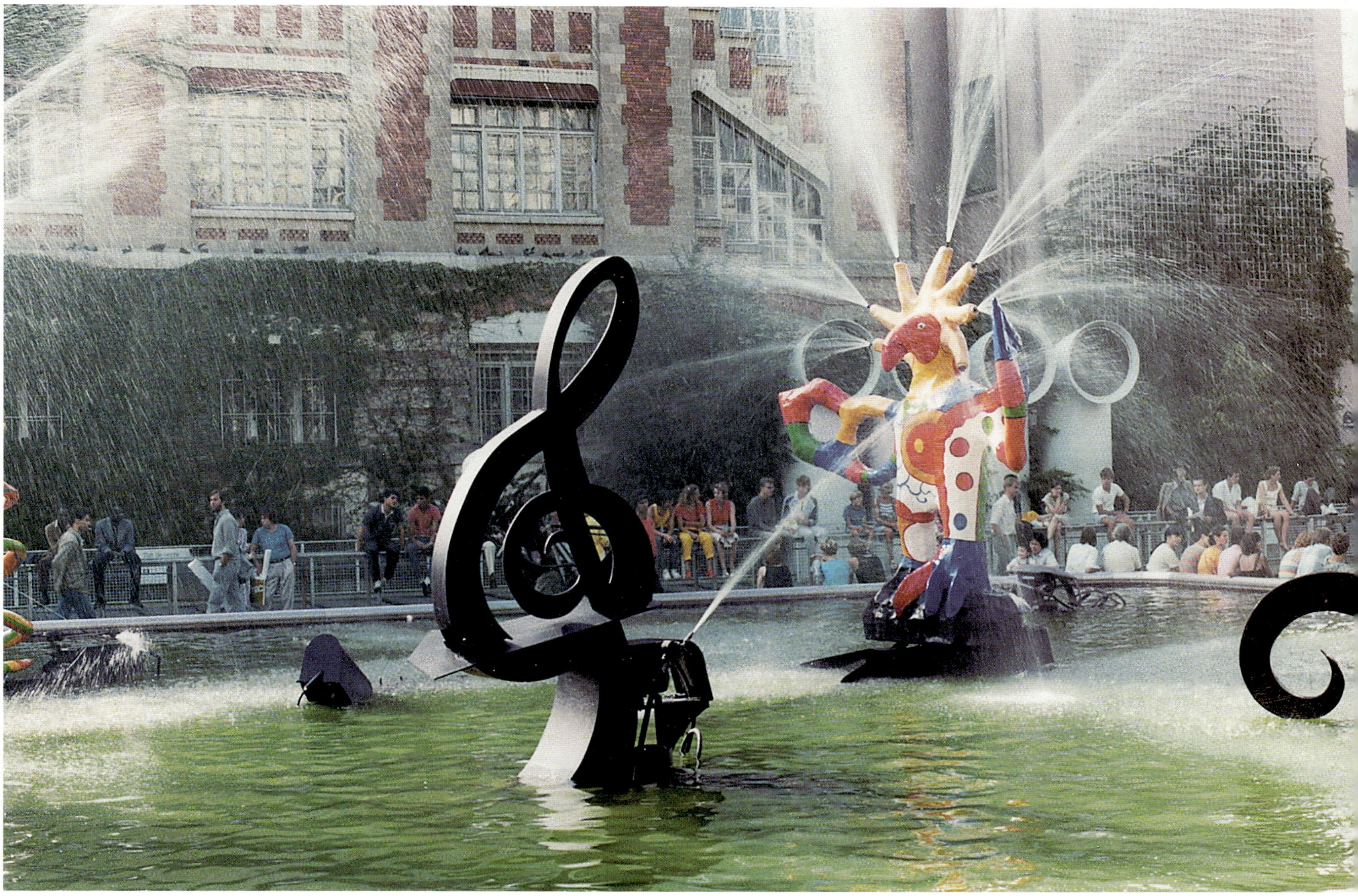

orchestrated play of drizzling, spraying, spouting, gushing, rippling and spurting water.

Tinguely and de Saint Phalle had been confronted with the architecture of the Centre Pompidou before they built the *Stravinsky Fountain*. Together with Bernhard Luginbühl, they had accepted an invitation from Pontus Hulten, then its Director, to construct a piece in the same vein as *Hon* for the centre's opening in 1977. The resulting scrap-iron fun house some 46 metres in length was named the *Crocrodrome* (fig. 53).[15] A dragon's head, with huge teeth and mobile jaws, was designed by de Saint Phalle; the body, complete with a ghost train, was Tinguely's responsibility. Luginbühl constructed the beast's behind and animated its internal organs. Material shaped like the hefty iron scrap Luginbühl uses in his sculptures was expelled from and returned to two open-ended tubes. Here, Luginbühl seemed to parody the sculptural method he and Tinguely had adopted. By recycling materials, the artists reclaimed industrial waste and shaped it into a poetic thing, which nonetheless, in the minds of many, was 'waste' material of a sort.[16] Amidst a jungle of mechanised wheels, the name *Crocrodrome* and the artists' alias Zig & Puce shone in neon letters like the signs in amusement parks. Spectators sat in open-mouthed shark-head chariots and were swallowed like Jonah and triumphantly resurrected after their journey through the monster's ghostly, fun-filled intestinal tract. They were then ready for the mock-serious art of Daniel Spoerri and his *Aberrant Boutique* and *Sentimental Museum* placed at the monster's side. The money collected from visitors was donated to charity.

Stravinsky Fountain, view from the Centre Georges Pompidou ▷

Niki de Saint Phalle, *Ragtime* (in the foreground), *Life* (right) and *Fire Bird* (in the background, right) at night

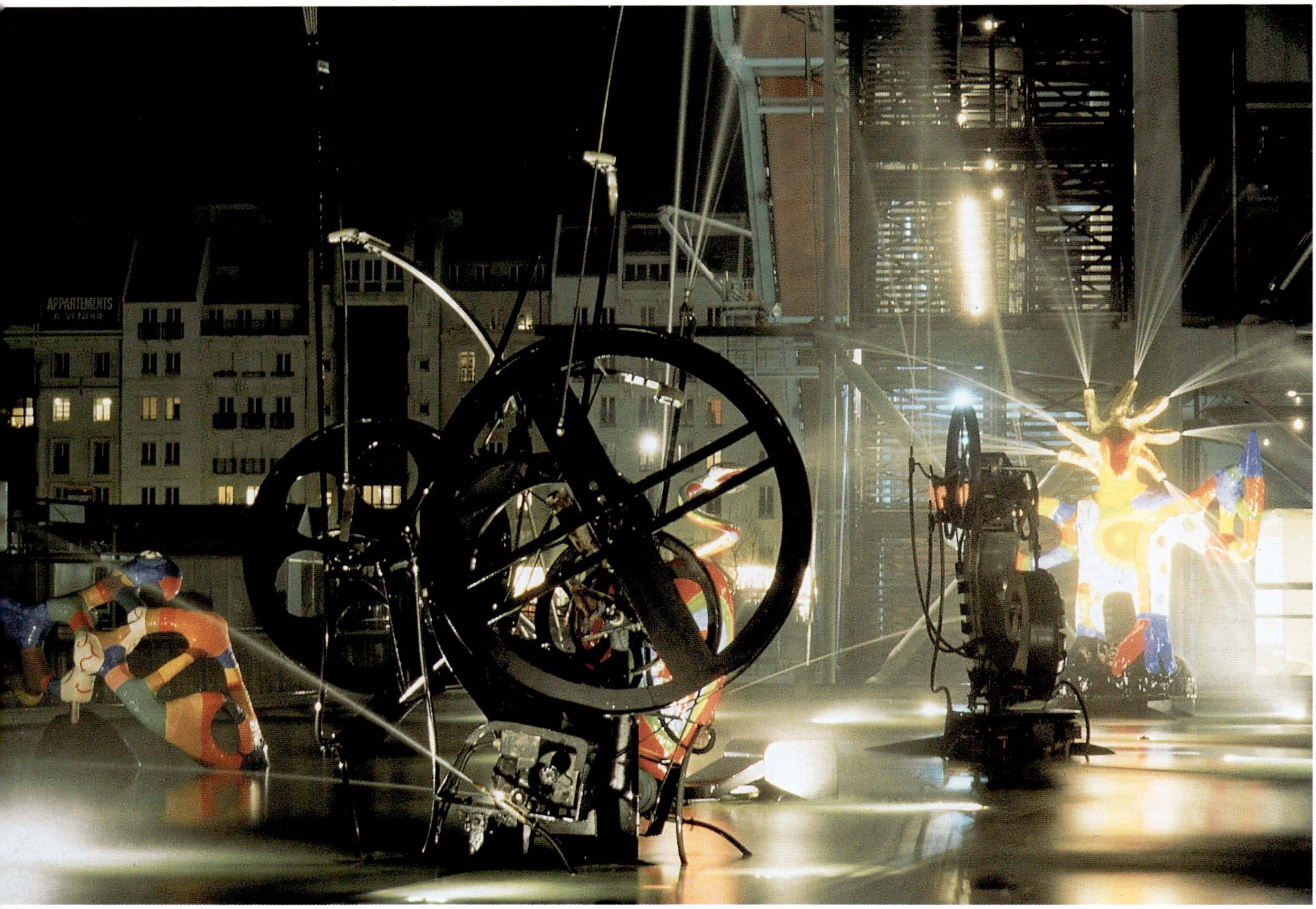

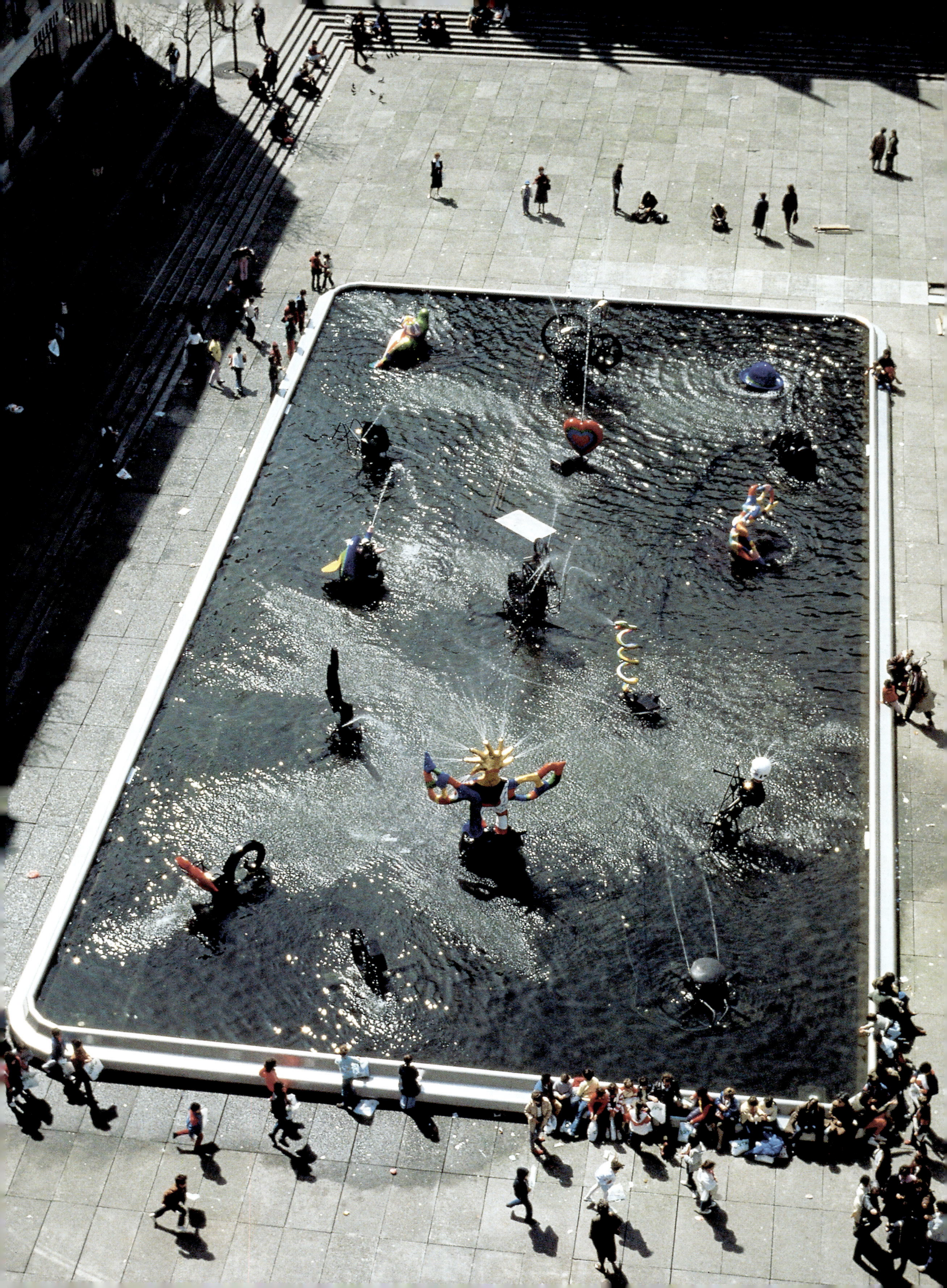

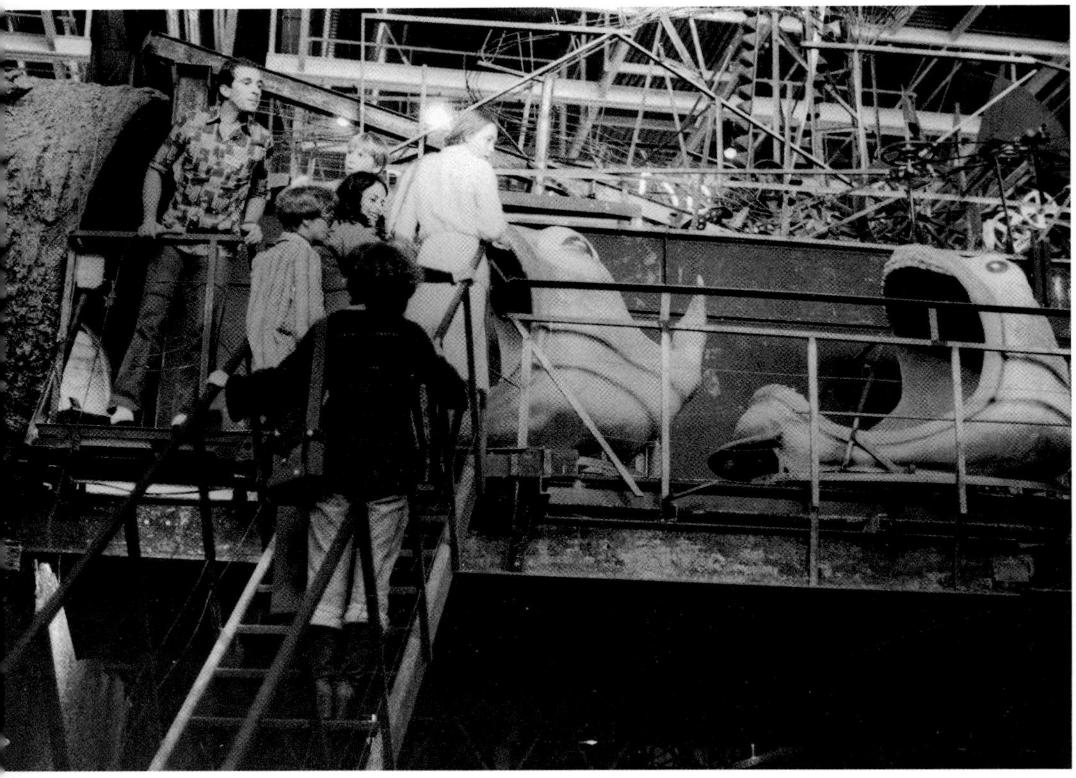

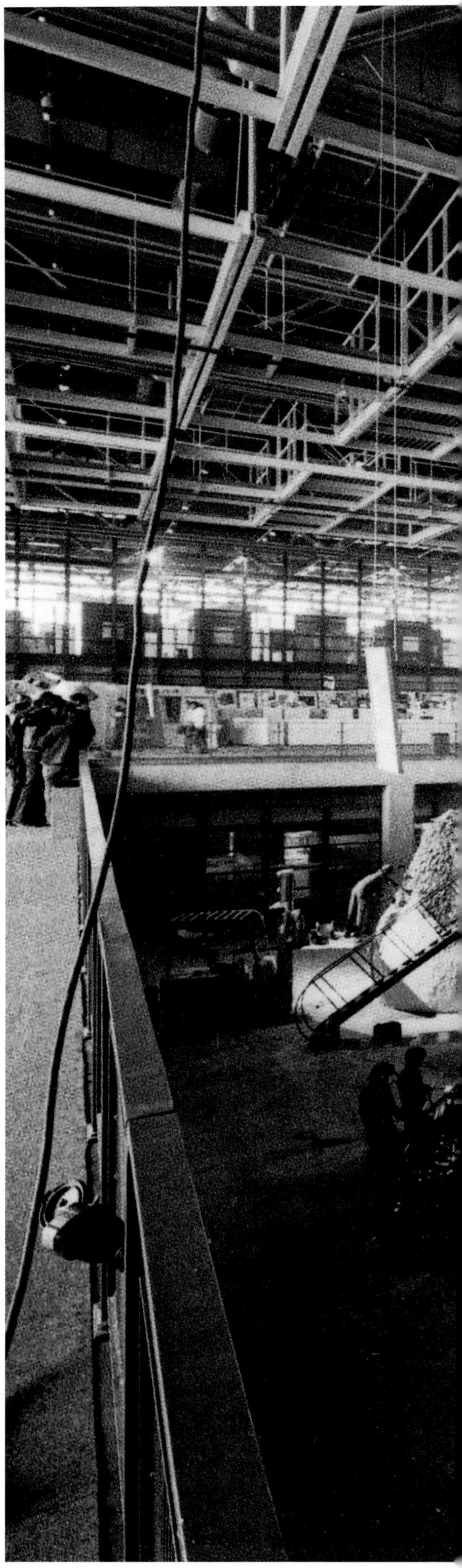

Two other large-scale works deserve mentioning here. The inauguration of a fountain in 1984 in Tinguely's native town of Fribourg became the occasion for a feast. The fountain was donated by Tinguely in memory of his friend the famed champion Grand-Prix racer Jo Siffert, who had been killed at Brands Hatch in 1971 (see fig. 55).[17] For the unveiling, Fribourg's citizenry enjoyed an epicurean feast offered by Tinguely and his artist-friends-turned-chefs Bernhard Luginbühl and family, Adolf Hofkunst and Jean-Pierre Corpataux. (The latter is a butcher and restauranteur who immortalises his trade in still-life paintings of meat.) The fountain, a single sculpture in the centre of a round basin, animates a grassy square not far from the train station. Its mechanical make-up is similar to that of its predecessors. Two large and two smaller wheels drive four arm-like rods to which hoses ending in different types of nozzles are connected. Each

53 *Crocrodrome*, Centre Georges Pompidou, Paris, 1977

Crocrodrome (view of the front) ▷

Entrance to the fun house

pair of wheels is driven by a motor. The motion of the rods depends upon the size of the wheel. An additional wheel, driven by its own motor and shaped like a spiral, whips the surface of the water. The fountain is painted black. A base that secures the sculpture in the water has a cylindrical extension around which the sculpture swings, pushed by a sturdy metal bar near the bottom. Thus, the sculpture presents a continuously changing spectacle of turning wheels, moving nozzles and variegated sprays. The wheels' quiet animation pays touching tribute to the

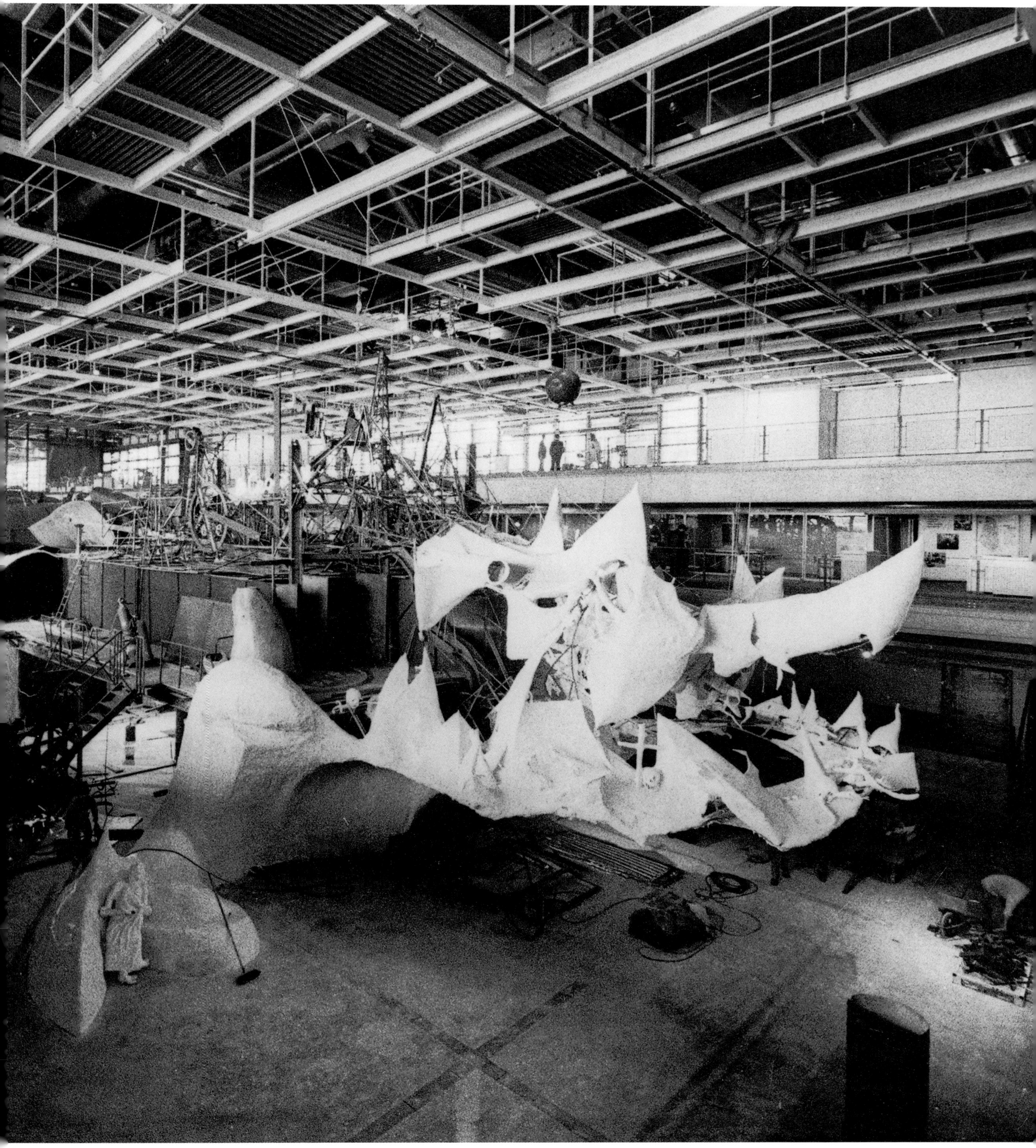

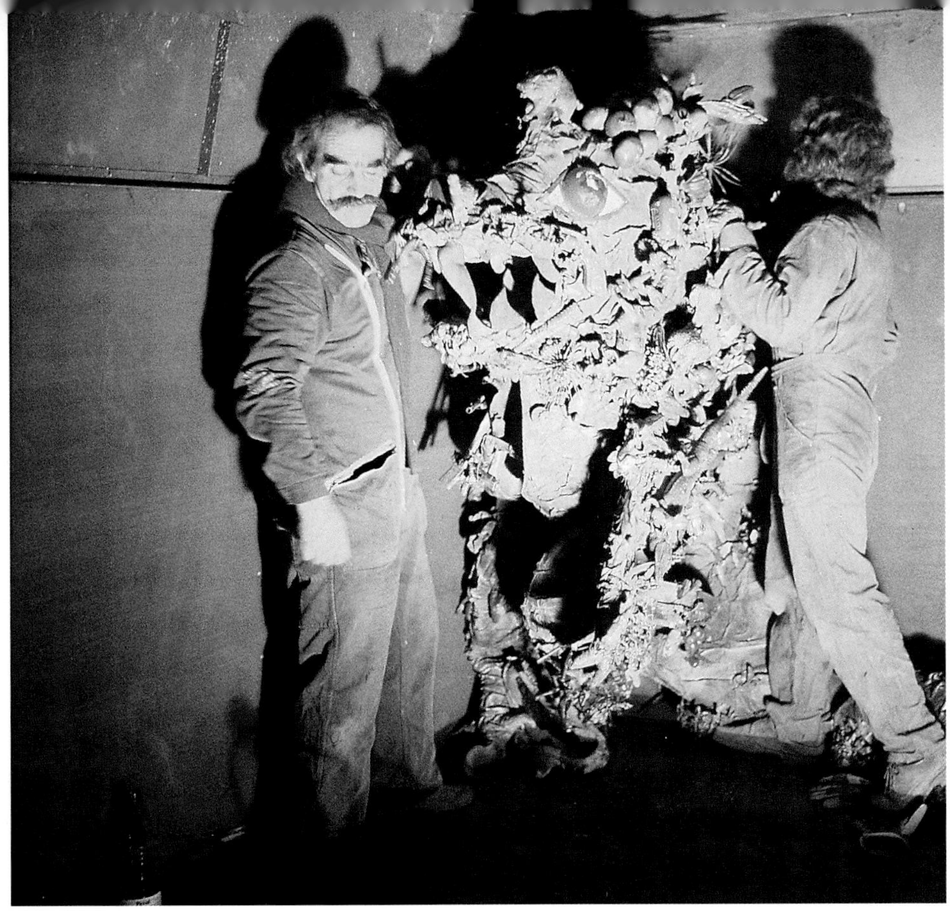

man who died behind the wheel of his racing car.[18]

Following the success of the fountains in Basel and Paris, Tinguely had been submerged with requests for waterworks. The artist refused all but one, from President François Mitterrand of France, for Château Chinon,

Crocrodrome (view from the inside)

Back leg of *Crocrodrome* with chocolate covering ▹

View of the forum at the Centre Georges Pompidou

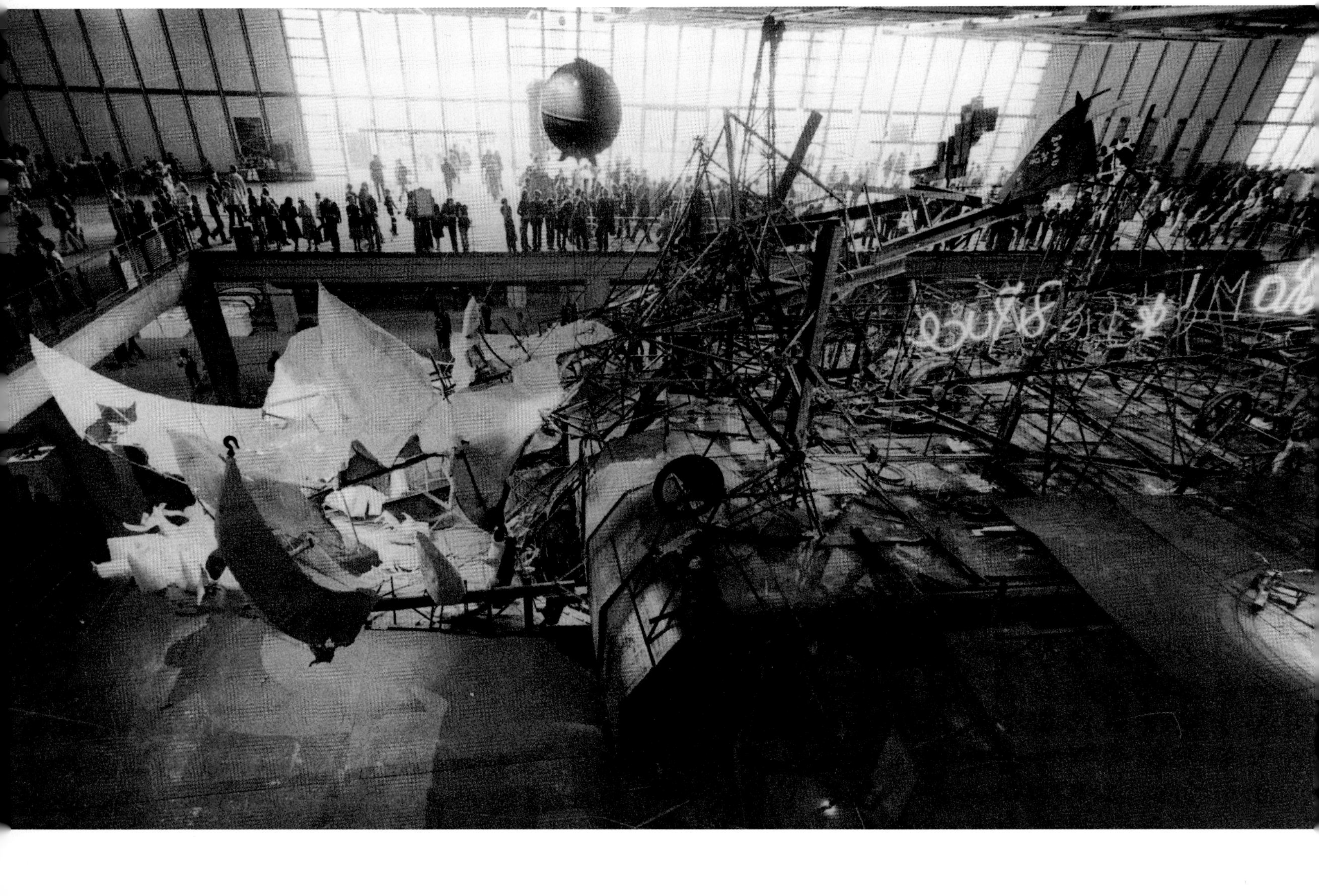

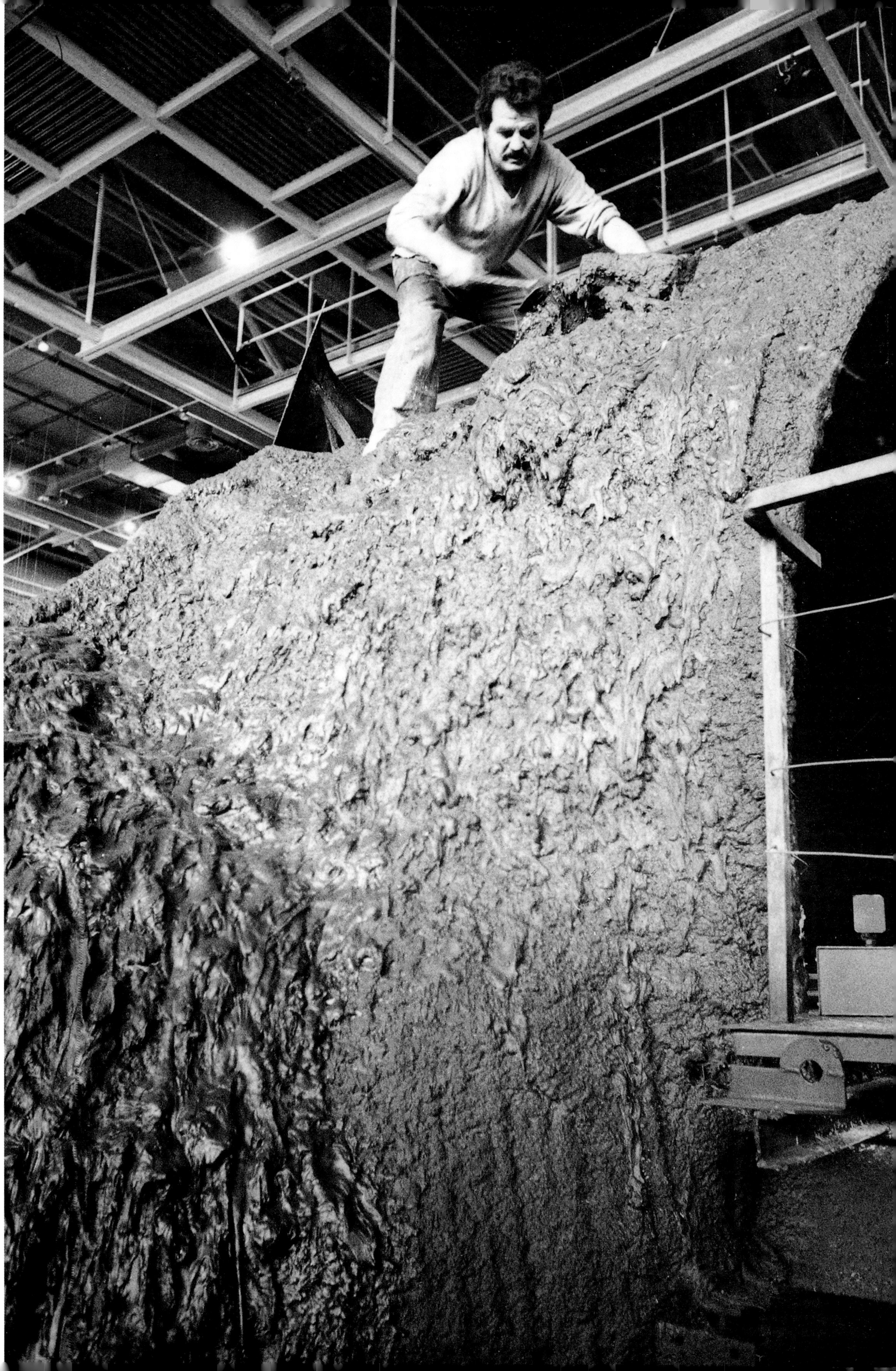

where Mitterrand had been mayor for 30 years. The President had shown genuine interest in the fate of *Head* and had accepted the artists' donation of it to France. Their thank-you took the form of a fountain as cheerful as the one in Paris (fig. 54). Tinguely stated that his participation consisted of providing the mechanisms to animate de Saint Phalle's figures, and that he therefore 'remained underground'. She provided the seven figures whose rounded, brightly coloured forms generously dispense water from a myriad of apertures.

Tinguely with Jo Siffert, Mötschwil, 1971

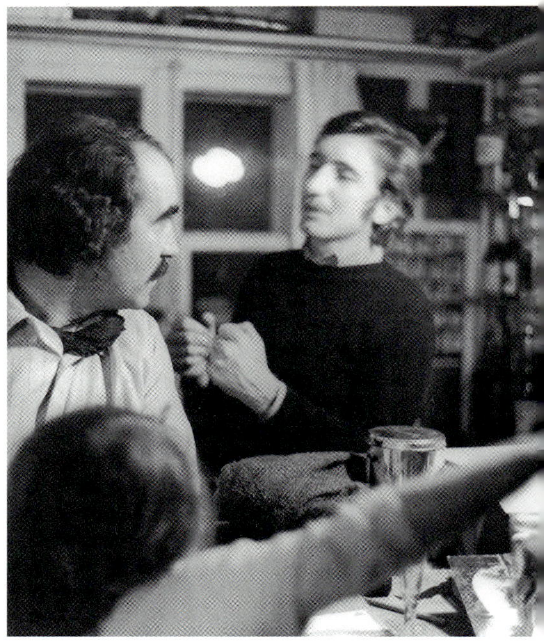

54 Niki de Saint Phalle with Tinguely, *Château Chinon Fountain*, 1988

55 *Jo Siffert Fountain*, 1984 ▷

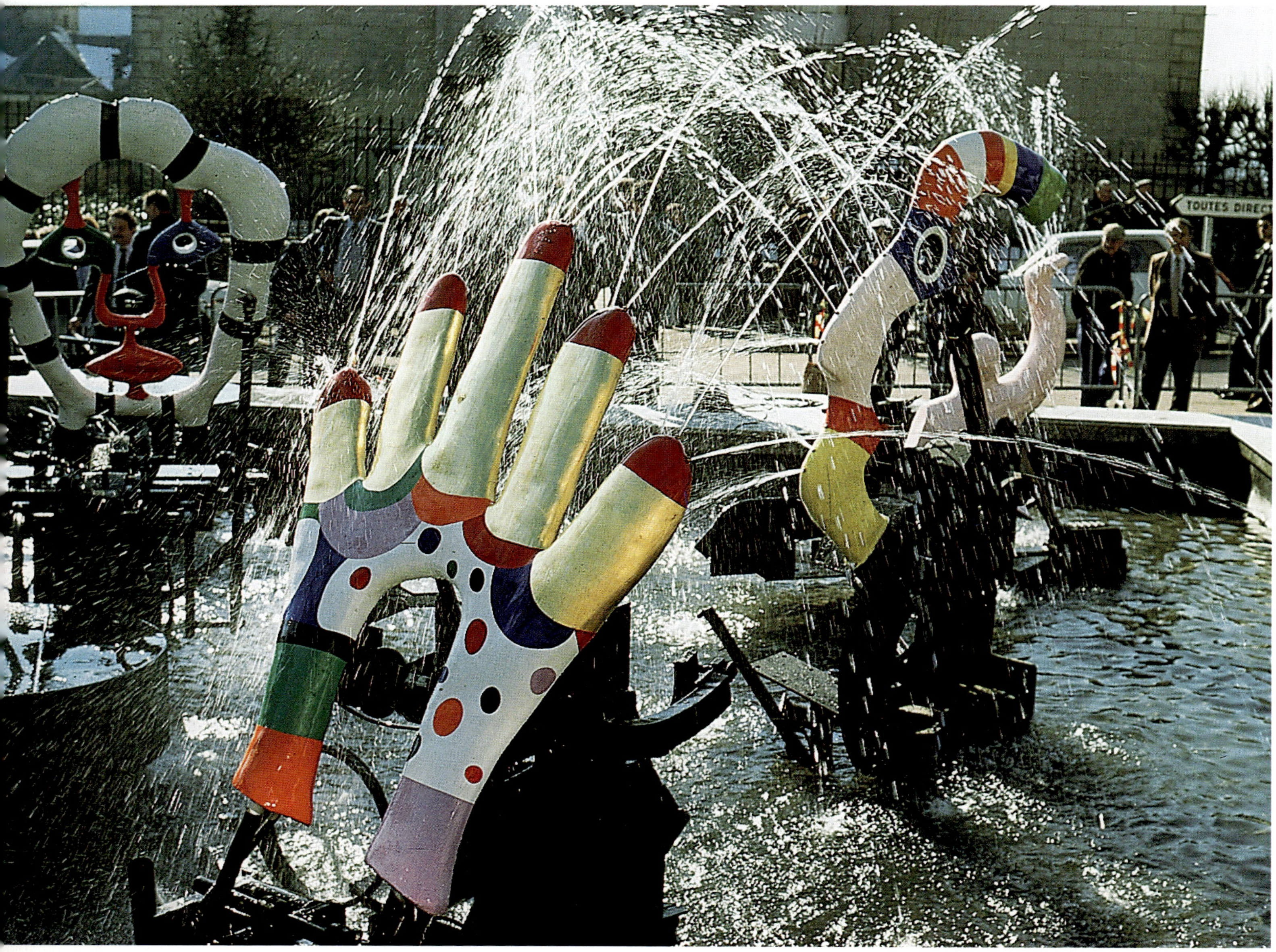

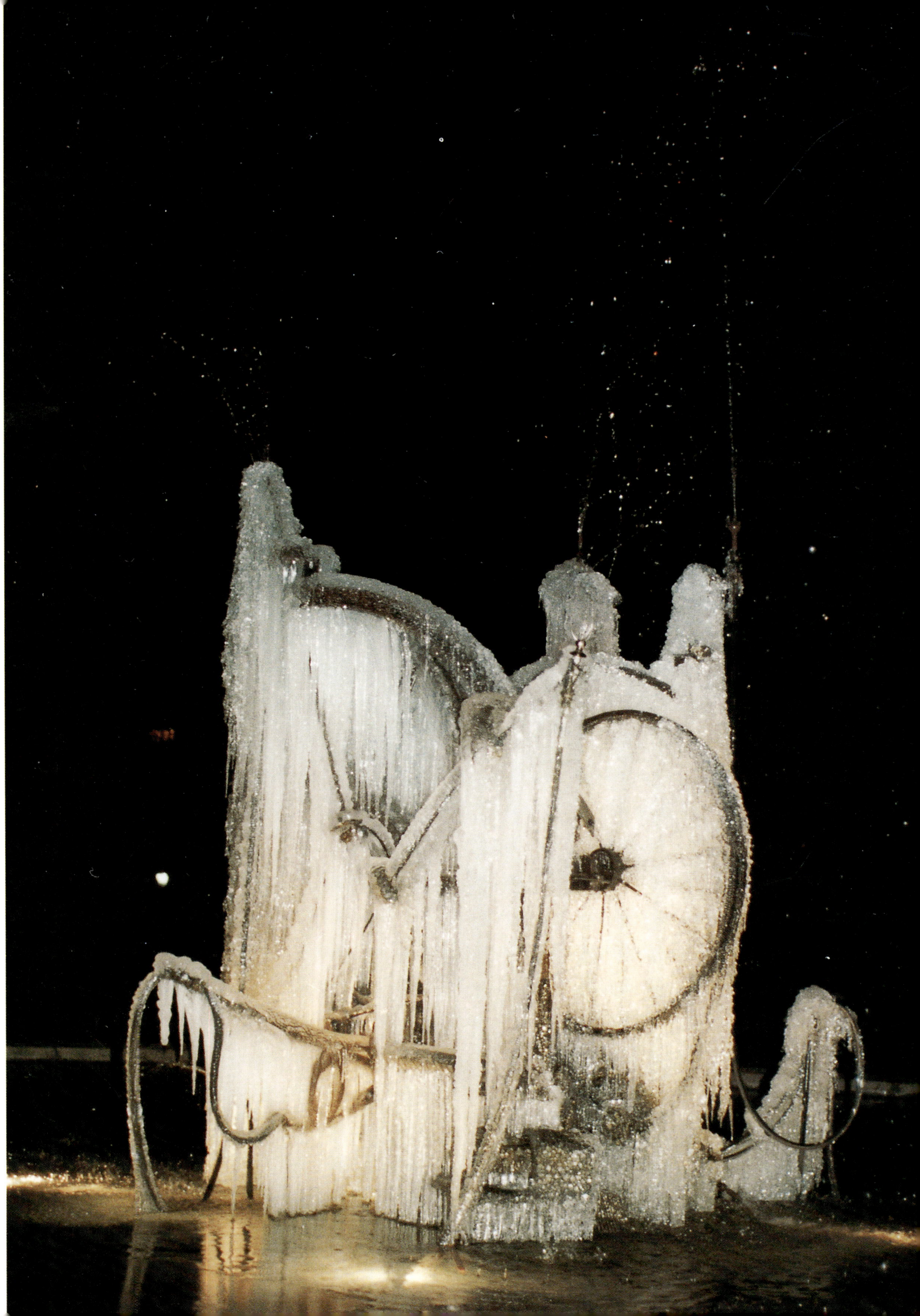

‘Art is nonsense and, like everything else, not senseless’

1978–85

In many of his works, Jean Tinguely attempted to connect his viewers with the intense creativity of childhood, when most learning occurs through play. Tinguely had preserved the child within himself, the positive narcissism, the intensity and concentration focused in the present, the naturally activist attitude. He appropriated the essence of play for his own needs—its fun and its primordial quality of facilitating communication.[1] His machine art is expressive of the total freedom of play and communicates on that level. In his junk assemblages, Tinguely created a poetic reality akin to the play world of the child by distorting reality rather than copying it. Like poetry, his works are transpositions of elements gleaned from the vernacular world and fashioned into new poetic arrangements and relationships. Thus, Tinguely's viewer can associate and merge with the poetic realm by proxy.

One of the most striking characteristics of Tinguely's works is their kinship with toys; indeed, he challenged the viewer to respond to them on that level. In his essay ‘A Philo-

56 *Machine Bar*, 1960-85

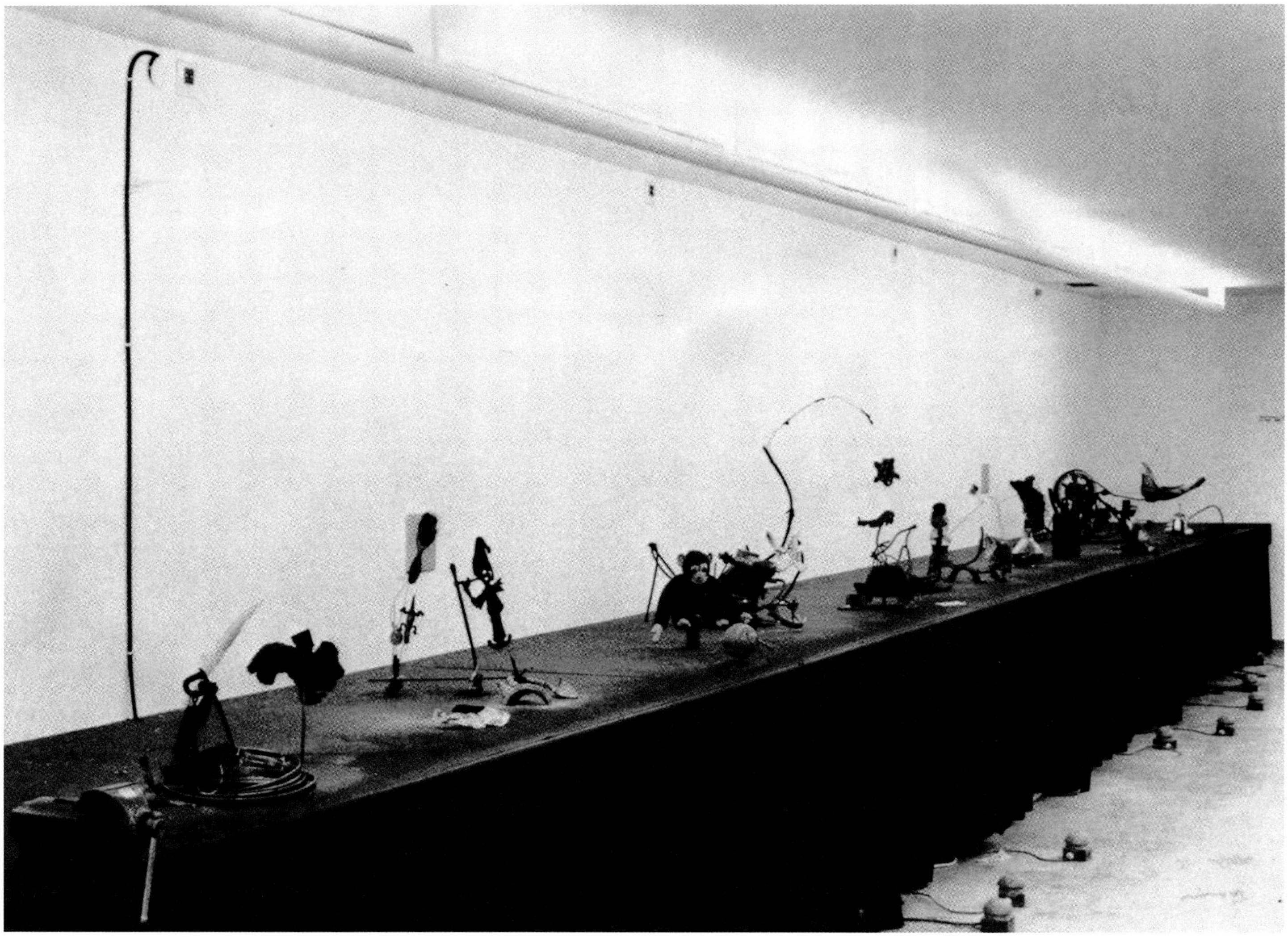

sophy of Toys', Baudelaire singled out toys as human beings' first exposure to art. The French poet argued that '[t]he toy is the child's earliest initiation to art, or rather for him it is the first concrete example of art, and when mature age comes, the perfected example will not give his mind the same feelings of warmth, nor the same enthusiasms, nor the same sense of conviction'.[2] It is to Tinguely's credit that he fashioned works of art which not only look like toys at times but which also succeed in being as communicative, surprising and exciting as the best of children's playthings. For example, the *Machine Bar* consists of seven miniaturesque objects built between 1960 and 1985 that sit on top of a counter, each object being connected to bright red push-buttons on the floor (fig. 56). The result is Las Vegas-style fun, only this slot machine row dis penses giggles. One of the objects is a dull-looking hollow metal building block. The press of a spectator's foot summons a witch, who plays peekaboo as she climbs in and out. An unlucky plush toy gets crushed by a huge hammer, and a plastic toy squeaks when it is squashed. This 'bar' offers liquor to grown-ups who play destructive games: a bottle of cognac is chained to one of the objects. A serious note is also struck by the jawbone of an ox used as a counterbalance at one end of a rocker: Death Opposite Life on the see-saw. When Tinguely said: 'I play furiously', he expressed the profound seriousness of play and his total freedom as a man and an artist. Or, as Schiller put it: 'A man plays only when he is a man in the full sense of the word, and he is fully human only when he plays.'[3]

Tinguely's works are generally greeted by his public with a certain amount of hilarity. Their humour, and the comic reaction they provoke, are perhaps their most striking characteristics. Tinguely was a cunning *agent provocateur* who was convinced that 'art is ideal when it is an assault, when it is subversive; art ought continuously to call into question everything, and doubt everything anew'.[4] The perplexities and difficulties of our civilisation were his inspiration; the potential for self-criticism provided him with hope.[5] By attracting viewers with his comic gifts, he made his ideological statements more palatable. The comic element in his works eliminates art-related preconceptions and conditioned behaviours. Tinguely used playful elements as shock troops in work whose artillery is meant to attack, disturb, unsettle. The comic was also a form of detachment, the mask that safeguarded the artist's innermost being. As he put it, 'I must build between me and the public a protective layer of irony'.[6] Above all, Tinguely played the fool, one who had cast himself in the role of Stultitia, Erasmus's paradoxical Folly preaching to an audience of fools, the truth-teller whose insights were thinly disguised as a form of insanity.[7]

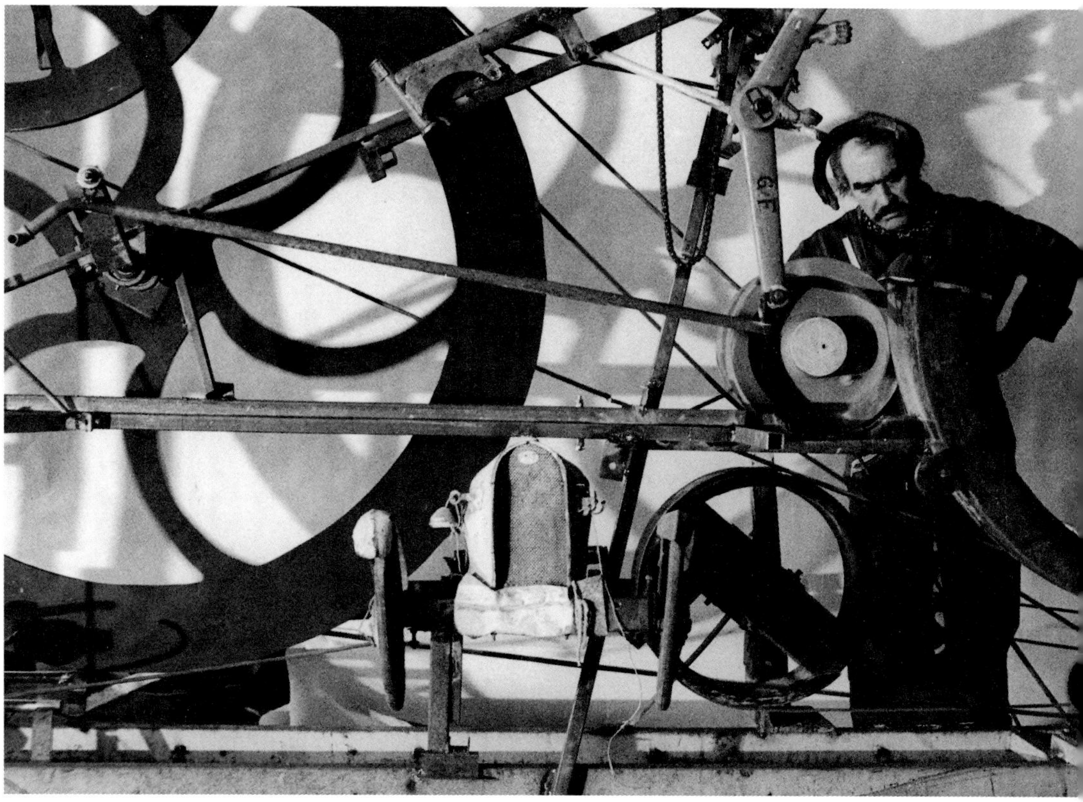

At work on *Fairy Tale Relief*, 1978

The comic element in the artist's work was also his personal ticket to freedom. In the mechanics of motion, he had discovered the idiom most congenial to his philosophy and artistic temperament, yet at times he felt constricted: 'The representation of my problems takes place far away from me, but nevertheless, it is obsessional. This is clear, and I feel it like a sickness, because I always do the same thing.'[8] A sculpture he made in 1963, *Mautz* (Switzerland, private collection), illustrates this state of mind. Frustration and anger are expressed through fast, repetitive movement and the sound of a ball chained

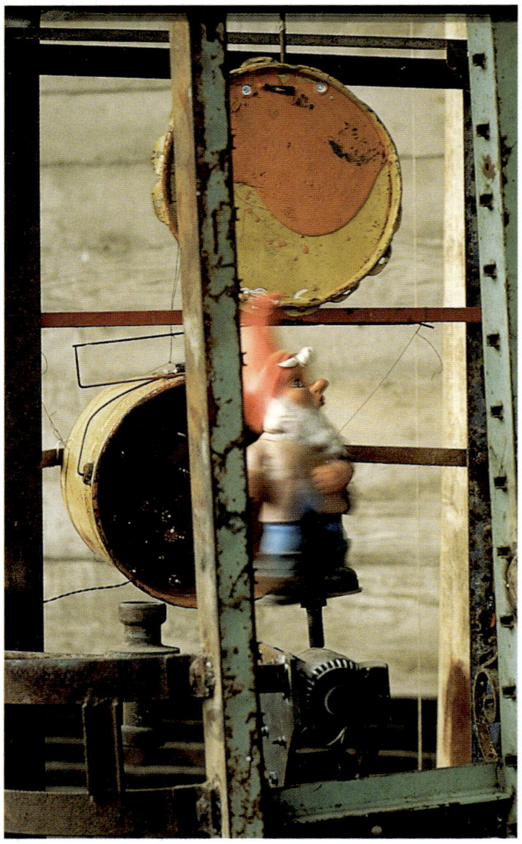

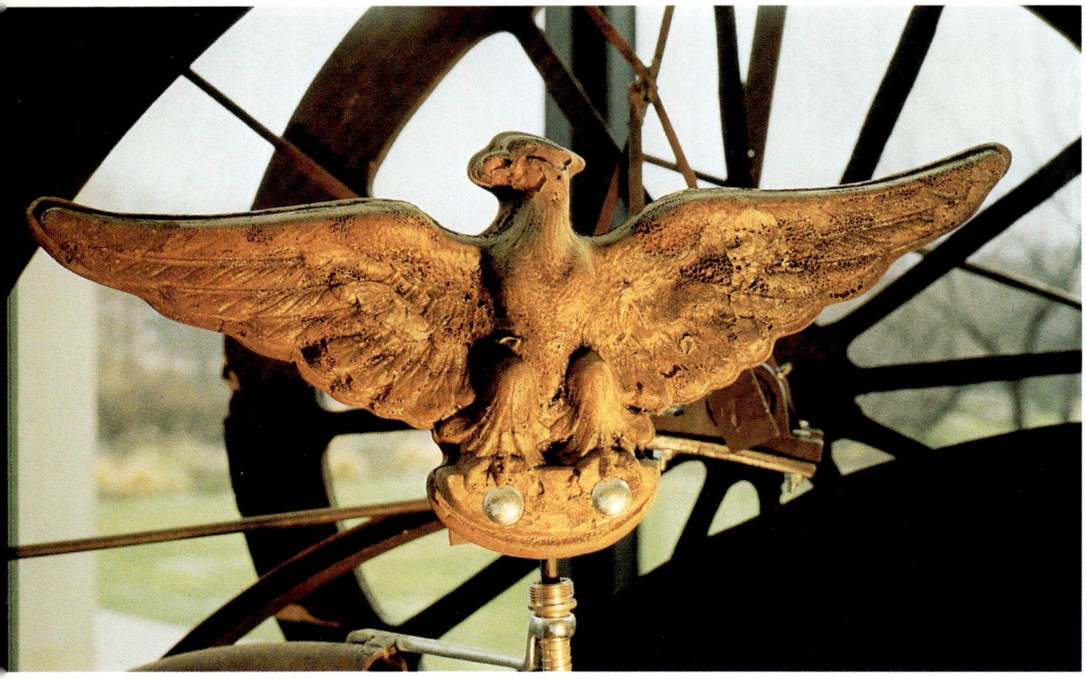

57 *Fairy Tale Relief*, 1978

The Proud Eagle
Der Rasende Gartenweg (Gnome)
The Frog
Bugatti

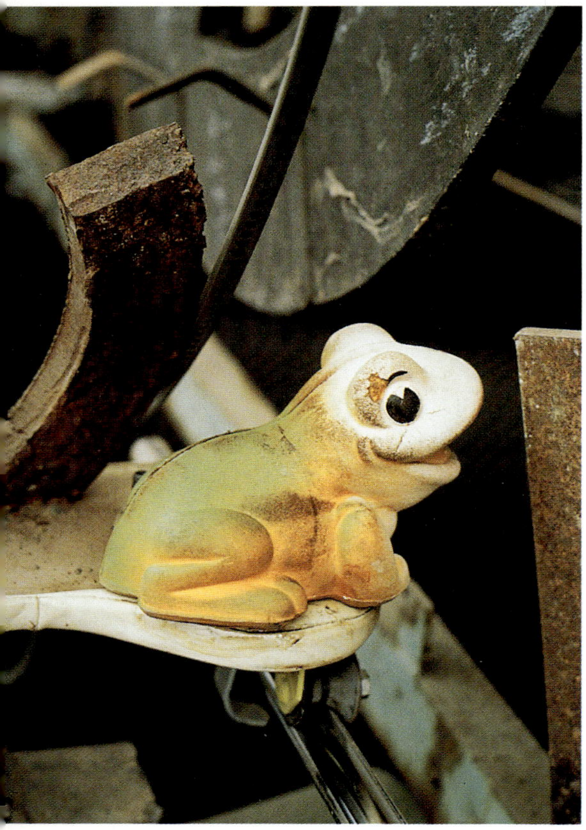

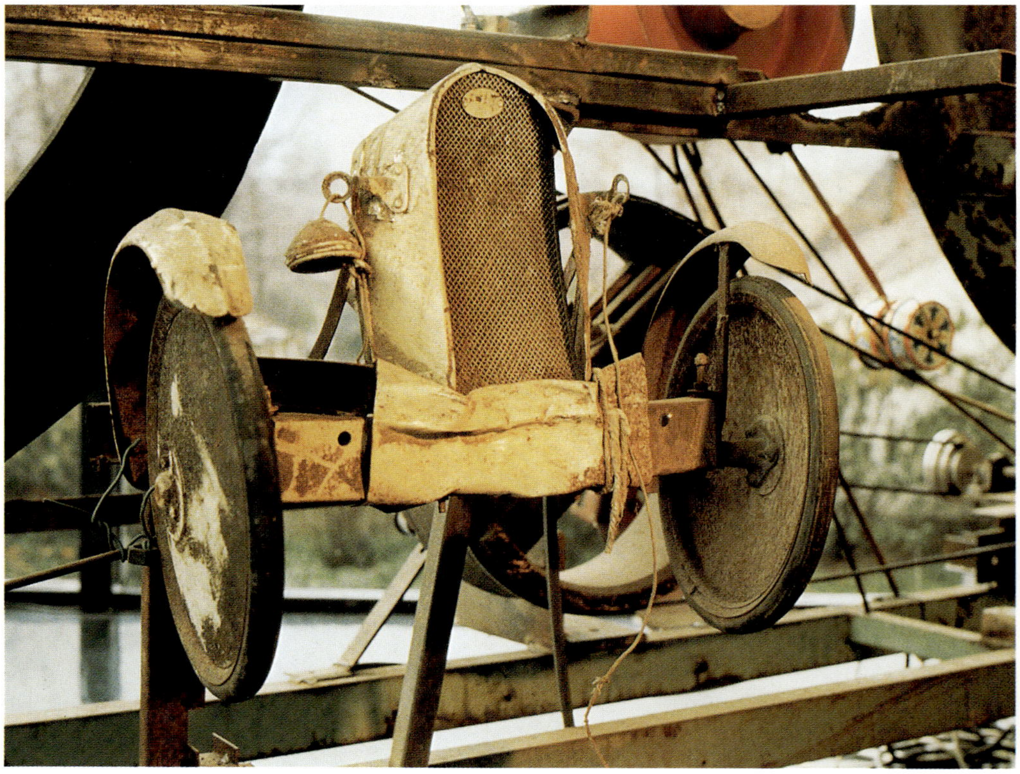

to a metal arm striking the pedestal, a compelling and tragic Piranesian image. Comedy and irony freed Tinguely: 'Irony in my work naturally gives me enormous possibilities and at any time I can wind myself past this condemnation to which I find myself sentenced. Irony . . . in the sense of the Dadaists, in the spirit of Marcel Duchamp . . . There is also a free field where I always can pass.'[9]

As the father of a young boy, the artist rediscovered the world of the child, with its toys and fairy tales. As

The *Fairy Tale Relief*, made in 1978, is the artist's most explicit exploration of the subject of fairy lore (fig. 57).[10] The open-work relief consists of a main section with an extension on each side. Three large wheels of different sizes and with different types of spokes and a variety of objects—some from Tinguely's son's playroom—are set in motion by motors. An eye-catching yellow duck stands out in the left-hand extension; its rear is brushed regularly by a small duster. There is also a frog in the main part of the

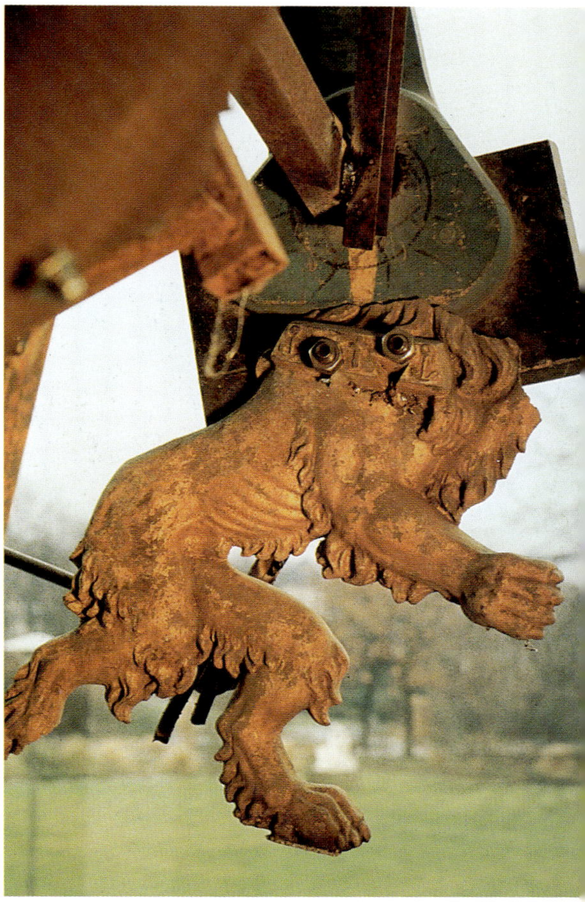

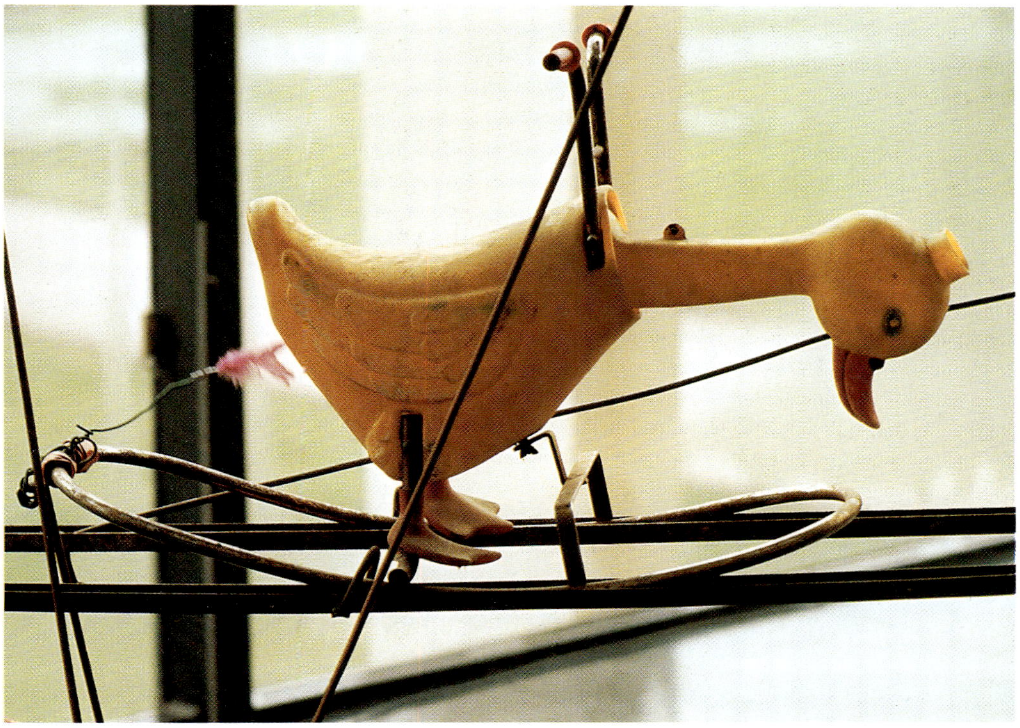

The Sad Lion

The Happy Duck

the child must create his or her own meaning out of fairy tales, so the viewer of Tinguely's art recognises his or her own projections of prototypical fantasies, refracted through the artist's chosen media. Tinguely's art confronts the realities of life in symbolic language, presenting existential dilemmas directly and unambiguously in a form accessible to any age group.

relief. A soaring eagle takes flight high above the frog. As befits his position as ruler of the animal realm, the lion's domain is the centre of the relief.

The other objects in the relief are playthings or other items close to the world of the child. The relief's bottom centre is occupied by the front section of a long-abandoned, rusty toy car, identified in a drawing by Tinguely as a fancy Bugatti whose front wheels navigate the curves of imaginary roads. A collection of broken wooden toys is nailed to a board fixed onto a further arm-like extension and lifted up into the neighbourhood of the lion. A sound-making toy is seen at the lower right. In the right-hand 'wing' of the relief, a brand new garden gnome perches on a thick metal rod and watches over a yellow paint barrel containing garlands of electric Christmas tree lights.

Gnomes figure prominently in many fairy tales. In his relief, Tinguely put the little creature into a fast twirl, describing him as the *Rasende Garten-*

zwerg.[11] Since he moves furiously but never goes anywhere, he really stands still. Tinguely's gnome does his frantic dance in front of a glittering treasure trove. In the fairy tale 'Snow White and Rose Red' he does the same thing just before the story resolves itself. One can also detect within Tinguely's relief elements that point to another tale, 'The Frog King'. Both stories are of the 'animal groom' type. Adults may need to know the title of the relief to set their imaginations onto the appropriate track. Children make connections between the figural elements and fairy tales spontaneously. Such tales reassure and confirm that maturity and love are needed to transform the perception of sexuality as animal-like. Tinguely alluded to the erotic significance of the frog by animating him with a back-and-forth motion and attaching him to a bent metal tube. The entire frog contraption is located near floor level, thus corresponding to the physical and psychological 'height' of a small child.

Psychic development from a lower to a higher state of being is also suggested through the presence and placement of the eagle and lion, ancient emblematic creatures and symbols of virility. In Tinguely's ornithological hierarchies, eagles, hawks, falcons and buzzards dominated. He associated these birds with the freedom that comes from a position of strength and identified with them. He enjoyed falconry, kept eagles and had a number of stuffed specimens at home.

As we have seen, Tinguely believed that although cars provided a certain freedom, they had also become, by their sheer quantity, impediments to that freedom. Thus, this icon of technological progress is also an image embodying the difficulties of that progress. The car in the *Fairy Tale Relief* is a toy that projects the child into adulthood and its conflicts. Brevity and recurrence are suggested by the lights inside the barrel, which blink on and off. The imagery of the relief evokes memories of childhood as fragmented as the bits and pieces nailed to the board. Speaking through a variety of images, Tinguely was tracing his perceptions of childhood as a period of both emotional and spiritual growth. He included the ideas of change, of development, of transitoriness, of power and aspirations, appealing to both the child and the child in all adults.

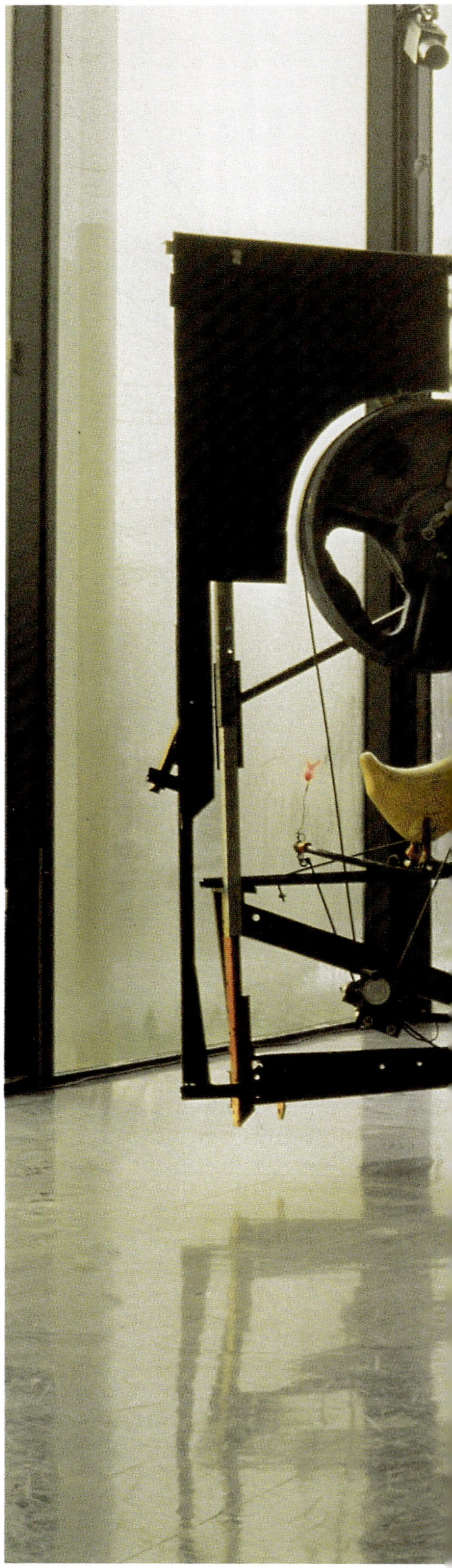

Fairy Tale Relief, 1978 (overall view)

At work on *Fairy Tale Relief*

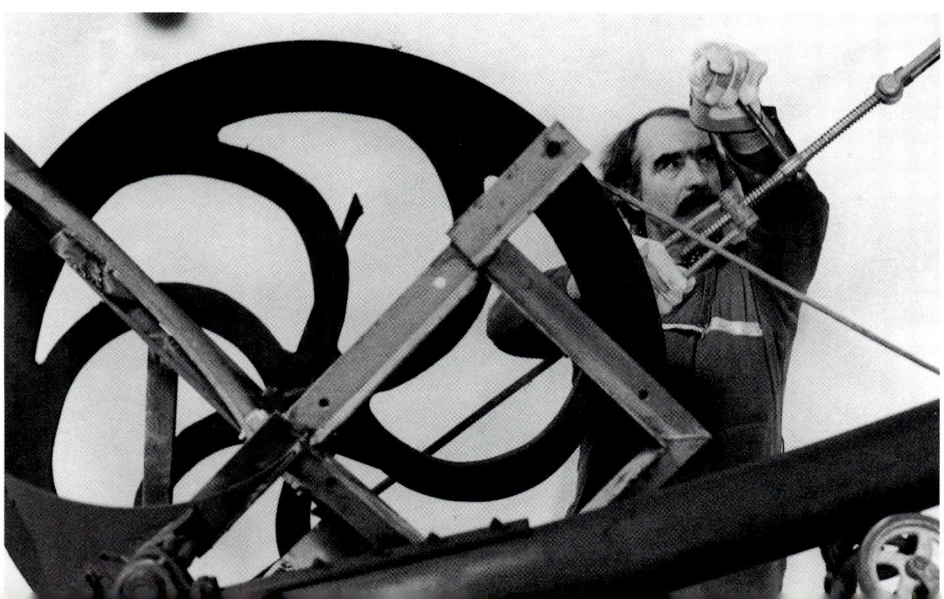

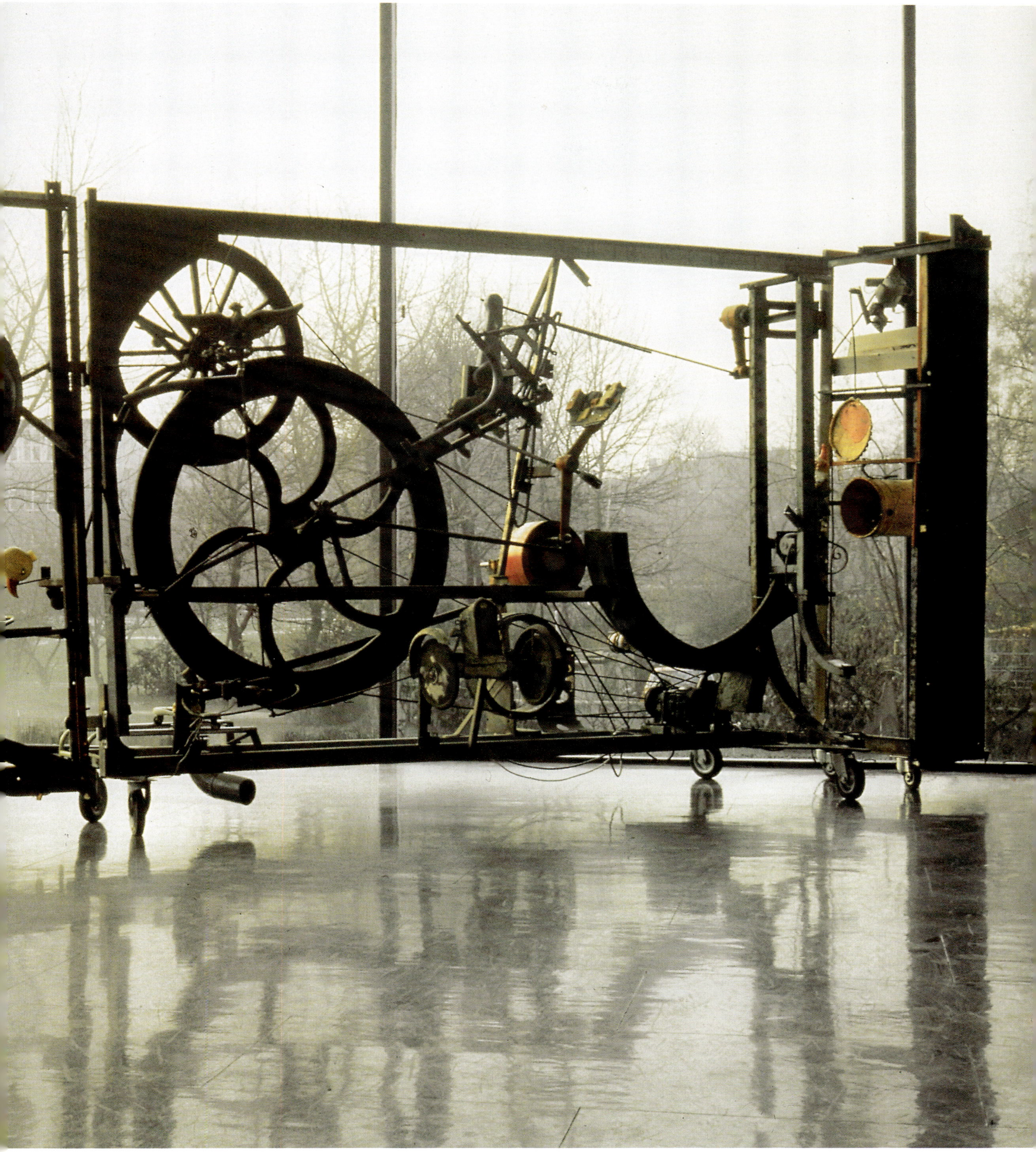

'I've always got on well with transitoriness'

1981–89

Throughout his career, Tinguely was commited to regenerating his poetic and artistic means and to expanding the boundaries of his idiom. In 1981, he once again surprised his audience by adding two new instruments to his arsenal, namely animal skulls and formal devices borrowed from traditional Christian art. Was it his experience of his mother's death in 1978 which led him to take up the theme of death unmasked? As he put it in a television interview, 'Death is unproblematic for me. In any case, everything dies all around us. Mama had problems with dying. After the death of my father, she suddenly stopped going to church. She only watched these horror things on television. So I sent her back to church. I did not want her to be crushed by the fear of dying. I wanted her to get free of the fear. I was with her when she died'.[1] Undisguised images of death in the form of a couple of canine and boar skulls appeared in the exhibition of 15 new sculptures that opened in the summer of that year at the Cistercian abbey of Sénanque in southern France. In December of the same year, his solo show at Galerie Bischofberger in Zurich centred on a large open-work relief entitled *Cenodoxus—Isenheim Altarpiece* (fig. 59) Here, the macabre element embodied in animal jawbones and crania is predominant. In addition, this piece has the classical tripartite structure characteristic of Christian altarpieces, a format unusual for Tinguely, who until then had avoided symmetry. With this work the artist paraphrased and subverted the formal and symbolic means of traditional religious art, thus opening a new chapter in his oeuvre.

The clues given by the structure and title of the relief are guides for deciphering its iconology. *Cenodoxus*, a Baroque play, is less well known than Matthias Grünewald's monumental *Isenheim Altarpiece* (illus. p. 119). Tinguely had first come into contact with *Cenodoxus* when asked by his long-time friend Werner Düggelin to build sets and design costumes (fig. 58) for the producer's restaging of the drama on the occasion of the 1972 Salzburg Festival. The play, written by the German Jesuit writer Jacob Bidermann, had had its first performance in Augsburg in 1602, becoming an immediate success.[2] Its hero was fashioned in the image of the self-absorbed Renaissance scholar who, like many of Bidermann's contemporaries, sought im-

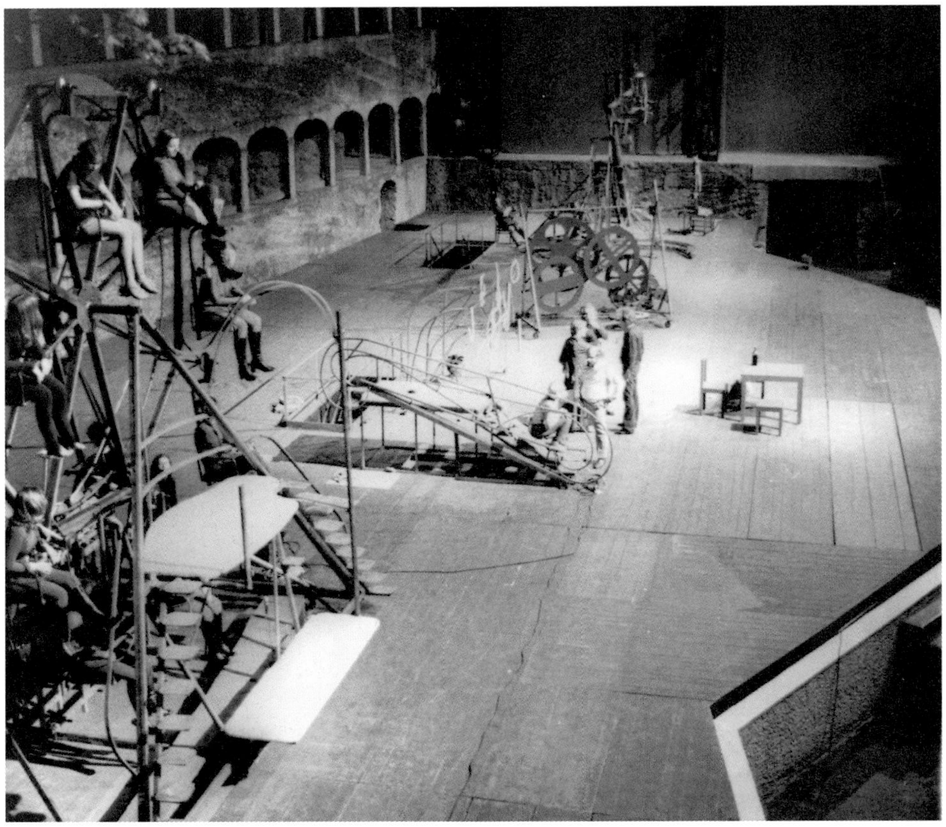

58 Stage set of Jacob Bidermann's *Cenodoxus*, produced by Werner Düggelin, Salzburg Festival, 1972. (*Hell, Earth* and *Heaven*)

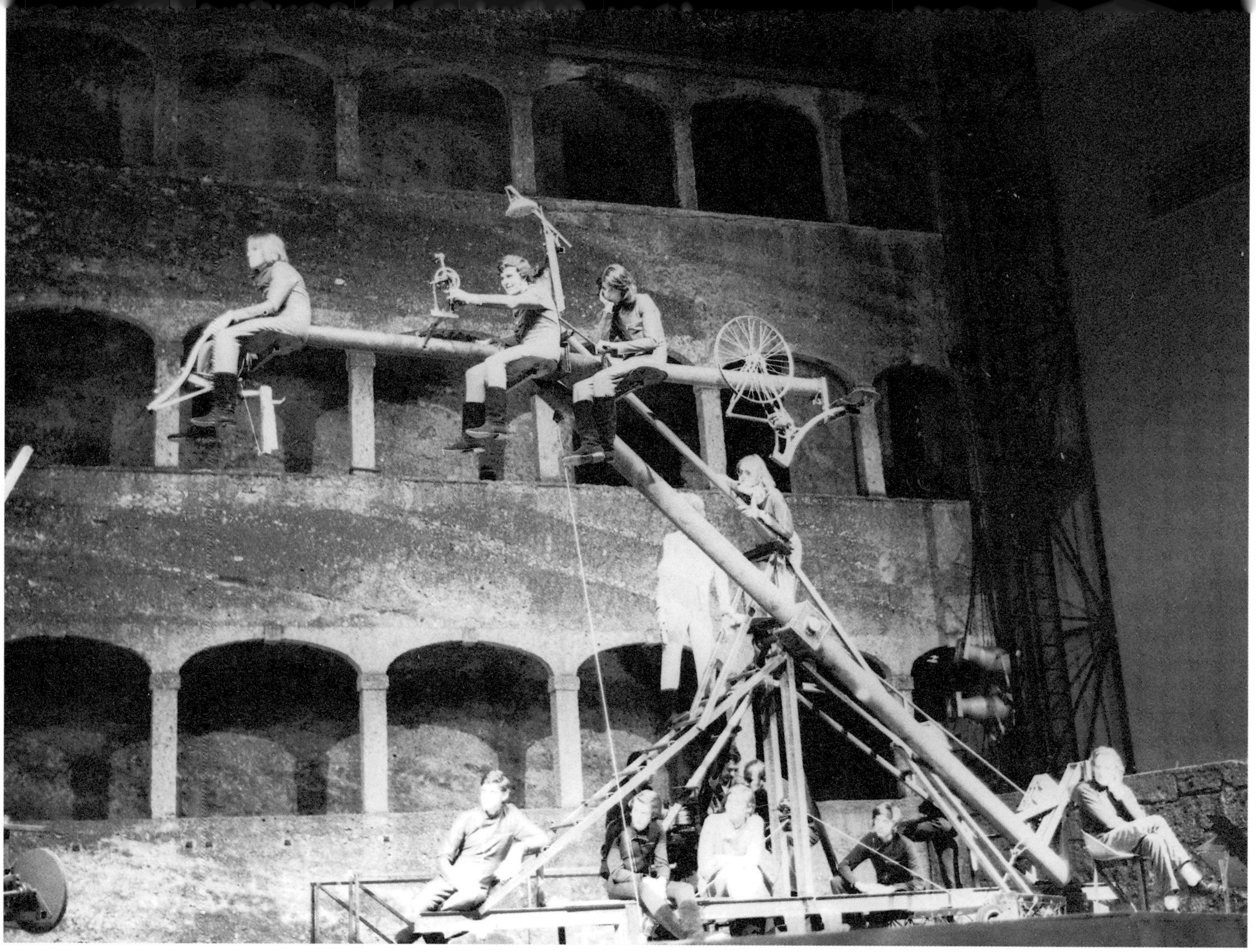

mortality through fame rather than through spiritual attainments and who was unwilling to subordinate his individuality to the will of God—in the manner of Doctor Faustus—or His emissaries.[3] For the 1972 Salzburg production, Tinguely created a mechanised triad of Hell, Earth and Heaven corresponding to the three settings in the play. Cenodoxus's worldly realm occupied centre stage; Düggelin recalled that it conveyed the impression of an alchemist's laboratory.[4] The structure of Heaven resembled and functioned much like a balance, with angels seated on one arm and God on the other. God's throne could be lowered by pedalling action on the part of the heavenly host, who would lower him to Earth in a most dignified manner. Once there, he could step out of his bucket-like ejection seat, a mock *deus ex machina*. The effeminate angels, whom Tinguely dressed in pink and light blue overalls, cleaned the heavenly machine while god was on earth. Hell was a Ferris wheel transformed by its occupants, a bunch of cavorting females, into a dynamic little bordello presided over by the panderer Satan. Death was given a very civilised, correct appearance.

Tinguely's first sketch of the stage props reveals his basic concepts: a static triangle for Heaven, subtitled *Nestlé*, and a dynamic wheel for Hell, compared in an inscription, *Von Roll*, to a steel and machinery works. Thus, he related the celestial realm to chocolate and sweet indulgence and connected Satan's territory with industry and progress. Death, which in the relief of 1981 became the principal subject, conformed at Salzburg to Bidermann's concept of a figure of transition, mediating on the threshold to Heaven or Hell. Düggelin recalls that Tinguely was made a generous offer by an American collector for the Salzburg sculptures and that he refused with the quip: 'I cannot sell heaven and hell, not even to an American.' This was amazing, since in 1972 the artist could certainly have made good use of the $ 30,000 offered by the collector, for example, to buy material for the *Head*, which was then under construction.

Cenodoxus (Heaven)

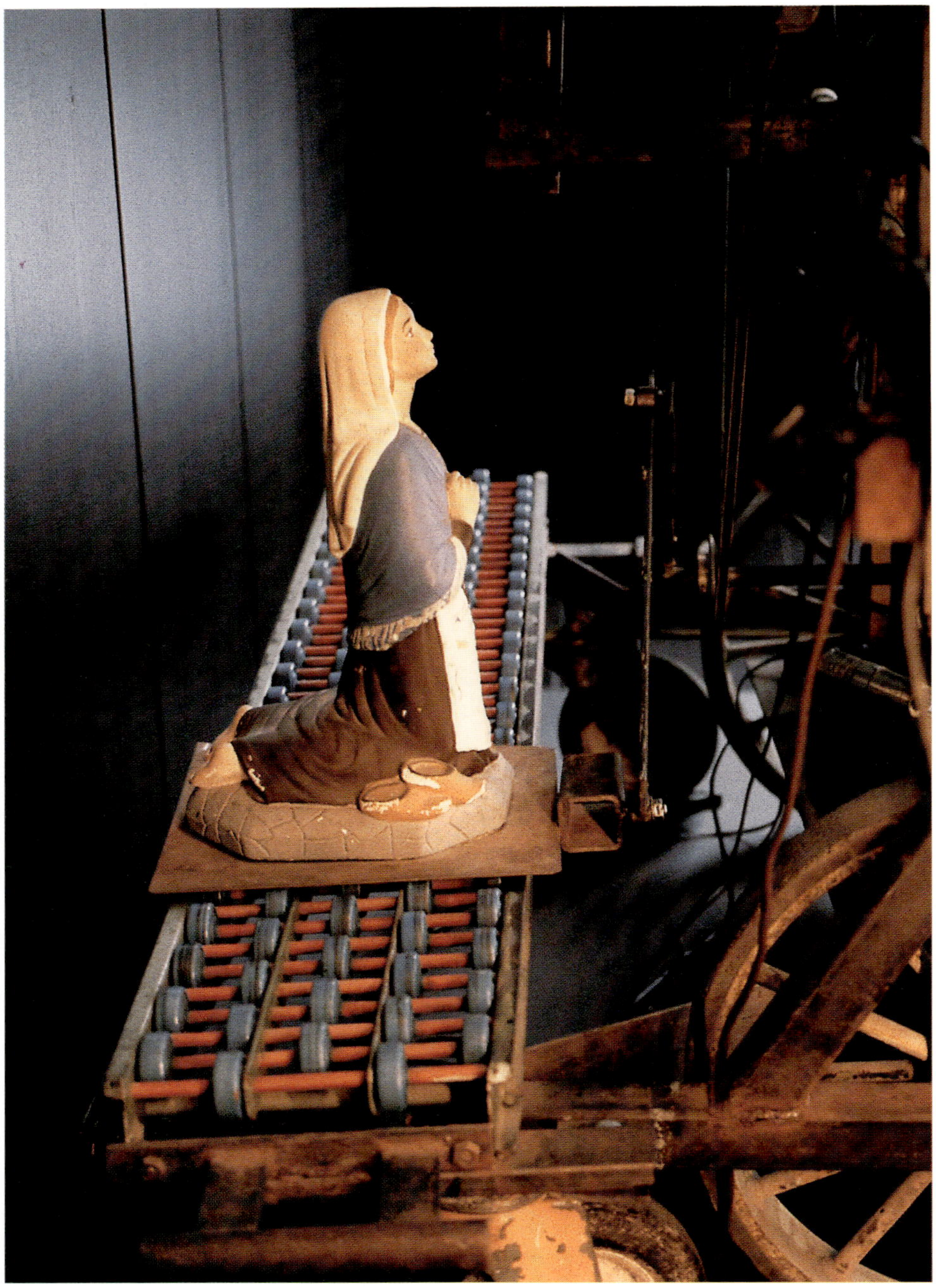

59 *Cenodoxus – Isenheim Altarpiece,* 1981 (penitent maiden)

Cenodoxus—Isenheim Altarpiece (fig. 59) is a motorised open-work relief consisting of red and yellow gleaming and rusty metal bars assembled to form three hinged rectangles. The centre frame stands atop a cart-like substructure whose elements extend to the front and back. Three rows of white light bulbs illuminate the piece like rows of candles. One row of nine bulbs is affixed to the top far right corner; another, with twenty-four bulbs, is affixed at the far left. These move as the two hinged 'wings' are pushed slightly, and almost imperceptibly, forwards and backwards. The third row, which terminates the bottom central section, holds nine bulbs and also moves. Eight twirling bouquets of feathers crown the top bar of the central frame, from which hangs a sizeable ox cranium with long, upward-twisted horns. The cranium is still partially covered with dried flesh. A rod connected to the wheel below pushes the cranium slowly up and down, a movement echoed by two corresponding jaws in each wing. The ox cranium is isolated visually at the apex of the composition.

Below the ox cranium, and forming the exact centre of the middle section, a solid, large blue wheel of wood turns slowly. In front of it swirls a rustic wooden cross (illus. p. 119). This small cross is flanked by two animal skulls that open and close their jaws busily. The latter are somewhat dislocated because Tinguely joined them to the cranium with a piece of old string.
A human skull made of solid foam is placed below the cross. In the background, a painted plaster figure of a penitent maiden,[5] kneeling and holding a rosary, slides from side to side on a kind of conveyor belt. There is a smaller wheel in each wing with a corresponding motor that activates the skulls. The right-hand section features in addition a ski and three peacock feathers connected to the wheel. The triptych is raised up on two recessed black platforms. Flanking it, a second pair of medium-sized sheep skulls decorate two urns placed on black pedestals. Tinguely directed that the entire structure be placed against a black backdrop.

If we compare Tinguely's relief with Grünewald's *Isenheim Altarpiece*, a number of direct and indirect correspondences become apparent. The cross and the penitent figure appear in both works. Tinguely's kneeling figure with its mechanical movement satirizes the reduction of a once-vibrant faith, which inspired artists like Grünewald, to observance by rote. Indirect references to Grünewald's work may include the cruciform ox cranium nailed to its support like the figure of the crucified Christ. Also, the skull-sprouting vessels placed to either side of the triptych like Eucharistic chalices are a visual counterpart as well as symbolical paradoxes of the chalice Grünewald placed beneath the Lamb to evoke Christ's sacrificial role. However, Tinguely provided no symbols of hope, confronting the viewer with inescapable death without the redemptive promise implied by Grünewald. By showing us death as the absolute limit of our existence, Tinguely calls our attention to the present, to life and its dynamic processes. Emphasising this message, the peacock feathers next to the ski suggest the prophecies of John the Baptist, since they are a Christian symbol of immortality and of Christ's Resurrection.[6] However, they get rough treatment, since with every full rotation of the wheel to which they are attached, they are hit and bent against the metal bars. Here,

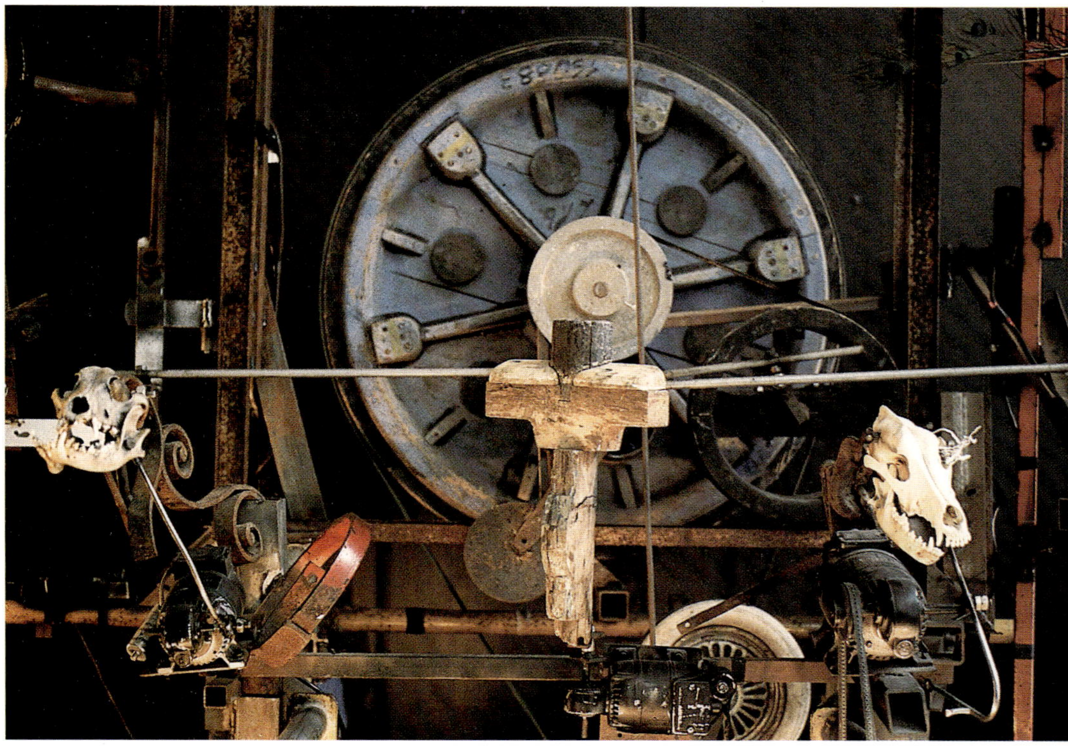

Cenodoxus – Isenheim Altarpiece (detail of the central section)

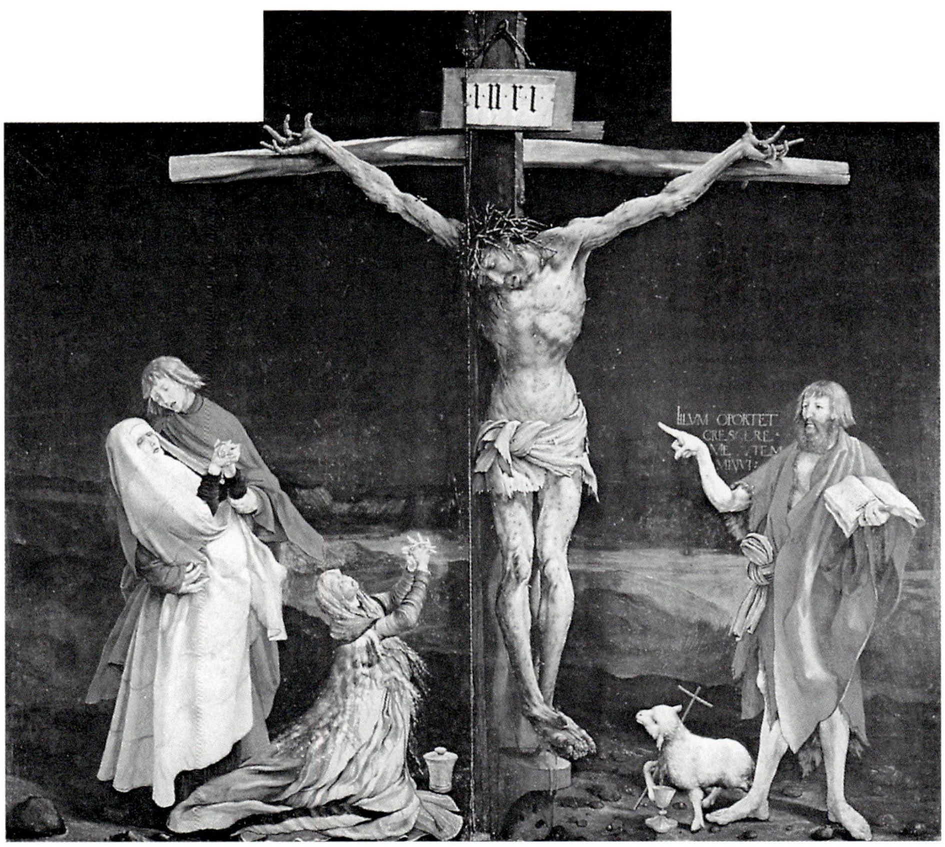

Matthias Grünewald, *The Crucifixion* from the *Isenheim Altarpiece*, 1513-15.
Musée d'Unterlinden, Colmar

Tinguely undercut the Christian symbol by pointing out the frailty of the object.

Both Tinguely's work and that of Grünewald make the most of the dynamics of movement and light. The two artists also addressed the element of time. For Grünewald, earthly, finite time is represented by the historical figures of the Virgin, St John and the penitent Mary Magdalene, and by Christ's death, while divine, eternal time is evoked by the figure of John the Baptist. Tinguely, however, restricted

Cenodoxus – Isenheim Altarpiece, 1981 ▷
(overall view)

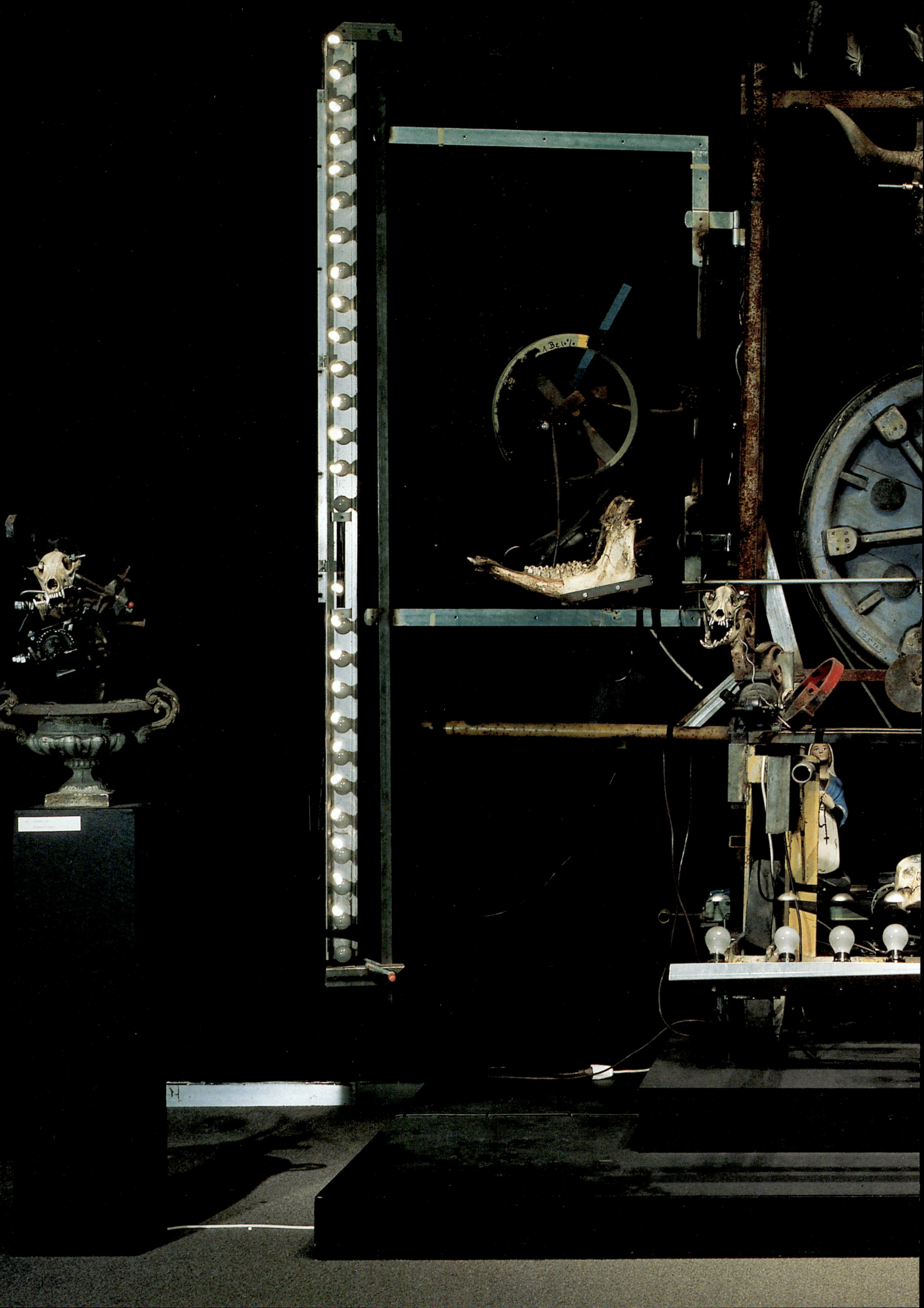

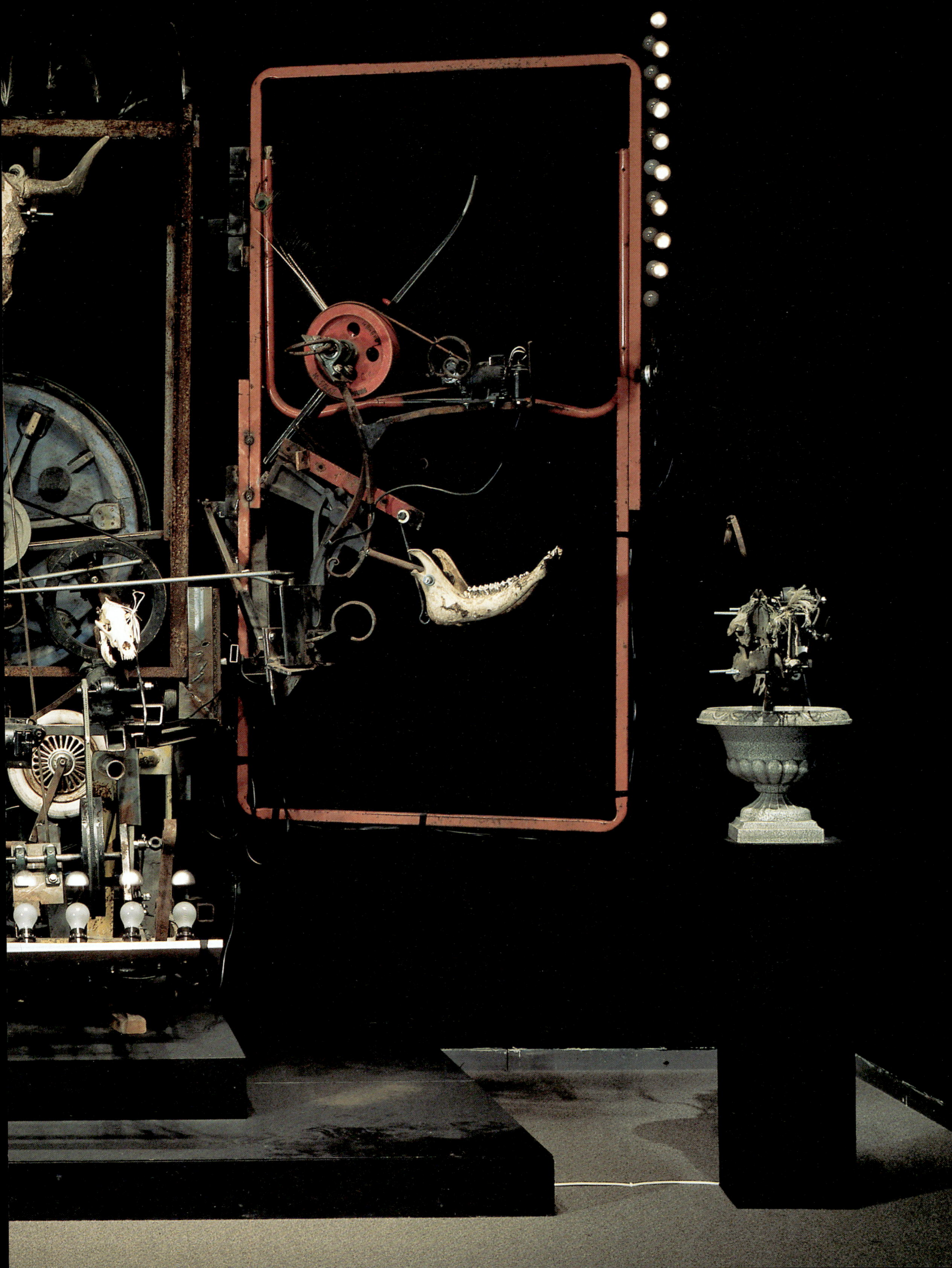

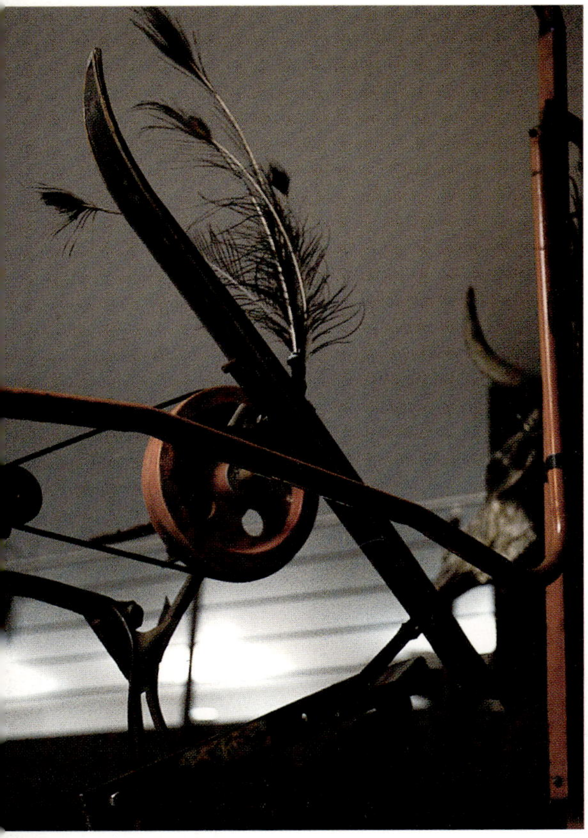

Cenodoxus – Isenheim Altarpiece (details)

his work to earthly time. Generally speaking, the visual elements in Grünewald's and Tinguely's Crucifixion scenes are distributed in the same way. The left wing of Tinguely's work has its counterpart in Grünewald's three figures standing on Christ's right. The spots of blue in this wing recall the colour traditionally associated with the Virgin. The dominant hue of the opposite wing is red, in Christian symbolism the colour of love, charity, fire and blood. This wing corresponds to Grünewald's figure of John the Baptist, while the central panel corresponds to his Christ on the Cross. Both artists used monumentalising effects achieved by isolating and silhouetting the main object—the crucified Christ and the ox skull, respectively—against an empty, dark space.

The focus can be seen to have shifted significantly from the production of *Cenodoxus* at Salzburg. In this revised scenario, it is Death that steals the show. Indeed, the most arresting element is the ox cranium, mirrored in the wings by the goat skulls. In medieval tradition, death is personified by a skull, a reminder of the transience of life, and as such it appears frequently in vanitas pictures. In this sense,

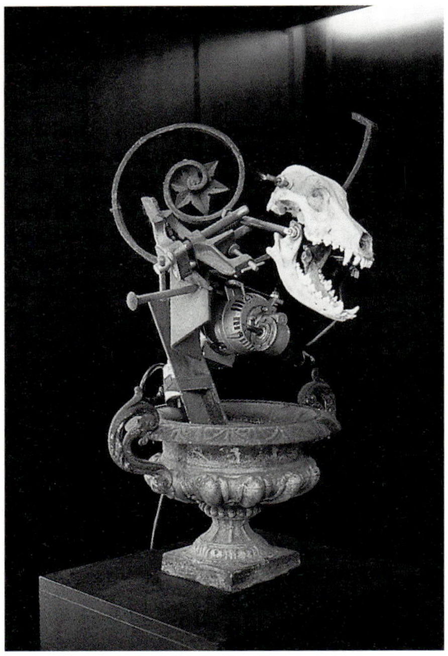

Cenodoxus can also be viewed as an allegorical still life.

Klaus Lankheit traced the process of secularisation of the triptych format back to the late Renaissance, when painters such as Hieronymus Bosch began to depict profane events in that sacred format. The liberated shell thus could serve to make the profane sacred, making possible an altar without God.[7] In *Cenodoxus*, Tinguely seems have to made use of the dramatic possibilities inherent in religious art, especially those apparent during the Catholic Mass, while opposing it with his own Carnival spirit. The two props holding up the chalice-like urns take up the positions of acolytes assisting at Mass just as Tinguely himself did as a child. Tinguely's goat

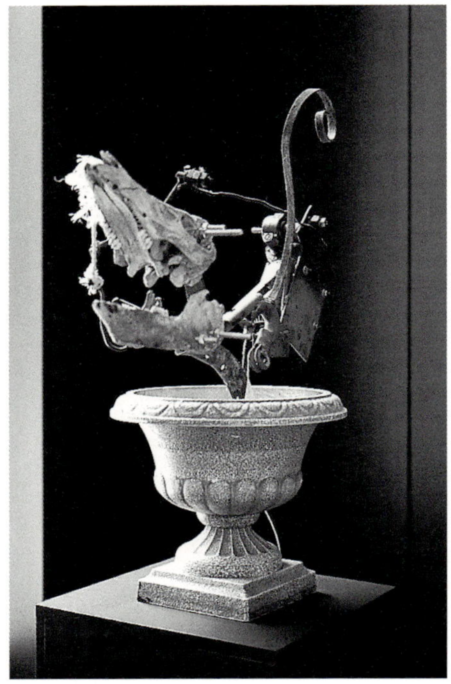

skulls vigorously chew the air—here death is active, indeed gleefully energetic. While these side figures comically ape the proceedings within the triptych itself, the similar motions of the skulls within the serious context of the work itself serve to suppress a humorous response from the viewer. The serious tone of the triptych as a whole is only enhanced by these notes of paradoxical humour, however.

At work on *Cenodoxus – Isenheim Altarpiece*, Neyruz, 1981

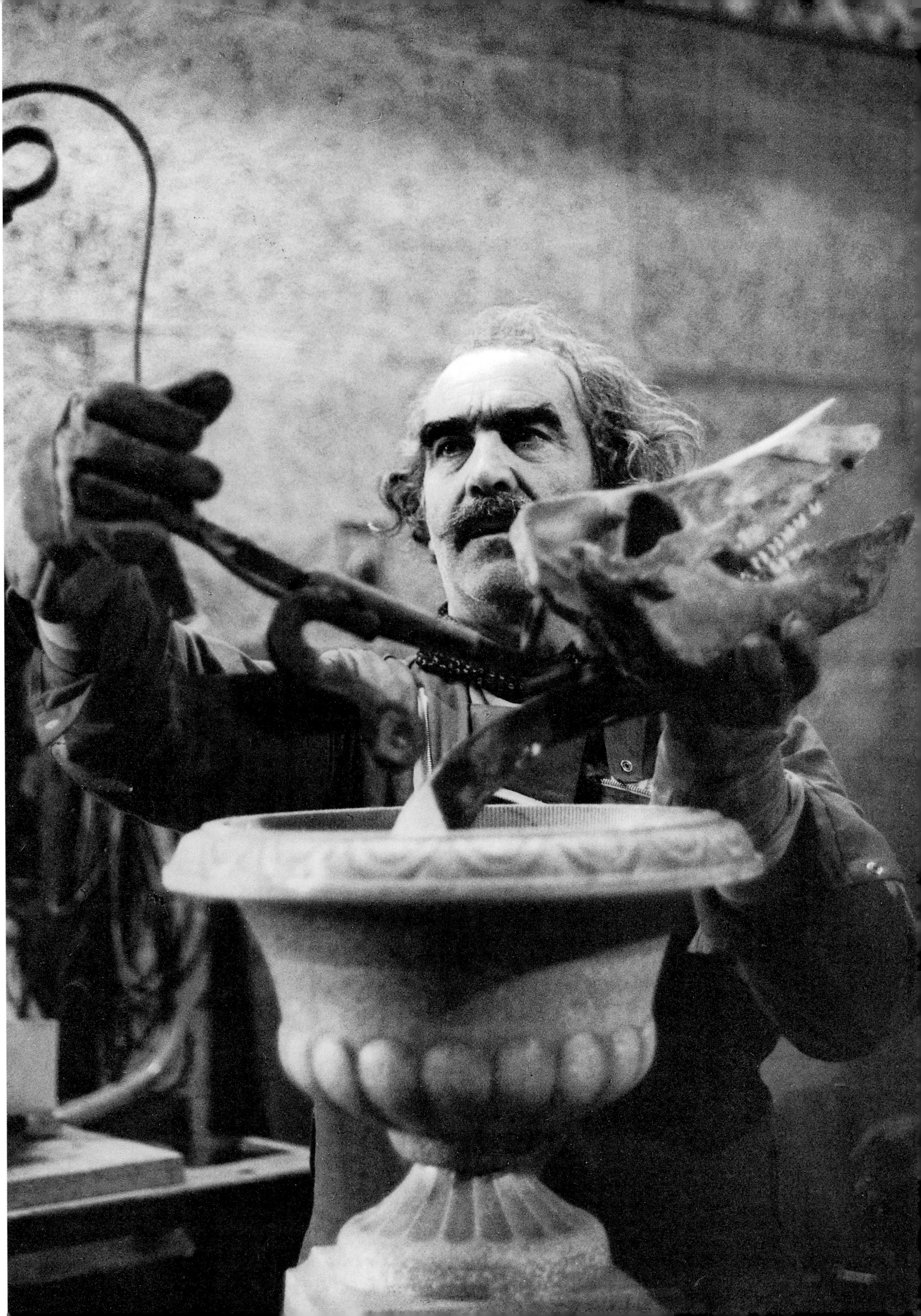

Cenodoxus was the most recent work in the artist's large retrospective that opened at Zurich's Kunsthaus in 1983.[8] At the end of the European tour, works belonging to the Stedelijk Museum, Amsterdam, were shown there together with a new triptych entitled *Poya*. This tripartite relief with two side sculptures is formally very similar to the mechanised *Cenodoxus* triptych (fig. 60). The work's title needs some explanation. For the people of Gruyère, near Fribourg, *poya* designates a mountain path and, by extension, the driving of cattle to Alpine pastures. The term also identifies painted or carved illustrations of this event.[9] The *poya* was part of the artist's store of memories. As a child, he spent summers with one of his grandmothers in Bulle. He recalled fondly the annual trips with his father from Bulle up to one of the pastures of Gruyère, where they would share for a few days the simple life of the herdsmen, and he returned to the area every now and then. Tinguely had grown up with the legends of the region, replete with black magic, witches, devils and ghosts. He spoke to me about this on one occasion, while driving his large Mercedes up a narrow mountain path without slowing down at all. Was it to comfort me that he told me in a low voice about the devilries of his maternal grandfather? The triptych *Poya* originated from within that tradition.

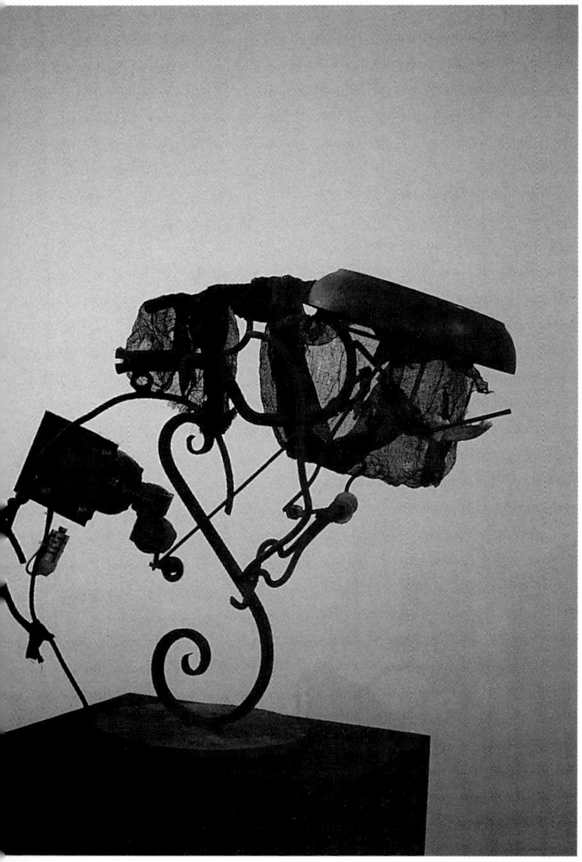

Driving the herds to pasture takes place at the end of May and is a festive event for which the cattle are garlanded with floral wreaths. Flowers also crown the ox skull in the centre of *Poya*. The tripartite relief consists of three equally large, rectangular metal panels splashed with acid to create different patinas, with colours ranging from a rich, rusty burnt sienna to a palish yellow. Standing out from this painterly background, the whitish, garlanded ox skull dominates the symmetrical arrangement completed by a jawbone in each wing. A whip dangles behind the skull, which slowly and mournfully raises and lowers its head. A quintet of black wheels conveys movement to the side panels, where the jaws, in profile, are made to nod. The turning of the wheels and the flogging, bowing and nodding of the accessories proceeds in near silence.

Because of the relative stillness of the triptych, its visual and auditory effects are amplified dramatically. The grating sounds, though hardly louder than those of a breathing beast, are disconcerting, like a kind of *chèta*, the term used in the area around Fribourg to describe the noises and spells produced by spirits.[10] The sculpture's skeletal remains perform a ghastly, not a joyful, rite; death has stripped these bones bare of any hope. Tinguely explained: 'To incorporate death into the extremely positive ascension rather than into the descent is naturally more effective—just as death is acceptable in old age but shocking in the young.'[11] The triptych hints at the cruelty, magic and myth of ancient rituals which survive in sublimated form in rational Christian rites and in rural traditions such as *poya*. The whip, the wreath and the bones of slain beasts are so

60 *Poya*, 1983

Overall view ▷

Details

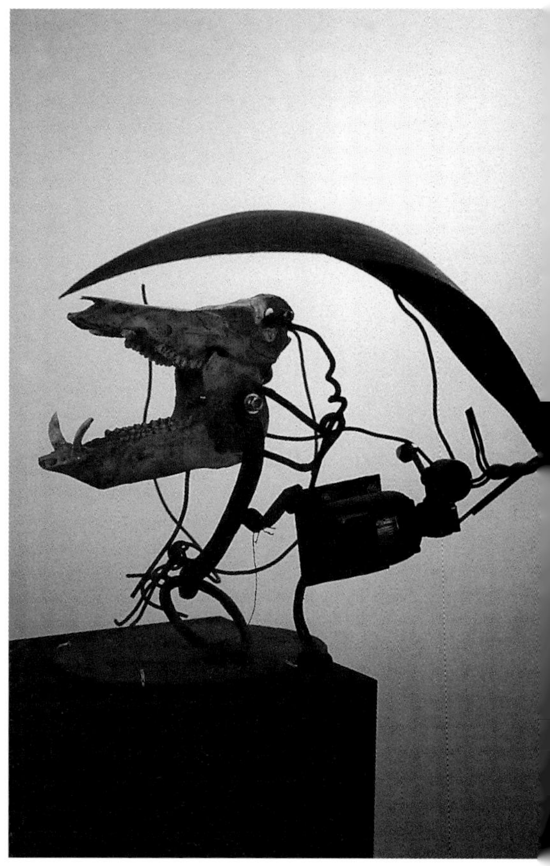

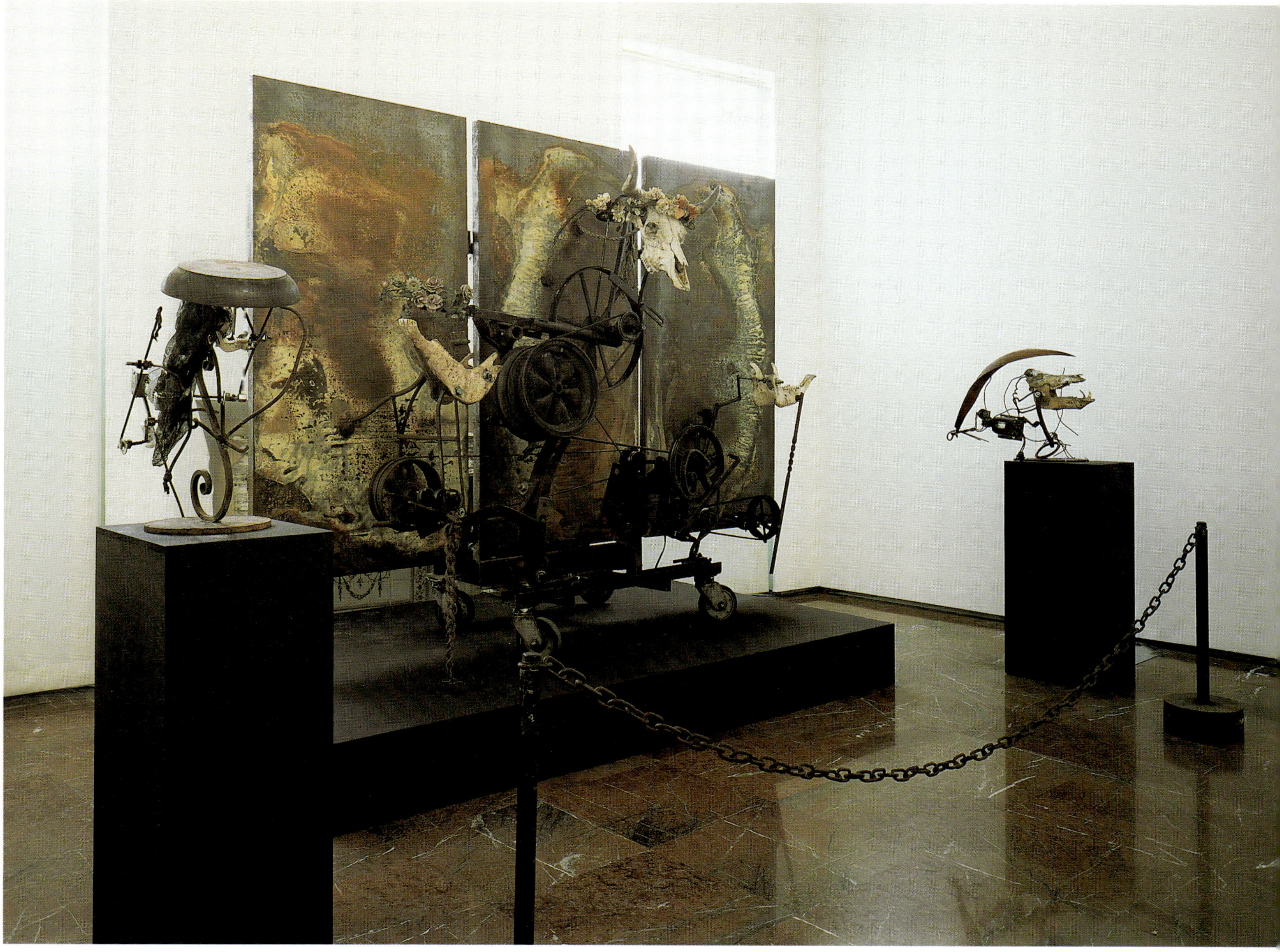

many props in the visual re-enactment of a rite Tinguely wished to make macabre and grotesque, opposing his dance of death to the folkloric ritual's hopeful promise. To the farmer's *poya*—his herd, the measure of his wealth—Tinguely opposed his own memento mori, death as the ultimate treasure that shows us the wealth of life.

As in *Cenodoxus*, the artist introduced comic relief in *Poya* by means of two side sculptures. They resemble the figures accompanying the earlier piece, but are not placed in chalices and are thus divorced from any Christian connotation. Each of two animal skulls is supported by a wrought-iron stand placed at eye level on a tall pedestal. The skulls' movement is made all the more grotesque by the oddments with which they are adorned: a frying pan and some black lace trimming as covering for one, a sheet of iron cut into a feather-like shape for the other. The pair bring a whiff of comedy to the triptych, and there is all-conquering carnivalesque laughter in the air.

Fribourg and its rural and urban traditions are also evoked in the *Small Animals' Altarpiece*, inaugurated in that city's Musée d'Art et d'Histoire in 1989 (fig. 61). The extension and renovation of the museum in 1981 had included the building adjacent to it, the city's old slaughterhouse. Tinguely explained that his triptych hangs on the

61 *Small Animals' Altarpiece*, 1989 ▷

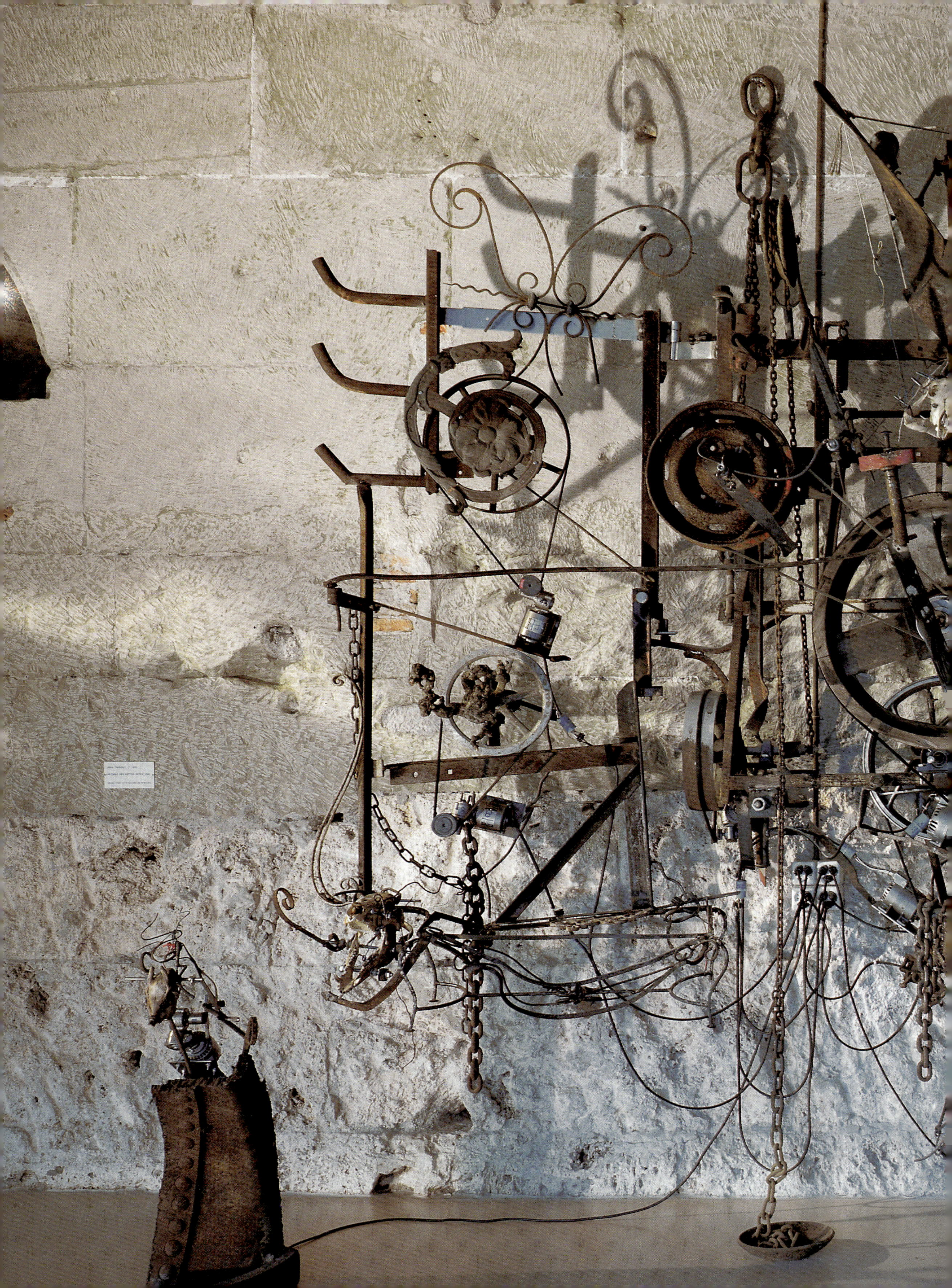

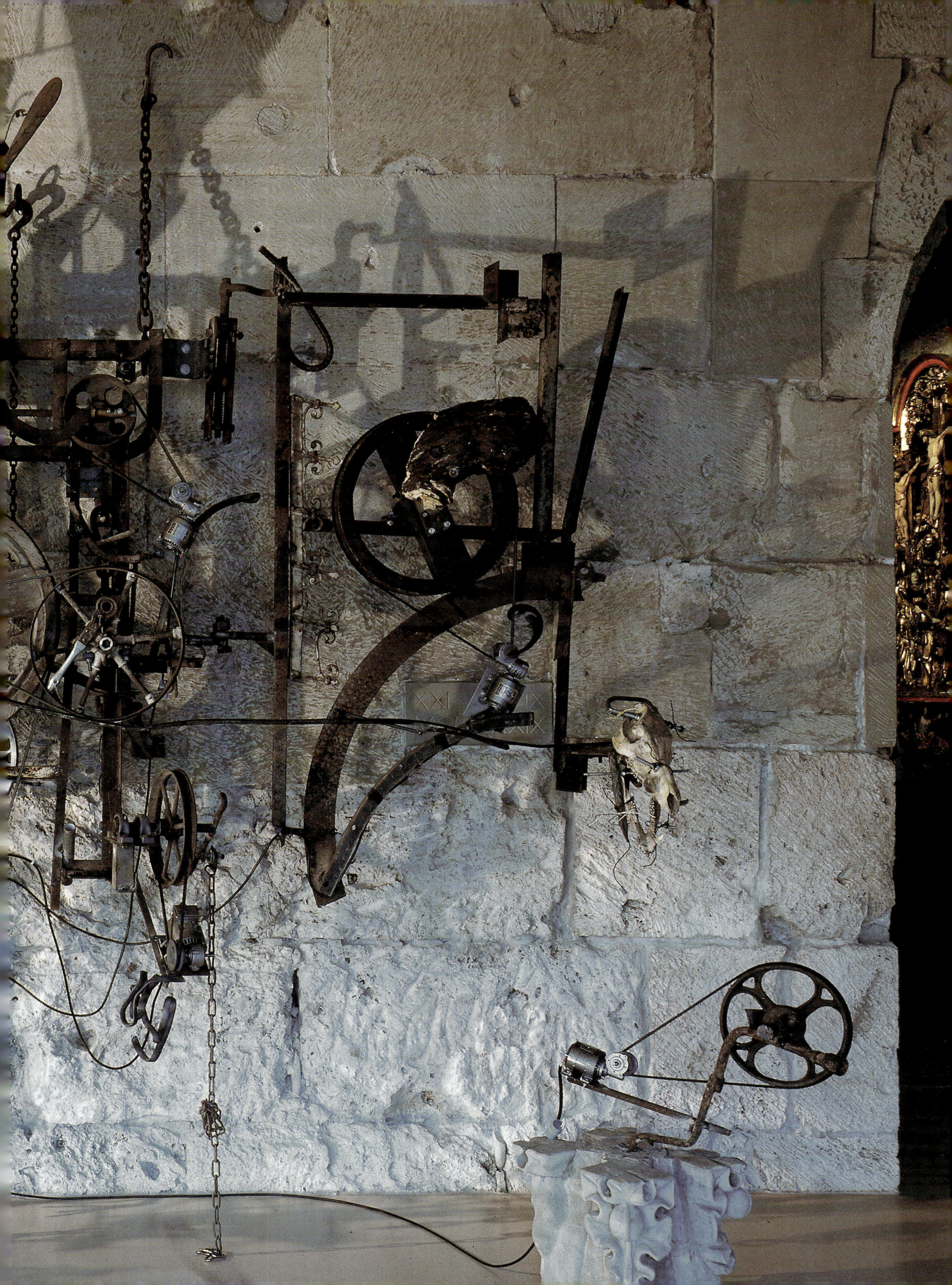

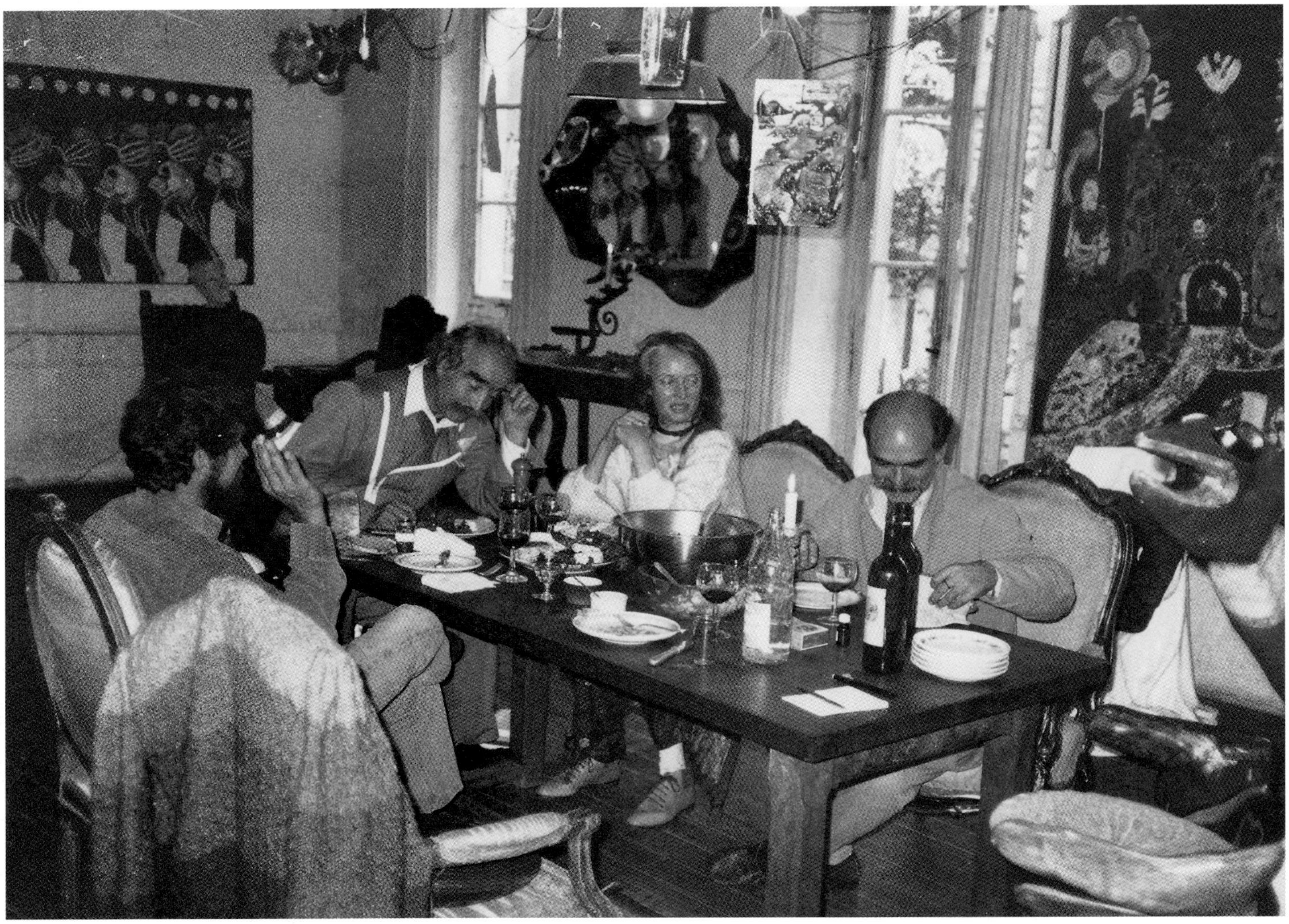

exact spot where animals such as goats and sheep were hung on hooks, head down, to be slaughtered. The bloody splatterings on the wall have all been removed, and the stench of death has long since evaporated—nothing of this routine sacrifice remains except Tinguely's memorial. The tripartite mechanised open-work relief is suspended on chains against the wall. The piece is flat, and a sense of depth is provided by accessories: goat and sheep skulls in the bottom right and left corners of the side wings and a ploughshare as the apex in the centre. One of the pair of subsidiary sculptures is fixed to a carved stone from the city's cathedral that was a gift to Tinguely when he received honorary citizenship in 1984. As in other important works, he was working with local materials.

Here, once again, the handyman of the absurd helped himself to the trappings of religious art.

Tinguely's altarpieces are programmed to unchain our innate fear of death. Their sacred format dignifies their subjects. Yet, he inserted sufficient elements of the derisory and of ridicule—a loose string or a forgotten tag, an odd movement—to undercut any weighty solemnity. His altars are dedicated to faith in action and to the demiurge of life.[12]

Joseph Imhof, Tinguely, Niki de Saint Phalle and Ricardo Menon, Soisy-sur-Ecole, 1986

Tinguely in Fribourg, 1988

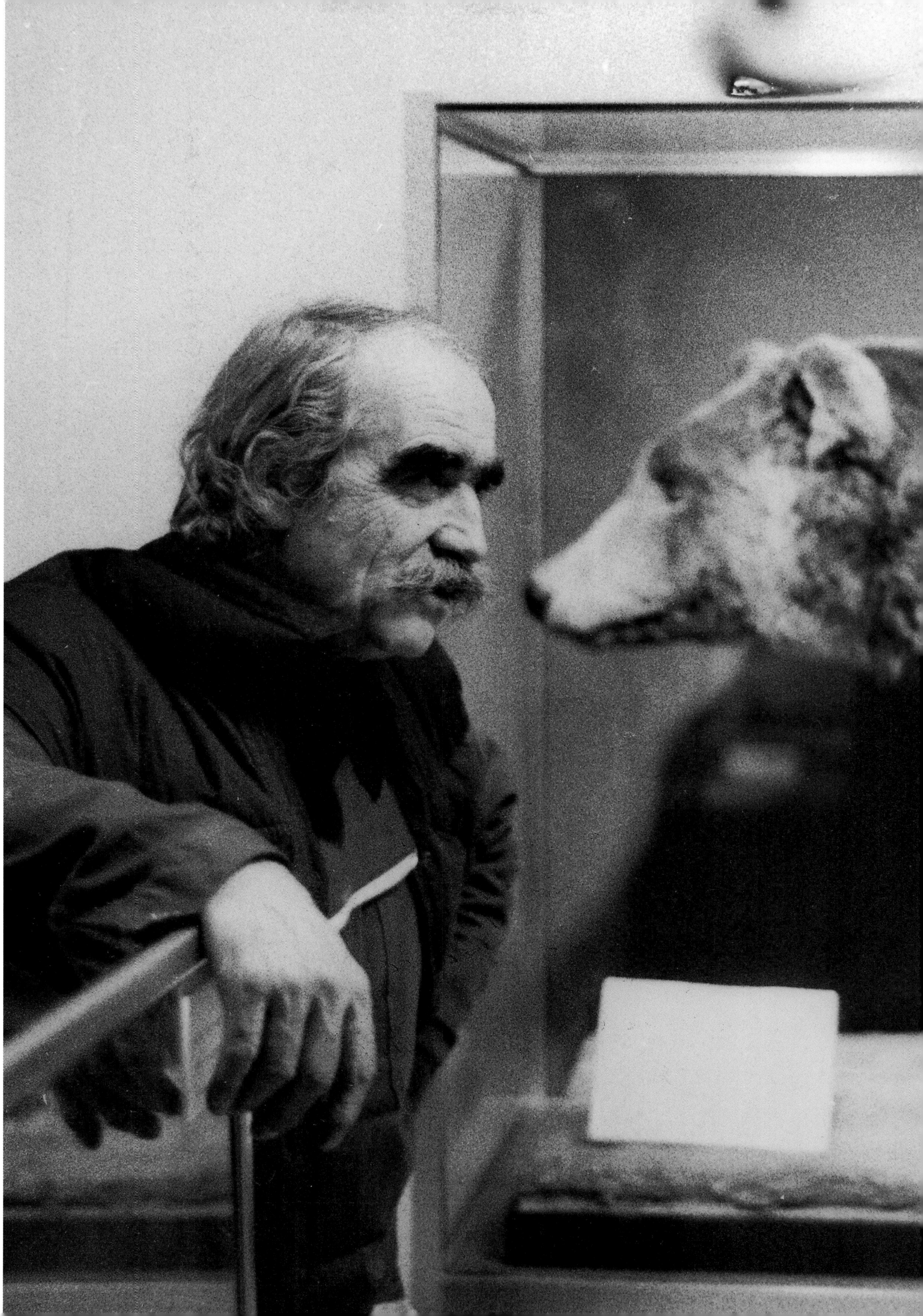

'Stagnation doesn't exist; it's not time to shut up shop yet'

1984–88

In the winter of 1984, Tinguely presented two majors new works in Berne, *Pit-Stop* at the Kunsthalle[1] and *Inferno* a few days later at the Kornfeld gallery. *Pit-Stop* was an assemblage of multiple parts from Renault Formula One racing cars attached to a central base (fig. 62). Four projectors fixed to mobile arm-like extensions growing out of the main body projected film via reflectors onto the surrounding walls. Upon entering the centre room occupied only by the Tinguely piece, the viewer was engulfed by the world of one of the most recklessly dangerous and exciting of sports, Formula One racing. Tinguely specified:

This [type of] pit-stop, which is prohibited today, happens at an unbelievable speed. It is a contest of precision, during which all the movements have to harmonise with one another. The whole thing is incredibly noisy, steamy, dangerous. I made nearly the opposite. The whole is like a paralysed sequence of movements, and for that I project images in slow motion. The whole thing is as submerged in a dream.[2]

Tinguely showed the worst possible outcome of a race in the sculpture: the moment of an accident, a split second after a car explodes into myriad parts. He thus recreated an event the eye could not perceive unless it had been filmed and replayed in slow motion. Downplaying sound, Tinguely caused a paradoxical silence to prevail.

An exemplary pit-stop could be viewed on the walls. Alain Prost, competing for Renault, went in for a routine tyre change and fill-up at the Zeltweg race-track during the Austrian Grand Prix in 1983, a race he won. The uncanny speed and perfect movements of an entire crew were dissected as the film unrolled in silent slow motion. An electronic timer in the top left corner of the image kept track of the second and fractions of seconds in 'real' time. Each of the four projectors showed the scene at a different moment, to hallucinatory effect. The artist expressed the hard facts of the sport through the wrecked supercar at centre stage and the more elusive side, of perfection and victory, through artificial images flickering on the walls. *Pit-Stop* was more than just a work around the theme of the automobile. After all, the race-car driver was Tinguely's absurd hero, a man propelled by an iron-willed determination to outsmart destiny, the heroic, gladiator-like embodiment of the absurd predicament. Technically and ideationally, *Pit-Stop* had affinities with *Rotozaza I* (fig. 43). But here, the driver and his crew played out the absurd game. The viewer was voyeur rather than being directly involved in playing ball with Tinguely's object.

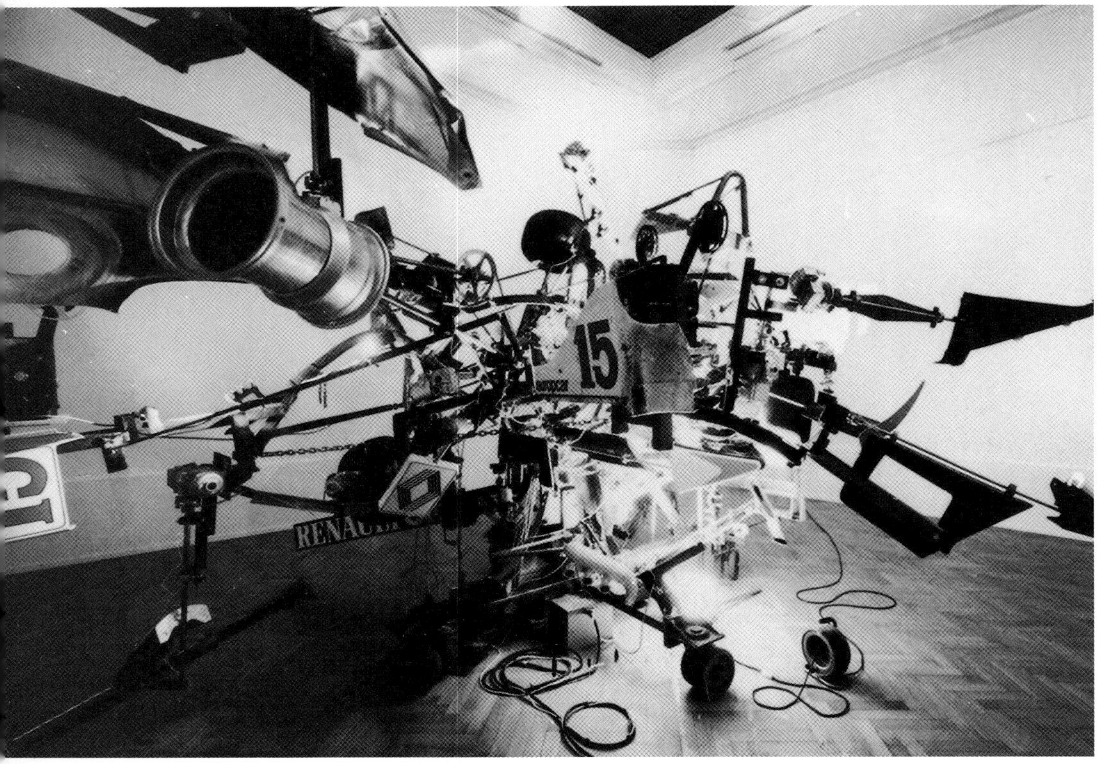

62 *Pit-Stop*, 1984

Pit-Stop, 1984

Pit-Stop was one of the high points in the 1985 Biennial at La Villette in Paris. While a commentator in Berne had raised the old issue of whether Tinguely's spectacular object was not pushing the other exhibits into the background, French critics emphasised his relevance to the current art scene. The work, described by the artist as a 'revival of civilization's leftovers',[3] was stimulating for young artists who saw themselves confirmed in their belief in art as an effective instrument of communication.

Tinguely also integrated parts of vehicles into works that do not overtly refer to racing or driving. The chassis of wrecked BMW motorcycles are associated with animals skulls in a 1985 work, *The Witches or Snow White and the Seven Dwarfs* (fig. 63).[4] Each skull moves a bit differently, for Tinguely fixed them variously to the rods connected to the machine-driven

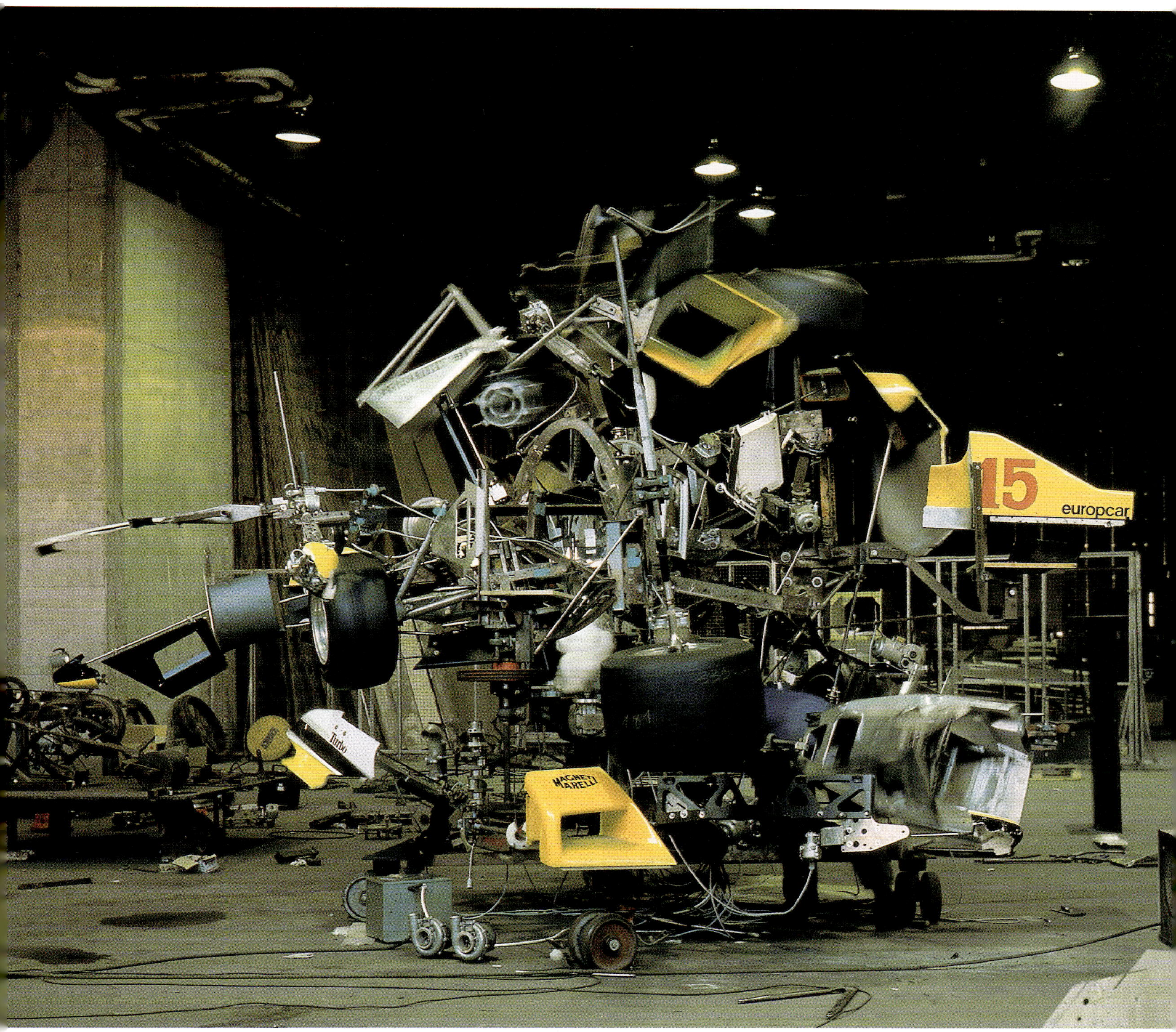

wheels. This group of eight sculptures was first shown in Munich in 1985, at the Kunsthalle of the Hypo-Kulturstiftung, placed off the main hall in an alcove-like space. Their aggressive quality was reinforced by the fact that they were 'gathered' behind barriers made of heavy chains. The nocturnal atmosphere was eerie; the monstrous shadows on the walls appeared to be spectral shades. Tinguely's ghostly mechanisms seemed caught in the endless pondering of a question confronting the viewers of Shakespeare's *Macbeth*: 'Do we live our lives because we all have these witches or do we have these witches because of the way we live our lives?' The paradoxical second subtitle, *The Widows*, is explained by the fact that the artist assembled this group of sculptures at a time when he was, in Niki de Saint Phalle's words, playing 'Russian roulette with his health'.[5] A few weeks

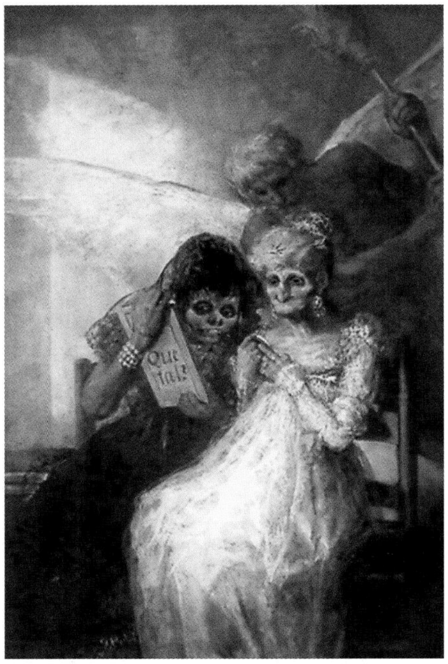

Francisco Goya, *Les Vieilles (Time and the Old Women), c.* 1810-12. Musée des Beaux-Arts, Lille

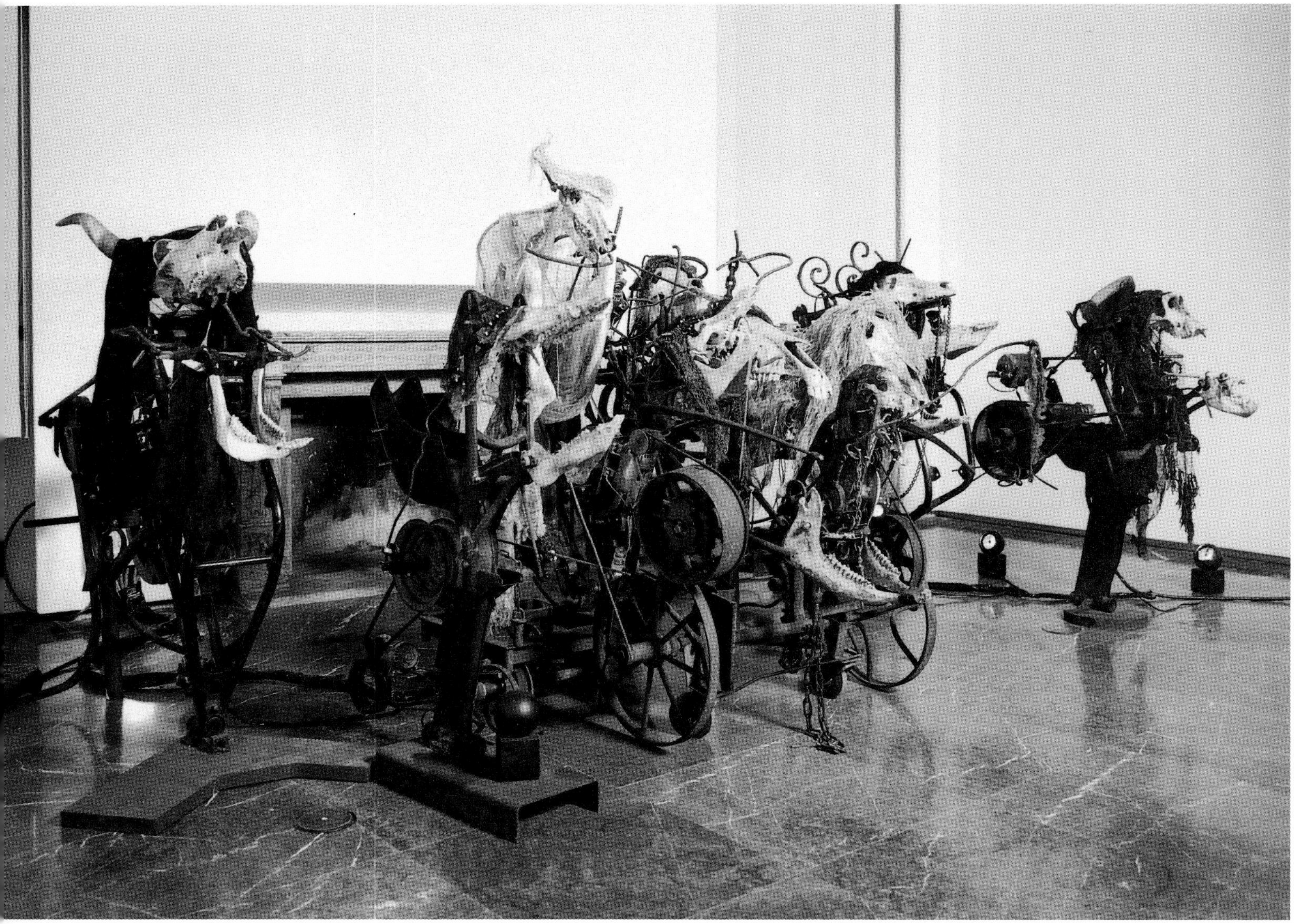

63 *The Witches or Snow White and the Seven Dwarfs*, 1985

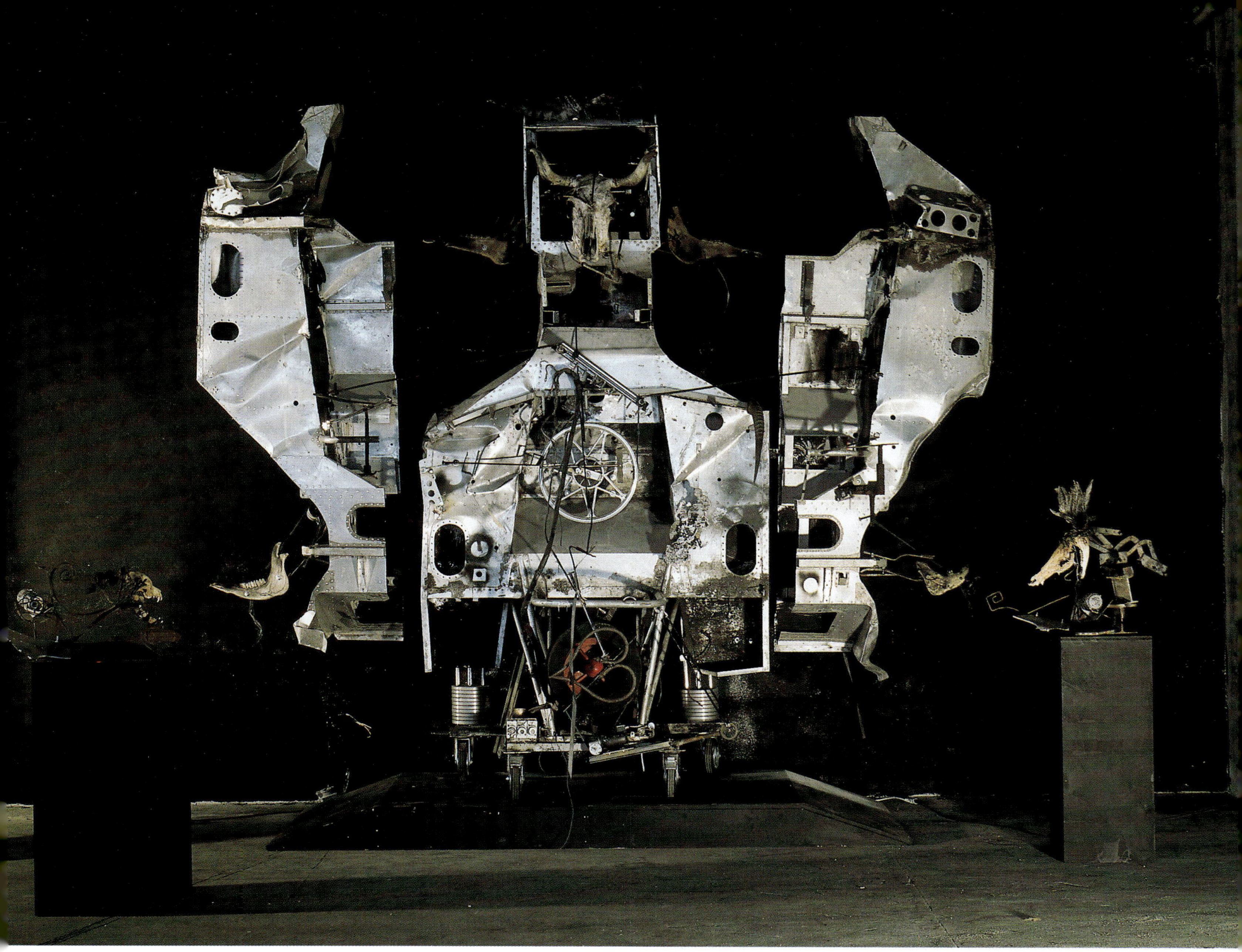

64 *Lola T. 180 – Memorial for Joakim B.*, 1988

after the opening in Munich, he had bypass surgery.

Thematically and visually, Tinguely's group matches a painting by Francisco Goya, *Les Vieilles (Time and the Old Women)*. With pitiless candour Goya revealed time's ravaging effect on female beauty, the blinding vanity of the bejewelled old maid and her toady companion. The fine mantillas and other frippery, the shadowy drama of lights and darks and the skeletal figures are similar in both works. Tinguely's witches were not simply mischievous poltergeists, but commented sardonically on the theme of ageing. Facing this bizarre banquet of biting, chewing and gnawing skulls, the viewers could imagine themselves as the next course on the goblins' menu. But unlike medieval sepulchral imagery, of which one was also reminded in the crypt-like space, death was not conjured up in terms of viewers' fear of hell but rather in relation to their fear of losing life. Tinguely affirmed that 'If I mock death and get her to mock us, it is to neutralise her.'[6]

In 1987, it was scrap from a particularly fashionable kind of deadly toy—Japanese motorcycles—that Tinguely repatriated as hanging chandeliers for a coffee-house in Kyoto. These ikebana-like lighting fixtures mix the brutal with the incandescent, combining images of speed and death with the message of light. The chandeliers were intended as a double homage, to honour a country that abounds in contradictions and to honour an old friend, the film-maker and ikebana master Hiroshi Teshigahara. Other works on the theme of motorised technology followed. *Lola T. 180—Memorial for Joakim B.* is a cenotaph for Tinguely's friend the racer Joakim Bonnier (fig. 64). Tinguely had met Jo Siffert through Bonnier and was very close to both drivers, each of whom died on the race-track. With the memorial to Bonnier, the material dictated the form. Tinguely actually had received parts of the Formula One prototype not long after Bonnier was killed at Le Mans in 1973. For years they remained stored in his atelier, untouched. Only after he had appropriated the formal vocabulary of religious art to express eschatological themes and had survived his own brush with death could he work with these elements, fashioning them into a triptych. Tinguely affirmed to Michel Conil Lacoste: 'After all that time, the pain was still locked in the wreck'.[7]

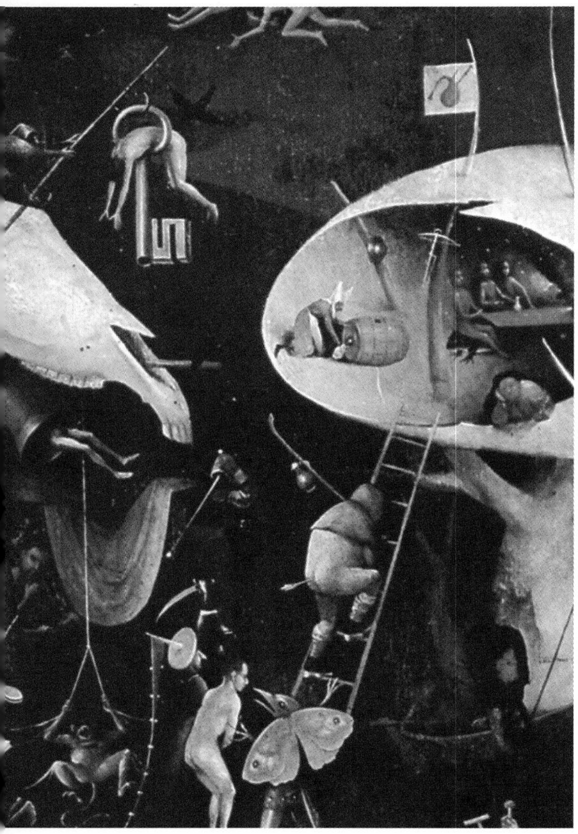

Hieronymus Bosch, *Garden of Earthly Delights, c.* 1500, Museo del Prado, Madrid (detail: *Hell*)

This subject was developed further in *Motorcycle of Death* and *Safari of Death*, built together in 1989 as part of a series of new works specially made for Tinguely's exhibition at the Tretjakowskaja Galerja in Moscow in the spring of 1990. *Motorcycle of Death* is made from the burnt carcass of a Honda 750 topped by an ox skull that moans and groans, compelled into a mournful gallop. *Safari of Death* is a functioning vehicle flagged with a scythe of death, a type of carnivalesque *Klamauk* (fig. 50). Joseph Imhof actually drove this *memento mori* on wheels on the snowy streets of Moscow. *Shuttlecock* is a sidecar variant on the motif and formally akin to *Pit-Stop*. Tinguely had actually sponsored a couple of René Progin's racing seasons by dabbing his 'colours' on the previous season's sidecar, thus creating a quickly sold rare art work, and by creating a print whose sales benefited the sidecar racer.

The other work that premièred in Berne at the end of 1984 was *Inferno*. The hall at the Kornfeld gallery, where the annual world-renowned auction takes place, was unrecognisable (fig. 65). Tinguely had shut out all natural light and created a room-sized ensemble of over 20 entangled elements.[8] The multi-sensory interweaving of sound, movement and light in the ensemble created a sense of web-like cohesion. A nexus of silhouettes was produced by light projectors installed within the work, which included the shadows of visitors in a film that instantly replayed the proceedings in black and white and two dimensions. Tinguely's 'infernal' terrain in which mechanisms, toys, animals and everyday objects noisily underwent symbolic adventures was an animated tableau literally loaded with subject matter. When the viewer sat down on the bench facing the piece, its rocking movement was likely to evoke childhood memories. Also, the adult's viewing level became equivalent to that of a child. Like the dramatic voice and expressive gestures of a good storyteller, the sounds and movements of the mechanisms became spellbinding. The magic world of early childhood was adumbrated by the diminutive black rocking horse standing idle in the foreground and, next to it, perched high and turning on an axial rod, a worn-out yellow wooden horse from a merry-go-round. The statue of a young girl in red with a barking dog inevitably suggested the Grimm brothers' tale 'Little Red Riding Hood'. The acrobatic jumping jack grinned in familiar fashion and articulated his limbs in odd positions. The white rubber head of a puppy, ears raised, big blue eyes gazing up at a master whose role the viewer immediately assumed, also belonged to childhood. *Inferno* was a mine-field of more or less hidden meanings, the unearthing of which was a game for anyone with an allegorical mind and a memory of childhood stories. The artist, who liked to repeat that his favourite public was children, believed that his work was able to 'return people to childhood'.[9]

The tale of 'Little Red Riding Hood'[10] articulates a universal mythical incident: the rebirth of a person out of the monster that has devoured her. Being in the belly of the wolf is a metaphor for transformation through experience. The most conspicuous animal in

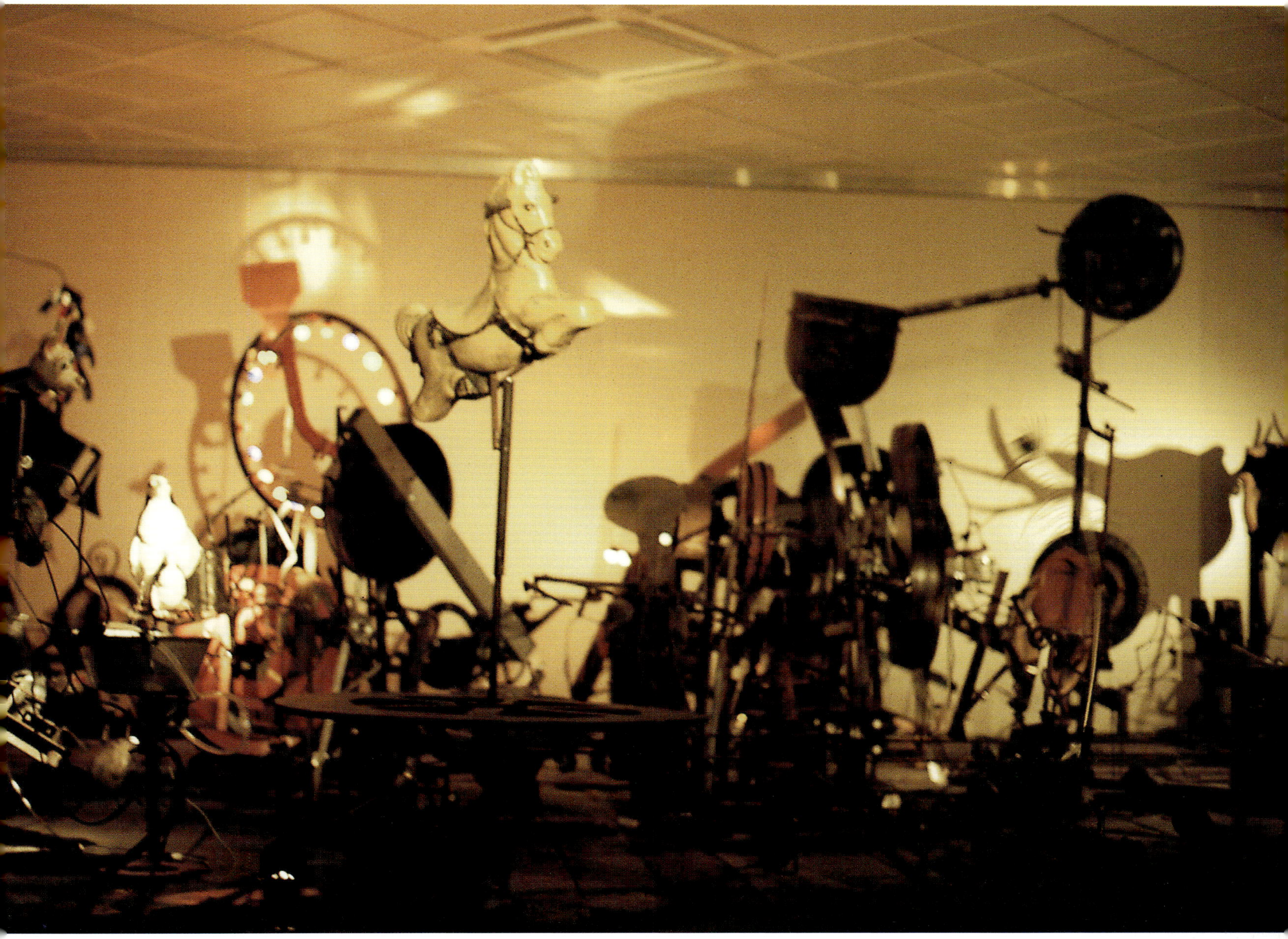

65 *Inferno,* 1984

Inferno, however, was the stuffed head of a moose with stately palmate antlers. This imposing specimen presided from an elevated position in one of the corners over the goings-on below, slowly turning its head from one side to the other. For Tinguely, the moose with its antlers was another fragment from nature exemplifying the principle of transmutation, which he upheld as a philosophical and artistic tenet. In *Inferno*, he also evoked the child's belief in an identification with all creatures by including a figure of Mickey Mouse, one of this century's most powerful graphic images in one of the corners.

Inferno was both a wilderness of twentieth-century rubbish and a philosophical landscape. Robert Hughes has shown that many visions of Hell start with a trial in the wilderness,[11] while Bruno Bettelheim argued that wilderness symbolises the near-impenetrable world of our unconscious in which we must find our way order to become ourselves.[12] Made up of urban and industrial, rural and agricultural parts, *Inferno* encompassed in turn the city and the country, man-made and natural things. Differentiated move-

Inferno, 1984 ▹

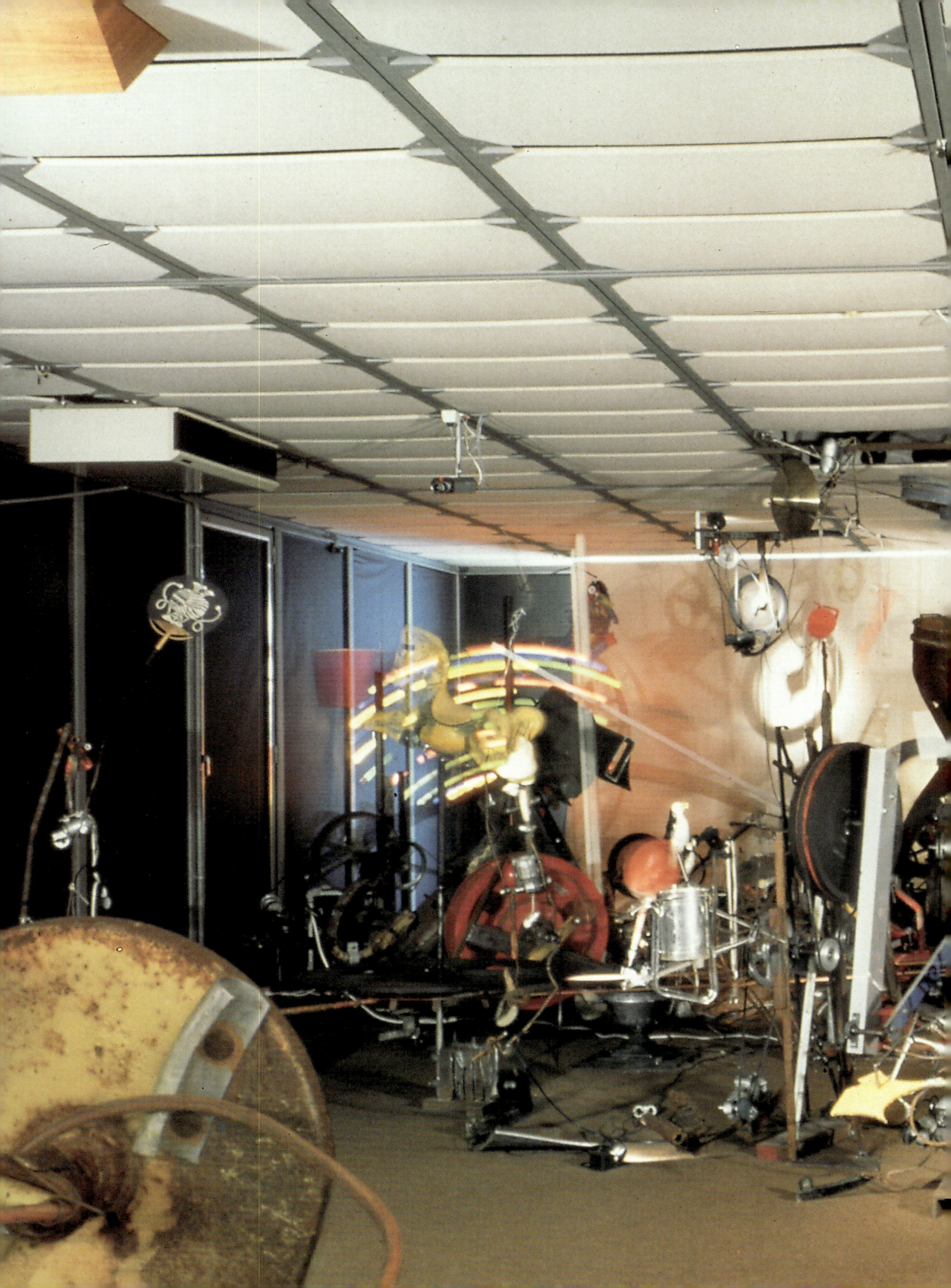

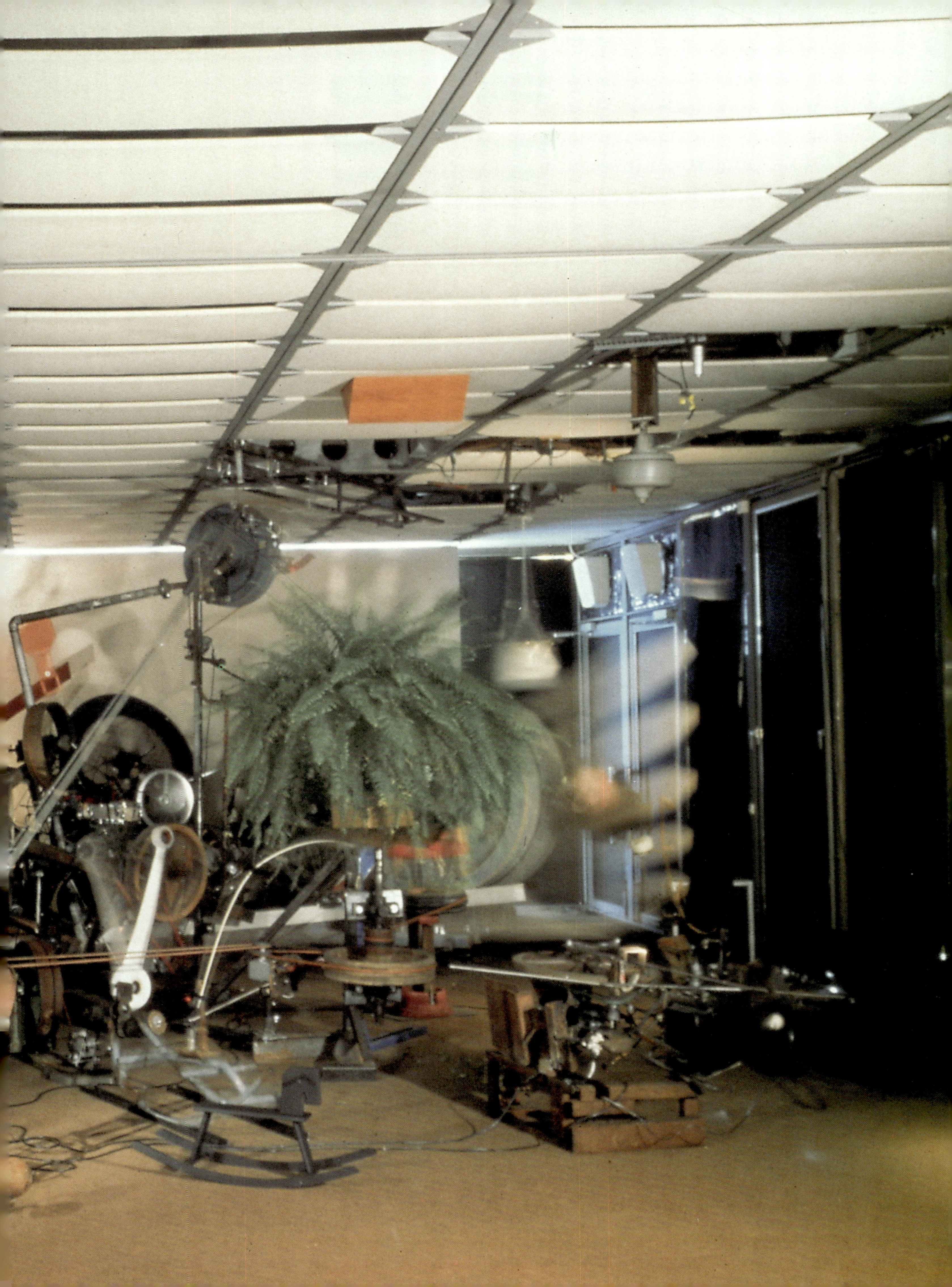

ments were enacted in the piece, such as the tilling of fields. Accelerated rotary movements suggested ant-like repetitious industriousness. All of this activity produced nothing tangible or material, however, nothing except sounds and shadows. The four elements were evoked: solid earth, liquid water, gas-like air and fire, agent of change. Water ran from the mouths of two penguins. Air was pushed out in ominous howling intervals from a ventilator, teasing a string of feathers into momentary flight. Life-giving earth was represented by the thriving fern, and fire was tamed in the bucket holding garlands of Christmas tree lights. Tinguely was reminding viewers of their journeys from childhood through conflict-filled adolescence to adulthood with anxieties, obsessions and destructive drives. The absurdity of daily labours was spelt out by the way in which a long beam was pushed slowly upwards but never reached a vertical, stable position, condemned to repetition without resolution. The pendulum-like swing of a large rubber ball referred to the precise measurement of time and its inevitability. In addition, by including references to fairy tales, Tinguely evoked a sense of timelessness. *Inferno*'s image of death was encapsulated by a sheep skull gnawing greedily on a metal bar, condemned to the endless repetition of its task.

Tinguely addressed the subjects of life and death throughout his oeuvre, but he first began a dialogue with traditional symbols in the props he built for Bidermann's *Cenodoxus*. His reasoned statement came with *Cenodoxus Isenheim Altarpiece*, for which he appropriated the triptych format, which he then used again for *Poya*. *Inferno*, recalling Hieronymus Bosch's *Garden of Earthly Delights* (illus. p. 134), continued this unorthodox elaboration on life's ultimate questions. The coexistence of heterogeneous elements and the suspension of the normal order of things served both artists as means to express the absurdities of their times. Both partook of the spirit of Carnival and are links in a tradition that originated in Greece with classical grotesques and that lived on in the drolleries, gargoyles and the like of the Middle Ages. *Inferno* was an admixture of the disquieting and the joyful, the disturbing and the reassuring. While in Bosch's frightful Hell, however, everything seems wrapped in a horrible silence, *Inferno* included a plethora of noisemakers and amplifiers, and its internal cacophony was the sound of life, of process. *Inferno* was Tinguely's cosmology

In the autumn of 1985, a retrospective exhibition opened in Munich, at the cultural foundation of the Hypobank. The show travelled to Knokke, Belgium, in the summer of 1986 and ended its tour in the fall at the Louisiana Museum of Modern Art in Humlebaek. For Munich and Knokke, Tinguely built two new 'Meta-Harmony'-type works. About the first one, entitled by Joseph Imhof *Fata Morgana*, Margrit Hahnloser-Ingold observed: 'The viewer is made to stop, to stroll, so as to understand. The work seems like a multicoloured drawing of wheels which has grown into something three-dimensional and monumental, like a mighty, festive clock without time'.[14] The *Meta-Harmonie No. 5*, also called *Meta Maxi*, premièred at Knokke. This giant relief had been built in the cavernous factory hall at Klus at the foot of the Juras. As Tinguely added the final touches to *Meta Maxi*, he unpacked toys and placed them like a painter adding final dots of colour to a painting. While he worked, he spoke about the difference between his latest creation and its predecessor, explaining that he had opened *Meta Maxi* up on top, giving it space and letting it go. He wanted the work to breathe, to suggest limitless, plant-like growth. This was Tinguely's first major work after the heart surgery that this quintessential man of action had found so traumatic. He translated his personal experience of recovery and regained freedom into this relief, but the space in Knokke was not quite high enough for it. The work seemed ready to burst through the ceiling, its blue lightning rod flashing upwards.

Inferno (detail)

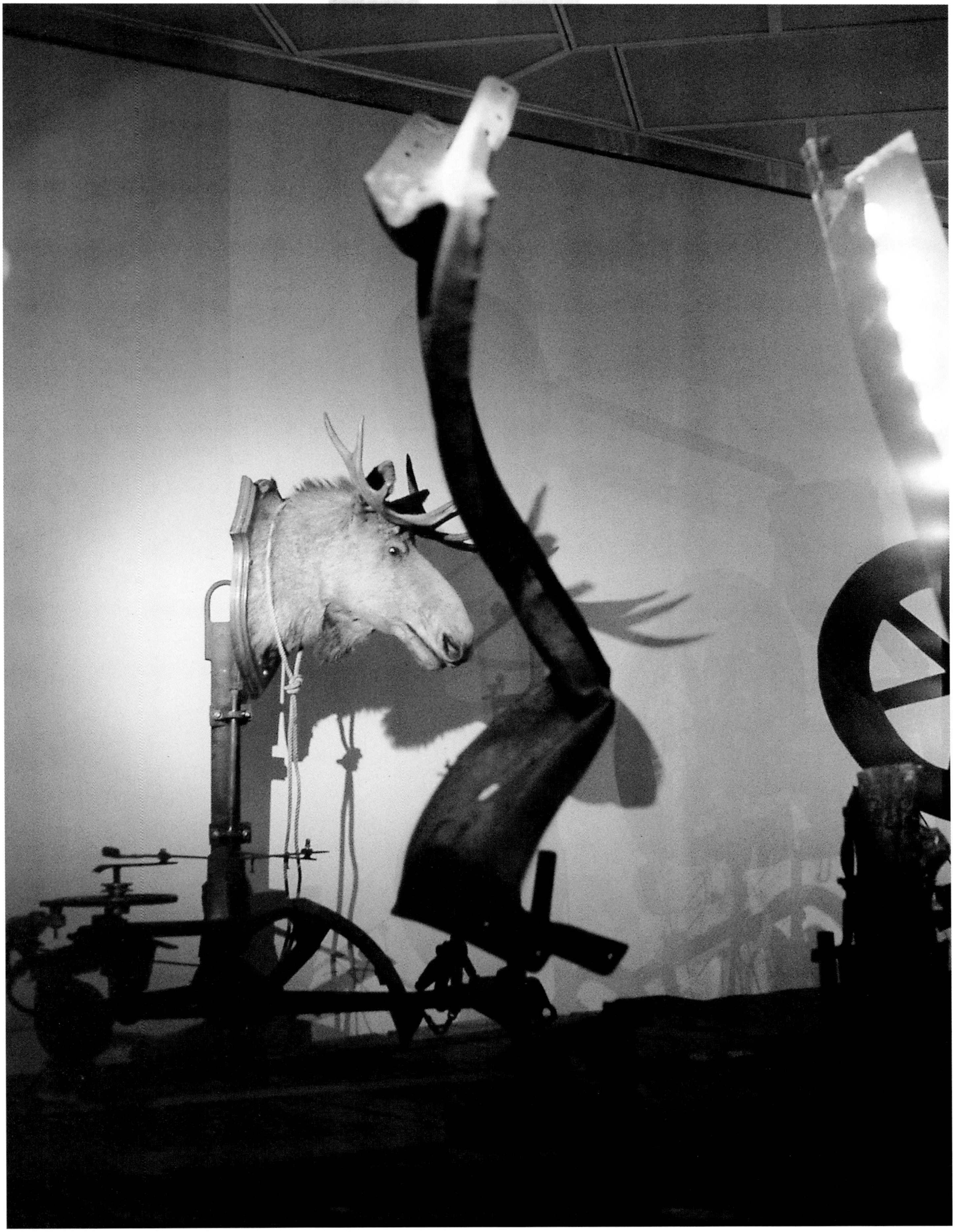

'It is beautiful to be transitory'

1987–91

In July 1987, the most comprehensive Tinguely retrospective to date opened in Venice, at the Palazzo Grassi; the following autumn, it travelled to Turin, to the Promotrice della Belle Arti. Organised by Pontus Hulten, then Director of Palazzo Grassi, the exhibition was as much a tribute to a great artist as a witness to an unusual friendship between two exceptional men. The show included over 90 mechanised assemblages, one of which (the *Big Meta Maxi-Maxi*) filled the atrium, and 77 works on paper.[1] The *Big Meta Maxi-Maxi* was a gigantic 'Meta-Harmony' that Tinguely had intended to be used by visitors to access the exhibit on the second floor. For security reasons, the public were not allowed to use its stairs and passageways (fig. 66). Thematically, the work was a homage to Venice itself and was as theatrical and showy as the place that inspired it. In the adjacent premises belonging to the Palazzo, formerly a church (San Samuele), Tinguely showed a Pandemonium enriched and moulded by events that had occurred some two years earlier. The group of 17 sculptures expressed a personal hell: the trauma of his major heart surgery in the winter of 1985. For about two weeks, he had been in a coma, an experience he considered to have brought about a twofold change:

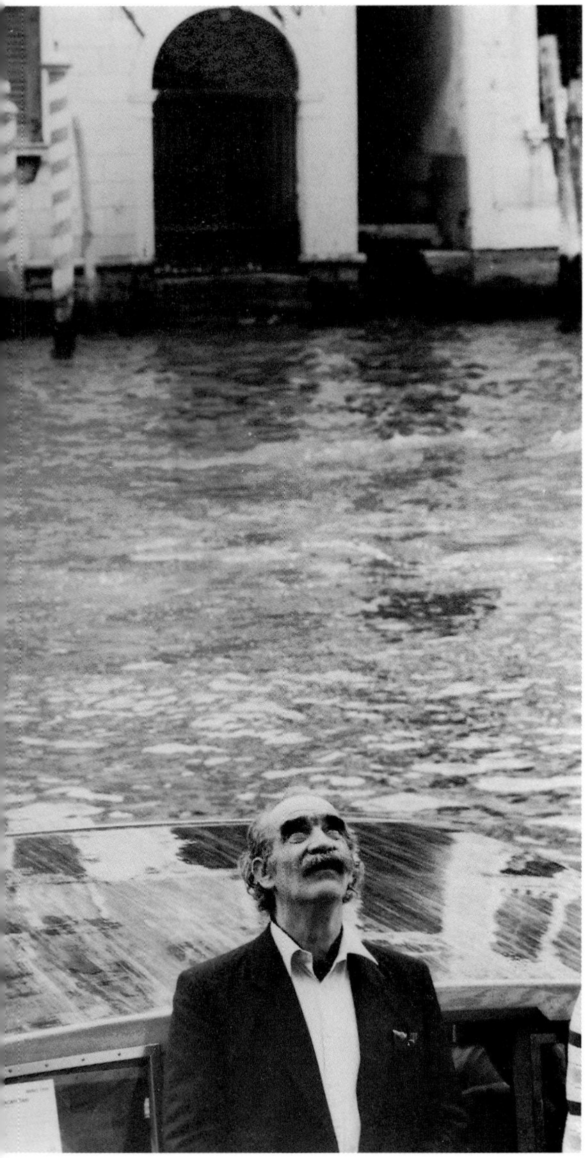

On the one hand, the long co-existence with death and all the drugs have confused me. As an artist, I have in any case a highly developed imagination, which, under the influence of drugs, exploded into a nightmarish universe of fantastical things. I wanted to fly, yet my hands and feet were bound. This is the one thing, the experience of terror. On the other hand, I now discover the world anew. Life. The erotic. Observe better, see more and experience more consciously. Light, shadows, the colours in between are now stronger, more intensive. I experience now my 'first' winter.[2]

The Pandemonium's 17 machines, collectively entitled *Mengele* after the largest of them (fig. 67), filled the old Venetian place of worship with visions of death in all its terror. Since building *Inferno*, Tinguely had been elaborating plans for a piece entitled *Hell*. In the late summer of 1986, a neighbouring farmhouse in Neyruz had been hit by lightning. Instantly set ablaze, the building burned completely. Its charred remains made a particularly strong impression on the artist, since he himself had so narrowly escaped death only a few months before. He freed himself from his terrible personal experience by expressing himself through items salvaged from the fire, working for three weeks in a highly charged creative frenzy. Having filled his studio to capacity, he brought forth enough objects to crowd the nave and apse of the church next door to the Palazzo Grassi.

Tinguely carefully planned the passage from the bright summer light of Venice and its festive, bustling atmosphere into the near darkness of the church by carefully positioning

◁ Tinguely in Venice, 1987

Tinguely at a press conference for his exhibition at the Palazzo Grassi, Venice, 1987

66 *Big Meta-Maxi-Maxi*, 1987 ▷▷

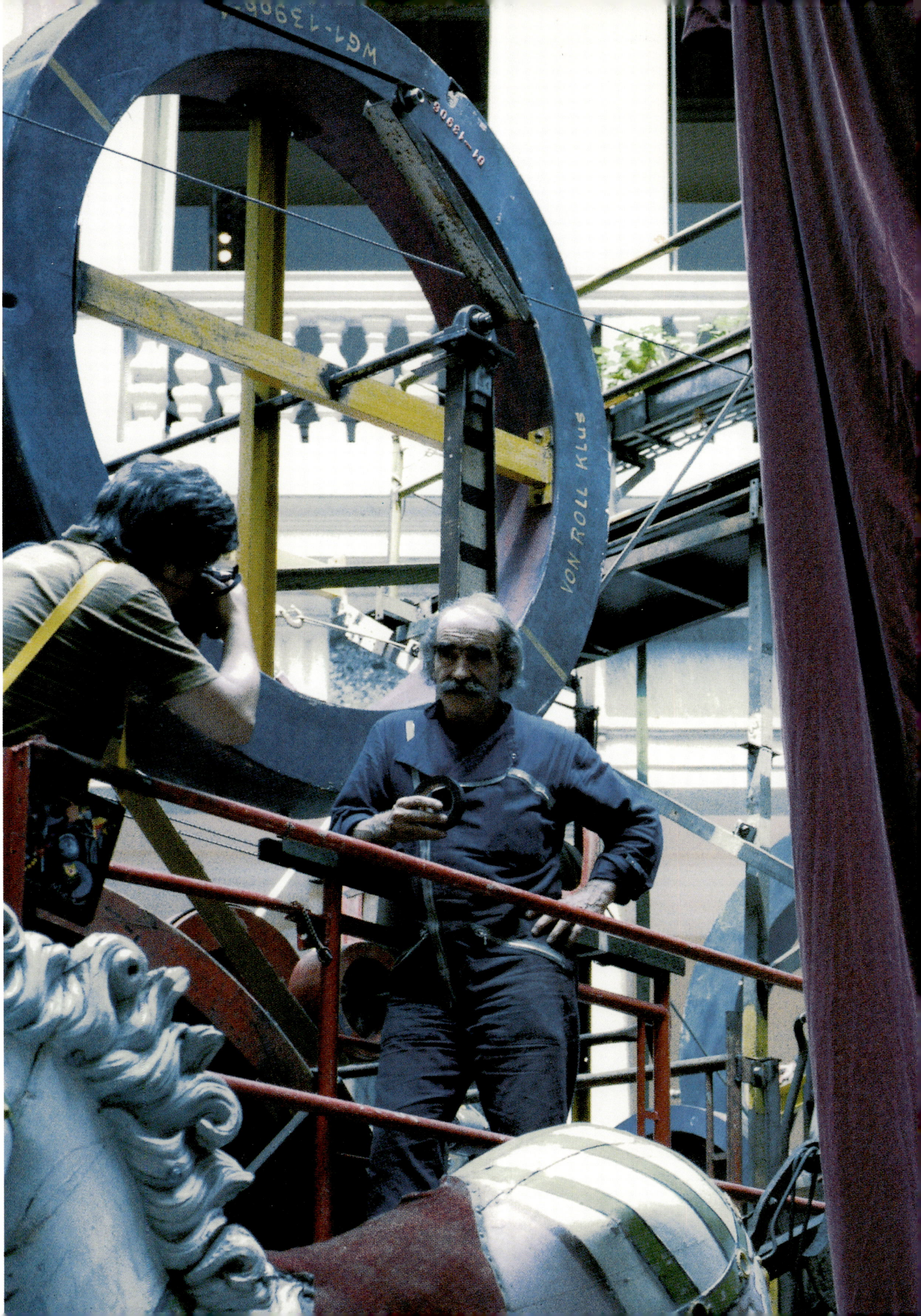
VON ROLL Klus

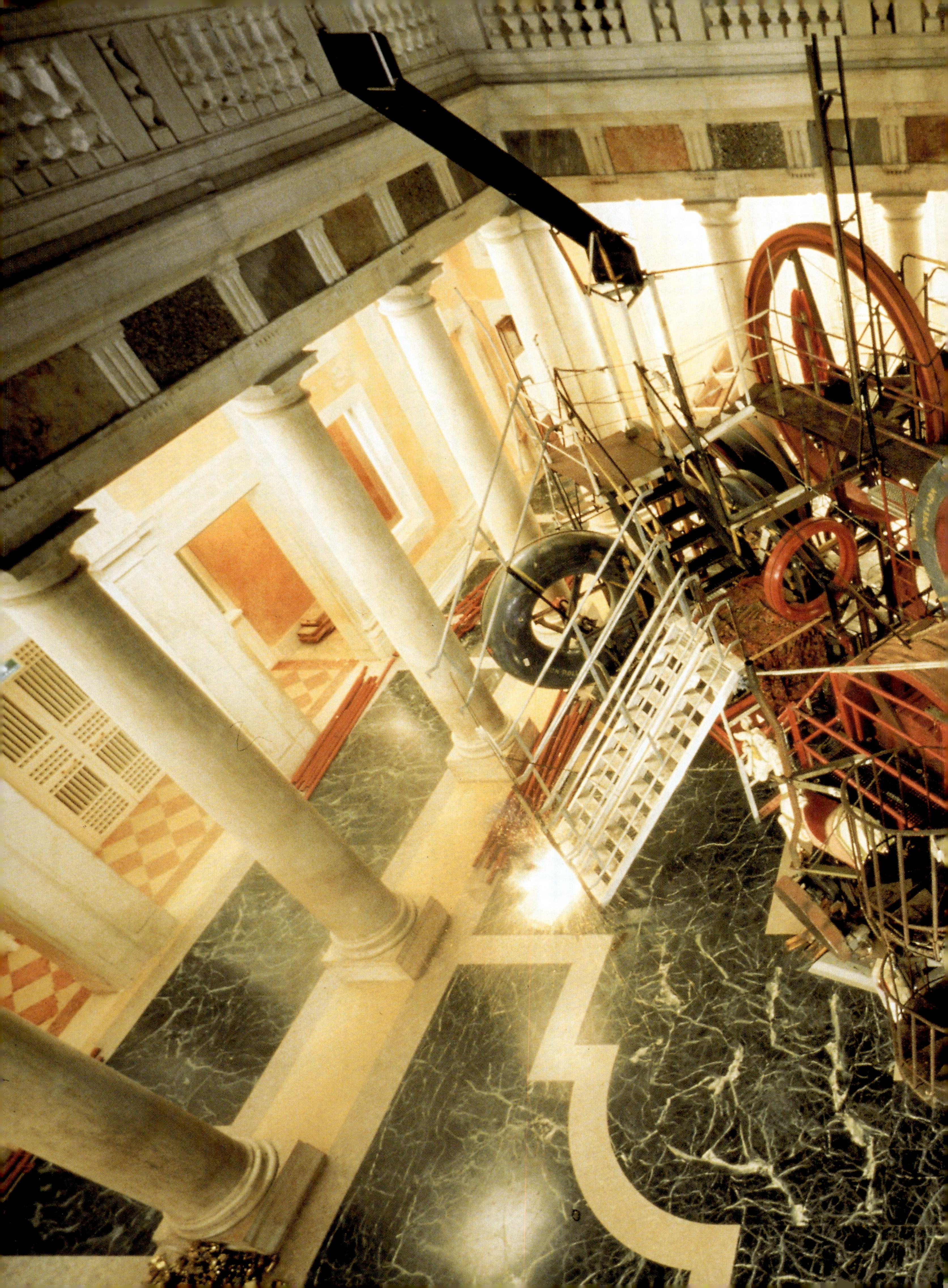

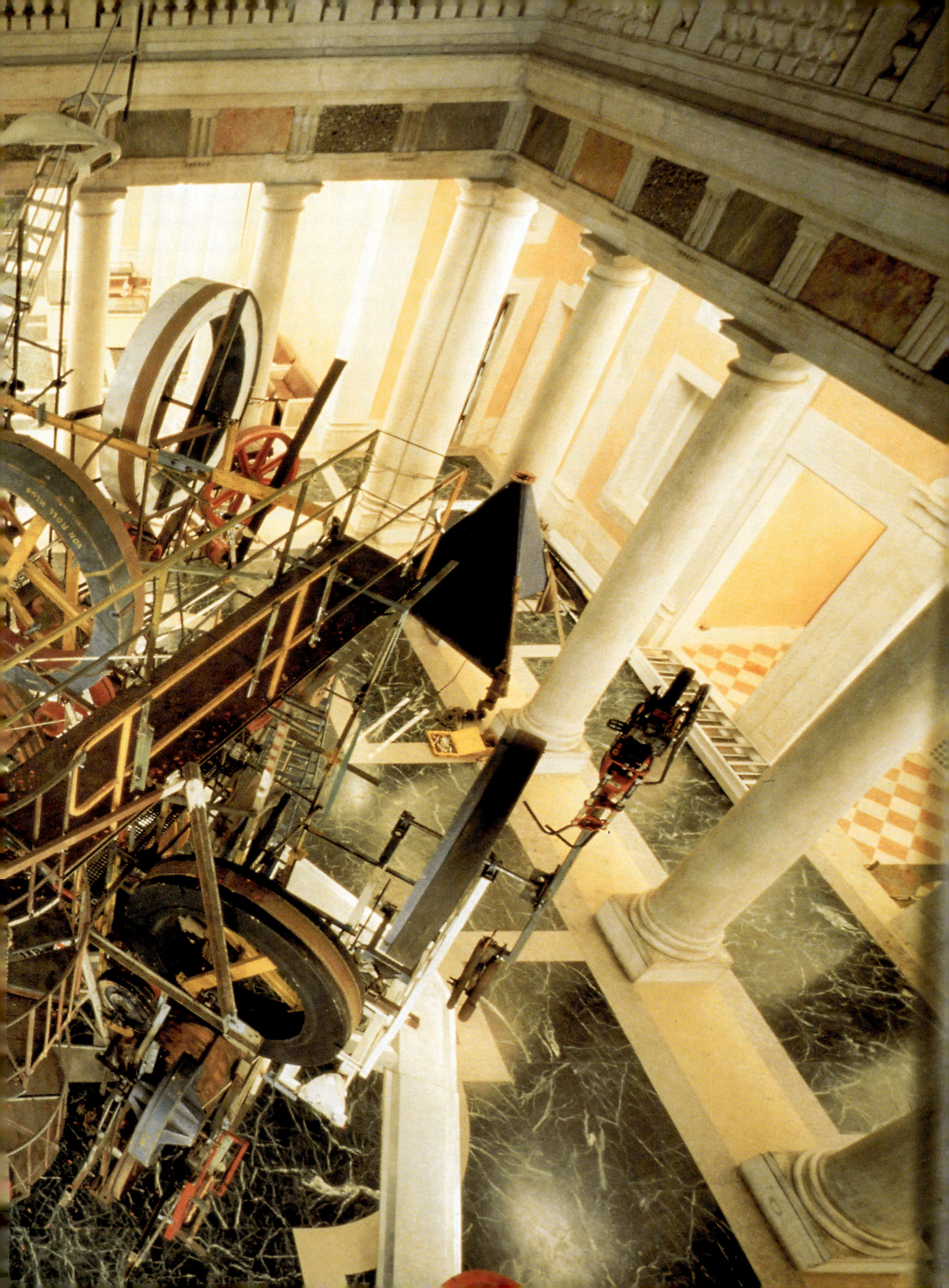

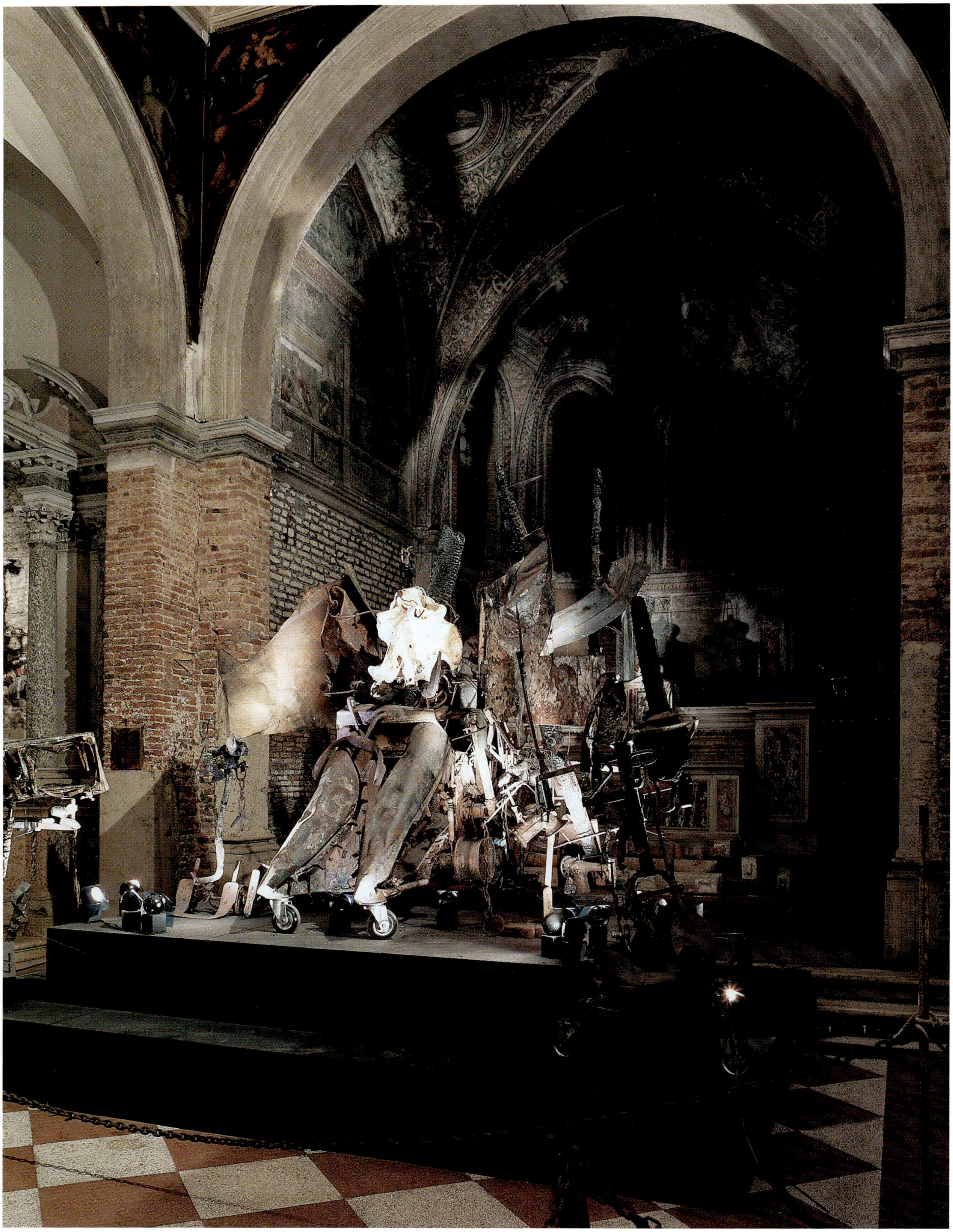

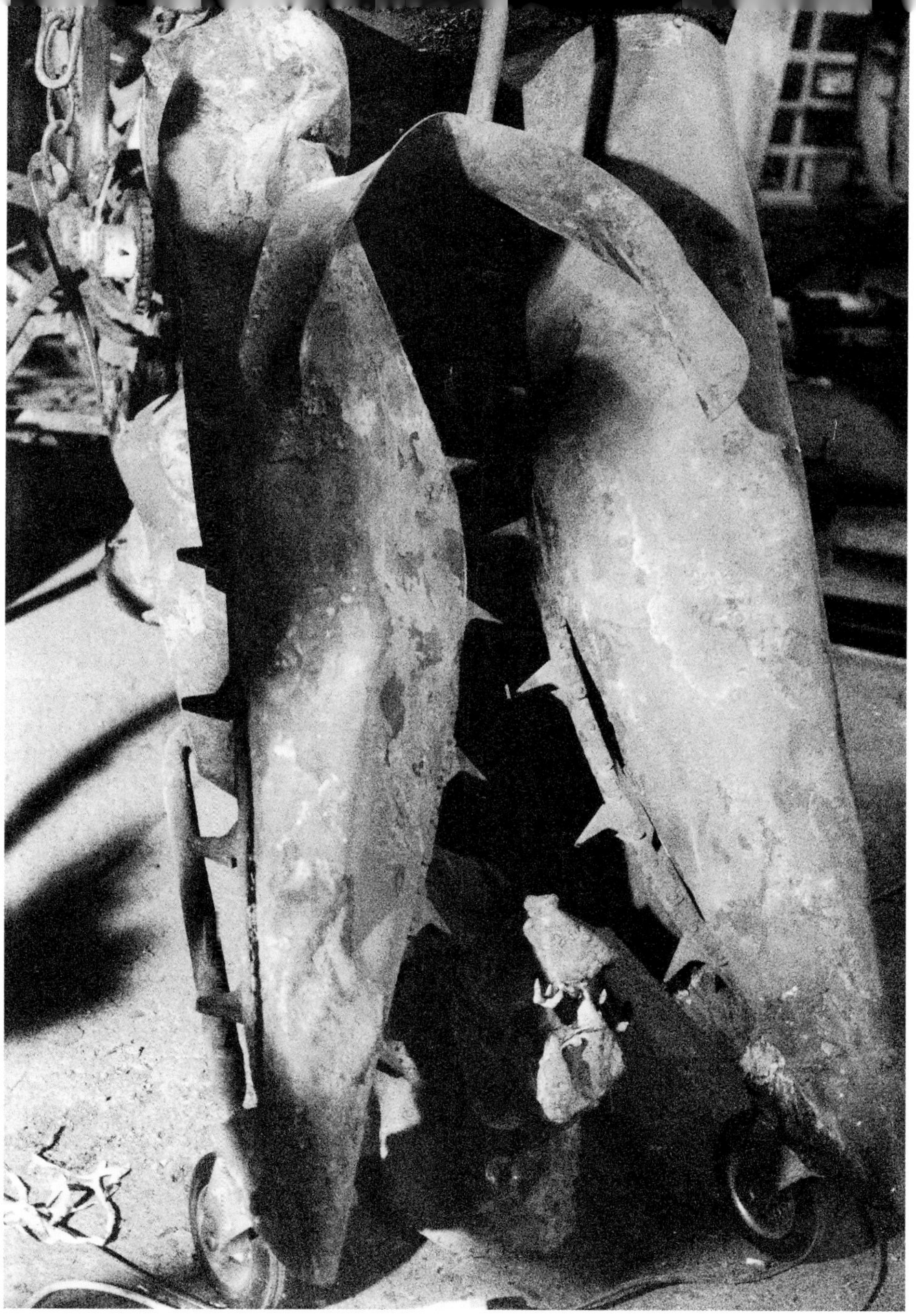

Mengele (detail)

◁ 67 *Mengele*, 1986

spotlights. To walk through the open door and small corridor into the nave was like participating in an initiation and the accompanying emotional transformation. The nightmarish ambience was an olfactory, auditory and visual assault. A foul odour hovered, the lingering smell of fire. Grating, sighing, creaking, murmuring sounds mixed in a discordant requiem. As one's eyes began to adapt to the semi-darkness, one saw a lurid scene. Surrounded by four subordinate sculptures, *Mengele* was enthroned in the raised apse, dominating all the other objects. *Mengele* combined an enormous hippopotamus skull set on a helical spring to a large corn-gathering machine produced by Mengele Augsburg, a manufacturer of agricultural equipment. The title of the work derived from the firm's name, which was embossed on the machine, and also referred to the doctor who performed murderous experiments at Auschwitz. The machine had a deep, vulva-like aperture lined with spikes. The cavity was lit from within and invited penetration, a threatening apparition of mutilation and castration. This typical 'bachelor machine' wedded the mechanical with the libidinal. Tinguely was exploring the violent potential in both erotic and mechanical actions, combining this notion with the idea of death.

Mengele was a monstrous enchantress. A mammoth memento mori, she wiggled her monstrous head and moved her burnt wings, an angel of death and obscene seductress. In the tradition of the carnivalesque-grotesque, she was an ambivalent and contradictory figure, showing both procreation and death, life in its contradictory aspects. Backing this central piece, three charred beams formed a burnt-out trio that performed eerie slow motion choreography. In this work, fire born of a thunderbolt was the purifying instrument of regeneration. The burnt wood signified death, but, as with all cremation, its ashes contained within it the wood's fertilising propensities. A similar idea is expressed in Paul Klee's *Death and Fire* (illus. p. 153, top). By creating a trinity of charred beams, Tinguely introduced the positive, regenerative aspect of destruction. The same symbolism informs *Targa-Florio* (alias *Die Gottesanbeterin* [*The Praying Mantis*]) a quartet of charred stumps aligned over a bent metal beam that ends in a tractor's seat. In a drawing, Tinguely referred to this piece as *The Passage of Fire*. A motor drives a wheel at the other end of *Targa-Florio*, moving the wooden quartet into continuously shifting positions via con-

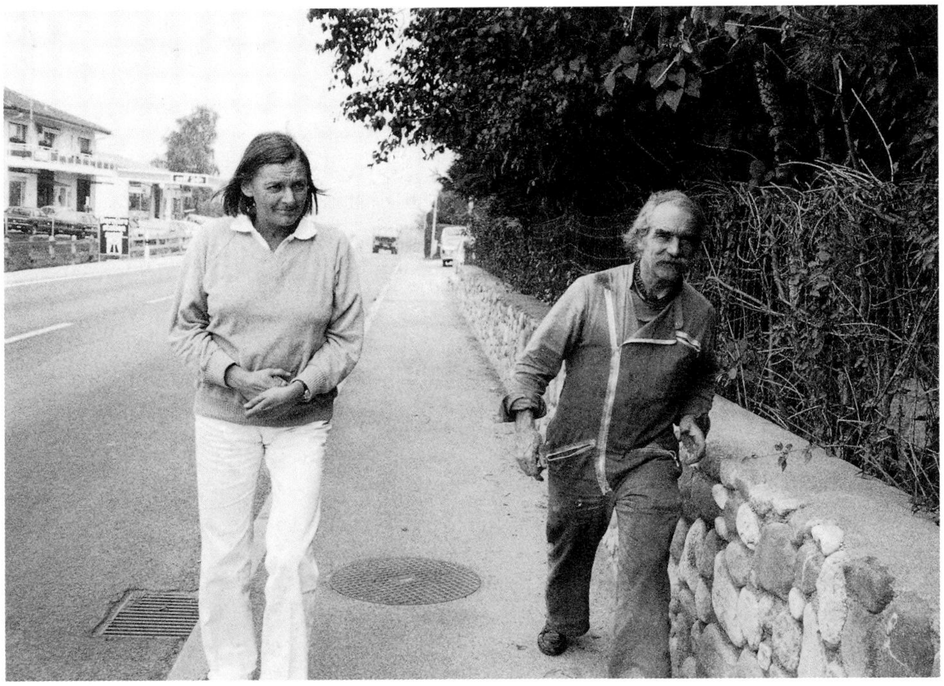

connecting metal rods resembling an assembly of standing worshippers.

Mengele, which Tinguely described as a '"High" altar with motorised wings & side accompaniment',[3] comprised in addition a sawing machine performing a relentless, absurd glissade on one track, unable to mend anything any more, and two pairs of 'acolytes': *The Television, The Bottle*

Tinguely with Micheline Gygax, Neyruz, 1986

68 *The Ram*, 1986

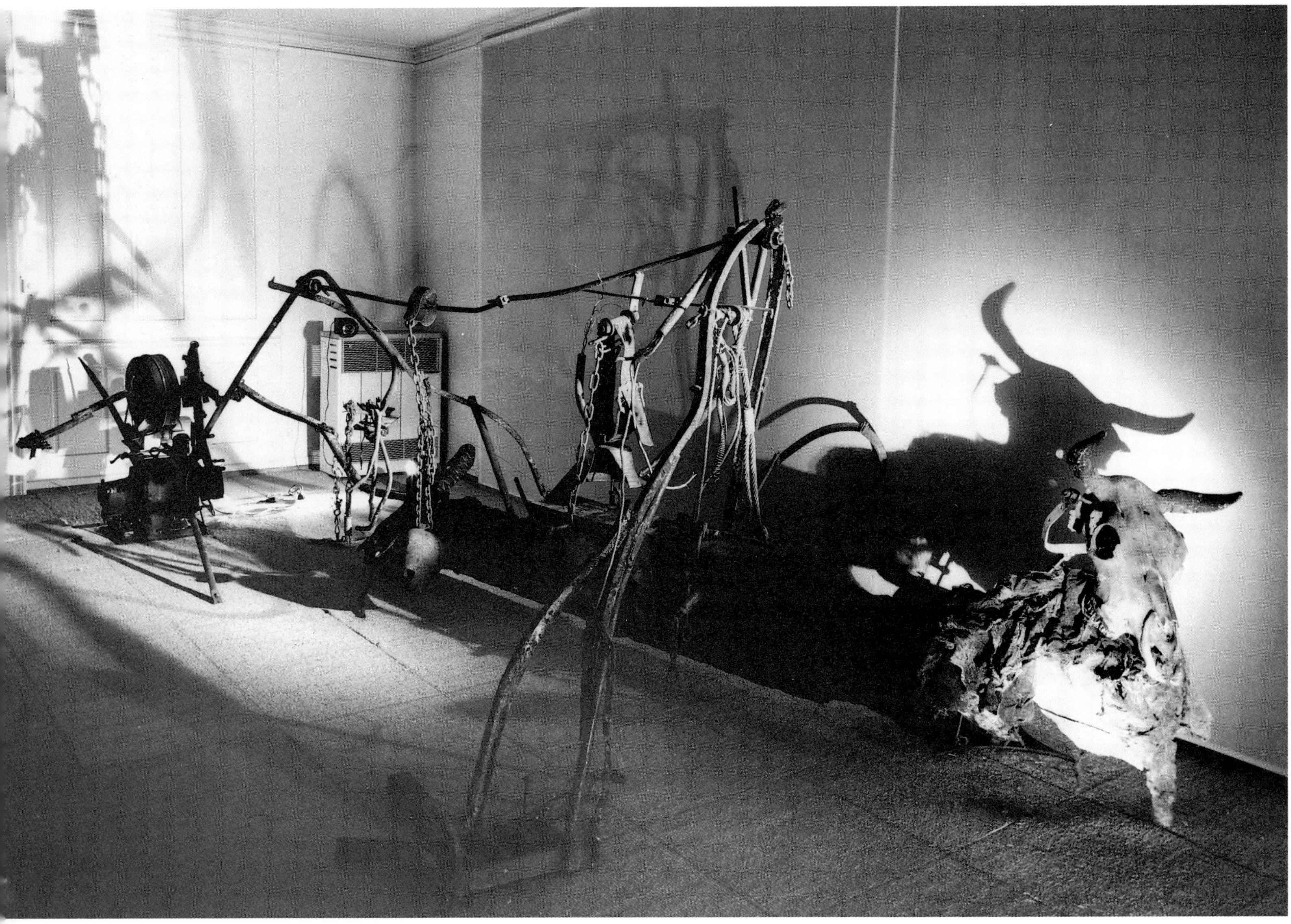

At Daniel Spoerri's home, Ueberstorf, 1986

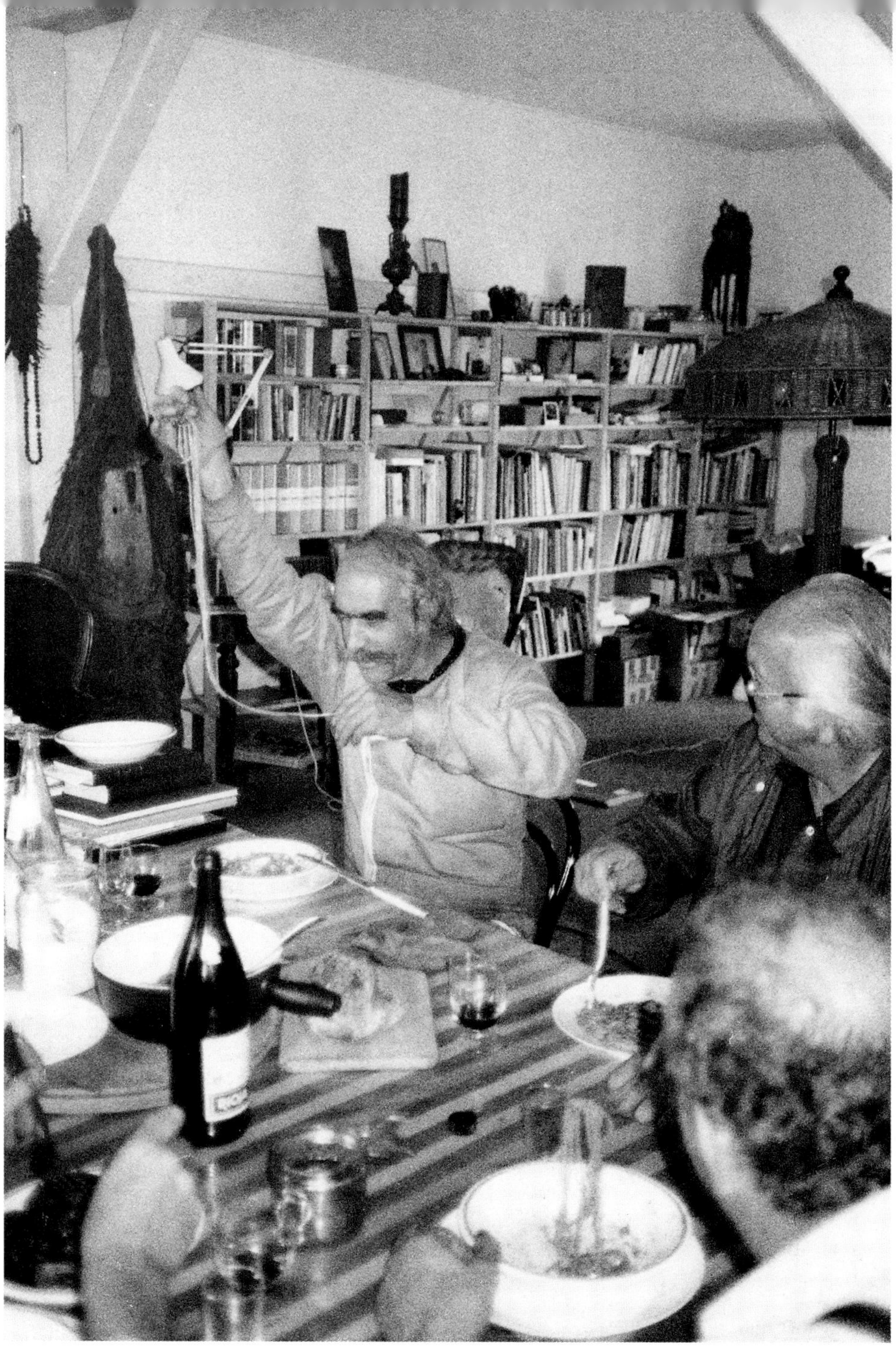

of Liquor, *Cosiness* and *The Bishop*. Like everything else in the assemblage, these elements had been salvaged from the calamity-stricken farmhouse in Neyruz. *The Television* was fixed by the artist to a bunch of metal rods. *The Bottle of Liquor* was an amalgam of unrecognisable things melted and crushed in the fire and welded to the farmer's hand trolley. His army rifle and bayonet and his saw formed an aggressive *Bishop*. His wife's meat-grinder and their cuckoo clock were combined in *Cosiness*. Because viewers recognised these rather banal household items, they were all the more empathic—after all, lightning can strike anywhere. Scarred by infernal heat, their patina resembling something caused by disease, these objects underwent metamorphosis twice over—first through natural disaster and second through artistic intervention. The burnt-out television set had become a metaphor for what Reinhardt Stumm called 'the deadly stare and empty eye'.[4] The saw, rifle and bayonet aimed bravely at the hippopotamus skull in a skirmish lost in advance. As with all of Tinguely's works, *Mengele* possesses a satirical undertone. The hippopotamus skull rocked as if moved by irresistible laughter. Tinguely had received the skull from Bernhard Luginbühl in 1984 and had used it for the 1985 Carnival in Basel. The *Requisit* he created was entitled *Monster-Witch* and combined a wheelchair draped in black with the skull. Both remained in a corner of his atelier, an oddity among oddities, until he used the skull to top another handicapped body in *Mengele*.

Thirteen further sculptures completed the gathering around *Mengele*: *Aggression* stood erect, wielding a tall thin metal bar ending in a chain like a halberdier, a shilhouette reminiscent of Luginbühl's 'Aggression' sculptures of 1960–62. *The Ram* was a battering contraption consisting of a heavy beam suspended from two connected arches (fig. 68). Its front was topped by an ox skull, and it swung back and forth, seemingly ready to storm any fortress head-on to the tolling of bells dangling on chains from its supporting rack. This is an image of relentless determination and single-minded struggle, the artist's visual equivalent of death's attacks and of his own determination to resist them. The devilish ram had its inspiring fairy, *The Ram's Fairy*, a tall, slender work crowned by a single feather. Again, a bell tolled, but the assemblage's most striking image—two pliers that held a large ring in a tight

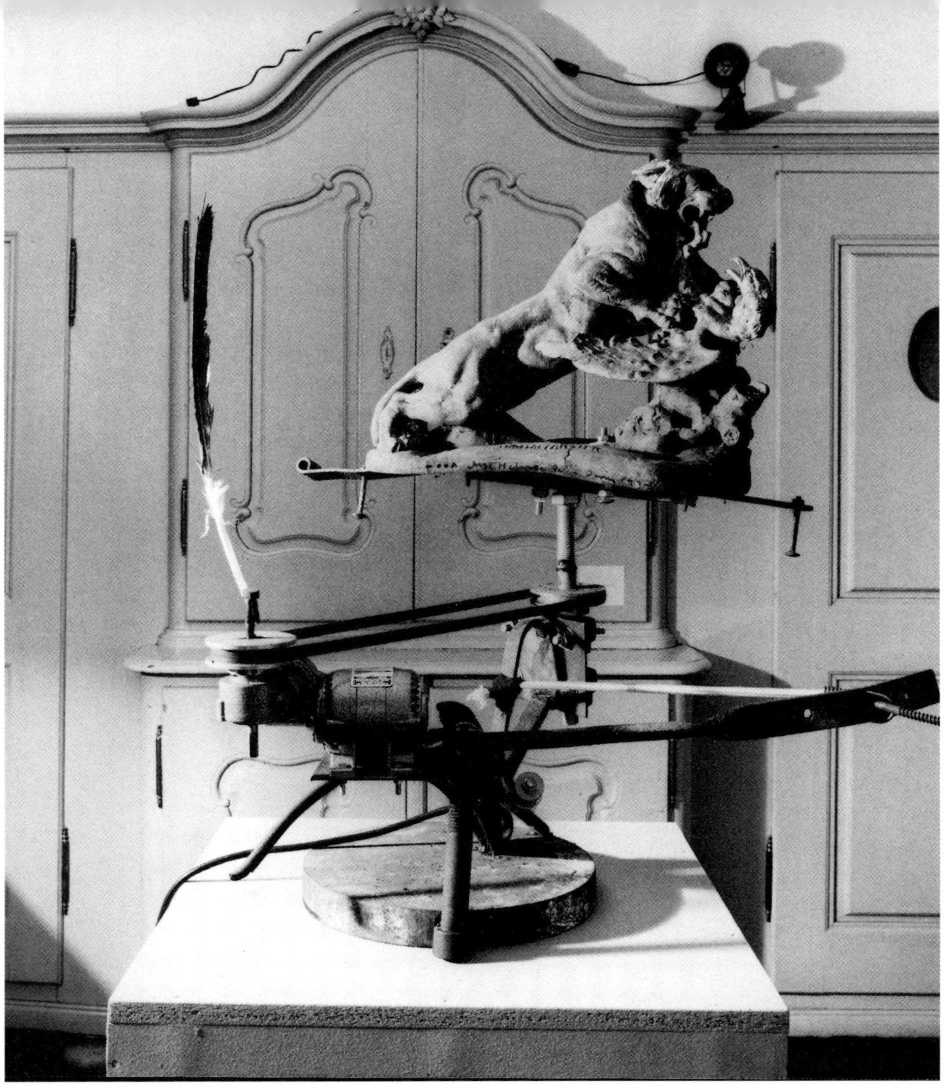

69 *Rotary Homage – The Furious Feather*, 1986

The *Scarab* was a rather low, squatting piece assembled from tools, including a rake and shovel. A chain attached to a metal bar was dragged back and forth across the floor. This metaphor for cyclical renewal was related to the symbolism of *The Spider*, a hornless cow cranium on top of a metal tube standing on a round sheet of metal to which a number of wheels were attached (fig. 70).[5] This spider's

At work on *The Spider*, Neyruz, 1986 ▷

70 The Spider, 1986

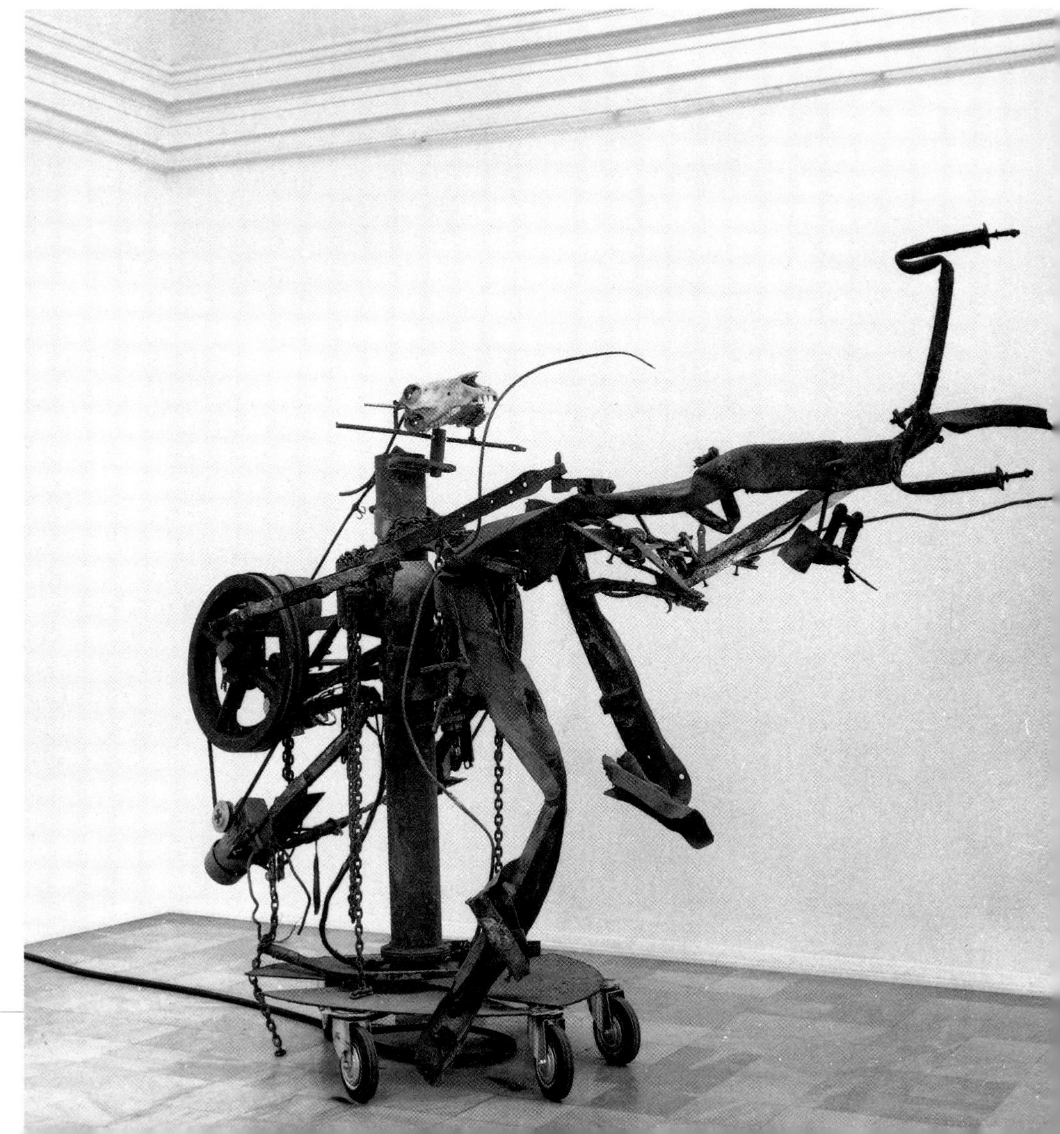

squeeze—suggested threat and torture. The proximity of the cutting tools to the wire holding the feather seemed to endanger this emblem of freedom. Tinguely here suggested how close he had come to losing his life. *Rotary Homage* was subtitled *The Furious Feather* (fig. 69). The artist had found a much-damaged reduced copy inspired by one of Antoine-Louis Barye's animal groups at a flea market. It was here engaged in a bizarre pas de deux with a long, roughed-up feather. On the one hand, this was a relic of Romantic pathos, a scene that catered to the late nineteenth-century fascination with the diabolical in all its manifestations. On the other hand, the single feather stood for flight and freedom, both spiritual and gravitational.

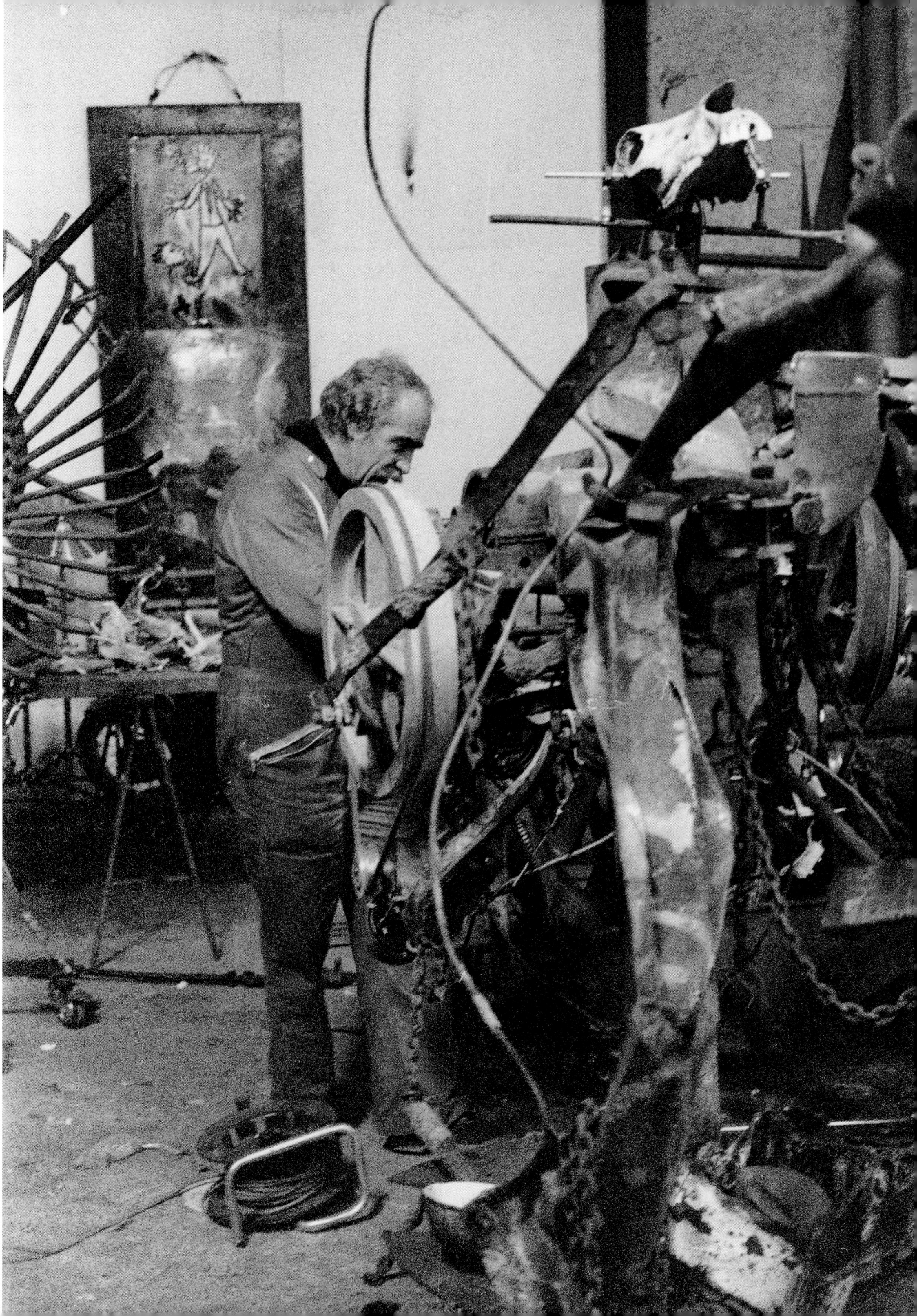

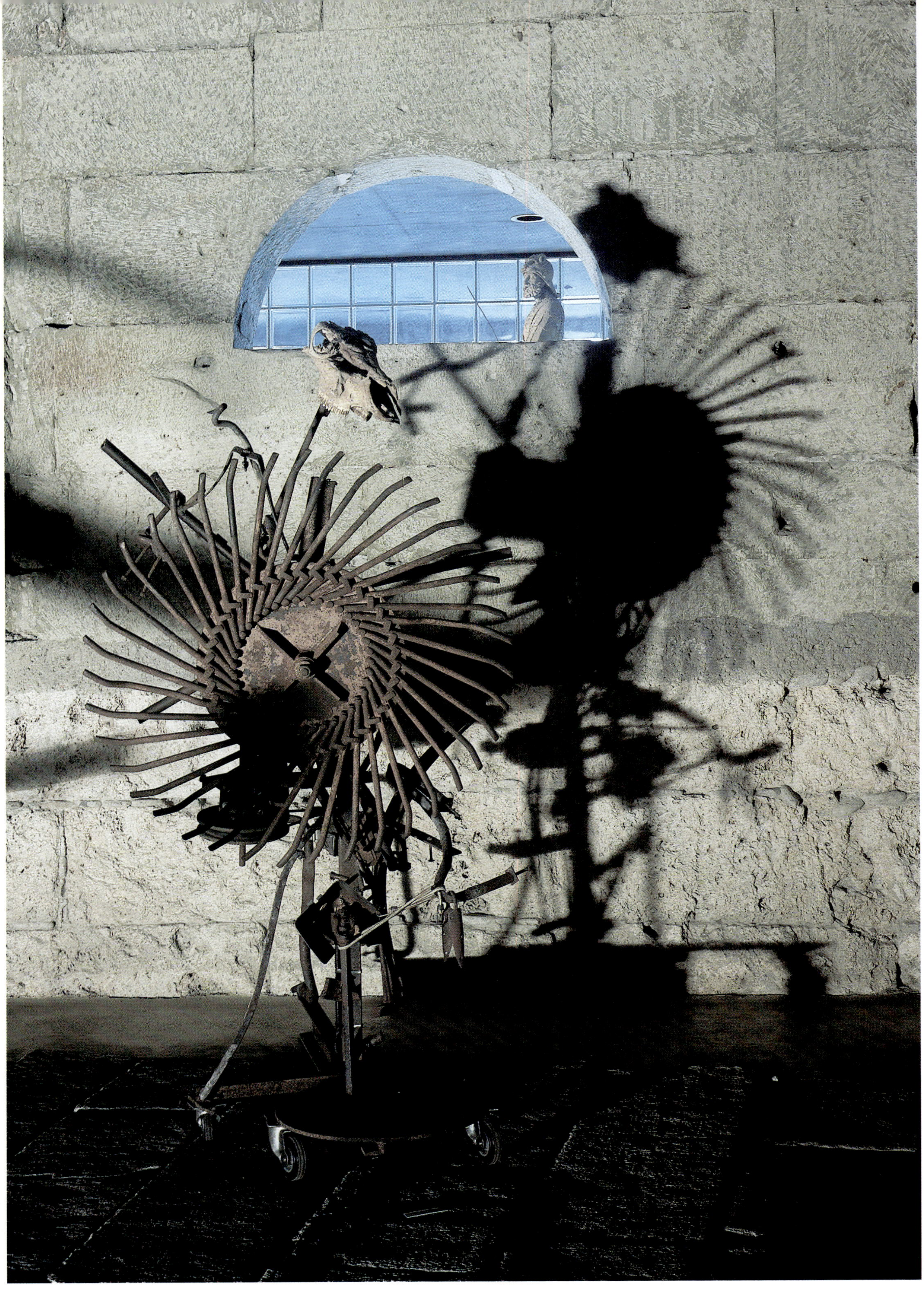

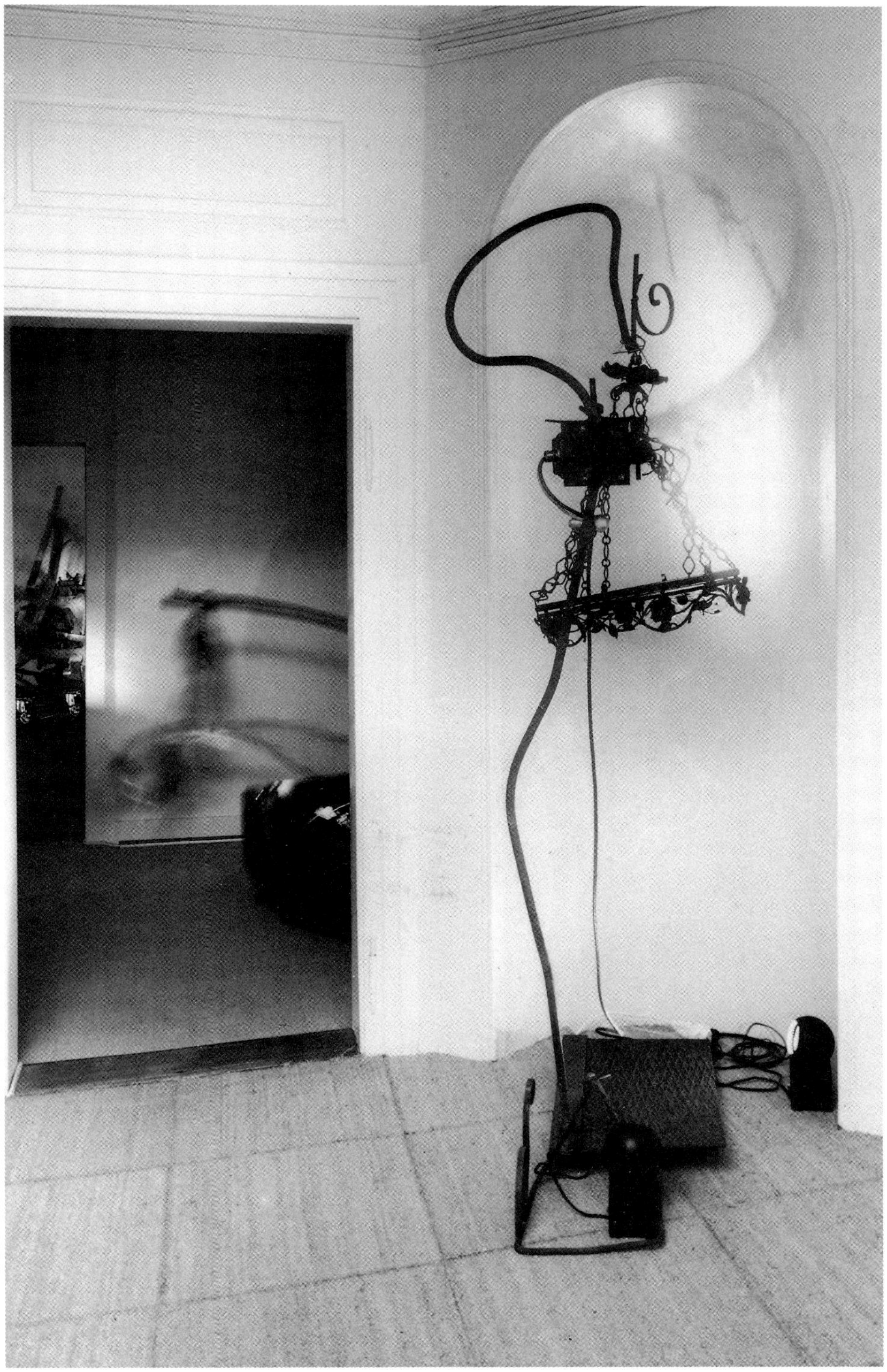

72 *The Moonshine Sonata*, 1986

◁ 71 *The Sun*, 1986

web was a chaos of chains, wheels and tentacles, some of which moved, searched and felt their way around, almost interlocking and separating again to the nodding acquiescence of the skull. Although this spider's ceaseless weaving to capture and kill was ominous, its activity can also be seen as being connected to the cycle of growth and death.

The Sun and *To The Moonshine Sonata* figured in the group as well. *The Sun*'s circular base, similar to that of *The Spider*, held up a part of an agricultural machine shaped like a huge petalled wheel that rotated, an overgrown metallic sunflower topped by a wiggling sheep skull on a pole (fig. 71). The sun, source of life and energy, can also burn and destroy, and Tinguely indicated its dual nature through the skull. *To the Moonshine Sonata* was a sort of standing lamp (fig. 72). Suspended from delicate chains, the crown-like frame of a chandelier without lights swung gently. Since it provided no light of its own, the object was a perfect personification of the moon. Like the moon also, its circular shape and shadows were modified by motion.

Two other sculptures in this group were made from automated agricultural machinery: *Transmission of Death* and *Mother* (figs. 73-74). The first was a nearly five-metre-high conveyor belt that carried a variety of animal skulls and one human cranium in place of bundles of hay. The skulls, affixed to helical springs, were a sorry sight, wobbling and quivering as the belt moved them up and down. *Mother* counterbalanced the mechanism of death with that of life. Assembled from the remains of an automatic feeding system, it included three bails set on top of a wheeled office machine stand. The axle connected to the motor was twisted into loops. When it turned, the bails connected by rods to the axle at different heights were pushed up or down with a great deal of clattering. Metal chains dangled from the axle, and a vacuum-cleaner tube was set in an arched loop above it. *Mother* expressed on the one hand the idea of dispensing and giving and on the other hand, that of grabbing and taking in. Tinguely was celebrating both the generative, food-giving earth-mother, the source of fertility, and the 'return to the mother', death.

Tinguely subtitled *Mother Der Ursprung – Vom Ursprung des Staates, des Privateigentums & der Familie; frei n. F. E.* (*The Origin of the Family, Private Property and the State adapted from F. E.*).[6] Critical of patriarchy, he favoured communalism and decentralist economics. Tinguely also believed strongly that '[the] most important [thing] is the absolute equality of men and women'.[7] The feminine principle was the theme of another work in the *Mengele* assemblage entitle *Crab*. Appropriately, this was a ground-hugging mechanism on wheels with a number of bent and twisted metal arms that stuck out like the pincers and legs of a crustacean. The fourth sign of the zodiac, the crab signifies mediation. *Balance*, the last piece in the *Mengele* group, was also an ideational synthesis that the artist had explored be-

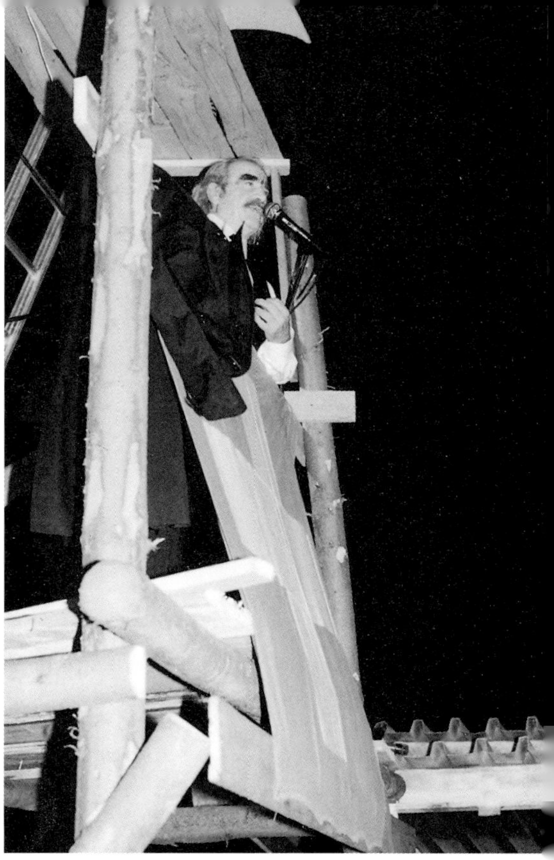

73 *Transmission of Death*, 1986

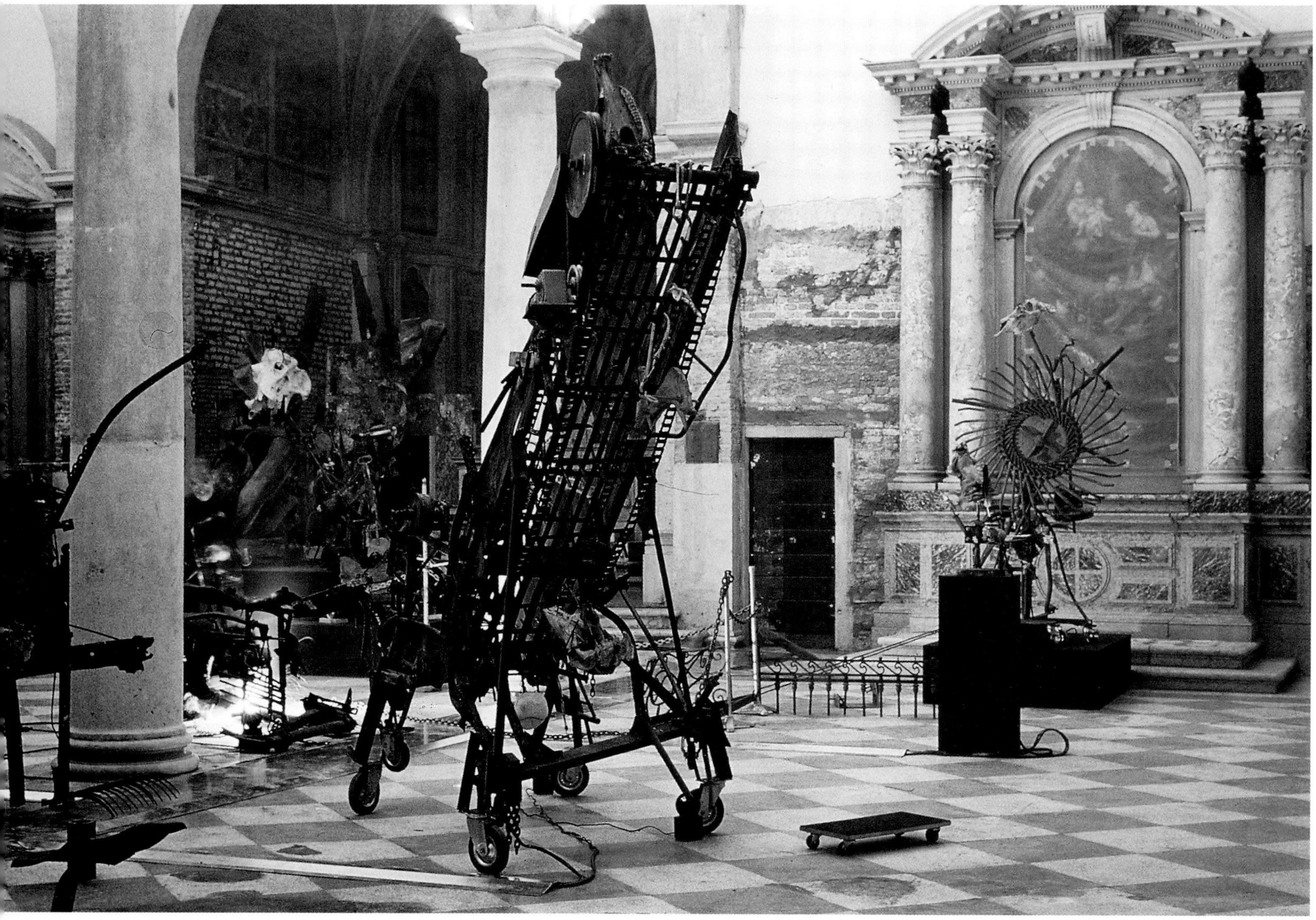

◁ Tinguely giving a speech on the Swiss national holiday, 1991

Paul Klee, *Death and Fire*, 1940, Kunstmuseum Bern

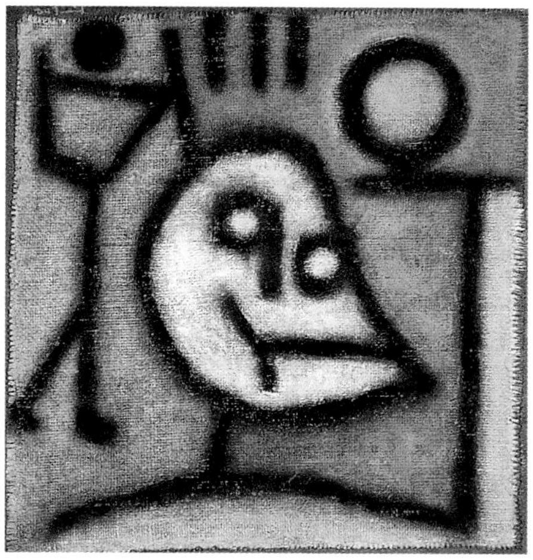

fore. It was assembled from a bent metal sheet set rocking by a motor-driven wheel. Two protruding bars were trimmed with lace; one branched upwards, the other reached horizontally across one of the rims of the curved metal sheet, its end emphasised by a cow's jawbone like the dot in the *t'ai-chi t'u* that symbolises the seed of its opposite.

Mengele and the objects created together from the charred debris of a farmhouse were unprecedented in their sustained, nearly paranoid vocabulary of terror and monomaniacal reiteration of the theme of death. This creative outpouring was an exorcism of Tinguely's nightmares, a process of healing by giving form to an overwhelmingly real vision of death. Powerful depicitions of death had surrounded the artist since his childhood in Basel, including Hans Holbein's *Christ in His Tomb* (1521; Kunstmuseum)[8] and the haunting personifications by Hans Baldung Grien, including *Death and the Maiden* (1517; Kunstmuseum). Tinguely once said: 'In Basel I lived with the Dance of Death',[9] referring to the life-sized frescoes along the wall of the Dominican cloister, destroyed in 1805 but known from prints, which were the most famous representations of the theme.

In works such as *Inferno* and *Mengele*, Tinguely brought death into our midst and reminded us of the vanity of all living things. In this he was opposing the hypocrisy of contemporary society, in particular the media. Contemporary Western culture is hostile to the idea of change and favours the permanent and rigid, the very things that Tinguely opposed. Asked what he hoped viewers would learn

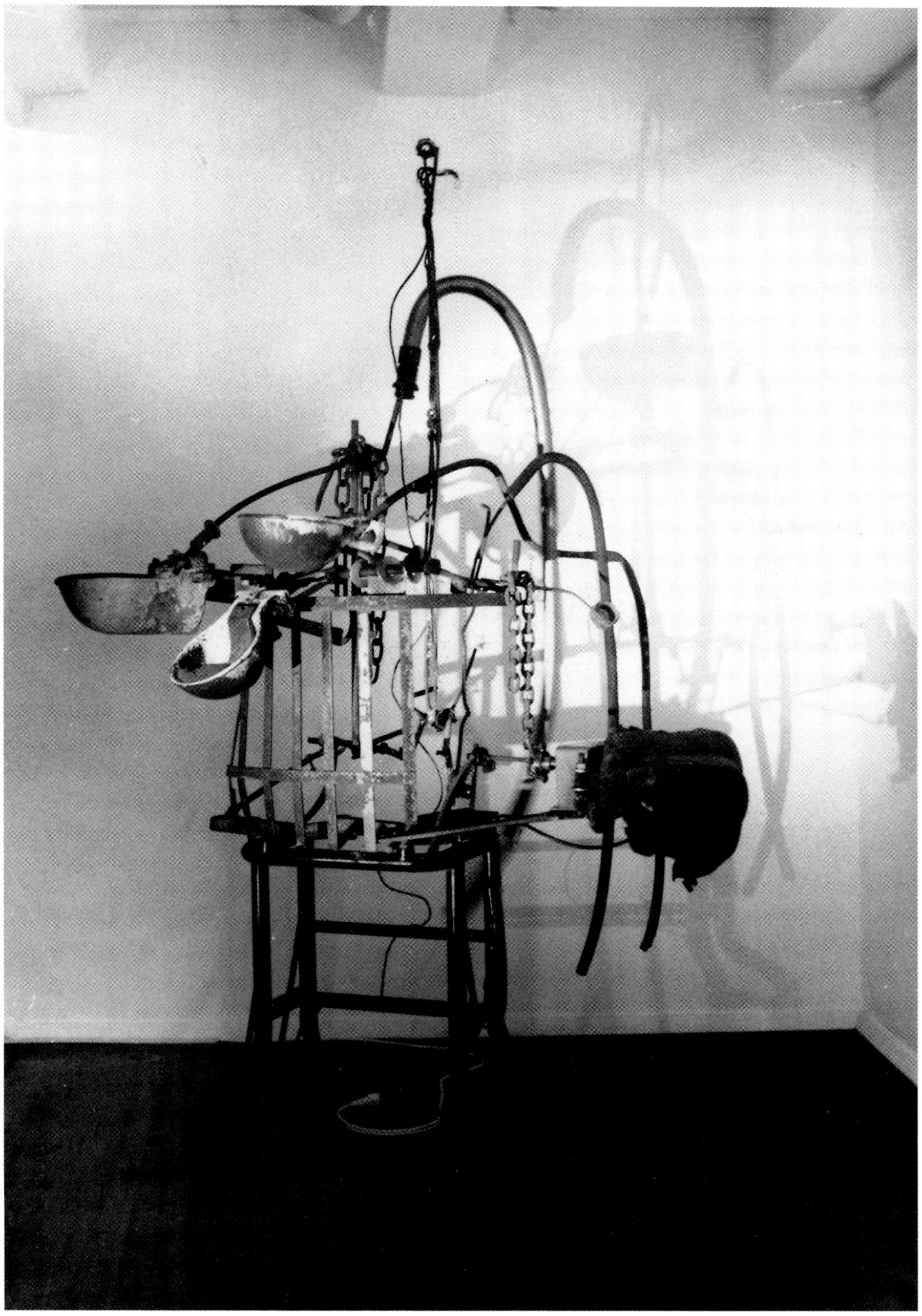

74 *The Mother*, 1986

about death from his work, he replied: 'To be more fond of life; & more real fear of death will produce more creativity—the media dehumanise death. Death is made synthetic'.[10]

Supplemented by several new works, the retrospective shown at Venice and Turin was reassembled and opened in December 1988 in Paris at the Centre Pompidou. The exhibition

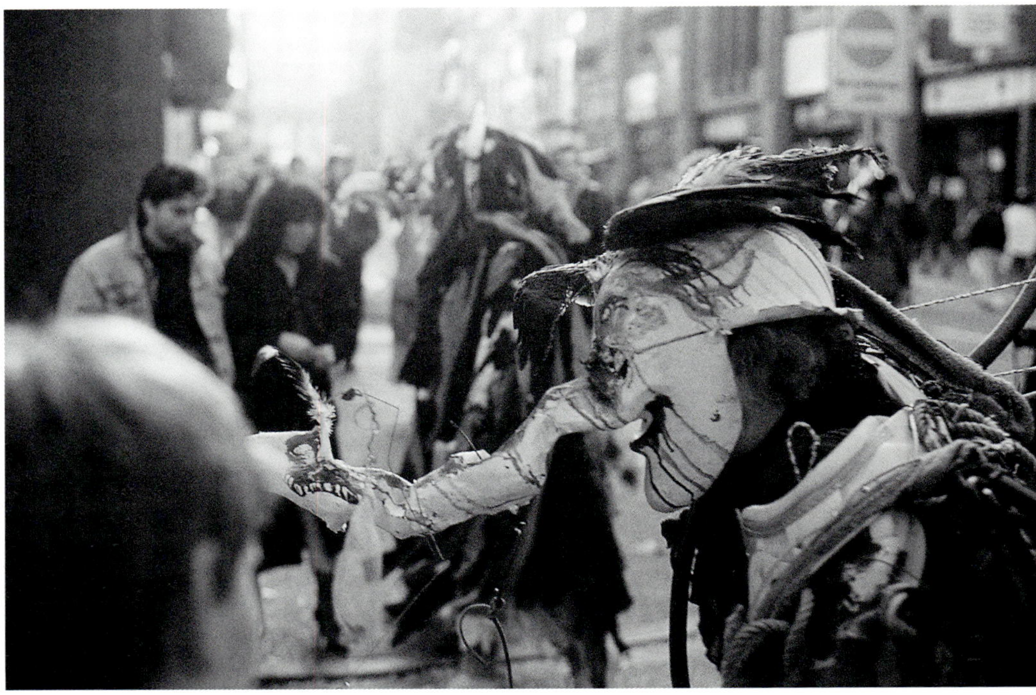

Tinguely wearing his 'down-and-out' costume at the Basel Carnival, 1988 (see plate 48)

75 *The Philosophers*, 1988, installation view at Centre Georges Pompidou

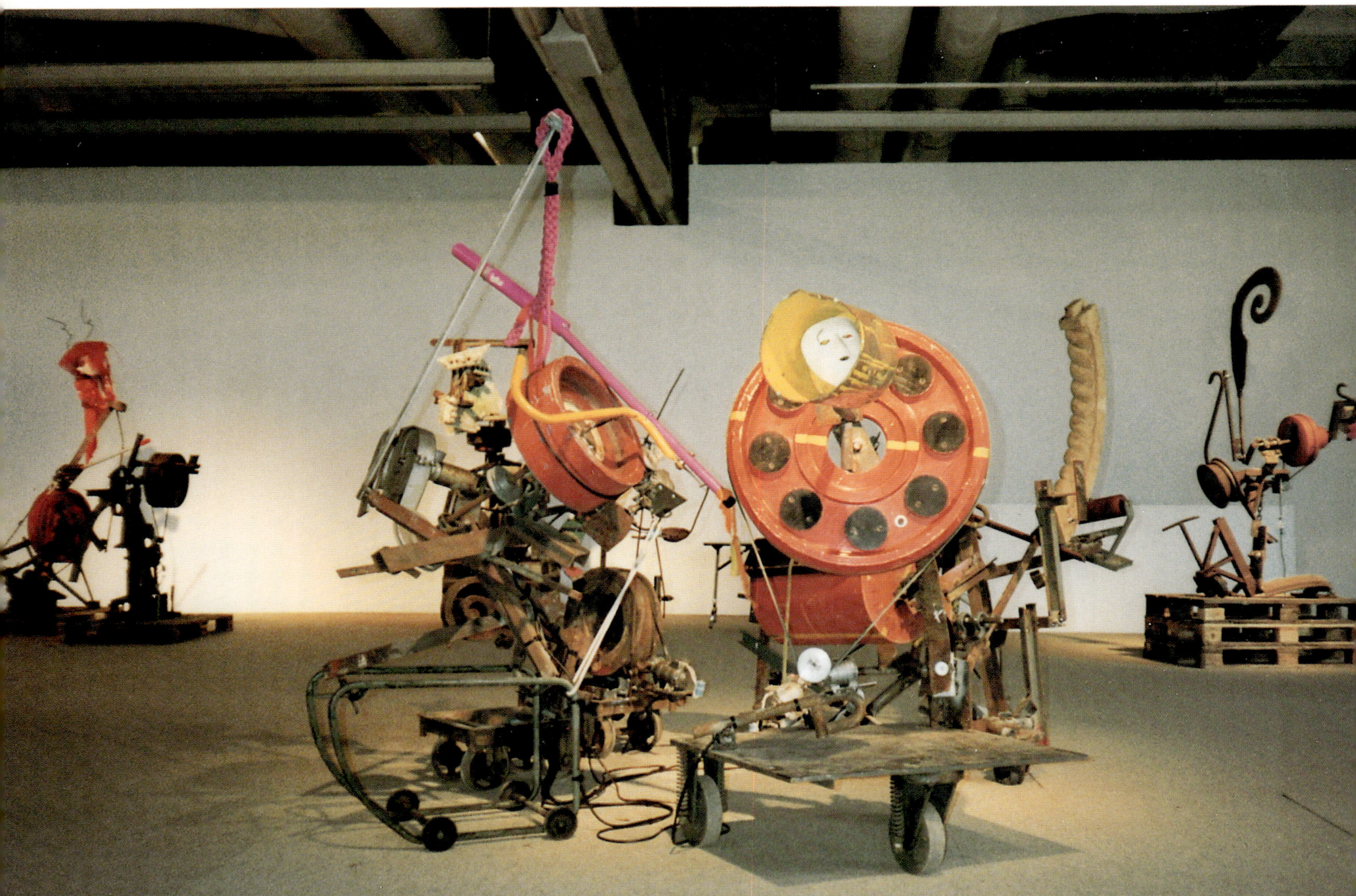

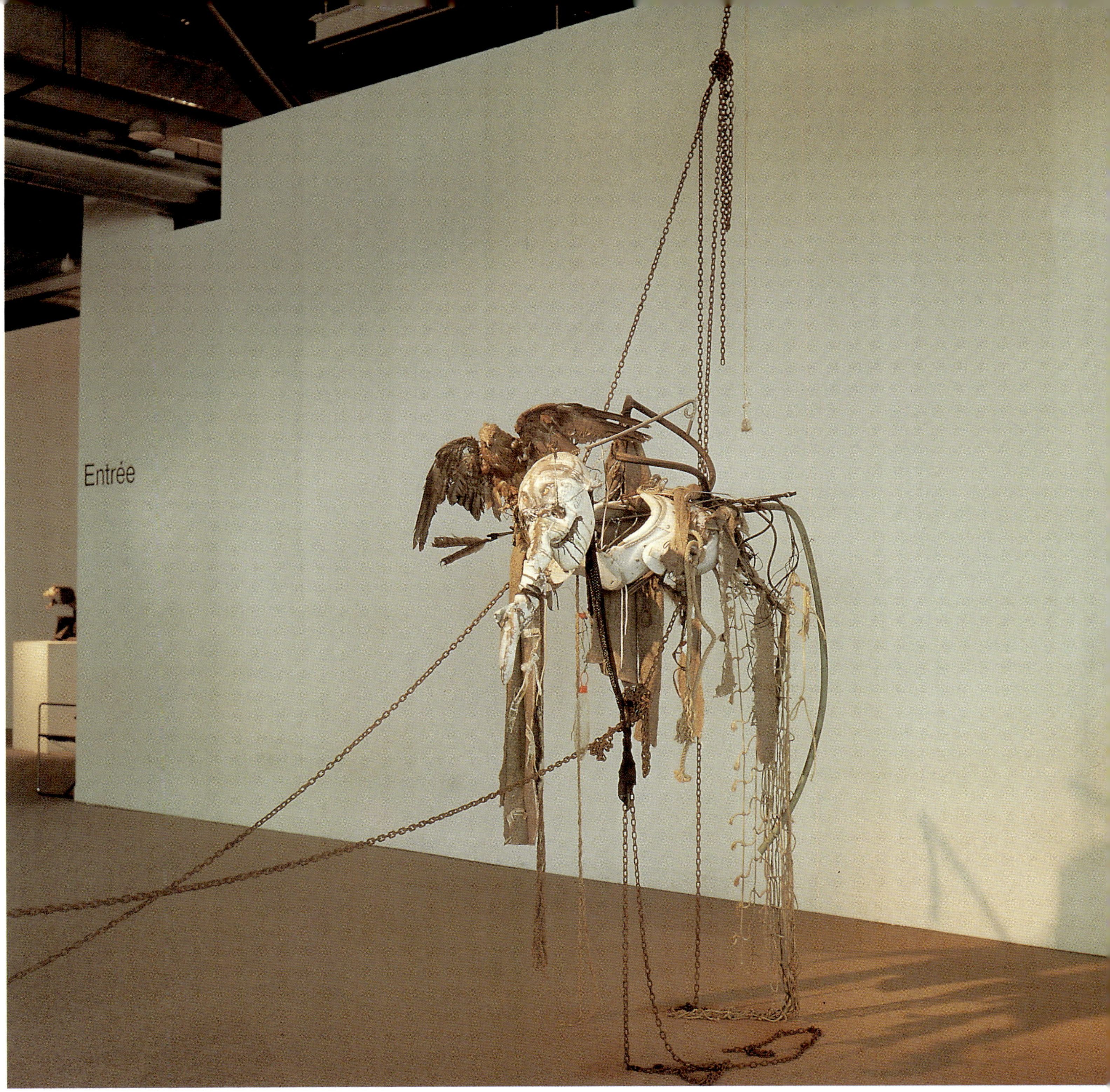

76 *Self-Portrait*, 1988 (detail)

occupied the entire large gallery on the fifth floor. An odd clique of anthropomorphic mechanisms greeted the visitor in the large entrance space where tickets could be purchased and coats deposited. *The Philosophers* (fig. 75) was the collective title of this welcoming coterie numbering 19 new sculptures in addition to a voluminous 'flatbed' relief, *Last Collaboration with Yves Klein* (1988; formerly collection of the artist). Alongside these homages to great scientists, innovators, creators and inventors stood a self-mocking self-portrait in which the artist's alias, tellingly dressed in his latest Carnival outfit, danced at the will of a large wheel (fig. 76). Women were absent from this gallery of famous thinkers except for the *African Queen*, named after the found object that was the pretext of this piece (formerly collection of

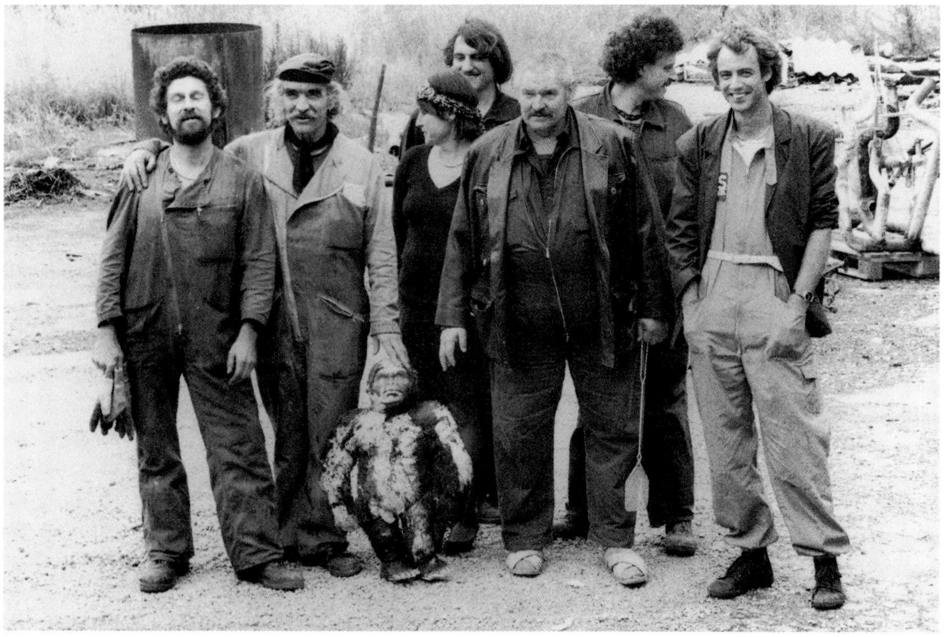

Left to right: Joseph Imhof, Tinguely, Ursi Luginbühl, Iwan Luginbühl, Bernhard Luginbühl, Basil Luginbühl and Reto Emch

Tinguely at a press conference, Moscow, 1990

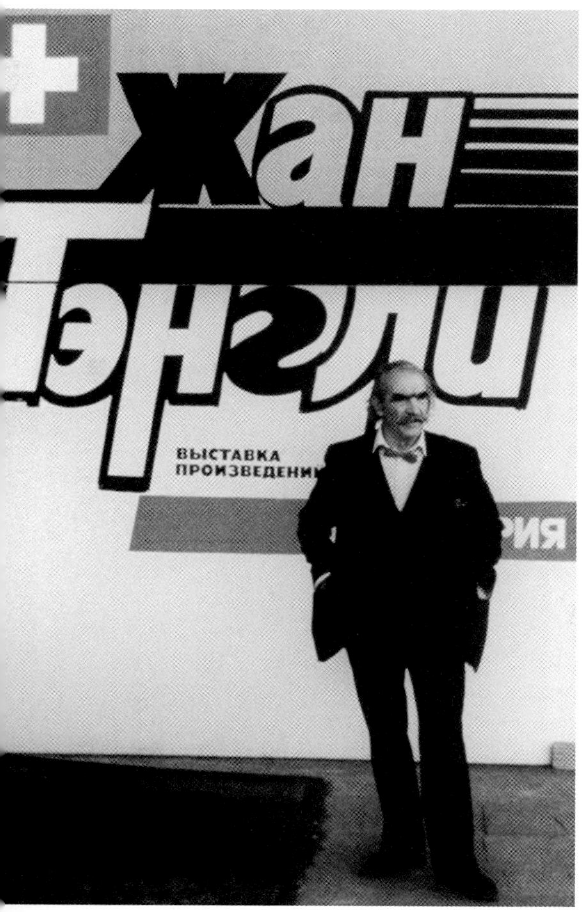

77 *The Triptych of Plenty and of Totalitarian Mercantilism*, Moscow, 1990 ▷

the artist). The animal realm was given its due with a work inspired by the artist's pet dachshund, Nona. Tinguely respected rigorous thought; indeed, it was the only reason for his optimistic outlook. Each one of these sculptures —named after Schopenhauer, Nietzsche, Hegel, Engels, Bergson, Kropotkin, Rousseau, Rudolf Steiner and Wittgenstein—presented a challenge to the viewer's imagination, sense of humour and ability to connect the work with the essential idea of each great man. For Tinguely these objects represented a 'summary of my relationships with the philosophers that I read. This short Nietzsche who scratches his belly, that's the way I feel it. The colour blue dominates my homage to Wittgenstein? Because for me he is a philosopher who is glacial'.[11] Tinguely was no stranger to the powerful hold ideals and ideas can have on human beings; he trusted the power of critical thought and the capacity of people to change.

In April 1990, Tinguely's retrospective opened at the Tretjakowskaja Galerja in Moscow. Even before they entered the gallery, visitors were confronted by a gigantic triptych entitled *The Triptych of Plenty and of Totalitarian Mercantilism* (fig. 77). Filled with gadgets and trivia, this triptych was a symbol of the absurdity of capitalist consumerism. Tinguely observed: 'I want to show the Russian people how richly we live—and at the same time how ridiculously ... With the altarpiece I wanted to take up the matter of the total, colossal idiocy of our industrial capitalism'.[12] Tinguely's provocative invitation to the Russian people to reflect on values and progress was probably better understood when the show went to Fribourg, where the same work welcomed visitors who had to pass under it to proceed to the museum's entrance. The retrospective was an unprecedented success there, as the exhibitions in Venice, Turin, Paris and Moscow had been. Tinguely had become a Swiss national hero, a songht-after speaker on the annual Swiss national holiday. He was omnipresent in the media and the recipient of numerous awards, including an honorary doctorate from the British Royal Academy of Arts in 1989.

Following his traumatic brush with death in 1985, Tinguely had lived at the edge, with death as his constant companion. The only concessions he had made to his doctors was that he had stopped smoking. Instead of slowing down, he accelerated his pace, producing a plethora of new work in his vast new studio at the Verrerie near Fribourg. Milena Palakarkina was his new young companion, a film-maker turned painter with whom he created a few collaborative works. Palakarkina was

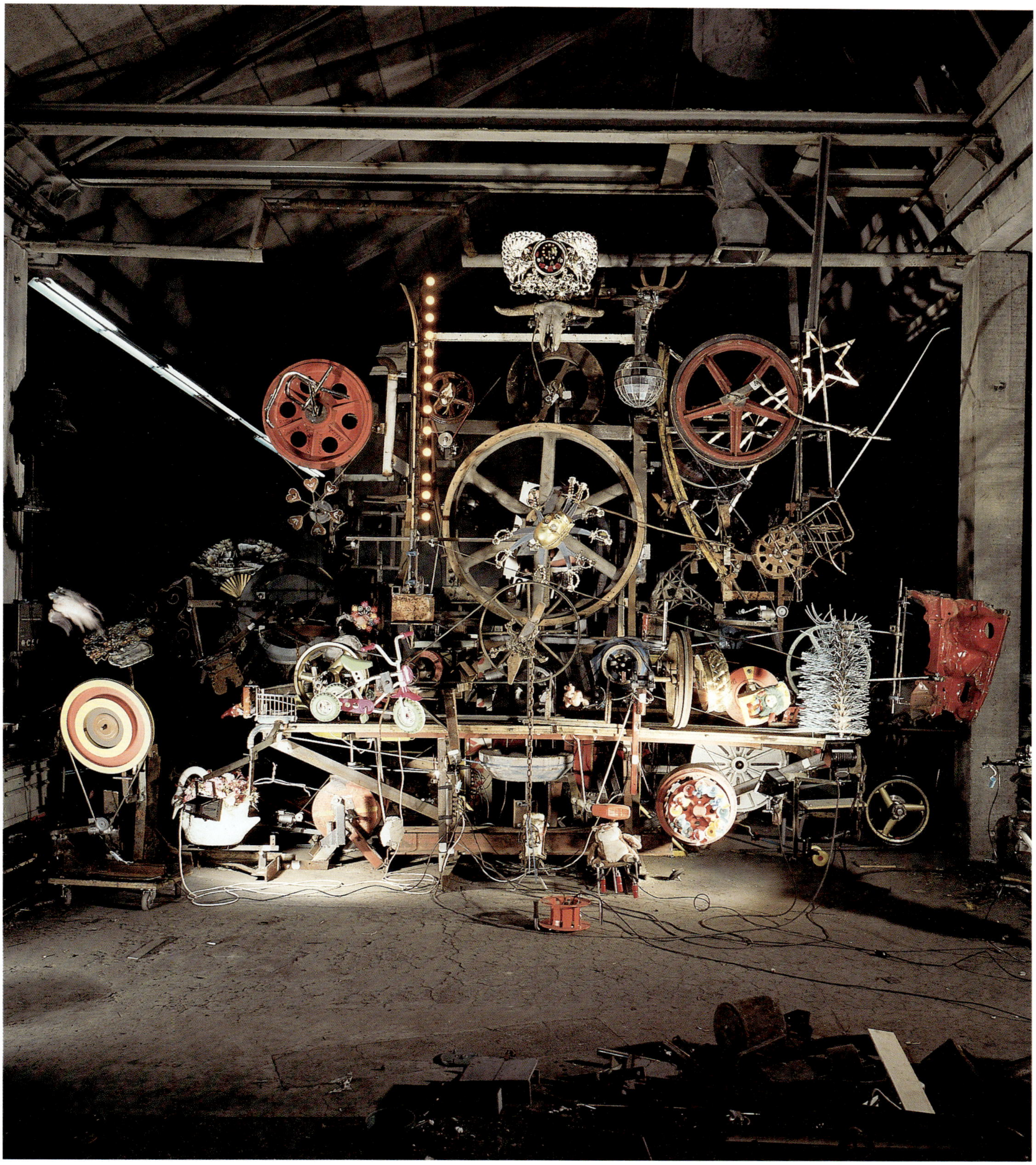

Left (from top to bottom):
Eva Aeppli's contribution to *Culture Freight Cars*, 1991
Milena Palakarkina's contribution to *Culture Freight Cars*, 1991
Bernhard Luginbühl's contribution to *Culture Freight Cars*, 1991

Below: Children searching for money under Tinguely's contribution to *Culture Freight Cars*, 1991
Ben Vautier's contribution to *Culture Freight Cars*, 1991

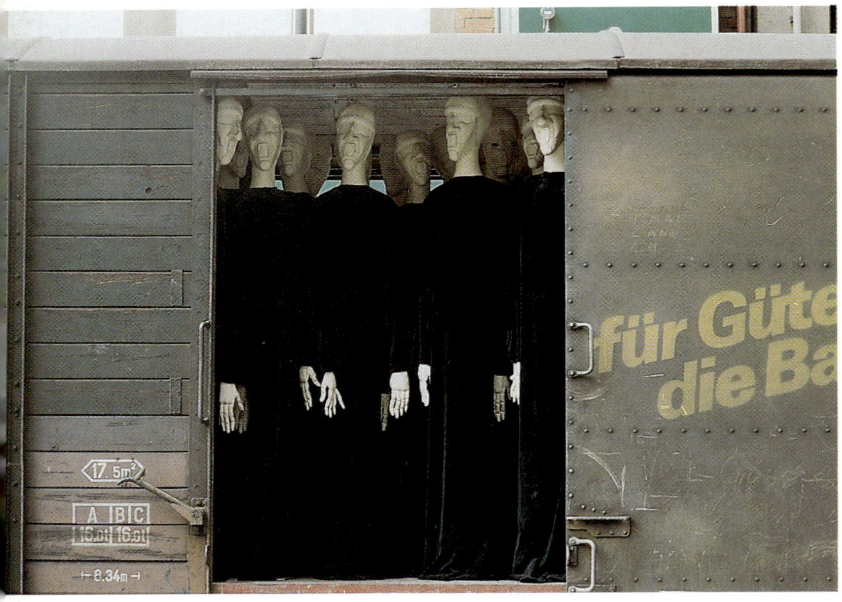

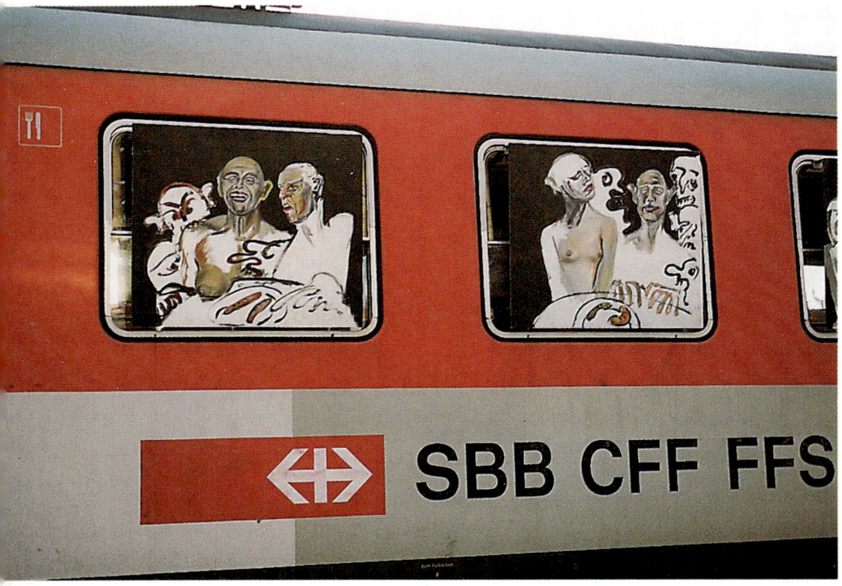

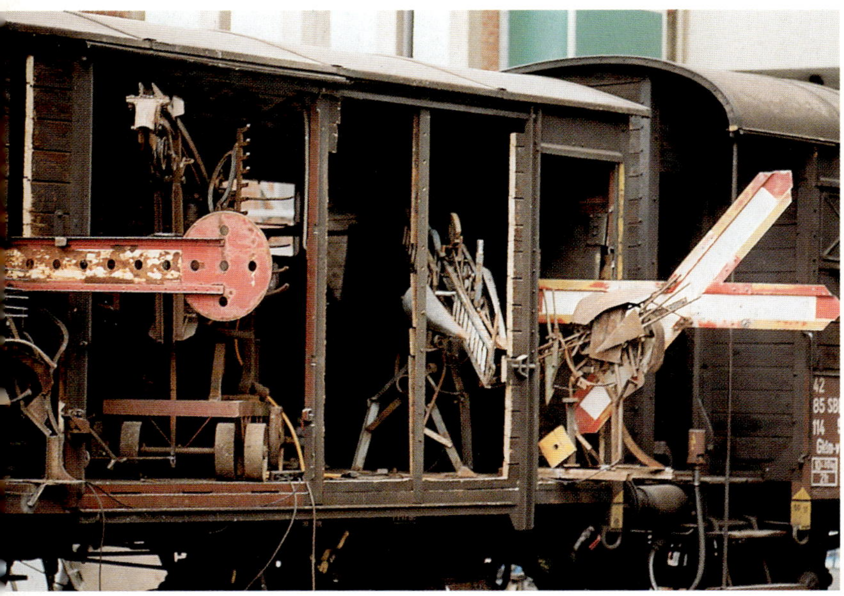

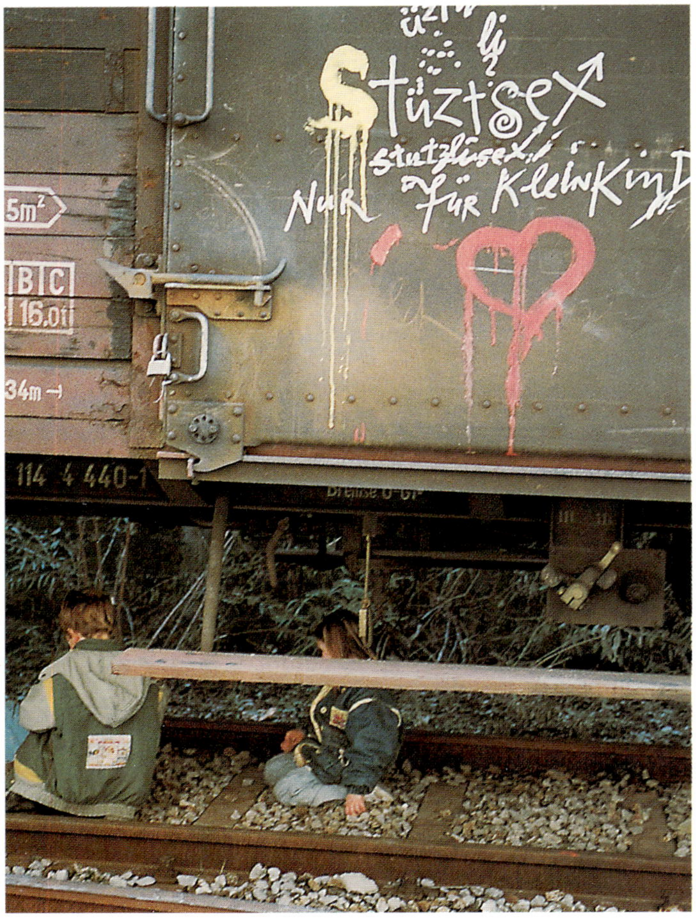

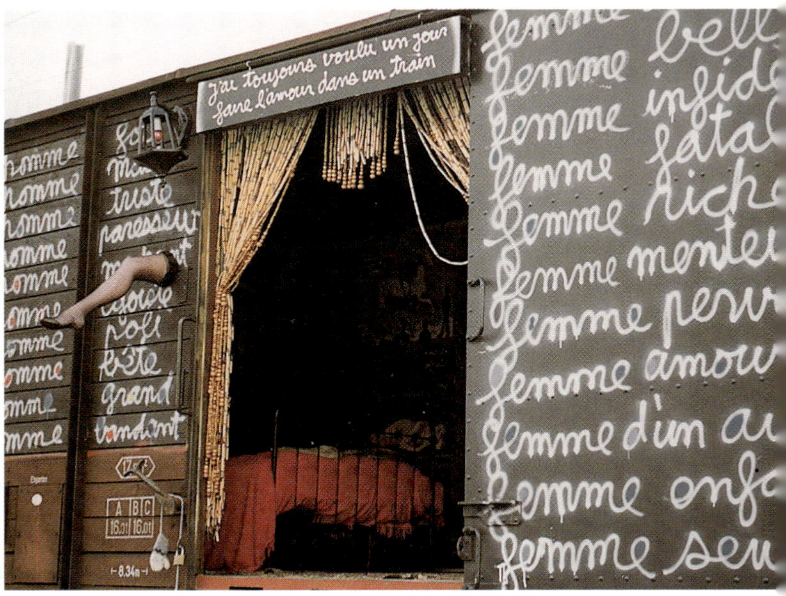

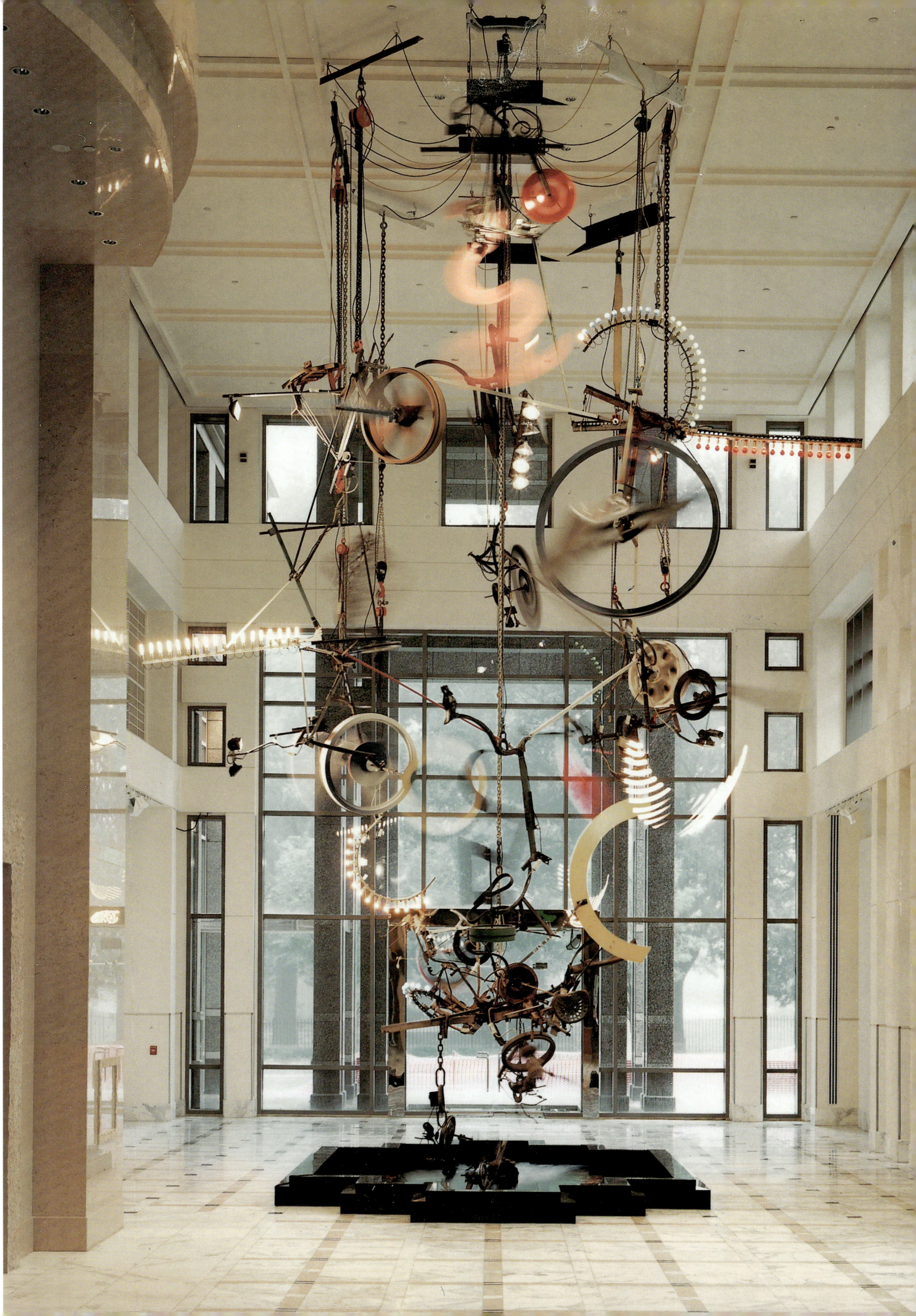

◁ 78 *Cascade*, 1991. Carillon lobby, Charlotte, North Carolina

among Tinguely's six artist-friends who collaborated with him on his last major project, the *Culture Freight Cars*, which premièred at the 1991 contemporary art fair in Basel (illus. p. 158). Eva Aeppli, Bernhard Luginbühl, Palakarkina, Daniel Spoerri, Ben Vautier, Jim Whiting and Tinguely each created a different environment within a freight car. Unlike the 1962 *Dylaby* (figs. 28-29), this time the installations were permanent and on wheels; when assembled into a train, the cars can bring their cultural message wherever there are tracks and have since travelled to several destinations within Switzerland and Germany.[13] At the Basel fair, they stood in an immense hall usually used to unload merchandise. Tinguely had also built a gargantuan lamp entitled *Luminator* which transformed the hall into a festive realm and which now greets travellers in the entrance hall of Basel's railway station. In the train, Aeppli's black-clothed figures that stare directly at visitors are a reminder of the Holocaust victims who were transported in similar freight cars to their final destinations. Luginbühl animated his car with cast-off railway tracks and signalling equipment. Palakarkina's paintings on the theme of gluttony and rapacity decorate the restaurant car, while Spoerri transformed his car into a vessel sprouting an array of weeds. Tinguely installed several new slot-machine type sculptures that moved only after the viewer had inserted a coin. The coins, however, were not collected, but fell through the floor onto the tracks, where children could wait to gather them up and play again. The artist entitled his own car *Stützlisex nur für Kleinkinder* (*Moolah Sex Only for Small Children*), a game for kids innocent of adult games and oblivious to the fact that most of the machines were engaged in frantic masturbation. Vautier created a cosy little bordello, while in Whiting's car a heterogeneous assortment of luggage developed a life of its own, snapping, zipping, popping and hopping, only to disappear behind closed doors.

Shortly before his death, Tinguely completed a major work in the United States. *Cascade* a 40-metre-high assemblage the artist suspended from the lobby ceiling of a building complex in Charlotte, North Carolina. The work dispenses light and joyful energy (fig. 78). Here too, the inhabitants of Charlotte can recognise elements from their immediate environment: the lion's head Tinguely salvaged from the old hotel that had been demolished to make way for the new building complex, or the balcony railing so typical of the American South. The old was integrated and given new life. As Tinguely put it: 'Art is communication. The only conceivable stability in life is development—is movement'.[14]

Although Tinguely was continuously on the move, his home base remained Neyruz, where Micheline Gygax lived with their son, Milan. The artist was touchingly concerned about his son's well-being. While Tinguely's daughter Miriam—a particularly gifted artist who lives in the United States—had suffered from his lack of attention, Milan almost got too much of it. In June 1991, Micheline Gygax died. A few months later, Tinguely himself passed away. The entire Swiss nation mourned the loss of their greatest artist in a grandiose state funeral on 4 September. *Cenodoxus Isenheim Altarpiece* and *The Sun*, one of the *Mengele* sculptures, were placed next to the artist's coffin. But life went on. On 1 February 1992, five months after Tinguely's death, Milena Palakarkina gave birth to Jean-Sébastien, his second son. And in 1996, a museum dedicated to Tinguely and built by Mario Botta will open its doors, and the public will have permanent access to Tinguely's unique poetry.

'Chez moi, c'est farce et attrappe, et rêve et oubli et promenade.'

Jean Tinguely, 1985

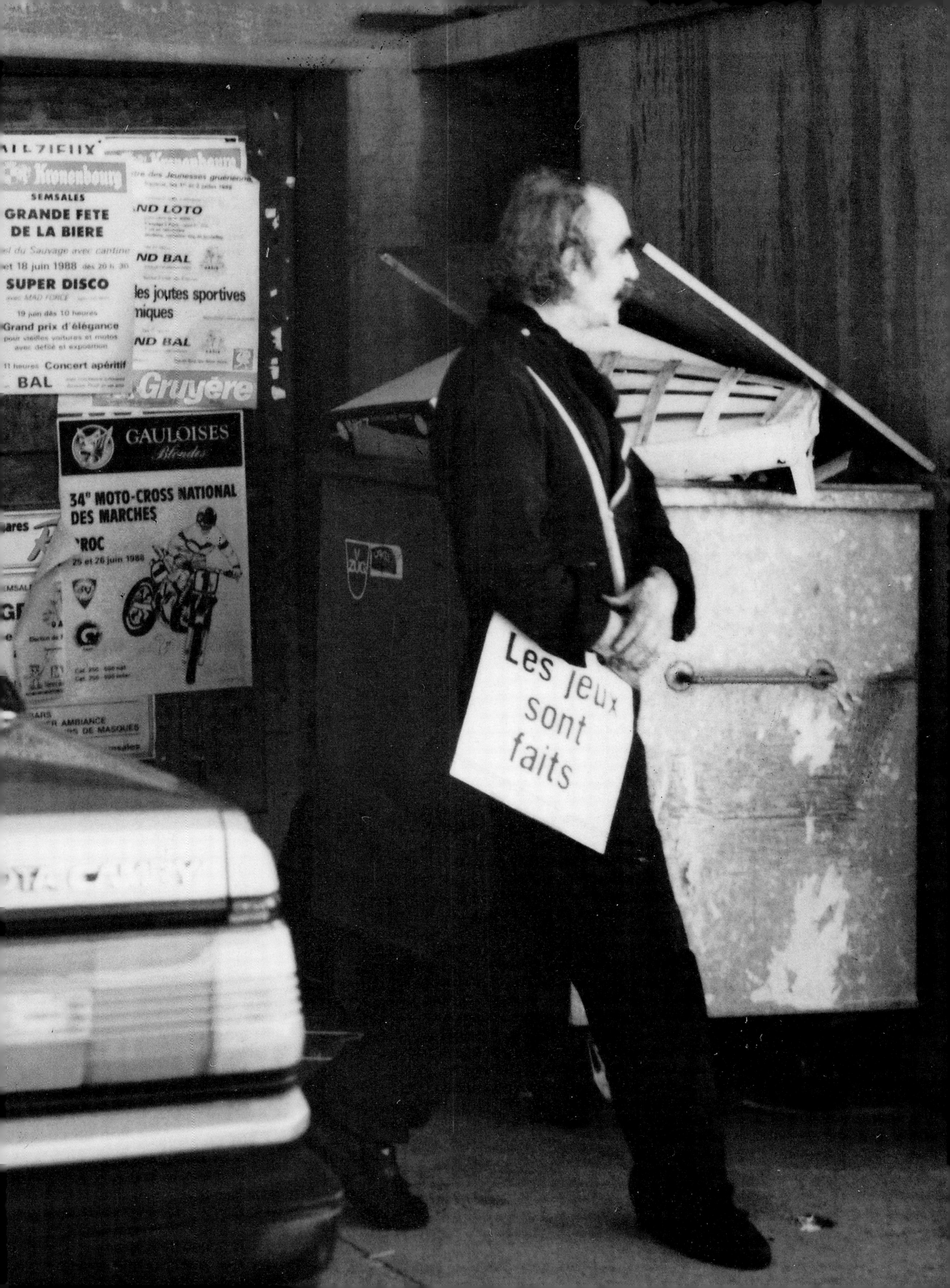
Kronenbourg
SEMSALES
GRANDE FETE
DE LA BIERE
SUPER DISCO
19 juin dès 10 heures
Grand prix d'élégance
pour vieilles voitures et motos
avec défilé et exposition
11 heures Concert apéritif
BAL
ND LOTO
ND BAL
les joutes sportives
ND BAL
Gruyère
GAULOISES
Blondes
34" MOTO-CROSS NATIONAL
DES MARCHES
25 et 26 juin 1988
Les jeux
sont
faits

Notes

19 Stefanie Poley and JT, 'Questions and Answers', in *Jean Tinguely*, exh. cat. (Munich: Kunsthalle Hypo Kulturstiftung, 1985), p. 105.
20 Rolf H. Ramstein, conversation with author, Basel, spring of 1986. Tinguely decorated windows in Basel during the years 1947–1954/55 and was paid a hundred Swiss francs per window by Ramstein & Cie.
21 Richard Calvocoressi, *Tinguely*, exh. cat. (London: Tate Gallery and Kunsthaus Zürich, 1982), p. 24.

'Luckily, there is no good and no evil': Introduction

Throughout the notes, Jean Tinguely is referred to as 'JT', Niki de Saint Phalle as 'NSP' and Pontus Hulten as 'PH'. Hulten's book *Jean Tinguely 'Méta'* (Boston: New York Graphic Society, 1975) is cited as 'PH (1975)', while his *A Magic Stronger than Death* (Milan: Gruppe Editoriale Fabbri Bompiani, 1987) is cited as 'PH (1987)'. The texts and illustrations in Hulten (1987) differ somewhat from those in Hulten (1975).

1 NSP, 'Jean', in PH (1987), p. 346.
2 JT reprinted in Otto Piene and Heinz Mack (eds), *Zero* (Boston: MIT Press, 1973), p. 119.

'Sink or swim': Formative Years

1 See Ernst Kris and Otto Kurz, *Legend, Myth, and Magic in the Image of the Artist* (New Haven: Yale University Press, 1979).
2 Transcribed in PH (1987), p. 13.
3 Unless otherwise noted, quotes by JT are from conversations with the author that took place between 1986 and 1991.
4 See similar statements in 'Jean Tinguely, Lecture, 10 Mai 1984, Cycle rencontre avec quelques artistes contemporains, du 9 au 11 Mai, 1984', Sonothèque Centre Georges Pompidou, BS 259. Unless otherwise noted, all transcriptions and translations are the author's.
5 Gustav Kyburz reminisced during a television show about JT, *Unbekannte Bekannte*, with Regina Kemp, Lukas Burckhardt and Niki Lauda, Suisse TV DRS, taped 13 May 1981, aired 1 June 1981.
6 JT interviewed by Kurt Wyss, in *Der Jeannot und der Karfreitag*, Radio Basel, 17 April 1981.
7 Gustav Kyburz, conversation with author, Basel, spring of 1986.
8 Hutter stated in his certificate, dated 12 April 1944: 'Mr Jeannot Tinguely is an above-average, talented young man, who is endowed with all the prerequisites of an efficient decorator.' JT worked under Hutter from 1 September 1943 to 30 April 1944.
9 JT and Julia Ris, conversation with author, Basel, spring of 1986. For similar statements, see JT, 'Parole d'artiste', in Charles Goerg and Rainer Michael Mason, *Jean Tinguely: Dessins et gravures pour les sculptures*, exh. cat. (Geneva: Musée d'Art et d'Histoire, Cabinet des Estampes, 1976). The interview is translated in PH (1987), p. 348.
alvin Tomkins, 4 April 1961 (author's archive). See also Calvin Tomkins, *The Bride and the Bachelors* (New York: Penguin Books, 1983), pp. 153–54.
11 Conversation with author, Basel, spring of 1986.
12 Conversation with author, July 1986.
13 Max Stirner, *The Ego and His Own: The Case of the Individual against Authority*, tr. Steven T. Byington; ed. James J. Martin (New York: Libertarian Book Club, 1963), pp. 4–5.
14 See Erich Fromm, *The Art of Loving* (New York: Bantam Books, 1967), pp. 48–53.
15 Albert Camus, *The Myth of Sisyphus and Other Essays*, tr. Justin O'Brien (New York: Alfred A. Knopf, 1955), pp. 61–74.
16 On Duchamp and Stirner, see Serge Stauffer, *Marcel Duchamp: Die Schriften*, vol. 1 (Zurich, 1981), pp. 240, 290, 301.
17 Stirner (note 13), p. 320.
18 JT in *Tinguely on Tinguely* (extract from radio debate), Radio Télévision Belge, Brussels, 13 December 1982, transcribed and translated in PH (1987), p. 350.

'You must steal your own freedom': 1953–57

1 JT in *Tinguely on Tinguely* (extract from radio debate), Radio Télévision Belge, Brussels, 13 December 1982, transcribed and translated in PH (1987), p. 350.
2 On the history of kinetic art, see Frank Popper, *Origins and Development of Kinetic Art* (Greenwich, Conn.: New York Graphic Society, 1968).
3 Daniel Spoerri, conversation with author, summer of 1986.
4 Franz Meyer, interview with author, spring of 1986.
5 While in Milan, he met Bruno Munari, who had written two manifestos, 'Useless Machines' (late 1930s) and 'Manifesto of Machinism' (1952). The ideas of his last surviving Futurist seemed particularly relevant to JT.
6 On the history of the Impasse Ronsin, see Claude Laugier, 'Impasse Ronsin', in *Paris—Paris 1937–1957*, exh. cat. (Paris: Centre Georges Pompidou, 1981), pp. 290–93. Brancusi's death date is mistakenly indicated in that text as 1958.
7 On the career of PH, see Calvin Tomkins, 'Profile: A Good Monster', in *New Yorker*, 16 January 1978, pp. 37ff.
8 Invited to Stockholm later in the year, he created a similar relief for his exhibition at the Galerie Samlaren.
9 *Musique concrète* was invented by the Frenchman Pierre Schaeffer. In this connection, JT was also influenced by the Futurists, particularly Luigi Russolo and his notions of the revival of music through noise explained in his manifesto 'The Art of Noises' (1913). *Musique concrète vocale*—sounds made by the vocal cords in a sort of organic automatism—was explored by the New Realist François Dufrêne (who also participated in

Fluxus events) and by Fluxus artist Joseph Beuys, among others.

10 Pierre Restany, Tinguely', *Cimaise*, 2 (November–December 1956), p. 36.

11 PH (1975), p. 47.

12 JT spoke at length about his interest in Grand-Prix racing and his perception of it as a disquieting and at times ridiculous 'circus of the absurd'. See *Jean Tinguely et le Grand-Prix*, Télévision Suisse Romande, 21 March 1985.

'Everything moves continuously. Immobility does not exist': 1958–59

1 JT's letter is reprinted in PH (1975), p. 62.

2 Iris Clert's autobiography gives a lively and detailed account of her association with Klein, JT and the other artists whose work she showed in her gallery; see *Iris time (l'art-venture)* (Paris: Denoël, 1978), pp. 159, 165.

3 JT, 'Der Künstler: Clown der modernen Gesellschaft?', interview with Stefanie Poley, January 1981, in *Unter der Maske der Narren*, exh. cat. (Wilhelm-Lehmbruck-Museum der Stadt Duisburg, 1981), pp. 221–27.

4 Norbert Kricke was the third artist selected to contribute works to the new opera house. For illustrations, see *Jean Tinguely: Meta-Maschinen*, exh. cat. (Wilhelm-Lehmbruck-Museum der Stadt Duisburg, 1978), p. 25.

5 Clert (note 2), p. 120. Tinguely's 'Concert' exhibition was a great success. Besides being featured in cinema newsreels, two radio programmes (Radio Monte Carlo and Europe No. 1) were devoted to it.

6 Clert (note 2), p. 132.

7 30 January 1959, at 8:00 p. m. See Leonardo Bezzola, *Jean Tinguely* (Zurich: Arche Verlag, 1974), pp. 192–93; *Jean Tinguely: Meta-Maschinen* (note 4), pp. 29–31.

8 See also PH (1975), pp. 78–79. The count of the leaflets varies between 15,000 and 150,000, with the artist having provided the more modest number.

9 Mrs Alfred Schmela, conversation with author, 1990.

10 JT, 'Kunst ist Revolte', *National-Zeitung* (Basel), 13 October 1967, reprinted and translated in PH (1975), pp. 326–27. JT also told the story of the accident with the marble sculpture to Alain Jouffroy; see 'Jean Tinguely', *L'Oeil*, no. 136 (April 1966), pp. 34ff.

11 JT quoted by Michel Conil Lacoste, in 'Tinguely: Is He a Sculptor?', *Studio International*, 42 (February 1965).

12 According to Pierre Restany (conversation with author, Paris, 1986), JT and Klein's intense involvement with each other's work led to subsequent developments in JT's approach to the machine. See also Pierre Restany, 'Des Machines célibataires aux machines inutiles', *XXème siècle*, no. 42 (1974), pp. 138–40.

13 The reduction of creation to a process of selection is perfected in computer-generated art. In the hands of British artist Harold Cohen, Tinguely's 'Metamatic' has become a flatbed plotter equipped with a conventional stylus and a computer. See Cynthia Goodman, *Digital Visions: Computers and Art* (New York: Harry N. Abrams, 1987), pp. 58–61.

14 The 'Metamatics' were shown in London at the Kaplan Gallery in October–November 1959.

15 Terry Hamilton's letter describing the event and the lecture JT delivered are published in PH (1987), pp. 66–67.

'Art is revolution – revolution is art': 1960

1 JT, 'Parole d'artiste', in Charles Goerg and Rainer Michael Mason, *Jean Tinguely: Dessins et gravures pour les sculptures*, exh. cat. (Geneva: Musée d'Art et d'Histoire, Cabinet des Estampes, 1976). In this catalogue, Goerg and Mason were the first to analyse JT's drawings and prints. For another examination of the relationship between JT's machine-art output and his graphic work, see Peter Baum, 'Jean Tinguely', in *3. Internationale Triennale der Zeichnung und Bildhauerzeichnung*, exh. cat. (Kunsthalle Nürnberg, 1985), pp. 110–42. See also Margrit Hahnloser-Ingold, *Briefe von Jean Tinguely an Maja Sacher* (Berne: Benteli Verlag, 1992).

2 Duchamp introduced JT to the painter William Copley, who mentioned JT to Sam Hunter, Curator at the Museum of Modern Art. Hunter informed his colleague Peter Selz of JT's arrival. Selz had been favourably impressed by the playful irony of JT's multisensory drawing machine, *Metamatic No. 17*, which he had seen the previous year in the courtyard of the Musée d'Art Moderne at the first Paris Biennale.

3 JT quoted in Calvin Tomkins, *The Bride and the Bachelors* (New York: Penguin Books, 1983), p. 166.

4 JT in *Tinguely: A Kinetic Cosmos*, film by François de Menil and Monique Alexander, FDM Foundation for the Arts Production, 1981.

5 JT in *Tinguely on Tinguely* (extract from radio debate), Radio Télévision Belge, Brussels, 13 December 1982, transcribed and translated in PH (1987), p. 350.

6 Billy Klüver, conversation with author, 1985. In 1960, Klüver, who was working in the Research Department at Bell Laboratories, New Jersey, was being encouraged in his frequent involvement with artistic projects that had nothing to do with the telephone business. He collaborated with Jasper Johns, Andy Warhol, John Cage and, most frequently, Robert Rauschenberg, co-founder in 1966 of Experiments in Art and Technology (E. A. T.). See *E.A.T. Proceedings*, no. 9 (19 May 1969); Billy Klüver, Julie Martin and Barbara Rose (eds), *Pavilion* (New York: Dutton Inc., 1972).

7 *Homage to Jean Tinguely's Homage to New York*, 16-mm b/w film with sound by Robert Breer. See also *Breaking It Up at the Museum*, 16-mm b/w film with sound by P. A. Pennebaker.

8 Klüver wrote his account of the building and destruction of *Homage to New York* two days after the event; it was first published in 1961 in *Rörelse I Konsten* (the Stockholm version of the *International Exhibition of Art in Motion* catalogue) as 'The Garden Party' (Moderna Museet, 1961, pp. 12–14). See also PH (1975), pp. 74–77.

9 Quoted in Tomkins (note 3), p. 173.

10 Quoted *ibid.*, p. 175.

11 Anonymous article, *Long Island Star*, 18 March 1960. See also John Canaday, 'Machine Tries to Die for Its Art'; 'Thoughts on Destruction and Creation after Suicide in a Garden', *New York Times*, 18 March 1960; 27 March 1960. Other newspaper clippings are on file at the Museum of Modern Art, New York.

12 'Jean Tinguely: Lecture', CNAC, 5 May 1971, Sonothèque Centre Georges Pompidou, BS 92.

13 *Ibid.*

14 The fifth work was untitled and was placed at the entrance to the gallery. See Christina Bischofberger, *Tinguely: Werkkatalog Skulpturen und Reliefs/Catalogue raisonné*

Sculptures and Reliefs, vol.1: *1954–1968* (Küsnacht and New York: Edition Galerie Bruno Bischofberger, 1992), no. 153.

15 Richard Calvocoressi, *Tinguely at the Tate Gallery,* exh. cat. (London: Tate Gallery, 1982), pp. 58–59.

16 JT's interests here converged with experiments by Moholy-Nagy and his *Light-Space Modulator* (1930; Cambridge, Mass., Harvard University, Busch-Reisinger Museum) and with Nicolas Schöffer's 'spacio-dynamic' oeuvre, especially the two artists' exploration of the limitless variety of light-and-shadow effects.

17 See JT's remarks in Dieter Daniels's interview with him on the subject of Duchamp, 'Klassiker schon—aber immer wieder vergessen', in *Übrigens sterben immer die Anderen: Marcel Duchamp und die Avantgarde seit 1950*, exh.cat. (Cologne: Museum Ludwig, 1988), pp. 129–42. In the same catalogue, see also Gerhard Kolberg, 'Aspekte der "Bewegung" im Werk von Marcel Duchamp und Jean Tinguely', pp. 115–28.

18 Quoted by James Johnson Sweeney, in *Jean Tinguely: Meta-Maschinen*, exh. cat. (Wilhelm-Lehmbruck-Museum der Stadt Duisburg, 1978), chap. 3, n. 4.

19 Restany published the first manifesto of the New Realists on 16 April in Milan; the official founding of the group took place on 27 October at Yves Klein's place in Paris. For detailed information, see *1960: Les Nouveaux Réalistes*, exh. cat. (Paris: Musée d'Art Moderne de la Ville de Paris, 1986).

20 JT in Erika Billeter, 'Das Interview: Jean Tinguely', *Art-Expo 85: Das Jahrbuch der Kunst* (Baar: Weltrundschau Verlag AG, 1985), pp. 236–40. Christo, for example, expressed a similar viewpoint when questioned by the author.

'In my work, somehow art is not art': 1960

1 Johannes Cladders, conversation with author, Krefeld, 1986.

2 Claude Lévi-Strauss, *The Savage Mind* (Chicago: University of Chicago Press, 1966), pp. 16–21.

3 However, for material to trigger Tinguely's creativity, it had to correspond with inquiries he was engaged in at the time. Animal skulls, for example, were collected by his artist friends Luginbühl and Spoerri and were available to him long before he began to feature them in his works.

4 This fountain was acquired by the Stedelijk Museum, Amsterdam, in 1961.

5 Gaston Bachelard, *L'Eau et les rêves* (Paris: J. Corti, 1976), p. 36.

6 Franz Meyer, conversation with author, Basel, 1986.

7 With the artist's authorisation, Alfred Otto Müller of Cologne was commissioned by 16 buyers of the plans to build the work. One of these multiples was sold by Christie's, London, on 29 June 1982 (lot 458), as a work by JT made by A. O. Müller.

8 *Ibid.* Newspaper articles on the exhibition located by the author—e. g. those in *Der Bund* (26 September 1960), *Berner Tagblatt* (27 September 1960) and *Die Weltwoche* (30 September 1960)—were all favourable.

9 JT, conversation with author.

10 See Maria Netter's commentary, 'Eisenplastik, mit und ohne Lärm', in *Die Weltwoche*, 30 September 1960, p. 20.

11 In French, *la jalousie* means both 'jealousy' and 'a Venetian blind'. *La Jalousie II* (Edinburgh, Scottish National Gallery of Modern Art) is another similar version of this work.

12 NSP, conversation with author, Soisy-sur-Ecole, 1986.

13 'Jean Tinguely, Lecture, 10 Mai 1984, Cycle rencontre avec quelques artistes contemporains, du 9 au 11 Mai, 1984', Sonothèque Centre Georges Pompidou, BS 259.

14 NSP in *Aventure Suisse*, exh. cat. (Fribourg: Musée d'Art et d'Histoire, 1993), pp. 7–28.

'... and anyway, the definitive is provisional, and chaos is order': 1961

1 Roland F. Pease Jr., 'New York Notes', *Art International*, 5:5–6 (June–August 1961).

2 'Tinguely at the Staempfli Gallery', *Arts* (May 1961).

3 *Monstrance* (1960; Switzerland, private collection) and *Makroko* (also known as *The Spider*) (1961; Geneva, Dominique Franck Collection).

4 Rauschenberg was in Europe for his first solo exhibition, which opened in April at the Galerie Daniel Cordier in Paris. In May, he participated in NSP's *Shooting Action* held in an old quarry near Stockholm during the *International Exhibition of Art in Motion*. In June, Rauschenberg once again fired at NSP's plaster reliefs during her exhibition *Fire at Will* at Galerie J, where Jasper Johns, Yves Klein, Jean Fautrier and Leo Castelli also practised their marksmanship.

5 Rauschenberg and Tudor had participated in what has come to be regarded as the prototypical Happening, John Cage's 'concerted action' at Black Mountain College in the summer of 1952. On *The Concert*, see Calvin Tomkins, *The Bride and the Bachelors* (New York: Penguin Books, 1983), pp. 228–29.

6 In its emphasis on common characteristics among an international group, the show prefigured *Art of Assemblage* that autumn and Sidney Janis's two-gallery exhibition *The New Realists* in November 1962.

7 Larry Rivers interviewed by Jean-François Canchy, February 1977, in *Paris—New York*, exh. cat. (Paris: Centre Georges Pompidou, Musée National d'Art Moderne, 1977), p. 590.

8 As reported by George Rickey, in 'The Kinetic International', *Arts Magazine* (September 1961), p. 16.

9 *Ibid.*, pp. 16–21.

10 Arthur Secunda, 'Two Motion Sculptors: Tinguely and Rickey', *Artforum*, 1:1 (June 1966), pp. 16–18.

11 PH (1975), p. 204.

12 JT's notations in PH (1975), pp. 216–17.

13 Knud Jensen, conversation with author, Humlebaek, September 1986.

14 As Siegfried Giedion explained, '[T]he idea of progress supposes a final state of perfection . . . Finality implies an approaching state of static equilibrium. This contradicts what the scientists have shown to be the essence of the universe, motion and unending change' (*Mechanization Takes Command* [New York: W. W. Norton & Company, Inc., 1975], p. 717).

15 JT, 'Parole d'artiste', in Charles Goerg and Rainer Michael Mason, *Jean Tinguely: Dessins et gravures pour les sculptures*, exh. cat. (Geneva: Musée d'Art et d'Histoire, Cabinet des Estampes, 1976), reprinted and translated in PH (1987), pp. 347–50.

'Don't stew in your own juice': 1962

1 'Jean Tinguely: Lecture', CNAC, 5 May 1971, Sonothèque Centre Georges Pompidou, BS 92.

2 JT quoted by William R. Byron, in 'Wacky Artist of Destruction' *Saturday Evening Post*, 21 April 1962.

3 *Izvestiya* 3 January 1963, reprinted and translated in PH (1975), pp. 247–48. One indication of the modified political climate was JT's welcome in Moscow for a major exhibition that opened on 3 April 1990.

4 JT cited in Byron (note 2).

5 On the Chelsea Hotel and European-American interrelationship of the period, see Pierre Restany, 'Chelsea 1960', in *Paris—New York*, exh. cat. (Paris: Centre Georges Pompidou, Musée National d'Art Moderne, 1977), pp. 142ff.

6 NSP in *Tinguely: A Kinetic Cosmos*, film by François de Menil and Monique Alexander, FDM Foundation for the Arts Production, 1981.

7 JT quoted in Calvin Tomkins, *The Bride and the Bachelors* (New York: Penguin Books, 1983), pp. 228–29.

8 John Wulp, 'Happening', *Esquire* (November 1962), pp. 134ff.

9 Following this collaboration, Rauschenberg, who thinks of 'painting as theatre or vice versa', would write his own theatre pieces, beginning with *Pelican* (1963). See Rauschenberg in conversation with Richard Kostelanetz, in *The Theatre of Mixed Means* (New York: RK Editions, 1980), p. 80.

10 Ad Petersen, conversation with author. See also *Forum*, no. 25–2; *Dylaby*, exh. cat. (Amsterdam: Stedelijk Museum, 1962).

11 Illeana Sonnabend opened her gallery in Paris in 1962, showing only American artists. NSP (in interview with art historian Roni Feinstein, 1982 [author's archive]) has remarked upon the inspiration she drew from Rauschenberg and lays much of the blame for their falling out during *Dylaby* at Sonnabend's door.

12 Quoted by Thomas McEvilley, in 'Yves Klein: Conquistador of the Void', *Yves Klein: A Retrospective*, exh. cat. (Houston: Rice University, Institute for the Arts, 1982), p. 78.

13 Reinhold Hohl, 'Wasserspiele im Kurpark', *National-Zeitung* (Basel), 16 September 1962. Lucius Burckhardt wrote a particularly witty comment on JT's waterworks, qualifying them, via Heidegger, as 'Anti-Design'. See 'Zu einer Demonstration von Jean Tinguely's Wassersprühern in Baden', *Werk-Chronik*, no. 11 (November 1962).

14 Rauschenberg was working on ideas similar to JT's and had incorporated a radio into his pieces *Broadcast* (1959) and *Oracle* (1965; Paris, Centre Georges Pompidou), in the making of which he was assisted by Billy Klüver's technical ingenuity. John Cage's *Imaginary Landscape No. 4*, a precedent for all of these radio works, had been written for twelve radios, each 'played' by two performers, in 1952.

15 Modern verbal grotesques have their predecessors in works by the Renaissance humanists Johann Fischart and his model, Rabelais. Wolfgang Kayser explained that 'the abysmal and terrifying aspects of Rabelais' and Fischart's works are not restricted to the content of their language but also extend to the elusiveness of language itself. The familiar and indispensable tool suddenly proves to be arbitrary, strange, demonically alive, and capable of dragging man into the nocturnal and inhuman sphere' (*The Grotesque in Art and Literature* [Bloomington: Indiana University Press, 1963], p. 157).

16 John Wideman, 'Playing, Not Joking, with Language' [review of Henry Louis Gates Jr., *The Signifying Monkey*], *New York Times Book Review*, 14 August 1988, p. 3.

17 NSP, conversation with author, 1987.

'I don't have to think about what to do; I just do it': 1963–65

1 JT, conversation with author, July 1986.

2 The hard, resilient golf-ball inspired other works such as *Mautz* and *Mechanised Frustration*, in which it was made into an object of obsession and frustration.

3 Virginia Dwan, interview with author, New York, 1986.

4 JT interviewed by Alain Jouffroy, in *L'Oeil*, no. 136 (April 1966), pp. 34ff.

5 Don Factor, in *Artforum*, 2:3 (September 1963), pp. 14–17.

6 JT, 'Parole d'artiste', in Charles Goerg and Rainer Michael Mason, *Jean Tinguely: Dessins et gravures pour les sculptures*, exh. cat. (Geneva: Musée d'Art et d'Histoire, Cabinet des Estampes, 1976), reprinted and translated in PH (1987), pp. 347–50.

7 This was intended as a temporary installation. As Peter Zimmermann reported (*Neue Zürcher Zeitung*, 4 March 1967), that *Eureka* was saved was indirectly due to Expo 67 at Montreal. Cinematographer A. Heiniger put pressure on the Zurich city fathers to assemble the work so that it could be featured as an example of contemporary Swiss art in the conclusion to a three-part film produced for the Swiss Pavilion at Expo 67.

8 *Ibid.* The expression 'Tinguely's machine' has entered common parlance. For example, journalists have referred to such institutions as the United Nations as 'Tinguely's machine'. *Eureka* was chosen by the Australian officials to represent Switzerland at the 1988 World's Fair at Brisbane.

9 In Switzerland: Geneva, Alexandre Iolas, 19 May–8 June 1964; Basel, Felix Handschin, 24 October–November); in Germany: Baden-Baden, Kunsthalle, 5–27 July; Cologne, Rudolf Zwirner, September; in France: Paris, Alexandre Iolas, 10 December–9 January 1965.

10 Jouffroy (note 4), pp. 34ff.

11 Quoted by Campbell Geeslin, in 'Museum Buys 12 Sculptures by Swiss Artist', *Houston Post*, 15 February 1965.

12 Ann Holmes, 'Wild Spasms, Rituals of Tinguely's Sculptures', *Houston Chronicle*, 4 April 1965.

13 *Chariot-Meta I* (also known as *Char* or *Meta I*) was built specially for this group exhibition in Paris and was destroyed—that is, recycled—by JT. See *Trois Sculpteurs: César, Roël d'Haese, Tinguely*, exh. cat. (Paris: Musée des Arts Décoratifs, 1965).

14 Quoted by Calvin Tomkins, in *The Bride and the Bachelors* (New York: Penguin Books, 1983), p. 186.

15 Olle Granath, interview with author, Stockholm, October 1986.

16 This exhibition opened on 23 November 1965 in New York; on 14 January 1966 at the Washington Gallery of Modern Art, Washington, D. C.; on 7 March at the Walker Art Center, Minneapolis; on 28 April at the Carnegie Institute, Pittsburgh, and on 27 June at the Seattle Art Museum, where it closed on 31 July.

17 Michael Gibson, 'Tinguely and His Machines', *Herald Tribune*, 28 May 1971.

18 Sam Hunter, *2 Kinetic Sculptors*, exh. cat. (New York: Jewish Museum, 1965), p. 11.

19 Hilton Kramer, 'One Inventor, One Pasticheur,' *New York Times*, 28 November 1965. Annette Michelson argued convincingly against Kramer's conclusions, demonstrating that he had misread Tinguely's stylistic appropriations. See *ibid.* and 'New York Letter', *Art International*, 10:2 (1966), pp. 58–60. Emily Genauer concluded that Tinguely, 'who used to be merely ingenious and witty, ha[d] learned both sculpture and mechanics, to emerge now a figure of stature'. See 'Critical Guide to the Galleries', *New York Herald Tribune*, 27 November 1965.

20 The play, announced as 'Mayhem on 92nd St.' by the *New York Times* (19 December 1965), took place on 22 December 1965. See Kenneth Koch, 'Change of Hearts', *Plays, Films and Other Dramatic Works 1951–1971* (New York: Vintage Books, 1973), pp. 19–41 (for *The Construction of Boston*) and pp. 131–50 (for *The Tinguely Machine Mystery* or *The Love Suicides at Kaluka*).

21 Grace Glueck, 'Show at Museum Stars Machines', *New York Times*, 24 December 1965.

'After all, it's the woman in a man that makes him a poet': 1966–70

1 The rest of the props for the ballet were created by Martial Raysse and NSP, who among other things contributed a number of bulbous female figures with which the dancers engaged in a wrestling match. *In Praise of Folly* now stands on the large staircase of the Kunsthaus in St Gall.

2 Ulf Linde kept track of the 'building' of *Hon*; see 'En Väldig Varelse', *Dagens Nyheter* (Stockholm), 4 June 1966. He also painted the fakes for the gallery in one of the legs. See also *Hon—en historia*, exh. cat. (Stockholm: Moderna Museet, 1967).

3 Frédéric-Auguste Bartholdi's *Statue of Liberty* in New York harbour can also be climbed and 'conquered' from the inside, from skirt to belly to head.

4 NSP, 'The Hon', in PH (1987), pp. 166–68.

5 Mikhail Bakhtin, *Rabelais and His World*, tr. Helene Iswolsky (Cambridge, Mass.: MIT Press, 1968), p. 26.

6 Arnold Schwengeler, 'Genug jetzt!' *Der Bund*, no. 265, 11 July 1966; j. [Dr. Erwin Jaeckle], 'Das Zeitalter der Schweine', *Die Tat*, 2 July 1966; H. D., 'Phall-Sucht', *Wochen-Express* (Schaffhausen), 5 July 1966. The critics' responses inspired a debate among their readers, a majority of whose printed responses supported the critics, not the artists.

7 JT, interview with Alfred Pacquemont and Françoise Cachin, CNAC, 5 May 1971, Sonothèque Centre Georges Pompidou, BS 92. See also PH (1975), pp. 339–52.

8 Michael Gibson, 'Tinguely and His Machines', *Herald Tribune*, 28 May 1971.

9 PH reported that the largest of the dailies, *Corriere della Sera*, referred, in only a single sentence,to '[a]n upright statue of a symbolic character, reminiscent of the Greek god of fertility'. JT's action-spectacles inspired his friend Luginbühl to build his first auto-da-fé. *Zorn* (into which JT incorporated fireworks), in 1976.

10 Marc Kuhn, 'Eine Nacht mit Tinguely', *Weltwoche*, 21 October 1966: 'Weitere 16 Tinguely-Maschinen nach Zürich', *Der Zürichbieter*, 3 October 1966.

11 Interview with Yves Robillard, in 'Jean Tinguely et ses machines,' *La Presse* (Montreal), 29 April 1967.

12 This move occurred despite the efforts of an association, 'Friends of Paradise', formed specifically to counteract a powerful group intent upon having the sculptures removed from their site on Skeppsholmen, across from the historic Royal Palace.

13 *L'Oeil*, no. 136 (April 1966), p. 38.

14 This exhibition originated at the Kröller-Müller Museum, Otterlo (15 July–27 August), and travelled to the van Abbemuseum, Eindhoven, and the Kunstmuseum, Lucerne (28 October–3 December).

15 Ulrich Seelmann-Eggebert, 'Unter Mitwirkung von Hannibal', *National-Zeitung* (Basel), no. 45, 29 January 1971.

16 JT, 'Kunst ist Revolte', *National-Zeitung* (Basel), 13 October 1967, reprinted and translated in PH (1975), pp. 326–27.

17 *Rotozaza II* and *III* were offspring of an idea first realised in *Hon*, where JT had built a bottle-smashing machine.

18 Charlotte Willard, 'The Way It Ends', *New York Post*, 23 December 1967, p. 42.

19 Harry Gilroy, 'Tinguely's Smashing Machine Deals Blow to Overproduction', *New York Times*, 20 October 1967, p. 54.

20 JT, Lecture, CNAC, 5 May 1971, Sonothèque Centre Georges Pompidou, BS 92.

21 Ambassador Dr Paul R. Jolles, interview with author, Berne, July 1988.

'Dreams are the best organisers': 1968–74

1 *Dada, Surrealism and Their Heritage*, Museum of Modern Art, New York, 27 March–9 June 1968; *The Machine as Seen at the End of the Mechanical Age*, Museum of Modern Art, New York, 25 November 1968–9 January 1969; *Sammlung Hahn: Zeitgenössische Kunst*, Wallraf-Richartz-Museum, Cologne, 3 May–7 July 1969. His work was shown comprehensively for the first time in Chicago at the Museum of Contemporary Art (2 March–7 April 1968).

2 The entertaining tale of JT's Japanese sojourn as told by his friend Luginbühl in letters to his wife is reprinted in Leonardo Bezzola, *Jean Tinguely* (Zurich: Arche Verlag, 1974), pp. 195ff.

3 The catalogue published on the occasion featured drawings by JT together with his comments; Eric Michaud compiled the biography and bibliography (originally published in 1970 as 'Jean Tinguely: Chronologie, Expositions, Bibliographie' by the Faculté des Lettres de Nanterre). The catalogue was part of the series 'Archives de l'art contemporain' edited by CNAC. After the show, *Meta II* was moved to the Parc Floral de Vincennes.

4 Gaston Bachelard, 'La Vocation scientifique et l'âme humaine', *Rencontres internationales de Genève, 1952* (Neuchâtel: Edition de la Baconnière, 1953), pp. 11–28.

5 *Dylabi* (an abbreviation for 'Dynamisches Labyrinth') was submitted by Luginbühl, Spoerri and JT for Expo 64 at Lausanne. In 1967, JT, Luginbühl and the architect Maurice Ziegler entered *Tiluzi* in the architecture competition for the Swiss Pavilion at Expo 70 in Osaka and won second prize.

6 Bernhard Luginbühl, 'Le Cyclope/Brief an Margrit Hahnloser', in Margrit Hahnloser-Ingold, *Pandämonium—Jean Tinguely* (Berne: Benteli Verlag, 1988), p. 282. See also JT and Bernhard Luginbühl, 'Kulturstation von Luginbühl und Tinguely', in *Kunstnachrichten*, 5:3 (November 1968).

7 JT in *Tinguely: A Kinetic Cosmos*, film by François de Menil and Monique Alexander, FDM Foundation for the Arts Production, 1981.
8 Quoted by Thomas McEvilley, in 'Yves Klein: Conquistador of the Void', in *Yves Klein: A Retrospective*, exh. cat. (Houston: Rice University, Institute for the Arts, 1982), p. 48.
9 See JT's statements, 'Einige Überlegungen von Jean Tinguely', *Jean Tinguely: Moskau—Fribourg*, exh. cat. (Fribourg: Musée d'Art et d'Histoire, 1991), pp. 23–32.
10 By Verlag Ullstein. In 1974, the book was published in French (Editions Pierre Horay) and in 1975, in English (Thames and Hudson, London, and New York Graphic Society, Boston).
11 JT in *Chaos No. 1*, film by John Denny, 1974.
12 Cesar Pelli, 'Piazza, American Style', *Progressive Architecture* (June 1976).
13 Susan Anderson, quoted by Marion Simon Garmel, in 'Chaos I Not Working, but Effective', *Indianapolis News*, 5 July 1974.
14 A second subtitle is *Speedy Jo*. For a drawing of *Chaos I*, see Bezzola (note 2).
15 JT in *Chaos No. 1*, film by John Denny, 1974.

'It's hard work to make people enjoy life': 1974–88

1 The term *Carnival* embraces a number of different types of festivities that share certain characteristic features. See Carol Clark, 'The Festive World: Carnival' in *The Vulgar Rabelais* (Glasgow: Pressgang, 1983), pp. 63ff.
2 Mikhail Bakhtin, *Rabelais and His World*, tr. Helene Iswolsky (Cambridge, Mass.: MIT Press, 1968), p. 218. Bakhtin investigated the relationship between the carnivalesque and farce in Renaissance theatre and literature in light of Rabelais' works.
3 The Carnival can best be documented through the various prohibitions against it. See Eugen A. Meier, 'Die Fasnacht im Alten Basel', *Die Basler Fasnacht* (Basel: Fasnachts-Comité, 1985), pp. 51–52. In its present form, the Carnival is believed to be about a hundred years old.
4 Roger D. Abrahams, The Language of Festivals: Celebrating the Economy', in Victor Turner, ed., *Celebration: Studies in Festivity and Ritual'* (Washington D. C.: Smithsonian Press, 1982), pp. 161ff.
5 The *Kuttlebutzer* were reported to the police and punished for their 'un-carnivalesque' action with a fine of 100 Swiss francs.
6 Most of this information on the *Kuttlebutzer* was provided by founding member and former archivist Joseph (Schosy) Schaub.
7 Monique Barbier-Müller and Jean-Paul Barbier were the appreciative recipients of JT's own mask, which is in congenial company among the family's superb collection of non-Western art.
8 The sponsor was the Swiss supermarket chain Migros and its dynamic Director of Cultural Affairs, Werner Muster, along with the city of Basel.
9 See Annemarie Monteil, *Der Tinguely-Brunnen in Basel* (Basel: Birkhäuser AG, 1980).
10 In the Swiss dialect, *Suuser* also denotes freshly pressed and fermented wine.
11 In the early morning hours at the beginning of Carnival, the *Cliques* are not yet dressed uniformly; rather, each member wears a different costume from a previous Carnival. This hodgepodge is called 'Charivari'.
12 In June 1987, the Swiss government issued a stamp in commemoration of the 10th anniversary of the fountain. In 1978, JT built *The Agricultural Platform* (formerly collection of the artist), the rustic counterpart of his *Carnival Fountain* in Basel. Assembled from parts of agricultural machines, these 'workers' are similarly absurd.
13 The institute was created and is directed by Pierre Boulez. See Pierre Boulez, PH, Franz Meyer and Stefanie Poley, *Jean Tinguely & Niki de Saint Phalle: La Fontaine Igor Stravinski* (Berne: Benteli Verlag, 1983) (photos by Leonardo Bezzola).
14 Stravinsky composed a short dance for the elephant act in a Ringling Brothers and Barnum & Bailey circus ballet.
15 For six months, the dinosaur-like dragon stood in the 'Forum' of the Centre Pompidou, filling this vast ground floor opposite the building's entrance. See '"Das Crocrodrome": Eine Bildreportage von Leonardo Bezzola', *Werk*, no. 64 (1977), pp. 18–19; Jean-Jacques Lévêque, 'Prenez le thé avec un gentil "crocrodrome"', *Le Quotidien de Paris*, 4–5 June 1977; PH (1987), pp. 252–57.
16 See also Bernhard Luginbühl, in *Tinguely & Luginbühl*, exh. cat. (Frankfurt: Städelsches Kunstinstitut, 1979).
17 It took Tinguely more than 10 years to convince the municipal authorities to accept his gift.18 In 1980, Tinguely built *Floating Fountain* in the Wenken Park at Basel; in 1986, for NSP, the *Fountain of Fortune* at Caravicchio; and in 1987, for Paul Sacher's estate near Basel, the *Schönenberg Fountain*.

'Art is nonsense and, like everything else, not senseless': 1978–85

1 For a brief overview of various theories of play, see D. E. Berlyne, 'Laughter, Humor, and Play', in Gardner Lindzey and Elliot Aronson (eds), *The Handbook of Social Psychology*, 2nd edn (Reading, Mass.: Addison-Wesley Publishing Co., 1968), vol. 3, pp. 795ff. See also Johan Huizinga, *Homo Ludens: A Study of the Play-Element in Culture* (Boston: Beacon Press, 1955).
2 Charles Baudelaire, 'A Philosophy of Toys', in *The Painter of Modern Life and Other Essays*, ed. and tr. Jonathan Mayne (London: Phaidon Press, 1964), p. 199.
3 Johann Christoph Friedrich von Schiller, *Die Piccolomini*, III, 4.
4 JT et al. in *Warum ist Ballett Kunst und Kunstturnen Sport?, Das Monatsmagazin*, Schweizer Fernsehen, 22 January 1975, Archive no. 0100824.
5 JT in *Jean Tinguely et le Grand-Prix*, Télévision Suisse Romande, 21 March 1985.
6 In conversation with author.
7 Another work framed around the motif of the Fool was Sebastian Brandt's *Narrenschiff* (Ship of Fools), published in 1494 in Strasbourg. Brandt identified 112 kinds of fools who journeyed aboard an imaginary ship with Wisdom preaching to them. JT was fond of Brandt's work and owned prints depicting the Ship of Fools.
8 JT with Reinhardt Stumm, *Jean Tinguely vorgestellt durch sich selber und durch seine Maschinen, Reflexe, ein Kulturmagazin*, edited and presented on Swiss Radio by Martin Walder, 7 December 1979. See also Reinhardt Stumm and Kurt Wyss, *Jean Tinguely* (Basel: F. Reinhardt Verlag, 1985), pp. 44–45.
9 JT interviewed by Mr Nakahara, in *Sogetsu Shuppun Inc., Magazine* (French transcription courtesy of Masa Yanagi, New York).
10 The work's subtitle is *Le Canard enchanté—Die freudige Ente—Der rasende Gartenzwerg—Dem traurigen Löwen—(Uns*

stolzem Adler)—Und die Ente Stefanie war zufrieden. As Bettelheim noted, English and French nomenclature emphasises the roles of fairies, though most stories do without them. The German words for 'fairy tale' and 'legend' or 'fable', *Märchen* and *Sage*, carry different connotations.

11 *Rasend* implies both fast, frenzied motion and an outburst of uncontrolled emotion, such as rage.

'I've always got on well with transitoriness': 1981–89

1 JT, cited in Reinhardt Stumm and Kurt Wyss, *Jean Tinguely* (Basel: F. Reinhardt, 1985), p. 38.

2 Jacob Bidermann, *Cenodoxus*, ed. and tr. D. G. Dyer (Austin: University of Texas Press, 1974).

3 The character of Cenodoxus is similar to the protagonist in Christopher Marlowe's *Tragical History of Doctor Faustus*, published around 1592. Goethe's Faust has become the best known of countless other characters whose intellectual striving brought about their downfall.

4 Conversation with author, Basel, January 1987.

5 She represents St Bernadette, to whom Our Lady of Lourdes appeared in 1858. The nearby waters are said to perform miraculous cures. The place was well known to JT, who as a young man worked as a tour guide for pilgrims from Switzerland.

6 The flesh of the peacock was believed not to decay, hence its association with Christ, the Resurrection and immortality.

7 Klaus Lankheit, *Das Triptychon als Pathosformel* (Heidelberg: Carl Winter Universitätsverlag, 1959), Preface, pp. 15, 84ff.

8 The exhibition tour included Zurich (11 June–8 August 1982); the Tate Gallery, London (8 September–2 November 1982); the Palais des Beaux-Arts, Brussels (15 December 1982–30 January 1983); and the Musée Rath, Geneva (12 March–23 May 1983).

9 A traditional *Poya* is a large work representing in detail the cattle owned by a peasant. It is painted either by the peasant himself or by an amateur artist on the peasant's barn or on panels or canvas placed over the entrance to the stable. Exposed to the weather, these works have to be repainted or replaced regularly. Given his attraction to the transitory, JT found this necessity appealing.

10 *Chètas* are to be avoided at all costs, lest one risk severe illness, folly or death. Only the image of a saint, holy water or a specific prayer can remove them and protect people from them. See Christine Détraz and Philippe Grand, *Contes et légendes de Fribourg* (Sierre: Monographic SA, Collection 'Mémoire Vivante', 1984), p. 18, n. 1.

11 JT's written answers to questions posed by Stephanie Poley, in *Jean Tinguely*, exh. cat. (Munich: Kunsthalle Hypo Kulturstiftung, 1985), p. 42.

12 In 1987, *Mengele* was the centrepiece of a group of thematically related sculptures. The *Altarpieces of the Tropics*, *Altarpiece of the Hunter* and *Lola T. 180–Memorial for Joakim B.* were all built in 1988. In 1990, JT collaborated with Milena Palakarkina on two altarpieces, *The Rococo Altarpiece (St Christopher)* and *The St Sebastian Altarpiece*; in spring of that year, *The Triptych of Plenty and of Totalitarian Mercantilism* premièred in Moscow.

'Stagnation doesn't exist; it's not time to shut up shop yet': 1984–88

1 As the guest artist of the *11. Berner Kunstausstellung*.

2 JT interviewed by François Grundbacher, in *Berner Zeitung*, 30 October 1984.

3 JT in *Tinguely par Jean Tinguely*, colour and b/w videotape, 30 feet, conceived and realised by Gianfranco Barberi and Marco Di Castri, with texts by Jean-Hubert Martin, PH, Jean-Yves Mock, Pierre Restany, NSP and Milena Palakarkina (Turin: Cataloga, 1988) (includes excerpts from international archives).

4 BMW is a Bavarian firm. The work was premièred in Munich during JT's major exhibition at the Kunsthalle, adding the kind of local flavour the artist was keen on.

5 NSP, conversation with author, Soisy-sur-Ecole, 1987.

6 Quoted by Philippe Cruysmans, in 'Jean Tinguely: L'Homme qui tape sur le fer', *Le Figaro*, 12 August 1986. Compare with similar statements made by JT in 'A Project by Pontus Hulten and Jean Tinguely', *Artforum* (January 1984), pp. 44ff.

7 Michel Conil Lacoste, *Tinguely: L'Energétique de l'insolence* (Paris: E.L.A. la Différence, 1989), p. 46. The author completed the text with a topographic drawing of the piece and asked whether deformations and modulations stamped into the metal by the impact of the accident were not as beautiful as the hips of the *Venus of Milo*.

8 The inventory of *Inferno* kept changing as JT added and subtracted elements depending on the exhibition space. Eberhard W. Kornfeld counted 35 individual objects at one point.

9 JT, conversation with Roger Anderegg, in 'Ich schaue meine eigene Maschine an, und dann gehe ich nach Hause und bin ganz verwirrt', *Sonntags Zeitung*, 11 March 1990.

10 The story was included in the Grimm Brothers' collection of fairy tales, which first appeared in 1812. Charles Perrault's well-known version published in Paris in 1697 has different psychological implications.

11 Robert Hughes, 'The Dark Wood', *Heaven and Hell in Western Art* (New York: Stein and Day, 1968), pp. 170ff.

12 In *The Uses of Enchantment* (New York: Alfred A. Knopf, 1977), pp. 93–94. In 1987, the same theme was taken up on Broadway in the Stephen Sondheim/James Lapine musical *Into the Woods*.

13 In 1985 Werner Düggelin was inspired by *Inferno* and *Meta-Harmony II* to create a film entitled *Mechanical Love or Harmony—Tinguely*. The film translates JT's ability to create a world in which each individual sees him- or herself projected, a world in which one can shed all disguises while trying to find a part of one's true self.

14 Margrit Hahnloser-Ingold, *Pandämonium—Jean Tinguely* (Berne: Benteli Verlag, 1988), p. 143.

'It is beautiful to be transitory': 1987–91

1 The exhibition catalogue was entitled *A Magic Stronger than Death*. The *valise* presentation of the 1972 text by PH with black and white photography was upgraded to a shoulder-bag version with colour photographs and a new text covering the period 1970–87. Published by Bompiani, it is available in Italian, French and English. The same catalogue, brought up to date and published in normal book form, was published in French for the exhibition in Paris in 1988–89.

2 JT quoted by Dagmar Wacker, in *Neues Sonntags Blatt*, no. 9 (1 March 1987), pp. 48–50. Compare the artist's statement in *Jean Tinguely*, exh. cat. (Basel: Galerie Beyeler, 1987). The group of 17 sculptures was first exhibited in Basel at the Beyeler gallery (28 February–15 May 1987).
3 *Jean Tinguely* (note 2). See also *Tinguely par Jean Tinguely*, colour and b/w videotape, 30 feet, conceived and realised by Gianfranco Barberi and Marco Di Castri, with texts by Jean-Hubert Martin, PH, Jean-Yves Mock, Pierre Restany, NSP and Milena Palakarkina (Turin: Cataloga, 1988) (includes excerpts from international archives).
4 Reinhardt Stumm, 'Tinguely's Kugelblitz-Kunst', *Basler Zeitung* (magazine), 28 March 1987.
5 JT made it a point that his sculptures be easily transportable, 'like a circus: here today, there tomorrow' (conversation with author).
6 JT in *Jean Tinguely* (note 2). He was referring to Friedrich Engels, *The Origin of the Family, Private Property, and the State*, first published in 1884.
7 Stumm (note 4). See also a similar statement in an interview with Lukas Burckhardt (*Jean Tinguely* [note 2]). JT defended this thesis whenever possible, as during an interview for a Swiss radio programme, *Persönlich*, DRS 1, 20 August 1989.
8 See Robert T. Stoll, 'Bilder vom Sterben und vom Tod im Basler Kunstmuseum', *Der Tod zu Basel: Didaktische Ausstellung im Kunstmuseum Basel*, exh. cat. (Basel: Kunstmuseum, 1979).
9 Quoted in *Jean Tinguely* (note 2).
10 JT in Stephanie Poley and JT, 'Questions and Answers', in *Jean Tinguely*, exh. cat. (Munich: Kunsthalle Hypo Kulturstiftung, 1985), p. 105.
11 'Tinguely, le Shakespeare de la ferraille', *Le Nouvel Observateur*, 14 December 1988.
12 'Jean Tinguely: Die Intelligenz kolossal, das Resultat total blödsinnig', *Basler Zeitung*, 31 March 1990.
13 Galerie Littmann, Basel, sponsored the *Culture Freight Cars*.
14 JT, 'Kunst ist Revolte', *National-Zeitung* (Basel), 13 October 1967. The Charlotte commission came from an old friend, Dr Walter A. Bechtler and his family, owners of Hesta Properties.

List of Illustrated Works

The abbreviation 'WK' refers to Christina Bischofberger, *Tinguely: Werkkatalog Skulpturen und Reliefs/Catalogue raisonné Sculptures and Reliefs* vol. 1: *1954–1968,* vol. 2: *1969–1985,* Küsnacht and New York: Edition Galerie Bruno Bischofberger, 1992

1
Bascule VII 1969
Metal base, wooden wheels, rubber belts, electric motor, black paint
Length: 220 cm
Louisiana Museum of Modern Art, Humlebaek
(WK 456)

2
Hegel 1988
Mixed-media assemblage
Museum of the Hoffmann-La Roche Foundation, Basel

3–7
Shop-window displays, Basel, 1949–51

8–9
Méta-Malevich 'Point rouge' 1954
Wooden panel, round and rectangular metal objects, wooden pulleys, rubber belt, metal fixtures, electric motor, black, red and white paint
61.3 x 49.3 x 10 cm
Private collection, Zurich
(WK 11)

Spirale éclatée 1957
Wooden panel, metal objects, wooden pulleys, rubber belt, metal fixtures, electric motor, white paint
104 x 58.5 x 31 cm
Private collection, Zurich
(WK 80)

10
Elément détaché I 1954
Steel tube frame, steel wire, cardboard objects, electric motor, white paint
81 x 131 x 35.5 cm
Private collection, Paris
(WK 20)

11
Moulin à prière III (Prayer Mill III) 1954
Wooden board, metal wire and rods
50 x approx. 40 x approx. 30 cm
Private collection, Stockholm
(WK 3)

12
Machine à dessiner No. 2 (Drawing Machine No. 2) 1955
Wooden board, metal plate, metal objects, wooden pulley, electric motor, white paint
Museum Jean Tinguely, Basel, Gift of Niki de Saint Phalle
(WK 52)

13
Auto-Mobile 1954
Metal tripod, wheel, rods and wire, various coloured metal objects, electric motor
Height: approx. 130 cm
Private collection, Switzerland
(WK 26)

14
Relief Méta-mécanique sonore I (Meta-Mechanical Sound Relief) 1955
Wooden panel, cardboard objects, metal rods and wire, bottles, funnel, saw, tins, electric motors, white paint
80 x 300 cm
Kunsthaus Zürich
(WK 37)

15
Meta-Kandinsky I (Wundermaschine)
1956
Wooden panel, various coloured metal objects, wooden pulleys, metal rods, rubber belts, electric motor
40 x 102 cm
Private collection, Paris
(WK 58)

16
Meta-Harmony II 1979
Iron frame, plastic, rubber belts, wooden and metal wheels, musical instruments, toys, electric motor
380 x 690 x 160 cm
Kunstmuseum Basel, Emanuel-Hoffmann-Stiftung, Gift of Maja Sacher-Stehlin
(WK 562)

17
Metamatic No. 1 1959
Metal, wood, electric motor, black paint
96 x 85 x 44 cm
Musée National d'Art Moderne, Centre Georges Pompidou, Paris
(WK 113)

18
Metamatic No. 17 1959
Iron, metal elements and wires, rubber balloon, rubber belts, petrol engine, black paint
330 cm
Moderna Museet, Stockholm
(WK 122)

19
Cyclograveur 1960
Welded scrap metal, bicycle parts, tin sheet, drums, cymbals
180 x 400 cm
Kunsthaus Zürich, Gift of the Artist
(WK 152)

20
Homage to New York 1960
In the Sculpture Garden at The Museum of Modern Art, New York, 17 March 1960

21
Gismo 1960
Metal wheels, rods, tin can, tin pitcher, helmet, iron frame, rubber belts, electric motor
200 x 560 x 170 cm
Stedelijk Museum, Amsterdam
(WK 150)

22
Homage to Marcel Duchamp 1960
Welded scrap metal bicycle wheel, automobile lamp, metal rods, fabric, stone pedestal from Brancusi's studio, electric motor
160 cm
Städtisches Museum Mönchengladbach
(WK 155)

23
Big Meta-Maxi-Maxi 1987
Mixed-media assemblage
1600 x 600 x 450 cm
Museum Jean Tinguely, Basel, Gift of Niki de Saint Phalle

24
Marilyn 1960
Welded scrap metal, bicycle and tricycle wheels, metal rods, calculator, carpet, electric motor
72 x 300 cm
Kunstmuseum Basel Gift of the Artist, 1976
(WK 187)

25
Scooter 1960
Scooter, helmet, rubber belt, electric motor
89 x 109 cm
Collection S. Perlstein, Antwerp
(WK 172)

26
Matrimonial Self-Portrait 1960
Scrap metal welded onto steel frame, ladder, tricycle wheels, chain, rubber band, stuffed bird, electric motor
180 x 141 x 41 cm
Kunstmuseum Basel, Gift of Franz Meyer, 1976
(WK 149)

27
Baluba No. 3 1961
Wooden trunk, steel bars, metal wheels, chain, spring, cow bell, feather, plastic, wheel cover, rubber belt, electric motors
Height: 144 cm
Museum Ludwig, Cologne
(WK 232)

28
Dylaby 1962
Installation by Robert Rauschenberg

29
Dylaby 1962
Plan of installation at the Stedelijk Museum, Amsterdam, 1962, by Robert Rauschenberg, Niki de Saint Phalle, Daniel Spoerri, Per Olof Ultvedt, Martial Raysse and Tinguely

30
Radio WNYR 1962
Plexiglass sheet, metal fixtures, radio, electric motor
62 x 62 x 12 cm
Galerie Bonnier, Geneva
(WK 277)

31
The Bamboo's Swan Song 1963
Scrap metal, wheels, metal rods, rubber belts, bamboo pole, electric motor
350 x 270 cm
Museum Jean Tinguely, Basel, Gift of Niki de Saint Phalle
(WK 306)

32
Hannibal I 1963
Iron bars and wheels, forged iron, rubber belts, chain, electric motor, black paint
117 x 102 x 274 cm
Collection Robert Rauschenberg
(WK 323)

33
Chariot M.K. IV 1966
Wooden base, metal wheels, rubber belts, wood, forged iron, electric motor, black paint
210 x 106 x 65 cm
Moderna Museet, Stockholm
(WK 393)

34
Eureka 1964
Iron bars, steel wheels, metal tubes, wooden wheels, metal pan, motors, brown paint
780 x 660 x 410 cm
Walter Bechtler-Stiftung, Zollikon (installed at Kasino Zürichhorn, Zurich)
(WK 347)

35
Chariot No. 8 1968
Wooden base, metal and wooden wheels, iron rods and bars, metal tube, rubber belts, electric motor, black paint
79 x 267 x 100 cm
Museum Ludwig, Cologne
(WK 438)

36
Dissecting Machine 1965
Window mannequin, saws, drills, electric motors, black paint
185.5 x 188 x 200 cm
Collection François de Menil
(WK 358)

37
Hon—A Cathedral 1966
Temporary installation, Moderna Museet, Stockholm, 1966, by Niki de Saint Phalle, Per Olof Ultvedt and Tinguely

38
In Praise of Folly, mechanical stage curtain, 1966
Aluminium frame, wooden wheels, wire, rubber belts, black paint
Approx. 350 x 600 cm
Kunstmuseum, St Gallen
(WK 401)

39
La Vittoria (The Victory) 1970
In the Piazza del Duomo, Milan, 1970 (various stages of the happening)

40
Requiem for a Dead Leaf 1967
Steel bar frame, wooden and metal wheels, rubber belts, welded leaf, electric motor and black and white paint
305 x 1150 cm
Fondation Renault, France
(WK 424)

41
Jean Tinguely and Niki de Saint Phalle, *The Fantastic Paradise* 1966–67
Wood, wires, wheels, fibreglass, plastic, electric motor, black paint

The Pierced Nana and *The Machine*
550 x 320 cm
The Fat Nana and *Drill*
420 x 280 cm; 135 x 325 cm
Gentle Creature and *Rotozaza*
450 x 480 cm; 230 x 310 cm
Tree-Nana and *Madwoman*
350 x 280 cm; 200 x 300 cm
Rasputin and *Baby Monster*
230 x 750 cm
Moderna Museet, Stockholm
(WK 413)

42
Hannibal II 1967
Wooden base with metal tracks, wooden and metal wheels, metal tubes, rubber belts, chain, electric motors, black paint
180 x 153 x 715 cm
Verkehrsverein Basel
(WK 428)

43
Rotozaza I 1967
Iron bars, steel plates, wooden and metal wheels, rubber belts, metal tube, balls, electric motor, black paint
220 x 410 x 230 cm
Collection Benedicte Pelse, Paris
(WK 432)

44
Cenotaph for a Kamikaze 1969
Iron base, wood, rubber belts, metal wheels and bars, electric motors
190 x 552 x 321 cm
Galerie Bonnier, Geneva
(WK 460)

45
Meta II 1971
Steel base, iron, wheels, bars, rubber belts, electric motors
150 x 600 x 300 cm
Stedelijk Museum, Amsterdam
(WK 472)

46
Head 1971-94
Jean Tinguely, Niki de Saint Phalle, Bernhard Luginbühl, Daniel Spoerri, Eva Aeppli, Rico Weber, Joseph Imhof, Paul Wiedmer, Jean-Pierre Reynaud, César, Arman, Larry Rivers, Jesus Raphael Soto and others
Steel, concrete
Height: 22.4 m
French state property, Gift of the Artists (installed in Milly-la-Forêt, near Paris)
(WK 471)

47
Niki de Saint Phalle, *Golem* 1972
Jerusalem

48
Chaos I 1973-74
Metal construction with moving balls on tracks, electric motors
915 x 854 x 458 cm
The Commons, Columbus, Indiana
(WK 495)

49
Ludwig Wittgenstein 1988
Mixed-media assemblage
230 x 172 x 102 cm
Museum Jean Tinguely, Basel, Gift of Niki de Saint Phalle

50
Klamauk 1979
Tractor, metal and wooden wheels, oil barrel, metal bars, rubber belts, found objects
330 x 700 x 300 cm
Museum Jean Tinguely, Basel, Gift of Niki de Saint Phalle
(WK 554)

51
Fasnachtsbrunnen (Carnival Fountain) 1977
Iron, rubber tubes, electric motors
Basin: 16 x 19 m
Dr Wäädel (The Wagger)
240 x 150 x 108 cm
Dr Suuser (The Whistler)
252 x 144 x 120 cm
D' Spinne (The Spider)
145 x 207 x 152 cm
Dr Theaterkopf (The Theatre Head)
155 x 130 x 123 cm
Dr Spritzer (The Squirter)
65 x 153 x 53 cm
Dr Schuufler (The Shoveller)
112 x 113 x 44 cm
Dr Seechter (The Sieve)
130 x 234 x 87 cm
Dr Waggler (The Rocker)
37 x 220 x 88 cm
D' Fontääne (The Fountain)
271 x 113 x 102 cm
Dr Schildchrott (The Turtle)
42 x 97 x 85 cm
Stadt Basel
(WK 541)

52
Jean Tinguely and Niki de Saint Phalle, *Stravinsky Fountain* 1983
Aluminium, steel, electric motors, black paint; polyester, steel
Basin: 0.35 x 36 x 16.5 m
Commune de Paris
(WK 609)

53
Crocrodrome 1977
Temporary installation at the Centre Georges Pompidou, Paris

54
Jean Tinguely and Niki de Saint Phalle, *Château Chinon Fountain* 1988
Motorised sculptures
Basin: approx. 5 m
Place de la Mairie, Château Chinon

55
Jo Siffert Fountain 1984
Iron wheels and bars, rubber belts and hoses, electric motors, black paint
Height: 440 cm; diameter of basin: 16 m
Stadt Fribourg
(WK 627)

56
Machine Bar 1960-85
Metal, found objects (mainly toys), animal skulls, electric motors mounted on wooden boards
Height: (max.) approx. 100 cm
Museum Jean Tinguely, Basel, Gift of Niki de Saint Phalle
(WK 549)

57
Fairy Tale Relief 1978
Iron frame on wheels, rubber belts, wood, metal wheels, toys, electric motors
280 x 620 x 130 cm
Wilhelm-Lehmbruck-Museum der Stadt Duisburg
(WK 549)

58
Cenodoxus 1972
Stage props, Salzburg Festival, 1972, produced by Werner Düggelin

59
Cenodoxus — Isenheim Altarpiece 1981
Metal frame, wooden and metal wheels and found objects, animal skulls, light bulbs, electric motors
310 x 408 x 260 cm
Schweizerische National-Versicherungsgesellschaft, Basel
(WK 587)

60
Poya 1983
Metal, wood, skull, found objects, rubber belts, electric motors
240 x 310 x 124 cm
Collection Barbier-Müller, Geneva
(WK 615)

61
Small Animals' Altarpiece 1989
Mixed-media assemblage, electric motors
400 x 210 cm
Musée d'Art et d'Histoire, Fribourg

62
Pit-Stop 1984
Parts of two Renault Formula-One racing cars, iron construction, film projectors, electric motors, black, yellow and white paint
360 x 600 x 600 cm
Museum Jean Tinguely, Basel, Gift of Niki de Saint Phalle
(WK 628)

63
The Witches or Snow White and the Seven Dwarfs 1984
Iron structures, metal bars, wheels, chains, animal skulls, fabric, electric motors
Height: (max.) approx. 200 m
Private collection
(WK 665)

64
Lola T. 180—Memorial for Joakim B. 1988
Mixed-media assemblage, electric motors
300 x 400 x 150 cm
Museum Jean Tinguely, Basel, Gift of Niki de Saint Phalle

65
Inferno 1984
Metal and wooden wheels, iron rods, plants, toys, electric motors
300 x 1020 x 970 cm
Musée National d'Art Moderne, Centre Georges Pompidou, Paris
(WK 661)

66
Big Meta-Maxi-Maxi 1987
Mixed-media assemblage, installation view at the Palazzo Grassi, Venice
Museum Jean Tinguely, Basel, Gift of Niki de Saint Phalle

67
Mengele 1986
Hippopotamus skull, fragments of farming machinery, remnants of a burned-down farmhouse, electric motor
Approx. 300 x 440 x 420 cm
Museum Jean Tinguely, Basel, Gift of the Hoffmann-LaRoche Foundation, Basel

68
The Ram 1986
Mixed-media assemblage, electric motor
160 x 550 x 220 cm
Museum Jean Tinguely, Basel, Gift of the Hoffmann-LaRoche Foundation, Basel

69
Rotary Homage—The Furious Feather 1986
Lead, remnants of metal sculpture, scrap metal, electric motor
77 x 75 x 70 cm
Museum Jean Tinguely, Basel, Gift of the Hoffmann-LaRoche Foundation, Basel

70
The Spider 1986
Mixed-media assemblage, electric motor
230 x 220 x 336 cm
Museum Jean Tinguely, Basel, Gift of the Hoffmann-LaRoche Foundation, Basel

71
The Sun 1986
Mixed-media assemblage, electric motor
250 x 160 x 190 cm
Museum Jean Tinguely, Basel, Gift of the Hoffmann-LaRoche Foundation, Basel

72
The Moonshine Sonata 1986
Mixed-media assemblage, electric motor
205 x 80 x 100 cm
Museum Jean Tinguely, Basel, Gift of the Hoffmann-LaRoche Foundation, Basel

73
Transmission of Death 1986
Assemblage of agricultural machinery, animal and human skulls
Museum Jean Tinguely, Basel, Gift of the Hoffmann-LaRoche Foundation, Basel

74
The Mother 1986
Mixed-media assemblage, office machines, electric motor
217 x 160 x 130 cm

75
The Philosophers 1988
Installation view at the Centre Georges Pompidou

76
Self-Portrait 1988
Mixed-media assemblage with Jean Tinguely's 'down-and-out' costume, 1988, electric motor
Musée National d'Art Moderne, Centre Georges Pompidou, Paris

77
The Triptych of Plenty and of Totalitarian Mercantilism 1990
Mixed-media assemblage
550 x 590 x 265 cm
Musée d'Art et d'Histoire, Fribourg, Gift of Niki de Saint Phalle

78
Cascade 1991
Installation in the lobby of the Carillon building, Charlotte, North Carolina

Selected Bibliography

Abrahams, Roger D. 'The Language of Festivals: Celebrating the Economy'. In Victor Turner, ed., *Celebration: Studies in Festivity and Ritual*, pp. 161ff. Washington D.C.: Smithsonian Press, 1982.

'Amusement Art'. *Artnews* (April 1988).

Bakhtin, Mikhail. *Rabelais and His World.* Trans. Helene Iswolsky. Cambridge, Mass.: MIT Press, 1968.

Baudelaire, Charles. 'A Philosophy of Toys'. In *The Painter of Modern Life and Other Essays*, pp. 199ff. Trans. and ed. Jonathan Mayne. London: Phaidon Press, 1964.

—— 'On the Essence of Laughter'. In *The Painter of Modern Life and Other Essays*, pp. 147–65. Trans. and ed. Jonathan Mayne. London: Phaidon Press, 1964.

Baum, Peter. 'Jean Tinguely'. In *3. Internationale Triennale der Zeichnung und Bildhauerzeichnung*, pp. 110–42. Kunsthalle Nürnberg, 1985.

Berlyne, D. E. 'Laughter, Humor, and Play'. In Gardner Lindzey and Elliot Aronson, eds., *The Handbook of Social Psychology*, vol. 3, pp. 795ff. 2nd edn. Reading, Mass.: Addison-Wesley Publishing Co., 1968.

Bettelheim, Bruno. *The Uses of Enchantment.* New York: Alfred A. Knopf, 1977.

Bezzola, Leonardo. *Jean Tinguely.* Zurich: Arche Verlag, 1974.

[——]. '"Das Crocrodrome": Eine Bildreportage von Leonardo Bezzola'. *Werk*, no. 64 (1977), pp. 18–19.

Bidermann, Jacob. *Cenodoxus.* Ed. and trans. D. G. Dyer. Austin: University of Texas Press, 1974.

Billeter, Erika. 'Das Interview: Jean Tinguely.' In *Art-Expo 85: Das Jahrbuch der Kunst*, pp. 236–40. Baar: Weltrundschau Verlag AG, 1985.

Bischofberger, Christina. *Tinguely: Werkkatalog Skulpturen und Reliefs / Catalogue raisonnée Sculptures and Reliefs,* vol. 1: *1954–1968,* vol. 2: *1969–1985.* Küsnacht and New York: Edition Galerie Bruno Bischofberger, 1992.

Boulez, Pierre, Pontus Hulten, Franz Meyer and Stefanie Poley. *Jean Tinguely & Niki de Saint Phalle: La Fontaine Igor Stravinski.* Berne: Benteli Verlag, 1983.

Camus, Albert. *The Myth of Sisyphus and Other Essays.* Trans. Justin O'Brien. New York: Alfred A. Knopf, 1955.

Christen, Hanns U. (text), and Hans-Jürgen Truöl (photographs). *Morgenstreich, Larven und Laternen: Ein Streifzug durch die Basler Fasnacht.* Freiburg im Breisgau: Eulen Verlag, 1986.

Clert, Iris. *Iris time (l'artventure).* Paris: Denoël, 1978.

Conil Lacoste, Michel. 'Tinguely: Is He a Sculptor?' *Studio International*, 42 (February 1965).

——. *Tinguely: L'Energétique de l'insolence.* Paris: E. L. A. la Différence, 1989.

Daniels, Dieter, with Jean Tinguely. 'Klassiker schon—aber immer wieder vergessen'. In *Übrigens sterben immer die Anderen: Marcel Duchamp und die Avantgarde seit 1950*, pp. 129–42. Exh. cat. Cologne: Museum Ludwig, 1988.

Débriscollages. Exh. cat. Zurich: Galerie Bruno Bischofberger, 1974.

Détraz, Christine, and Philippe Grand. *Contes et légendes de Fribourg.* Sierre: Monographic SA, Collection 'Mémoire Vivante', 1984.

Düggelin, Werner. Quoted in '"Tinguely-Paraphrase": Ein Musikfilm von Werner Düggelin'. *Basler Zeitung*, 23 May 1985.

Dylaby. Exh. cat. Amsterdam: Stedelijk Museum, 1962.

Elliott, Robert C. *The Power of Satire: Magic, Ritual, Art.* Princeton, N.J.: Princeton University Press, 1960.

Erikson, Erik. *Toys and Reason.* New York: Norton, 1977.

Farine, Pierre. 'Die Strassenfasnacht'. In *Die Basler Fasnacht*, pp. 81–122. Basel: Fasnachts-Comité, 1985.

Finkelstein, Haim N. *Surrealism and the Crisis of the Object.* Ann Arbor: UMI, 1979.

Foster, Stephen C. *'Event' Arts and Art Events.* Ann Arbor: UMI Research Press, 1987.

Fromm, Erich. *The Art of Loving.* New York: Bantam Books, 1967.

Glauser, Alain. *Poyas de la Gruyère.* Paudex: Editions de Fontainemore, 1974.

Glueck, Grace. 'Show at Museum Stars Machines'. *New York Times*, 24 December 1965.

Hahnloser-Ingold, Margrit. *Pandämonium—Jean Tinguely.* Berne: Benteli Verlag, 1988.

——. *Briefe von Jean Tinguely an Maja Sacher.* Berne: Benteli Verlag, 1992

Hansen, Al. *A Primer of Happenings and Time/Space Art.* New York: Something Else Press, 1965.

D'Harnoncourt, Anne, and Kynaston McShine, eds. *Marcel Duchamp.* Exh. cat. New York: Museum of Modern Art, 1973. Repr. Munich: Prestel, 1989.

Hobi, Viktor. 'Das "Innere" der Basler Fasnacht: Versuch eines Psychogramms'. In *Die Basler Fasnacht*, pp. 375–83. Basel: Fasnachts-Comité, 1985.

Hon—en historia. Exh. cat. Stockholm: Moderna Museet, 1967.

Hughes, Robert. *Heaven and Hell in Western Art*, New York: Stein and Day, 1968.

Huizinga, Johan. *Homo Ludens: A Study of the Play-Element in Culture.* Boston: Beacon Press, 1955.

Hulten, Pontus. *Jean Tinguely 'Méta'.* Boston: New York Graphic Society, 1975.

——. *A Magic Stronger than Death.* Milan: Gruppe Editoriale Fabbri Bompiani, 1987.

Hutchinson, Donna. 'Tanz, Musik und Musikinstrumente im Totentanz'. In *Der Tod zu Basel: Didaktische Ausstellung im Kunstmuseum Basel*, unpaginated. Exh. cat. Basel: Kunstmuseum, 1979.

Jouffroy, Alain. 'Jean Tinguely'. *L'Oeil*, no. 136 (April 1966), pp. 34ff. Interview with the artist.

Kayser, Wolfgang. *The Grotesque in Art and Literature*. Bloomington: Indiana University Press, 1963.

Klein, Yves. 'Preparation and Presentation of the Exhibition of 28 April 1958'. In *Yves Klein: A Retrospective*, p. 226. Exh. cat. Houston: Rice University, Institute for the Arts, 1982.

Klüver, Billy. 'The Garden Party' (1960). In *The Machine as Seen at the End of the Mechanical Age*. Exh. cat. New York: Museum of Modern Art, 1968.

——. *E. A. T. Proceedings*, no. 9. New York, 19 May 1969.

——, Julie Martin and Barbara Rose, eds. *Pavilion*. New York: Dutton Inc., 1972.

Kolberg, Gerhard. 'Aspekte der "Bewegung" im Werk von Marcel Duchamp und Jean Tinguely'. In *Übrigens sterben immer die Anderen: Marcel Duchamp und die Avantgarde seit 1950*, pp. 115–28. Exh. cat. Cologne: Museum Ludwig, 1988.

Kostelanetz, Richard. *The Theatre of Mixed–Means*. New York: RK Editions, 1980.

Kris, Ernst. *Psychoanalytic Explorations in Art*. New York and London, 1952.

Lankheit, Klaus. *Das Triptychon als Pathosformel*. Heidelberg: Carl Winter Universitätsverlag, 1959.

Laugier, Claude. 'Impasse Ronsin'. In *Paris-Paris, 1937–1957*, pp. 290–93. Exh. cat. Paris: Centre Georges Pompidou, 1981.

1960: Les Nouveaux Réalistes. Exh. cat. Paris: Musée d'Art Moderne de la Ville de Paris, 1986.

Lévêque, Jean-Jacques 'Prenez le thé avec un gentil "crocrodrome"', *Le Quotidien de Paris*, 4–5 June 1977.

Luginbühl, Bernhard. *Tinguely & Luginbühl*. Exh. cat. Frankfurt am Main: Städelsches Kunstinstitut, 1979.

McEvilley, Thomas. 'Yves Klein: Conquistador of the Void'. In *Yves Klein: A Retrospective*, pp. 19–87. Exh. cat. Houston: Rice University, Institute for the Arts, 1982.

Meier, Eugen A. 'Die Fasnacht im Alten Basel'. In *Die Basler Fasnacht*, pp. 51–52. Basel: Fasnachts-Comité, 1985.

——, and Robert B. Christ. *Fasnacht in Basel*. Basel: Pharos-Verlag, 1968.

Millar, Susanna. *The Psychology of Play*. New York: Penguin Books, 1968.

Mohler, Hans, with Franz K. Opitz (photographs). *Fasnacht*. Zurich: Orell Füssli Verlag, 1963.

Müller, Rolf Arnold. *Komik und Satire*. Zurich: Juris Druck and Verlag, 1973.

Neumann, Erich. *Art and the Creative Unconscious*. Princeton, N.J.: Princeton University Press, 1974.

Pelli, Cesar. 'Piazza, American Style'. *Progressive Architecture* (June 1976).

Petersen, Ad. 'Jean Tinguely & Co.'. *Forum*, 25–2.

Piddington, Ralph. *The Psychology of Laughter: A Study in Social Adaptation*. New York: Gamut Press, Inc., 1963.

Poley, Stefanie, and Jean Tinguely. 'Questions and Answers'. In *Jean Tinguely*, pp. 34–105. Exh. cat. Munich: Kunsthalle Hypo Kulturstiftung, 1985.

——. 'Der Künstler: Clown der modernen Gesellschaft?'. In *Unter der Maske der Narren*, pp. 221–27. Exh. cat. Duisburg: Wilhelm-Lehmbruck-Museum, 1981.

Rang, Florens Christian. *Historische Psychologie des Karnevals*. Berlin: Brinkmann and Bose, 1983.

Rank, Otto. *The Myth of the Birth of the Hero*. New York, 1913.

Restany, Pierre. 'Des Machines célibataires aux machines inutiles'. *XXème Siècle*, no. 42 (1974).

Rickey, George. 'The Kinetic International'. *Arts Magazine* (September 1961), pp. 16–21.

——. 'The Morphology of Movement: A Study of Kinetic Art'. In Gyorgy Kepes, ed., *The Nature and Art of Motion*. New York: Georges Braziller, 1965.

Rosenthal, Nan. 'Assisted Levitation: The Art of Yves Klein'. In *Yves Klein: A Retrospective*, pp. 91–135. Houston: Rice University, Institute for the Arts, 1982.

Rubin, William S. *Dada, Surrealism, and Their Heritage*. Exh. cat. New York: Museum of Modern Art, 1968.

Schmidt, Johann Kaspar [Max Stirner]. *The Ego and His Own: The Case of the Individual Against Authority*. Trans. Steven T. Byington, ed. James J. Martin. New York: Libertarian Book Club, 1963.

Seckler, Dorothy G. 'The Audience is His Medium'. *Art in America*, no. 2 (1963), p. 62.

Seitz, William C. *The Art of Assemblage*. Exh. cat. New York: Museum of Modern Art, 1961.

Sorell, Walter. *The Other Face: The Mask in the Arts*. London: Thames and Hudson, 1973.

Stoll, Robert Th. 'Bilder vom Sterben und vom Tod im Basler Kunstmuseum'. In *Der Tod zu Basel: Didaktische Ausstellung im Kunstmuseum Basel*, unpaginated. Exh. cat. Basel: Kunstmuseum, 1979.

Stumm, Reinhardt. 'Tinguely's Kugelblitz-Kunst'. *Basler Zeitung* (magazine), 28 March 1987.

——, and Kurt Wyss. *Jean Tinguely*. Basel: Friedrich Reinhardt Verlag, 1985.

Tatar, Maria. *The Hard Facts of the Grimms' Fairy Tales*. Princeton, N.J.: Princeton University Press, 1987.

Tinguely, Jean. *Manifesto für Statik*. Düsseldorf, March 1959.

——. 'Kunst ist Revolte'. *National-Zeitung* (Basel), 13 October 1967.

——. 'Lecture'. Paris, CNAC, 5 May 1971. Sonothèque Centre Georges Pompidou, BS 92.

——. In Otto Piene and Heinz Mack, eds., *Zero*, p. 119. Boston: MIT Press, 1973.

——. 'Parole d'Artiste'. Interview by Charles Goerg and Rainer Michael Mason. In *Jean Tinguely: Dessins et gravures pour les sculptures*, pp. 9–16. Exh. cat. Geneva: Musée d'Art et d'Histoire, Cabinet des Estampes, 1976.

——. 'Was mir gefällt'. *DU* (April 1977), pp. 23ff.

——. In *Rheinische Post* (Düsseldorf), 21 December 1978.

——. 'Die Appenzeller Kläuse finde ich eigentlich doch noch besser als meinen "Klamauk"'. Interview by Reinhardt Stumm. *Tages-Anzeiger*, 21 June 1980.

——. 'Die Frauen entscheiden alles von A–Z'. Interview by Yvonne-Denise Köchli. *Annabelle*, no. 19, 16 September 1982.

——. Quoted by Thomas McEvilley. 'Yves Klein: Conquistador of the Void'. In *Yves Klein: A Retrospective*, p. 48. Exh. cat. Houston: Rice University, Institute for the Arts, 1982.

——. 'Tinguely on Tinguely'. Extract from a radio debate. Radio Télévision Belge, Brussels, 1982.

——, and Pontus Hulten. 'A Project by Pontus Hulten and Jean Tinguely'. *Artforum* (January 1984), pp. 44ff.

——. 'Jean Tinguely, Lecture, 10 Mai 1984, Cycle rencontre avec quelques artistes contemporains, du 9 au 11 Mai, 1984, Sonothèque Centre Georges Pompidou, Paris, BS 259.

——. 'Jux muss meine Kunst sein—und vor allem unseriös'. *Neues Sonntags Blatt*, no. 9, 1 March 1987.

——. Interview by Dr Lukas Burckhardt. In *Jean Tinguely*. Exh. cat. Basel: Galerie Beyeler, 1987.

——. Interview by Dieter Daniels. 'Die Wirklichkeit der Utopie: Jean Tinguely über den "Kopf"im Wald'. *Kunstforum*, 91 (October-November 1987), pp. 258–64.

Tomkins, Calvin. 'A Profile of Jean Tinguely: Beyond the Machine'. *New Yorker*, 10 February 1962, p. 44 *et passim.*

——. *The Bride and the Bachelors.* New York: Penguin Books, 1983.

——. 'Profiles: A Good Monster'. *New Yorker*, 16 January 1978, p. 37 *et passim.*

Trebay, Guy. 'Machine Dreams'. *Village Voice*, 24 May 1988, pp. 19–20.

Trois Sculpteurs: César, Roël d'Haese, Tinguely. Exh. cat. Paris: Musée des Arts Décoratifs, 1965.

Trümpy, Hans. 'Wesen und Ursprung der Fas(t)nacht'. In *Die Basler Fasnacht*, pp. 12–19. Basel: Fasnachts-Comité, 1985.

Turner, Victor, ed. *Celebration: Studies in Festivity and Ritual.* Washington D.C.: Smithsonian Press, 1982.

——. *Dramas, Fields and Metaphors.* Ithaca, N.Y.: Cornell University Press, 1974.

Violand, Heidi E. 'Jean Tinguely's Cenodoxus Isenheim Altarpiece'. *Arts Magazine* (October 1987), pp. 80–85.

——. 'Les Leçons de Tinguely'. *Journal de Genève*, 7 September 1987, p. 2.

——. *Jean Tinguely's Kinetic Art, or A Myth of the Machine Age*. Ann Arbor: UMI Research Press, 1990.

Wulp, John. 'Happening'. *Esquire* (November 1962), pp. 134ff.

Index of Names

Photograph Credits

Leonardo Bezzola, Bätterkinden: pp. 2, 9, 24-25, 28-29, 32, 37, 45, 47, 57-58, 61 (top), 64–65, 67–69, 71, 76–80, 83, 84 (bottom), 85-89, 91, 92 (top), 93–98, 99 (top), 100 (top), 102–8, 110–17, 120–21, 123–27, 129–31, 133, 136–37, 140, 142–44, 146 (bottom), 148, 150–51, 152 (bottom), 153 (bottom), 154 (top), 155-57

Lukas Burckhardt, Basel: p. 81

Michelle Facos, South Euclid: pp. 16, 35, 49, 63, 73

Courtesy Galerie Bruno Bischofberger, Zurich: pp. 26 (top), 38–39, 46

Hans Hammarskiöld, Stockholm: p. 66

François Lalanne, Ury: p. 31

Peter Möschlin, Basel: pp. 18–19

Jean-Marc Rey, Villars-sur-Glâne: pp. 109, 152 (top)

Courtesy Jean-Marc Rey: pp. 10–11

Stedelijk Museum, Amsterdam: pp. 53–55

Josy Schaub, Basel: p. 90

Heidi E. Violand-Hobi: pp. 7, 13, 17, 20–23, 26 (bottom), 27, 41, 43, 59-60, 61 (bottom), 62, 70, 72, 74-75, 82, 84 (top), 92 (bottom), 99 (bottom), 100 (bottom), 101, 118, 119 (top), 122, 128, 135, 139, 141, 145, 146 (top), 147, 149, 154 (bottom), 158, 161